The Royal Naval Air Service in the First World War

AN·AVIATOR'S·LIFE·CONSISTS·OF·PERIODS·OF·GREAT·LEISURE —

— PUNCTUATED·BY·MOMENTS·OF·INTENSE·FEAR.

This First World War postcard neatly encapsulates the life of a Royal Naval Air Service pilot.

The Royal Naval Air Service in the First World War

Aircraft and Events as Recorded in Official Documents

Philip Jarrett

Pen & Sword
AVIATION

First published in Great Britain in 2015 by
Pen & Sword Aviation
an imprint of
Pen & Sword Books Ltd
47 Church Street
Barnsley
South Yorkshire
S70 2AS

ISBN 978 1 47382 819 3

Typeset in Ehrhardt by
Mac Style Ltd, Bridlington, East Yorkshire
Printed and bound by Replika Press Pvt. Ltd.

Pen & Sword Books Ltd incorporates the imprints of Pen & Sword Archaeology, Atlas, Aviation, Battleground,
Discovery, Family History, History, Maritime, Military, Naval, Politics, Railways, Select, Transport, True
Crime, and Fiction, Frontline Books, Leo Cooper, Praetorian Press, Seaforth Publishing and Wharncliffe.

For a complete list of Pen & Sword titles please contact
PEN & SWORD BOOKS LIMITED
47 Church Street, Barnsley, South Yorkshire, S70 2AS, England
E-mail: enquiries@pen-and-sword.co.uk
Website: www.pen-and-sword.co.uk

Dedication

*In fond memory of J.M. ('Jack') Bruce, to whom all researchers into the
history of First World War aviation owe so much.*

*In memory of the late Barry Ketley, with whom I initiated this project
years ago, but who sadly did not live to see its completion.*

Philip Jarrett

Contents

Introduction

This book is based on several original documents relating to the work of Britain's Royal Naval Air Service (RNAS) during the First World War. The aim is not to analyse their content or present a coherent account of the RNAS; the latter has already been done by Brad King in his book *Royal Naval Air Service 1912–1918* (Hikoki, 1997). It is simply to make these rare documents readily available to students and historians. To complement them and add some visual interest, a large collection of photographs, many hitherto unpublished, have been added. Whilst some of these relate directly to the aircraft and events mentioned in the documents, many are included to show developments before and after the periods covered.

THE DOCUMENTS

Diary of Important Operations, Flanders, 1916

I bought this large ring binder and its contents many years ago, and it has sat on the shelf ever since. Covering the period from 29 June to 9 September 1916, it comprises reports of a number of reconnaissance and bombing operations, and includes a number of photographs and maps of the targets. Although it is neither comprehensive nor complete in its coverage, and lacks the detail sought by many modern historians, it is valuable as a primary source.

0001
COMBINED FRENCH AND ENGLISH OPERATION NO.1.
Destruction of BATTERY TIRPITZ – 4, 12″ guns.

0002/3/4

COPY. No.6

Headquarters.
R.N.A.S.,
Dunkerque.
June 29th. 1916.

SECRET OPERATION ORDER, No. 7.

On the occasion of the big Naval Gun and the two French Guns opening fire, it is of the utmost importance that the enemy are unable to locate its position by aircraft or to spot their artillery on to the position.

With this object in view, a constant patrol will be maintained on the areas shewn in the attached map. Two machines should, if possible, be always maintained in each Sector, and if this is found impossible, assistance should be asked for from Headquarters.

The Spotting Machines together with their attendant Fighters, will be quite separate to the Patrol, but, in the event of the former being attacked in force, they will be in a position to fall back on the Patrol line for support.

Commanding Officers of Wings may make their own arrangements for carrying this out, but should bring me their proposals at 6pm on Friday next.

The length of each Sector is about 8 miles, and the two Machines should patrol this length.

If an enemy machine is seen, it is to be immediately attacked, but should not be pursued unless inside the Sector or if approaching X Position.

It is difficult to lay down the heights at which the patrol will be maintained owing to the various types of machines used, and also the varying efficiency of the enemy anti-aircraft guns. If necessary to go to 14,000 feet, or over, a good look out should be kept for enemy machines breaking through underneath.

In the event of a forced landing, machines should endeavour to reach FURNES Aerodrome, but in any case they should report themselves to Headquarters by telephone, who will inform their Unit.

Great secrecy should be observed until the day of operations, but, on the commencement, Officers and Men should be impressed with the importance of maintaining a continuous patrol and hence of maintaining as many machines as possible in flying condition.

Pilots should be impressed with the necessity of attacking every German machine seen, but that the chief object of the Patrol is to prevent the enemy locating the gun, and hence that the machines should NOT be pursued over their own lines. After chasing the enemy off the machines should return at once to their Sector.

One Flight of Baby Nieuports will be held in reserve but will occasionally fly round the Patrol.

When the operations have commenced, the telephone service to H.Q., and La Panne should be restricted entirely to messages regarding the operations. All other important communications, should be sent by Despatch Rider.

The Spotting Machines will be marked with broad vertical bands on the sides of the fuselage, and broad horizontal bands on the top of the fuselage abaft the passenger.

All clocks should be set accurately by No. 1, Wing time, who will give a "STOP" over the telephone.

No. 1. Wing will give the time signal to X Position, and the W/T. Stations.

Copy No.1. – No.1.Wing.
Copy No.2. – No.1 Wing.
Copy No.3. – No.4.Wing.
Copy No.4. – No.5.Wing.
Copy No.5. – Seaplane Base.
Copy No.6. – Intelligence Officer. HQ.
Copy No.7. – S.O., H.Q.
Copy No.8. – S.O.,
Copy No.9. – Commodore.
Copy No.10. – French Aviation Militaire
Copy No.11. – French Aviation Navale.

[Signed]
Acting Captain.

0005

<u>SCHEME OF BARRAGE USED IN CONJUNCTION WITH THIS OPERATION.</u>

0006

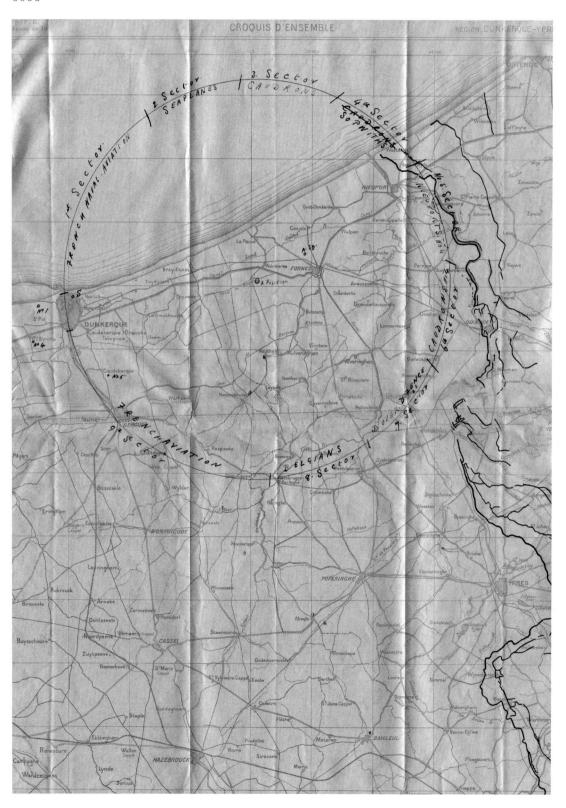

0007

PLAN OF TIRPITZ BATTERY.

Four 12 inch guns.

0008

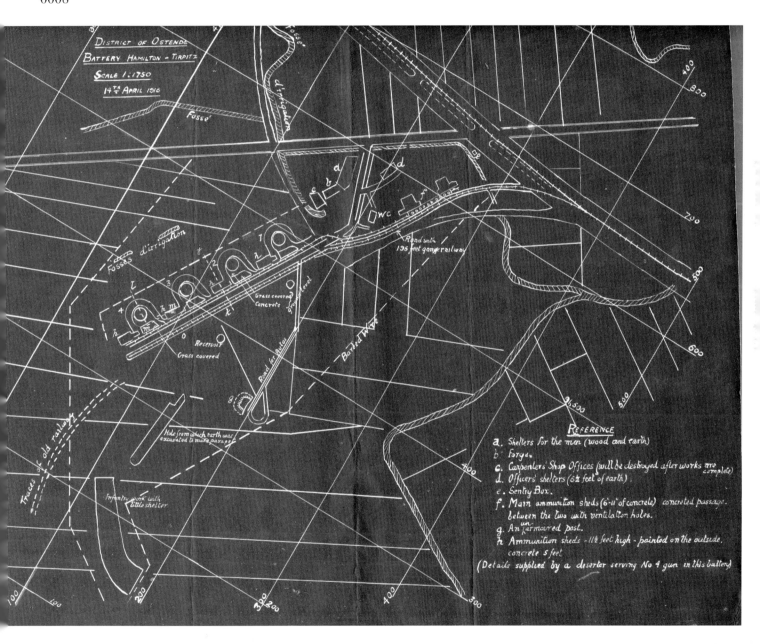

0009
Flying Map.

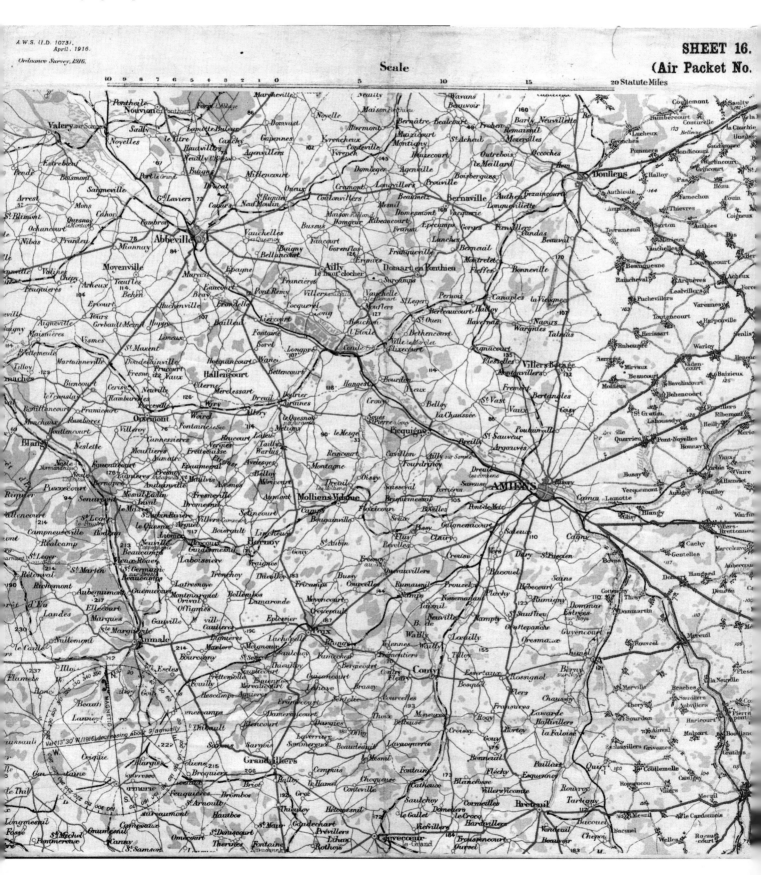

0010

Figure 1 : Maquette vue par l'avant.

Figure 2 : Maquette vue par l'arrière.

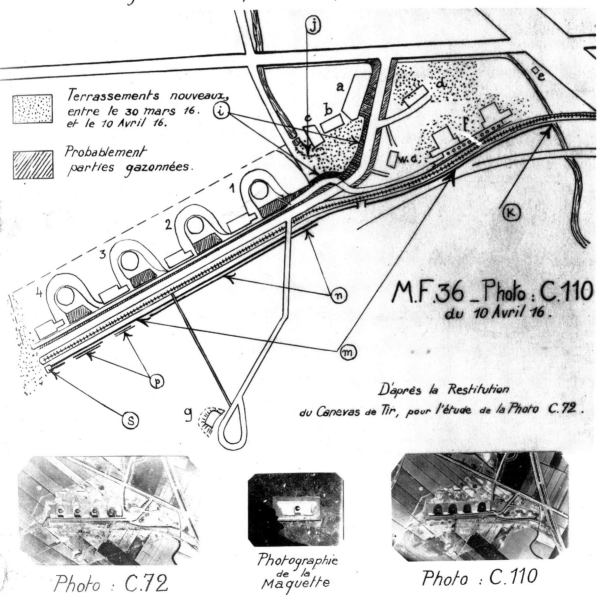

Terrassements nouveaux,
entre le 30 mars 16.
et le 10 Avril 16.

Probablement
parties gazonnées.

M.F.36 _ Photo : C.110
du 10 Avril 16.

D'après la Restitution
du Canevas de Tir, pour l'étude de la Photo C.72.

Photo : C.72

Photographie
de la
Maquette

Photo : C.110

0011/0012/0013

ROYAL NAVAL AIR SERVICE.

DAILY SUMMARY.

July 8th. 1916. (Midnight to Midnight.)

RECONNNAISSANCES:-

5.00 a.m. to 6.45 a.m. – Seaplane patrol over Special Area.

5.45 a.m. – One armed trawler 5 miles N.E. of OSTEND, steering towards Harbour.

2.19 p.m. to 4.29 p.m. – Seaplane Patrol. – No hostile vessels or submarines observed.

Coastal Reconnaissances:-

12.15 p.m. – OSTEND. – One dredger between the PIERS. One destroyer moored alongside the QUAY outside the BASSIN DE LEOPOLD. No railway activity.

3.20 p.m. – OSTEND. – One small coasting steamer steering S.W. one mile from Harbour.
One vessel (tank steamer) proceeding E.
Two large barges in the OSTEND Canal.
No railway activity observed.

3.35 p.m. – One small steamer under lee of MOLE and several barges in ZEEBRUGGE Harbour. One large steamer under way.
Five barges at various intervals in the ZEEBRUGGE-BRUGES Canal.
Coast between OSTEND and ZEEBRUGGE clear of shipping.

FIGHTER PATROLS:-

From 2.00 p.m. till 9.00 p.m. 100 Fighter Patrols were carried out in conjunction with the one English and two French guns firing on the Tirpitz Battery.

These patrols successfully prevented hostile machines from:-

(1). Attacking French and English machines spotting for the land guns.
(2). Observing position of land guns.
(3). Attacking Kite Balloons which were also observing.

Seven engagements with hostile machines occurred during the afternoon, one of which appeared to be decisive in our favour.

At 3.05 p.m. a new type of Fokker was observed. Pilot dived down on enemy and fired ¾ of a tray into him, whereupon enemy dived towards OSTEND. Pilot fired a full tray at the Fokker at ranges decreasing from 200 yards to 20 feet, at which the hostile machine was observed to roll right over to the left and fall nose first towards the sea. Pilot flattened out his machine to reload and, on looking again, could see no trace of the enemy machine.

Tracer bullets appeared to enter cockpit of Fokker and pilot is of opinion that the machine was absolutely out of control when last seen.

At 6.05 p.m, the same pilot, when off WESTENDE, at 11,000 feet, encountered a second Fokker monoplane at rather lower altitude. Pilot manoeuvred into position behind enemy and dived 3,000 feet on to him, firing 1½ trays at ranges decreasing from 200 to 30 yards. The enemy dived steeply towards OSTEND and was afterwards lost sight of.

At 6.45 p.m. the same pilot again, when 3 miles off MIDDELKERKE, observed an Aviatik coming towards DUNKERQUE at a much lower altitude. Pilot followed him as far as NIEUPORT. Aviatik then turned and pilot dived 6,000 feet and attacked, firing 2 trays at close range. The enemy promptly dived towards MARIAKERKE.

Both these machines were observed to be hit, but the pilot does not think that either were [*sic*] badly damaged.

5.53 p.m. – Two hostile aeroplanes were observed near WESTENDE. Pilot fired a tray whilst diving from 12,500 to 7,000 feet. Both hostile machines dived towards the shore and kept close under protection of the shore batteries. Pilot, therefore, returned from patrol.

Two other hostile machines were observed patrolling the coast between MIDDELKERKE and OSTEND at very low altitudes.

The WESTENDE A.A. Battery 95.74 showed a certain amount of activity during the afternoon, but as a whole the A.A. guns were not very active, nor was the firing very accurate.

One Fighter Patrol had the misfortune to fall into the sea, but both pilot and observer were picked up.

WIRELESS TELEGRAPHY.

Successful spotting for the operations in hand was carried out from 2.00 p.m. till 8.00 p.m. by four machines, which relieved each other at intervals throughout this time.

Machines flew at heights between 11,000 and 16,000 feet.

The visibility was, at first, bad, but later it was very good, deteriorating again later in the evening.

At 4.50 p.m. a spotting observer reported that it was thought that the second gun from OSTEND in the Tirpitz Battery was apparently out of action, as the cupola had disappeared.

Spotting operations were not interfered with by hostile aircraft owing to the efficient protection afforded them by our machines.

Considering the exposed position of our machines, very little A.A. firing was experienced.

NO.11 KITE BALLOON SECTION:-

One ascent was made from 2.10 p.m. to 8.10 p.m.
Height 1,400 to 1,700 feet.
Visibility very poor.

The target was only visible occasionally, owing to mist and smoke screens used by the land batteries. It is thought probable that the enemy used smoke screens to hide the target, as big smoke clouds were frequently seen in the vicinity of the target. Owing to this only four out of the 21 shots from the English Battery and three out of the 70 from the French Batteries were observed.

The Tirpitz Battery replied with 21 shots, all of which fell where the smoke screen had been started.

During the afternoon the hostile battery 86.52 was observed in action seven times and battery 95.74 was in action at 3.58 p.m.

Hostile Kite Balloon at LEFFINGHE (close to Battery Tirpitz) was observed in the air during the afternoon.

NO.9 KITE BALLOON SECTION:-

H.M. Barge "Arctic" left the Harbour in the early morning and arrived at her appointed position later. Two ascents were made as follows:-

(1). At 1.40 p.m. – Duration 2 h. 10 m.
(2). At 4.11 p.m. – Duration 1 h. 35 m.

Owing to the bad visibility no record of shots by the land batteries could be made, as for the most part, the shore was only visible at intervals.

[Signed]

Acting Captain.

Belonging to No.9 Kite Balloon Section, RNAS, H.M. Barge *Arctic* is seen here with its observation balloon inflated ready for ascent. The second view shows the vessel's hold, with a few gas cylinders against the cabins at the far end. (Bruce/Leslie)

0014

No.1

TIRPITZ BATTERY.

Belgian Photograph.

Date:- July 9th. 1916

Time:- 12.30 p.m.

0015

0016

No.1a.

TIRPITZ BATTERY Enlargement of Photograph No.1.

0017

0018/19/20/21

ROYAL NAVAL AIR SERVICE.

DAILY SUMMARY.

July 9th (Midnight to Midnight.)

RECONNAISSANCES:-
5.00 a.m. to 7.25 a.m. ⎫ Seaplane patrols over
3.20 p.m. to 5.35 p.m. ⎭ Special Area. Nothing to report.

During the Photographic Reconnaissance at 3.50 p.m., the following observations were made:-

One large steamer in OUTER Harbour alongside Jetty.

One Kite Balloon over MIDDELKERKE.

Five hostile seaplanes observed in formation between OSTEND and NIEUPORT one mile from the coast at a height of about 2,000 feet.

During the remainder of the day, practically no shipping activity was observed in OSTEND Harbour.

5.51 p.m. – Three vessels, apparently destroyers, manoeuvring quickly off OSTEND.

PHOTOGRAPHIC RECONNAISSANCE:-

10.30 a.m. – A Photographic Reconnaissance was carried out over BATTERY HAMILTON at 13,000 feet. Very heavy A.A. fire was experienced, especially from the BAESLER BATTERY. The machine was hit in five places, but neither pilot nor observer were [sic] touched.

3.50 p.m. – A second Photographic Reconnaissance carried out over BATTERY HAMILTON. Five plates were exposed and three very successful results wore obtained. Heavy A.A. fire was again experienced and the machine was hit twice in the Wings. Fortunately the pilot and observer sustained no injuries.

WIRELESS TELEGRAPHY:-

W/T spotting for the English gun continuing the same operations as on the previous day.

Six machines carried out spotting for the British gun in rotation and continuously from 10.50 a.m. to 7.00 p.m. and with almost complete immunity from attack by hostile aircraft; and, considering the exposed position of these machines, an extraordinarily small amount of A.A. fire was experienced.

The visibility during the morning was better than on the previous morning and excellent during the afternoon and evening.

FIGHTER PATROLS:-

Just over 100 Fighter Patrols were carried out during the operations and successfully prevented the English and French Spotting machines from being harassed by enemy machines and also prevented enemy machines from breaking through the BARRAGE, which was swarmed by a constant patrol.

Numerous engagements took place during the day, three of which appeared to be decisive in our favour.

2.35 p.m. – Pilot encountered a Fokker, which was of a light colour underneath and dark brown on top. Pilot opened fire at a range of 1,000 yards decreasing to about 50 yards. Tracers were seen to hit cowl and fuselage behind pilot, whereupon he nose dived and landed S. of YPRES just over his own lines.

Pilot then returned and continued patrol of his sector.

Fourteen escorts to French Spotting machines were carried out during the day:-

Twenty-four hostile machines were encountered, eleven of which were brought to action, and at least two, both Fokkers, were totally destroyed.

The following are extracts from reports of these combats:-

Encounters with Fokker monoplanes occur frequently in the diary reports. These are Fokker E.IIIs attached to the Fokker Staffel of the IX Army, at Vouziers in 1916. The pilot lying by the wheels of the nearest machine is Lt Kurt Student.

An air-to-air study of a Fokker E.III eindecker over the Western Front.

3.10 p.m. – Pilot, when 12,000 feet above MARIAKERKE AERODROME, suddenly observed a FOKKER quite close to him. Both machines quickly manoeuvred for the attacking position. Pilot, however, out-manoeuvred the enemy, forcing him to turn to the right in small circles becoming more and more steep. The Fokker could not keep the steep bank, and breaking away presented a perfect target at point-blank range, and the Nieuport emptied a full tray into him at a distance of a few yards. The Fokker then stalled suddenly and the pilot was clearly seen to fall back, partially out of his seat, and with both hands hanging in the air – obviously having been killed instantly. The Fokker was last seen falling vertically.

On his return journey pilot met a French Maurice-Henri Farman No.2 engaging a large enemy bi-plane, which he also attacked, firing one tray; the result was not observed, but machine dived away apparently in difficulties, and steering an erratic course.

3.00 p.m. – Pilot, when at 10,000 feet, one mile seawards off MIDDELKERKE, encountered a Fokker monoplane slightly lower. Pilot dived to within 50 or 100 feet and fired 20 rounds with one gun which jambed, and then a few rounds with his second gun, which also jambed. The Fokker then fell over and went down vertically spinning, and was without doubt destroyed.

Whilst attending to his guns, pilot observed an enemy bi-plane close to him attacking, and at the same moment he saw bullets striking and holing his top plane. Simultaneously his engine cut-out, and pilot was forced to glide down and land on the beach at NIEUPORT-BAINS, being subjected to heavy A.A., machine-gun and rifle fire. Pilot was forced to abandon his machine, being under shell fire and it was soon entirely destroyed.

This encounter was observed by one of the officers of the Lewin Camp, who considers that the Fokker fell down spinning and uncontrollable.

4.00 p.m. – Another pilot, when at 13,000 feet off MIDDELKERKE, sighted a squadron of five enemy machines working in a "V" wedge. They appeared to be two Fokkers, one L.V.G. and two Aviatiks. Pilot immediately attacked, single handed, all five machines, whereupon four out of the five turned and dived towards the coast. About 20 rounds were fired into the Fokker monoplane, which was last seen diving steeply towards the sea off OSTEND. Meanwhile the Fokker bi-plane was firing down from above, and the L.V.G. was firing backwards from below, at the Nieuport Scout.

Pilot then turned sharply to the right and found himself close to a large Aviatik with a green-coloured fuselage, into which he fired the remainder of the tray. The Aviatik dived away steeply towards the coast.

The same pilot encountered yet another Aviatik, which was at about 8,000 feet, near MARIAKERKE. Pilot dived at the Aviatik from 12,000 feet, emptying one tray at long range. The enemy promptly descended towards MARIAKERKE.

One pilot, whilst returning from escorting the French Spotting machines experienced a sudden total failure of his engine at 7,000 feet, when off LA PANNE. Pilot was unable to reach the shore, but was able to bring his machine down without turning over, in the sea off LA PANNE, where, unfortunately, it sank after a very few minutes. The pilot swam to shore, a distance of over a mile, his floating jacket failing to inflate.

Several engagements with German LVG reconnaissance aircraft are recorded. Here, LVG C.Vs prepare to depart on a mission. The aircraft in the distance on the left has broad stripes painted chordwise across its elevator.

NO. 9 KITE BALLOON SECTION:-

H.M. Barge "Arctic" did not leave Harbour during the day, as she was replenishing supplies and certain repairs were being made.

NO. 11 KITE BALLOOM SECTION:-

The KITE Balloon ascended at 11.30 a.m. and remained up till 8.15 p.m.

Height from 1,500 to 2,300 feet.

The visibility was at first difficult, but became excellent later on.

During the long ascent the observers were spotting and recording the shots from the English gun. Thirty-nine shots in all were fired, the first at 11.40 a.m. and the last at 7.30 p.m. BATTERY HAMILTON replied with 102 shots up to 7.52 p.m. at the French guns.

At 7.52 p.m. BATTERY HAMILTON fired a shell into COXYDE-LE-BAINS, apparently causing a fire.

The following additional observations were made:-

12.13 p.m. – Battery No.86.52 in action.
12.41 p.m. – German Balloon at LEFFINGHE ascended.
4.01 p.m. – Batteries Nos. 86.52 and 490.928 in action.
4.20 p.m. – Battery No. 91.72 engaged by our artillery.
4.41 p.m. – Battery No. 91.72 replying to the Dunes.
5.33 p.m. – Small vessel observed entering OSTEND Harbour.
5.40 p.m. – Another small vessel at end of OSTEND Pier, giving out smoke.
5.50 p.m. – Three vessels, apparently destroyers, manoeuvring quickly off OSTEND.
5.51 p.m. – The LEFFIGHE Balloon moved to STEEN.
7.41 p.m. – Battery 36.52 in action.

[Signed]

Acting Captain.

NOTE:-
On July 8th from 1.30 p.m. till dusk 194 hours flying.
On July 9th from 10.30 a.m. till dusk 248 hours flying.

———————————————

Total: 442 hours.

0022

No.2.

TIRPITZ BATTERY.

Date:- July 9th 1916.

Time:- 3.50 p.m.

Height:- 13,200 feet.

Pilot:- Flight Sub-Lieut. Mack.

Observer:- Sub-Lieut. Sims.

0023

0024

No.3.

TIRPITZ BATTERY.

Date:- July 9th 1916.

Time:- 3.50 p.m.

Height:- 13,200 feet.

Pilot:- Flight Sub-Lieut. Mack.

Observer:- Sub-Lieut. Sims.

0025

0026

No.3a

TIRPITZ BATTERY.

Enlargement of Photograph No.3.

0027

0028

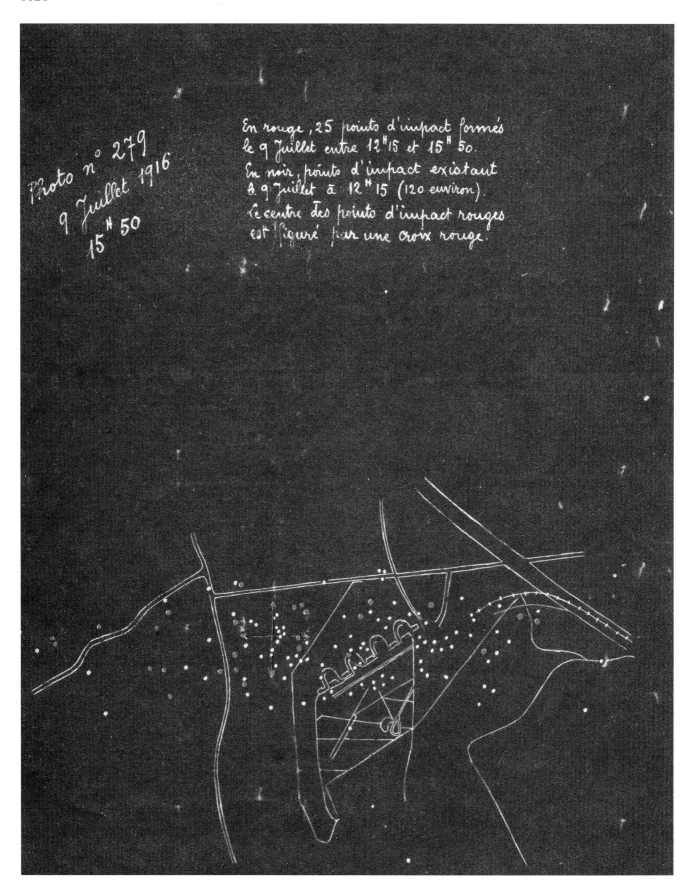

0029/30/31

ROYAL NAVAL AIR SERVICE.

DAILY SUMMARY.

July 19th. 1916. (Midnight to Midnight.)

RECONNAISSANCES:-

5.00 a.m. – Seaplane patrol attempted, but abandoned owing to the thick mist.

9.40 a.m. to 11.30 a.m. ⎫
9.45 a.m. to 12 noon.   ⎬ Seaplane Patrols.

10.16 a.m. – OSTEND. – Two hostile trawlers 5 miles N.E. of OSTEND.

10.45 a.m. – ZEEBRUGGE. – One small vessel, stationary, 2 miles W. of ZEEBBRUGGE, close to the shore.

11.45 a.m. – OSTEND, – One hostile trawler 5 miles N.N.W. of OSTEND, surrounded by six small boats.

One hostile trawler 3 miles N.W. of OSTEND steaming towards Harbour.

No submarines or hostile machines observed.

6.15 p.m. to 7.34 p.m. – Seaplane patrol over special area. No hostile shipping observed.

Coastal Reconnaissances:-

2.46 p.m. – OSTEND. – One small steamer entering the Harbour.

One vessel in the Outer Harbour, thought to be a submarine, but owing to the haze it was impossible to make clearer observations. This reconnaissance was carried out at a height of 5,000 feet.

Photographic Reconnaissance:-

At 4.20 p.m. a Photographic Reconnaissance was carried out over the TIRPITZ BATTERY at 14,000 feet.

Heavy anti-aircraft fire was experienced on the return journey as far as DIXMUDE.

Although the visibility was hazy one excellent result was obtained.

The last photograph taken of this Battery prior to this was taken at 3.50 p.m. on the 9th instant.

During the last 3½ hours firing considerable damage was inflicted.

No.1 Gun is practically untouched, but No.2 Gun shows the cement emplacement very badly damaged and a big sector of the cement work completely knocked away.

No. 3 Gun, which at 3.50 p.m. showed 3 hits on the cement parapet, has had many more hits.

No.4 Gun, which had also received one hit, has been hit again in the same place several times.

The only signs of repair work since the 9th instant seem to be on the spare railway line running in the rear of the Battery. Two trucks are visible on this line behind No.4 Gun.

Comparison of All three Photographs:-
(A). Represents Belgian Photograph taken at 12.30 p.m. on July 9th.
(B). Represents English Photograph taken at 3.50 p.m. on July 9th.
(C). Represents English Photograph taken at 4.20 p.m. on July 19th.

(A).
Gun No.1. – Trained on WESTENDE BAINS.
Gun No.2. – Trained on RAVERSIJDE BAINS.
Gun No.3. – Trained on SLYPEBURG.
Gun No.4. – Trained on ST. PIERRE CAPPELLE.

(B).
Gun No.1. – Trained on the two French Gun Positions.
Gun No.2. – Trained on MIDDELKERKE BAINS.
Gun No.3. – Trained on SLYPEBURG. (Exactly the same position as above.)
Gun No.4. – Trained on the two French Gun Positions.

(C).
Gun No.1. – Trained on RAVERSIJDE BAINS.
Gun No.2. – Trained on WESTENDE.
Gun No.3. – Trained between MARIAKERKE and RAVERSIJDE.
Gun No.4. – Trained approximately towards ANTWERP BATTERY.

Throughout the operations there were always two guns trained seawards.

No. 4. Gun in the first photograph is shown pointing inland over ST. PIERRE CAPPELLE, (possibly anticipating an attack from inland).

In the second photograph this gun was trained on the two French Gun Positions.

In the third photograph all four guns are trained towards the sea, as if an attack from ships was anticipated.

It is thought that the No.3 Gun may have been injured, as during the whole of the second day up to 3.50 p.m. it was pointing somewhat in the direction of the English Gun position and yet never fired a shot.

The shaded portions of the following sketches show the positions where the cement work has been damaged.

Sketch No.1. Damage caused on July 8th and up to 3.50 p.m. on July 9th.

Sketch No.2. Damage caused from 3.50 p.m. to 7.30 p.m. on July 9th.

NO. 9 KITE BALLOON SECTION:-
The barge "Arctic" stood by ready to leave Harbour.

NO.11 KITE BALLOON SECTION:-
Owing to the bad visibility, no ascents were made during the day.

FRENCH AVIATION:-
Four French Seaplane patrols were carried out during the day, but nothing of importance was observed.

NOTE:-
At 1.15 a.m. a hostile machine dropped four bombs on the Aerodrome at FURNES. No damage was done.

[Signed]

Acting Captain.

0032

No.4.

Tirpitz Battery.

Belgian Photograph.

Date:- July 19th. 1916.

Height:- 14,000 feet.

0033

0034

No.4a.

Tirpitz Battery.

Enlargement of Photograph No.4.

0035

0036

No.5.

Tirpitz Battery.

Date:- July 19th. 1916.

Time:- 4.30 p.m.

Height:-

Pilot:- Flight Sub-Lieut. Mack

Observer:- Sub-Lieut. Sims.

0037

0038

No.5a.

Tirpitz Battery.

Enlargement of Photograph No. 5.

0039

0040

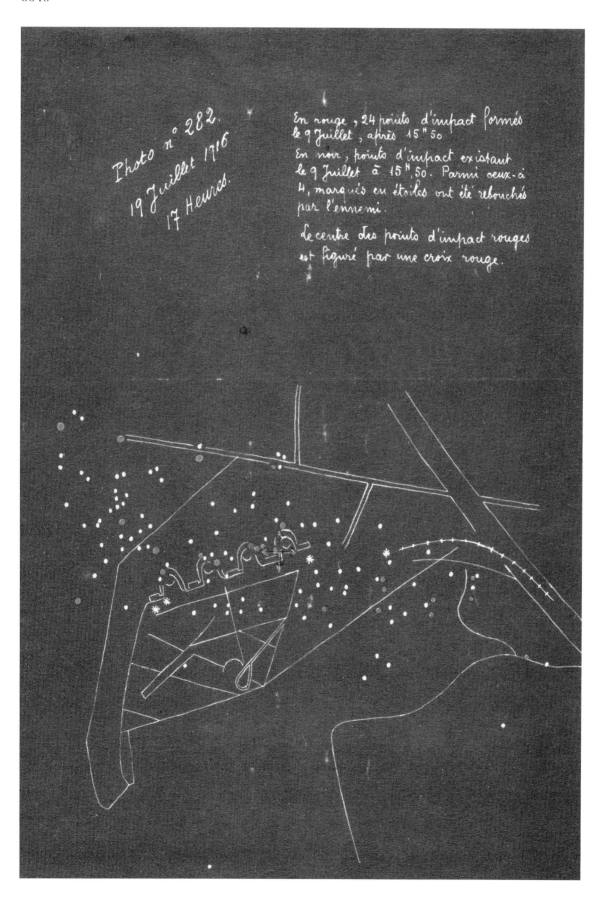

0041/42

ROYAL NAVAL AIR SERVICE.

DAILY SUMMARY.

July 20th. 1916. (Midnight to Midnight.)

RECONNAISSANCES:-

5.10 a.m. to 5.55 a.m. – Seaplane patrol attempted but was forced to return owing to mist.

9.44 a.m. to noon. – Seaplane patrol over special area. – Nothing of importance to report.

Owing to the bad visibility, no Coastal Reconnaissance to OSTEND or ZEEBRUGGE could be carried out.

WIRELESS TELEGRAPHY, SPOTTING ETC.

Operations of the 8th and 9th instant were resumed at 1.30 p.m. B.S.T.

Two spotting machines left at 1.25 p.m. and 2.20 p.m. respectively, but although various positions were tried, including that of a vertical one over the target, observations were absolutely impossible owing to the clouds which were drifting from the N.E.

A smoke screen was observed proceeding from the N. of Battery TIRPITZ, but if the visibility has been good, this would not have interfered with the spotting.

Heavy anti-aircraft fire was experienced over OSTEND.

FIGHTER PATROLS:-

64 Fighter Patrols, including 8 seaplane patrols, were carried out during the afternoon, in conjunction with the operations; protecting the English and French spotting machines and maintaining a perpetual barrage.

3.00 p.m. – A seaplane observed a hostile seaplane patrolling between WESTENDE and OSTEND. The pilot immediately gave chase, but the hostile seaplane was able to make good its escape in the clouds, which were drifting from a N.W. direction.

6.00 p.m. – An enemy biplane was observed coming in from the sea over LA PANNE. Two machines left in pursuit. A third machine had already gone up a few minutes sooner, on the report of two hostile machines spotting.

The hostile machine, whilst crossing over FURNES, making for DIXMUNDE, was encountered by a Nieuport. The latter machine succeeded in chasing the hostile machine over the lines, but was unable to get within close enough range to open an effective fire.

6.18 p.m. – Hostile machine sighted over HOUTHEM. It was chased for a short time, when it was lost sight of in the clouds in the direction of POPERINGHE.

A hostile Kite Balloon was observed close to the Church near the village of D'HOULTHULST, Sheet 12,S.E., 1/40,000 p.13.b.

The only heavy anti-aircraft fire was experienced by the Fighting Escort machines over OSTEND.

One shell burst at a height of 14,000 feet. This was probably fired by the GROOSHERZOG Battery, situated close to the ATELIER DE LA MARINE.

NO. 9 KITE BALLOON SECTION:-

The Barge "Arctic" was in readiness throughout the day, to be put to sea at the shortest notice.

A short ascent was made to test the lift of the balloon, which was found satisfactory.

NO. 11 KITE BALLOON SECTION:-

An ascent was made from 1.34 p.m. to 7.50 p.m.

Altitude 1,700 feet.

Observations were rendered somewhat difficult by the smoke screens which were lit up in front of Battery TIRPITZ, just before the English Battery was due to fire.

The English Battery fired 12 shots and Battery TIRPITZ replied.

2.21 p.m. to 6.57 p.m. – German balloon at LEFFINGHE was up at a great height.

Battery 86.52 was in action at 3.52 p.m.

[Signed]
Acting Captain.

0043/44/45/46

ROYAL NAVAL AIR SERVICE.

DAILY SUMMARY.
July 21st, 1916.
(Midnight to Midnight.)

RECONNAISSANCES:-
2.47 a.m. to 6.40 a.m. – Seaplane patrol over special area. No hostile shipping observed.
5.00 a.m. to 7.40 a.m. – Seaplane patrol, 1 small trawler steering N. magnetic 8 miles N.N.W. of WESTCAPPELLE.

3 vessels, unknown type, 1 mile W. of WESTENDE. No other hostile shipping observed.

10.45 a.m. to 1.15 p.m. – Seaplane patrol. Nothing to report.
3.00 p.m. to 5.00 p.m. – Seaplane patrol. Nothing to report.
6.30 p.m. to 8.30 p.m. – Seaplane patrol. No hostile shipping observed, 1 hostile seaplane sighted, which withdrew on approach.

Coastal Observations:-
10.41 a.m. – 3 small boats lying off OSTEND between 2 and 3 miles seawards.
11.44 a.m. – 2 of the above boats were still off OSTEND and 2 other small boats off the end of OSTEND PIERS.
3.00 p.m. – Coast reported clear of enemy shipping as far as OSTEND.
3.50 p.m. – A long whitish boat entering OSTEND Harbour.
4.45 p.m. – Coast reported clear of enemy shipping as far as BLANKENBERGHE.
6.45 p.m. – 1 large vessel observed between BLANKENBERGHE and ZEEBRUGGE, which appeared to be stationary. Owing to the distance was unable to distinguish the type.

WIRELESS TELEGRAPHY, SPOTTING ETC.
Operations of the English Battery firing on the TIRPITZ Battery were recommenced at 3.40 p.m.

Spotting machines were sent up, but just before operations actually commenced, the spotting machines were recalled.

The visibility at 2,000 feet was good, but at 5/6,000 feet it was very bad.

PHOTOGRAPHIC RECONNAISSANCE:-
At 6.15 p.m. 3 plates were exposed over Battery TIRPITZ at a height of 14,000 feet. Again very heavy A.A. fire was experienced, the machine being hit in the fuselage. The visibility was good, but the light poor for photographing and, in consequence, the prints are rather weak. The same pilot and observer have succeeded in taking the photographs which were obtained on the 9th, 19th and 21st instant. On each occasion their machine came under very heavy A.A. fire; the machine being hit each time.

FIGHTER PATROLS:-
During the afternoon and evening perpetual patrols against enemy aircraft were carried out.

4.10 a.m. – Report was received that a hostile machine was over DUNKERQUE, but owing to the low mist and fog no machines were able to leave to give chase.

10.10 a.m. – Hostile machine was reported over BOURBOURG, which was later reported going in the direction of CALAIS. Machines were sent up to patrol the sector between NIEUPORT, DIXMUDE to seawards and towards CALAIS in the hope of cutting off the hostile machine. Unfortunately no news could be obtained as to the direction in which the hostile machine was returning. A later report states that it was thought that the machine returned by an inland course.

Two pilots reported seeing a very large fire in the direction of ADRINEQ, S.S.W. of GRAVELINES. [Audruicq (current spelling) was the site of a German ammunition dump. Ed.]

3.15 p.m. – Pilot on a Sopwith Fighter Seaplane encountered a hostile Aeroplane (2 seater biplane) of a chocolate colour, with bright cowl, iron crosses painted on white squares, rectangular tail plane.

The hostile biplane was at 10,000 feet and the Sopwith at 11,000 feet.

Pilot dived on the hostile machine, which, in the meantime, was manoeuvring for the position under his tail, opening fire at the same time.

Both machines met nose on, both firing. Pilot fired one tray at close range, machines passing within 20 feet of each other. The hostile machine then turned and made up the coast. The Sopwith gradually began to overhaul the enemy, who was descending and who finally flew over OSTEND at about 5,000 feet. By this time the pilot had practically no petrol left and was forced to return.

5.50 p.m. – Pilot, on a Nieuport, encountered a hostile 2 seater biplane 3 miles E. of DIXMUDE at 9,000 feet. Whilst pilot was manoeuvring for position, the hostile machine opened fire, but pilot eventually was able to get behind and open fire at a range of 100 yards, which was reduced to 30 yards before the complete tray was fired. Tracers were seen entering the enemy's fuselage. The enemy machine was then seen to nose dive and spin with engine full on and black smoke issuing from the machine. Pilot was able to see machine falling at 6,000 feet, obviously entirely out of control. On changing tray the hostile machine had disappeared.

The R.M.A. at LAMPANISSE report that at about 6.00 p.m. a machine was observed E. of DIXMUDE descending at a greater speed than a machine under control usually descends.

Two Fighter Patrols accompanying the Photographic Reconnaissance came under very heavy A.A. fire, one machine being hit in 3 places. One pilot experienced two salvoes at close proximity from WESTENDE A.A. Battery.

NO 9 KITE BALLOON SECTION:-
Barge "Arctic" stood ready to be put to sea. No ascents were made during the day.

NO. 11 KITE BALLOON SECTION:-
An ascent was made from 10.18 a.m. to 1.35 p.m. and two weather reports were signalled. Visibility at 12.45 p.m. was bad, owing to the low lying mist.

A second ascent was made from 3.15 p.m. to 6.30 p.m. Visibility moderate at first, improving later.

Spotting was carried out for Dominion Battery firing on TIRPITZ Battery. Smoke screens were again used by the hostile Battery, which somewhat interfered with the Balloon observations. Dominion Battery opened fire at 3.25 p.m., seven shots in all being fired.

5.05 p.m. – A very bright light, not unlike a flashlamp, was observed in a line with target, but a shade to the left, about opposite MIDDELKERKE.

A hostile Kite Balloon was observed near the coast. Bearing 1/40,000 Belgium, Sheet 12, H.31,c.l.l.

The hostile Kite Balloon at LEFFINGHE was also observed up at a great height.

THE FOLLOWING OBSERVATIONS WERE MADE BY THE FRENCH:-

10.40 a.m. to 12.20 p.m. – French Seaplane patrol. 3 T.B.D's about 2 miles N. of OSTEND. 1 very large T.B.D. between BLANKENBERGHE and ZEEBRUGGE and 5 leaving OSTEND Harbour.

3.10 p.m. to 5.00 p.m. – French Seaplane Patrol.

3.55 p.m. – 2 merchant vessels off OSTEND.

4 vessels moored in the W. Quay of the BASSIN D'ECHOUAGE.

4.10 p.m. – 2 vessels moored in ZEEBRUGGE Roads, apparently merchant vessels. 1 Kite Balloon over HEYST at a height of about 5,000 feet.

The HEYST Batteries were trained towards the sea.

3.40 p.m. to 5.05 p.m. – French Seaplane Patrol.

4.05 p.m. – 2 small boats off OSTEND.

4.15 p.m. – 5 small boats off OSTEND, 1 of which appeared to be a T.B.

One Kite Balloon in the direction of ZEEBRUGGE.

HEYST Batteries observed to be in action and dense smoke clouds over MARIAKERKE.

[Signed]

Lieutenant, R.N.V.R.,
for Acting Captain.

0047

No.6.

TIRPITZ BATTERY.

Date:- July 21st. 1916.

Time:- 6.15 p.m.

Height:- 14,000 feet.

Pilot:- Flight Sub-Lieut. Mack.

Observer:- Sub-Lieut. Sims.

0048

0050

No.8.

BATTERY TIRPITZ.

Showing repair work. Cementing No.2 parapet and preparations in progress for cementing No.2 dug-out.

French Photograph

Date:- August 9th. 1916.

Time:- 3.00 p.m.

0049

0052

No.8a.

Enlargement of No.8.

0053

0054

Bombing Raid carried out on August 2nd. 1916 on the ST. DENIS AERODROME and MIERELBEKE AMMUNITION SHEDS, by Nos.4 and 5 Wings.

0055/56

ROYAL NAVAL AIR SERVICE.

DAILY SUMMARY.
August 2nd. 1916.
(Midnight to Midnight.)

RECONNAISSANCES:-
5.15 a.m. – Seaplane patrol was attempted, but owing to the bad visibility was forced to return.

Owing to the low lying mist throughout the day, no other patrols were carried out.

BOMBING RAIDS:-
At noon 14 machines took part in a bombing raid on:-

(1). ST. DENIS WESTREM AERODROME, and
(2). AMMUNITION DEPOT AT GHENT.

(1). The actual damage inflicted on the objective is difficult to estimate, but it is certain that a number of the sheds and billeting buildings of the Aerodrome were badly damaged.

During the attack eight hostile machines were observed on the Aerodrome and bombs were seen to fall close to them.

(2). Bombs were clearly seen to fall on the ammunition depot and Arsenal close by; also 2 or 3 bombs hit railway trucks on the siding.

REMARKS:-
No anti-aircraft fire seems to have been experienced over the objectives and only a few shots were fired from the coast batteries.

What appeared to be a destroyer and submarine were observed making circles under the lee of ZEEBRUGGE MOLE. These were probably in fear of an attack from the air and were consequently, making evolutions.

A new Aerodrome at KNOCKE was located, but the number of sheds could not be ascertained.

FIGHTER PATROLS:-
10 Fighters accompanied the Bombing machines on their journey, working in two "V" formations.

3 hostile seaplanes were observed leaving ZEEBRUGGE Harbour, which were immediately attacked by one of the machines of the Fighter escort. One tray was fired, upon which the hostile seaplanes returned.

Whilst these machines were circling over GHENT, in order to allow the Bombers time to reform for the return journey, observations were able to be made and a number of explosions were seen on the objectives and several fires started, but owing to the smoke which by this time was considerable, it was difficult to observe anything precise.

At the time of the raids reported in the diary, 5(N) Sqn was commanded by this man, Lt Cdr Spencer Grey. (Bruce/Leslie)

No anti-aircraft fire was experienced over the town of GHENT or in the neighbourhood.

Ranken darts were dropped over the Aerodrome by one of the Fighter escort machines.

METHOD OF ATTACK:-

A rendezvous was made at a pre-arranged place, the Bombing machines being in the middle and supported by a "V" wedge of Fighters on each side.

One Bombing machine acted as leader throughout the journey, both there and back.

On approaching the objectives the bombing machines divided off into two sections, each attacking their objective in a pre-arranged formation, after which both Bombers and Fighters reformed in similar formation and returned.

FIGHTER PATROLS (cont.):-

11 Fighter machines proceeded to meet the returning Bombing machines and their Fighter escorts, and patrolled the lines between NIEUPORT, DIXMUDE, YPRES, ROULERS, THOUROUT.

No hostile machines were observed during this patrol.

CASUALTIES:-

One pilot from the second set of Fighters, patrolling the lines, did not return. A pilot who was flying close by observed a shell burst near this pilot, and his machine immediately nose dived for several thousand feet, flattened out and again nose dived out of sight. Approximate position about 4 miles N. of YPRES, close to the lines.

Nos. 9 AND 11 KITE BALLOON SECTIONS:-

No ascents were made during the day, owing to the unfavourable weather.

[Signed]
WING CAPTAIN.

0057/58

ROYAL NAVAL AIR SERVICE.

DAILY SUMMARY.
September 7th. 1916.
(Midnight to Midnight.)

RECONNAISSANCES:-
10.00 a.m. to 12.30 p.m. – Seaplane reconnaissance accompanied by seaplane fighter machine.

11.45 a.m. – 2 hostile T.B.D's observed 4 miles magnetic N. of ZEEBRUGGE. This was reported to the Fleet by W/T.

The SCHOUWEN Lightship was not observed in its old position and no trace of the new one could be found; nor were the positions of Nos. 13 and 4 buoys picked up although the visibility was good and the seaplane made a thorough search for both lightship and buoys.

On the return journey a bright light like a searchlight was observed at 12.5 p.m. when the seaplane was to seawards off NIEUPORT. This light appeared to come from the direction of RAVERSIDJE and was stationary.

No submarines were observed.

Coastal Reconnaissances:-
A signal was received that the Belgian Kite Balloon had observed great train activity on the OSTEND-BRUGES railway line.

3.35 p.m. to 5.15 p.m. – A special reconnaissance was therefore made, but was unable to confirm the above report. The following observations were made:-

1 train at OSTEND on the Loop-line proceeding to the town station.

No activity at the DOCKS and none on the railway lines to BRUGES and THOUROUT.

No activity in OSTEND either in the form of smoke from Factories or movement of Barges.

1 small trailer in the Fairway of OUTER HARBOUR and 1 dredger between the PIERS.

BOMBING RAID:-
18 machines left at noon to bomb ST. DENIS WESTREM AERODROME at GHENT.

6 of these machines, when opposite ZEEBRUGGE, were forced to return owing to the strong wind.

One of those pilots, whilst returning, was shelled from KNOCKE and chased from ECCLOOS to KNOCKE by an L.V.G, which was firing intermittently. Pilot was later attacked by a small seaplane which followed him from ZEEBRUGGE to OSTEND, firing continually. This seaplane was very much like a Schneider Cup [seaplane: i.e. single-engined, single-seat tractor floatplane. Ed.]. The hostile machine gave up the chase when about 1 mile N.E. of NIEUPORT PIERS at 800feet and landed on the water.

Pilot was able to make a successful landing, although his machine was severely damaged. Amongst other damage, the warp control was cut through, one elevator wire cut, oil tank punctured, there being in all 49 holes in the machine.

An LVG C-type two-seat reconnaissance aircraft over the Front, as it might have appeared to an Allied fighter pilot. Although its tailplane is quite effectively camouflaged, the chordwise stripes across its wings render the machine highly visible.

Another of these pilots was attacked by a Fokker monoplane, but the hostile machine was successfully driven off by the Fighter escort.

The remaining machines succeeded in finding their objective, and dropped their bombs from heights varying from 1,000 feet to 2,000 feet. It is estimated that considerable damage was done but, although the sheds were clearly visible at this low altitude, it was impossible to observe the actual damage owing to the heavy hailstorm in progress.

All the machines returned except one.

The following observations were made:-

1.15 p.m. – 3 vessels observed moored to the quay in the OUTER HARBOUR, OSTEND.
1 vessel at the entrance to OSTEND HARBOUR.
2 vessels inside ZEEBRUGGE MOLE.
1 large vessel outside the MOLE.
3 hostile seaplanes observed getting off the water outside ZEEBRUGGE MOLE.

On the return journey one pilot was followed by a Fokker from the vicinity of BRUGES as far as 3 miles off DIXMUDE, when hostile machine turned off in the direction of GHISTELLES.

Attack on hostile Kite Balloon about 1 mile S.E. of STEENE, (OSTEND)

At 2.10 p.m. a signal was received from No. 11 Kite Balloon stating that the hostile Kite Balloon was up at WILSKERKE, one pilot was immediately dispatched.

Pilot proceeded out to sea and hung about off NIEUPORT for about 10 minutes and then proceeded towards WILSKERKE. Observing the balloon arriving at its position E. of STEENE, pilot flew out to sea until the balloon had reached a considerable altitude and then proceeded over OSTEND, throttling down at 16,000 feet, pilot dived, attacked the balloon and immediately afterwards saw the balloon with at least three, if not more, flaming points in her. When last observed, the balloon was falling, a mass of flames, with a large column of smoke above.

Kite Balloon was observed to fall approximately at OSTEND 1/40,000. I.17.b.7.4. (See detailed report appended).

Photographic Reconnaissance:-

A photographic machine accompanied the bombers on their raid on ST. DENIS WESTREM AERODROME. The thick layer of clouds prevented photographs being taken of the Aerodrome during the raid, although the photographic machine remained in the vicinity about half an hour endeavouring to find a pocket. [Copy ends here; final page apparently missing. Ed]

0059/60/61

ST. DENIS – WESTREM.

Sketch Map showing Aerodrome.
REFERENCE.

(1).   Small wooden hut, about 8 ft. square and 10 ft. height, used as the wireless operator's cabin. Close by it are the antennae.

(2).   Wooden shed, about 30–36 ft. broad by 48 ft. long, painted so as to have the appearance of a house, ground floor, first storey and garret; sham door painted green with imitation windows and curtains, green shutters. This frontage which is moveable forms the door of the shed.

(3).   A building in all respects similar to No. 2.

(4).   A shed having the outward appearance of six small cottages, with one door and two windows each, painted grey and green. This shed is used for aeroplanes and part of it as a garage for motor cars.

(5).   An aeroplane shed with a painted frontage representing a house, with ground floor, one storey and a garret with painted doors and windows.

(6).   Two small houses, ground floor only, painted red, white windows, light red door. All this frontage can be removed and forms the door of the shed. This shed is 36 ft. broad by 48 ft. long.

(7).   An aeroplane shed having the appearance of a house, with ground floor, one storey and a garret, painted red with white windows and light red door; a door with a window on each side of it, two windows on the first storey, with a skylight at the top.

(8).   One of the race-course stands with a corrugated iron roof, tiers, etc., about 40 metres long by 12 in depth.

(9).   Another stand, rectangular in shape, without a roof, greyish in colour, 30 metres in length by 12 in depth.

(10).   Close by this stand is a dug-out for the men in case of bombardment.

(11).   A small "café", red brick building with black tile roof.

(12).   "Tir aux Pigeons" house, red brick building with wooden ornamental work.

(13).   A large chateau, Flemish Renaissance style, red bricks, slate roof, leading to which is a drive planted with oak trees.

(14).   Poplar trees plantation in the middle of meadows, known in Flanders as a "Dries".

(15).   Straight race Course, used for the 1800 yards for the four year old.

(16).   A grass bank running all round the plain with a double line of trees planted all the way round.

(17).   A paved road lined with poplar trees.

(18).   A paved road partly lined with poplar trees.

(19).   A road called in the country "CHAUSEE de la PRAIRIE" paved and lined with young poplar trees.

(20).   Café "au Derby" gable roof, white-washed building with a garden attached to it. A meeting place for men employed at the aerodrome.

(21).   Small woods and plantations.

(22).   A large school with several brick buildings around a central square.

(23).   A small house, red bricks, dark roof.

(24).   A white house, one storey, red roof.

(25).   A small farm, white with a low reddish roof.

(26).   A red house with a black roof.

(27).   A white house with a black roof.

Ch. I. A large chateau, Gothic Style, red bricks with a tower, situated in the middle of a well timbered park.

Ch. II. Another chateau consisting of a red brick building on the St. Denis side and a white building on the Ghent side. This building stands on a small island surrounded by a moat, bridged in three places. There are several hothouses in the middle of orchards on the Ghent side of the Chateau.

Ch.III A white chateau with a slate roof.

COURTRAI to GHENT Road. –A large paved main road, lined with trees at irregular intervals and a cycle track in cinders running along one side of the road.

N.B.
(1). The waterways are at this time of the year (summer) covered with a mossy vegetation, which in part render them from the air hardly discernable from the neighbouring meadows.
(2). The Flying Ground as shewn in the sketch Map is partly covered with grass with a huge patch of bare sand.
(3). Up to quite recently there were no fixed defences in the way of guns and anti-aircraft guns at the aerodrome.

------OoO------

EXTRACT FROM D.A.R. NO. 115.

St. Denis Westrem. – Changes have been made at this flying ground. Five sheds, which were said to come from another aerodrome on the Western Front, have been brought here and erected close to the stand, on the western side of the flying ground. Two other sheds are under construction on the eastern side of the ground.

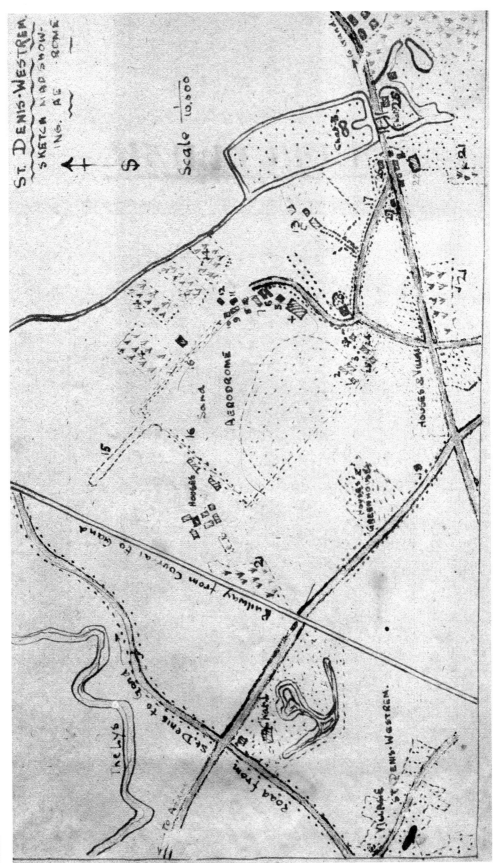

0063

MEIRELBEKE.

Sketch Map showing position of Ammunition Sheds.

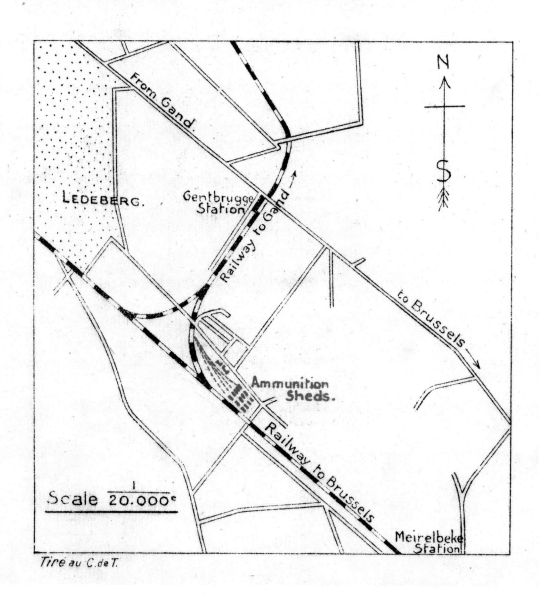

Tiré au C.de T.

0064

Newspaper cutting, source unidentified

BOMBS WRECK "ZEPP"
BASE IN BELGIUM.
40 British Airmen Drop
2 Tons of Explosives.

HAVOC IN ARSENALS

The raid on the Germans' Zeppelin base near Ghent by forty British naval aeroplanes seems, from yesterday's messages, to have been on a much bigger scale than the Admiralty's modest communiqué claimed.

Two tons of bombs were dropped on various important aerodromes, arsenals, a railway junction and railways as set out in the reports below.

AMSTERDAM, Saturday.

The *Telegraaf* gives the following additional details of the British naval air raid on the German establishments at Ghent on Wednesday, obtained from a correspondent on the frontier.

About noon some forty aeroplanes arrived above the town. They attacked aircraft sheds and workshops on the Place Farman, near Port Arthur, which were hit by several bombs.

A great hangar where 150 men were working was totally ruined, and other buildings were badly damaged.

The Germans are now constructing defence works along the road from Amandsberg to Oostacker.-Reuter.

The *Echo Belge* says the aeroplanes bombed the arsenal at Ghent and various other strategical points.

The squadron arrived in several detachments. One, which was composed of ten machines, flew along the eastern frontier of Flanders, at a height of from 2,500 to 3,000 metres, and passed Selzaete at 2.30 in the afternoon, flying towards Ostend.-Reuter.

A Central News version of the *Telegraaf's* new account says that the effect of the bombs on the biggest railway junction in Belgium, for such is the station lying in the northern suburb of Ghent, was terrific.

It is also understood that bombs were dropped on a munition factory in the suburb of Ledeberg, which was completely destroyed.

Newspaper cutting, source unidentified:

MUNITION FACTORY BLOWN UP

AMSTERDAM, Saturday.

The *Telegraaf* gives the following additional details of the British naval air raid on the German establishments at Ghent on Wednesday, obtained from a correspondent on the frontier.

About noon some forty aeroplanes arrived above the town. They attacked aircraft sheds and workshops on the Place Farman, near Port Arthur, which were hit by several bombs.

A great hangar, where 150 men were working, was totally ruined and other buildings were badly damaged.

The Germans are now constructing defence works along the road from Amandsberg to Oostacker.–Reuter.

A Central News version of the *Telegraaf's* new account says that the effect of the bombs on the biggest railway junction in Belgium, for such is the station lying in the northern suburb of Ghent, was terrific. It is also understood that bombs were dropped on a munition factory in the suburb of Ledeberg, which was completely destroyed, while the arsenal was damaged.

0065

Bombing Raid carried out on the 9th of August, 1916 on the ZEPPELIN SHED at EVERE by (Sub-Lieutenant COLLET and HARKNISS) No. 5 WING.

0066/67

SPECIAL REPORT ON BOMBING RAID ON ZEPPELIN SHEDS AT BRUSSELS ON THE MORNING OF THE 9TH, AUGUST, 1916.

First pilot left at 4.30 a.m. B.S.T., and set a course up the coast and turned inland East of ZEEBRUGGE. He had no difficulty in finding BRUSSELS and arrived within view of his objective at 12,000 feet. Whilst gliding down, this pilot had a good view of the shed at BERCHEM ST. AGATHE, of which the eastern door was open and the shed was seen to be empty, he therefore decided to attack EVERE shed and came down to within 300 to 500 feet of the ground, which corresponds to 150 and 350 feet above the shed. All twelve bombs were released in a diagonal line across the shed and at least eight direct hits were registered. Huge masses of black smoke were seen pouring out of the shed throughout the whole of its length, and gave place shortly afterwards to dense clouds of white smoke. Pilot distinctly heard eight detonations from his own bombs and concludes that the remaining four did not have time to mix properly on account of the low altitude from which they were dropped. No anti-aircraft fire was experienced until the bombs had been dropped, but immediately afterwards this machine was subjected to very heavy rifle, machine-gun and shrapnel fire from all directions. Pilot attained a height of 1,000 feet shortly after dropping his bombs and then steered a zig-zag course across the Town in order to present as difficult a target as possible. Return journey was made via GHENT and DIXMUDE. Notwithstanding the very heavy fire this machine was subjected to, no damage was caused to the machine, which only shows a few small holes caused by rifle and shrapnel bullets in both planes. While on this outward journey, this pilot observed a white light, which flashed every second on the northern edge of the BASSIN DE CHASSE at OSTBND. Returned to Aerodrome at 7.50 a.m. Machine – Sopwith No.9395.

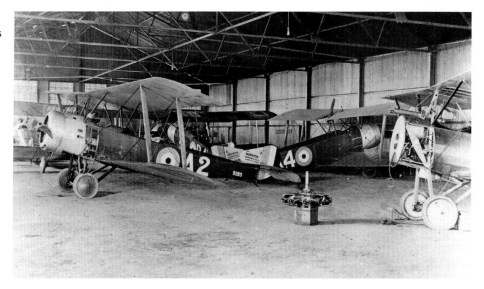

Single- and two-seat Sopwith 1½ Strutters of 5(N) Sqn in various states of repair or readiness. The aircraft on the left, 9395/A2, was one of the two that took part in the raid on the airship shed at Evere on 9 August 1916.

Second pilot left at 4.40 a.m. B.S.T. and steered the same course as the first pilot and arrived over the shed at EVERE at 6.25 a.m. B.S.T., when he observed bombs from the first machine, falling in a line across the Zeppelin Hangar, a large hole being blown by one of these in the eastern end of the roof, through which immense volumes of black smoke were emitted. Smoke was also pouring out of the other end of the Hangar. Meanwhile this pilot was gliding down with the object of attacking the same Hangar from a low altitude, but the anti-aircraft fire that he was subjected to became so dense that he dropped his bombs from a height of just under 9,000 feet. Eight bombs were released in a line north to south across the shed, of which some were certainly direct hits, for immediately after the bombs were dropped still greater quantities of black smoke appeared out of both ends of the shed. This pilot then steered west to the shed at BERCHEM ST. AGATHE, where the remaining four bombs were released. The anti-aircraft fire was, during the whole of this time, increasing in volume, although rather erratic, and pilot was therefore unable to observe whether any damage was caused by the four bombs dropped over the second shed, although they appeared to fall in a line straight across it. This pilot returned by the coast route, steering N.W. to ZEEBRUGGE, where he attained a height of 12,000 feet. On return journey two torpedo boats were seen manoeuvring near ZEEBRUGGE MOLE, and two smaller vessels were seen a mile N.W. of ZEEBRUGGE, steering H.W. A fleet of about nine War Vessels were seen 15 miles out to sea off OSTEND. This machine returned to the Aerodrome at 8.20 a.m., when it was found that the third bomb had failed to release. Machine – Sopwith No.9420.

A group of 5 Wing pilots in front of 1½ Strutter 9378 after it had been crashed by Hewson. Left to right: Moir, Reynolds, Hervey, Hewson, Fowler and Harkniss. Flight Sub-Lieutenant D.E. Harkniss, a New Zealander, piloted one of the two aircraft in the raid on the Evere airship shed on 9 August. (Bruce/Leslie)

Harkniss is on the left of this group, posing in front of a 5 Wing Breguet Z at Coudekerque in the spring or summer of 1916. (Bruce/Leslie)

0068

24.8.15.   N.A.S.F.161.

AIRCRAFT.

EVERE AIRSHIP SHED.

0069

This photograph was taken on the 13th August from the roof of a house in the EVERE-SAVENTHEM Road. (Vide Sketch Map and reference in airship stations in Belgium 2nd Edition N.A.S.F. 10th August 1915).

The following details of the airship shed often mentioned in the reports may be noticed on this photograph:

(1) The new sliding-doors at the end of the shed facing towards BRUSSELS. These doors have been erected since the air raid on the 7th June. The portion that was destroyed and then repaired was at the same end of the shed.

(2) The iron framework.

(3) The gangway above the sliding-doors.

(4) The protective colouring of the shed.

(5) Some of the huts and small sheds of the aerodrome built between the shed and the HAECHT Road may be seen to the left of the sliding-doors in the photograph.

0070

24. 8. 15.

AIRCRAFT.

THE ZEPPELIN-LUFTSCHIFF LZ 38

Destroyed at EVERE on 7th June, 1915.

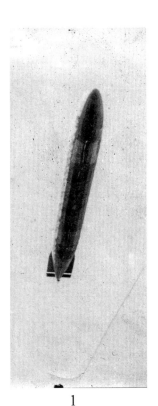  

1   2   3

1. The LZ 38 flying over EVERE. The distinctive marks can be seen on the airship. Three black crosses on the fore and two aft on either side of the aft gondola; the letters and figures LZ 38 also appear although faintly at the bows on either side of the fore black cross.
2. The LZ 38 leaving the shed at EVERE. This photograph was taken from the HAECHT road seen in the foreground.
3. The LZ 38 clear of the shed and ready to ascend.

The LZ 38 completely destroyed at EVERE on 7th of June 1915 by Flight Lieut. J.S. Mills, R.N. and Flight Lieut. J. Wilson, R.N. had taken part in all the raids on England at the end of May and the beginning of June. (Vide N.A.S.F. Monthly Record for May and June.)

0074

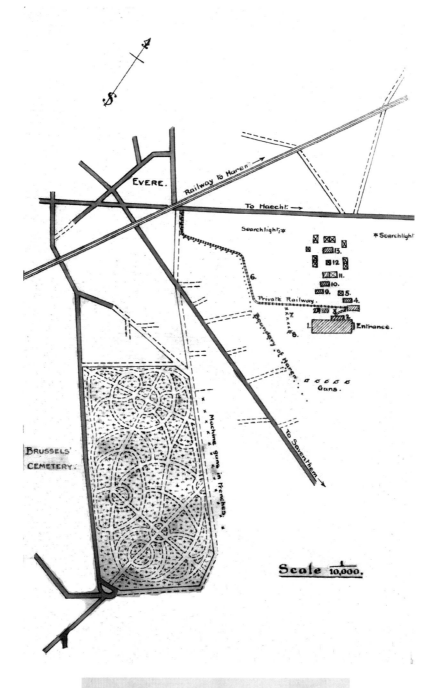

EVERE.

SKETCH MAP SHOWING ZEPPELIN SHED.

TO ACCOMPANY N.A.S.F.

0075

BOMB RAID ON THE LICHTERVELDE AMMUNITION DUMPS by Flight Lieutenant Wood and Flight Sub-Lieuts, Collett, Harkness and Jamison, on August 18th, 1916.

0076

ROYAL NAVAL AIR SERVICE.

DAILY SUMMARY.

August 18th. 1916.

(Midnight to Midnight,)

RECONNAISSANCES:-

1.50 p.m. to 3.45 p.m. – Seaplane patrol over special area, accompanied by a Fighter machine.

One black buoy observed 5½ miles N.W. of OSTEND. Heavy white smoke observed at the back of OSTEND Harbour.

5.04 p.m. to 6.05 p.m. – Seaplane patrol over special area accompanied by a Fighter machine. Nothing to report.

1.55 p.m. to 2.30 p.m. – Photographic Reconnaissance attempted, but was forced to return owing to the heavy clouds at 3,000 feet.

BOMBING RAID:-

At noon 4 machines left on a Bombing Raid on the LICHTERVELDE AMMUNITION DUMPS.

48–20 kilo. bombs were dropped on the objective. The pilots found it extremely difficult to locate the target, owing to the low altitude of the clouds. Pilots, therefore, were only able to pick up their bearings through holes in the clouds and then dive through them before releasing their bombs. Very heavy anti-aircraft fire was experienced, but the firing in the vicinity of the target was inaccurate.

Two large fires were observed at the S. end of the DUMP, near the road which leads to LICHTERVELDE VILLAGE. All four machines returned safely.

FIGHTER PATROLS:-

Fighter patrols were carried out from 7.30 a.m. onwards:-

(1). Patrolling the NIEUPORT-DIXMUDE lines.
(2). Accompanying the attempted Photographic Reconnaissance.
(3). Two machines accompanied the four bombing machines, one of which went the whole journey there and back and circled over the objective for about 15 minutes, until all the bombing machines were on their return journey.

Owing to the thick low clouds the observer was unable to make any observations as to the results of the raid.

No hostile machines were observed during the day.

NO. 9 KITE BALLOON SECTION:-

The barge "Arctic" stood ready to be put to sea, if required.

0077

BOMB RAID ON THE THREE COGNELEE ZEPPELIN SHEDS AT NAMUR

by Lieut. Wood and Flight Sub-Lieuts. Collet

and Jamieson of No. 5 Wing. August 25th. 1916.

Flight Sub-Lieut. Jamieson did not return from the raid and it has since been learnt that he was forced to land in HOLLAND and has been interned as a prisoner of War.

Lieut. Woods, owing to thick clouds, lost his bearings and was forced to return.

Flight Sub-Lieut. Collet succeeded in reaching the objective. (Detailed report attached.)

Flight Sub-Lieut. Jamieson flew with Flight Sub-Lieut. Collet as far as NAMUR and news as to the results of his bomb dropping are not yet to hand.

*T*HE Secretary of the Admiralty makes the following announcement :—

BRITAIN.

Early yesterday (Friday) morning an attack was carried out by naval aeroplanes upon enemy airship sheds near Namur.

The sheds were successfully bombarded and two of them hit, but, due to low-lying clouds, it was not possible to observe the amount of damage done.

One of our machines has failed to return.

.·. An interesting feature of this announcement is that our raid on Namur and the Zeppelin raid on the outskirts of London and the East and South-east Coasts appear to have been taking place simultaneously.

Though no definite hour is mentioned in the Admiralty communiqué, it has been announced that the German airships' visit lasted from midnight to three o'clock yesterday morning.

Namur is thirty-four miles south-east of Brussels. Last Friday at noon, it will be recalled, British naval aeroplanes dropped forty-eight bombs on ammunition-dumps at Lichtervelde, near Bruges.

0078

BOMBING RAID ON ZEPPELIN SHEDS AT GOGNELEE, NAMUR,

AUGUST 25th, 1916.

(Detail Report By Pilot Who Reached The Objective.)

Pilot left at 05.27 (B.S.T.) and set compass course 125 degrees, crossed the lines at 10,000 feet and increased his height to 13,000 feet on the way out. When he arrived at what he judged to be the target, he had to descend to 5,000 feet to see the ground at all. Whilst searching for Namur, he kept in the lower layer of clouds in order to present as difficult a target as possible[;] even at this height it was only after 25 minutes search that he picked up the target. In this he was considerably helped by a sudden burst of shrapnel close to the machine. This Pilot dropped his twelve bombs in a line along the two northern sheds from a height of 5,000 feet, but on account of bad weather conditions and heavy and extremely accurate A.A. fire, he was not able to observe any results. He then steered for home by compass, but a strong S.W. wind blew him out of his intended course and eventually he picked up Bruges Ship Canal at a distance of 25 miles, and shaped his course to cross the lines at Dixmude. Three miles west of our lines, his engine stopped on account of an internal breakage, but he managed to glide down and land safely on the beach at La Panne. Heavy A.A. fire was experienced in the neighbo[u]rhood of Dixmude and Thourut, both on outward and return Journey. This Pilot flew in close company with Third Pilot all the way to Namur and the last glimpse of this machine was when he shut off his engine and glided down to search for the target.

0079

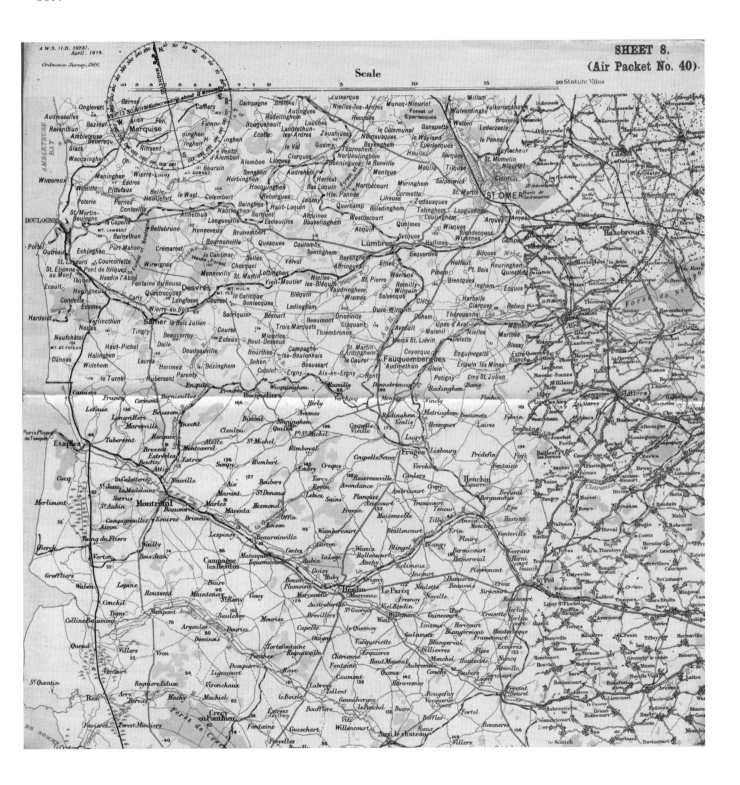

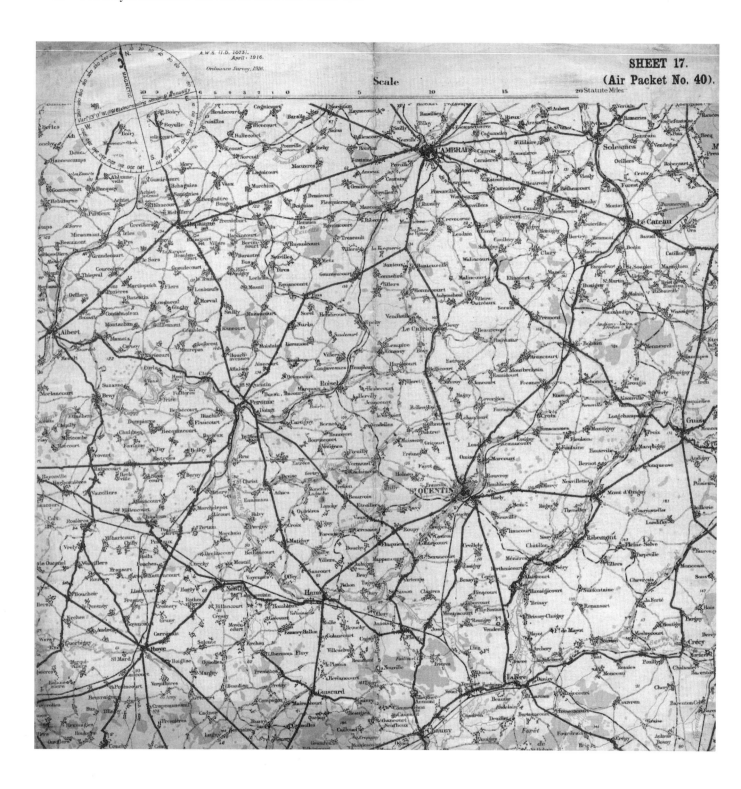

SHEET 17.
(Air Packet No. 40).

0080/81

ROYAL NAVAL AIR SERVICE.

DAILY SUMMARY.
September 2nd, 1916.
(Midnight to Midnight.)

RECONNAISSANCES:-
12.50 p.m. to 2.00 p.m. ⎫ Seaplane patrols accompanied by
 3.40 p.m. to 6.15 p.m. ⎭ Fighter machines. Nothing to report.

Owing to the overcast sky, no Coastal Reconnaissances were carried out during the day.

BOMBING RAID:-
3.10 p.m. – Four pilots left and carried out a bombing raid on the shipbuilding yards at HOBOKEN, ANTWERP.

The first pilot to leave, although in the vicinity of ANTWERP, was unable to pick up any landmarks owing to the thick layer of clouds and was forced to return.

Whilst on the return journey pilot observed two vessels leaving ZEEBRUGGE, one of which appeared to be a large destroyer.

The other three pilots succeeded in reaching the objective, but this was only done by steering a compass course above the clouds, and when they thought they had reached the objective, diving down through the clouds to pick out the shipbuilding yards. This they succeeded in doing, although some time elapsed before the objective could be clearly observed.

34 bombs were dropped from heights varying from 1,000 to 3,000 and 4,500 feet. No results as to the damage done could be observed, as during the actual time that the bombs were being dropped a heavy hailstorm was in progress.

No anti-aircraft fire was experienced from ANTWERP, but one machine had a quantity of fire balls fired at it. The balls were of an incendiary nature and the shooting was good, several passing quite close.

All three machines were subjected to heavy anti-aircraft fire off ZEEBRUGGE and one pilot, as soon as he was out of range of the shore batteries was attacked by a hostile monoplane. Pilot fired 9 rounds at this machine and then got into the clouds once again and lost sight of it.

Owing to gaps in the clouds between ZEEBRUGGE and NIEUPORT, all coast batteries kept the machines under continuous fire.

FIGHTER PATROLS:-
Three Fighter patrols were sent out to meet the bombing machines on their return from HOBOKEN. Owing to the thick layer of clouds the coast was hardly ever visible and it was impossible to locate the returning machines. No hostile aircraft were observed.

A few other Fighter patrols were carried out over NIEUPORT, WESTENDE and DIXMUDE, but there was nothing of importance to report.

NOS. 9 & 11 KITE BALLOON SECTIONS:-
Owing to the unfavourable weather conditions, no ascents were made during the day.

[Signed]
WING CAPTAIN.

0082/83

ROYAL NAVAL AIR SERVICE.

DAILY SUMMARY.

September 3rd. 1916.

(Midnight to Midnight.)

RECONNAISSANCES:-

Owing to the extremely low altitude of the clouds, no Coastal Reconnaissances were carried out during the day.

5.37 a.m. to 7.50 a.m. ⎱ Seaplane patrols over special area
1.02 p.m. to 2.12 p.m. ⎰ accompanied by Fighter machines.

No hostile shipping or submarines were observed.

The visibility on both occasions was very bad owing to low lying clouds.

BOMBING RAID:-

17 machines left about 4.45 a.m. and bombed GHISTELLES AERODROME.
85 Bombs were dropped.

Owing to the early hour and the bad visibility, the exact damage done was difficult to observe, but one of the last machines to leave distinctly saw columns of smoke rising from the AERODROME and two hits were observed on the railway side track which leads to the large sheds on the S. side of the AERODROME.

Bombs were dropped from an average height of 5,000 feet.

One of the Pilots had just crossed the lines when he was attacked by a Fokker, which completely outmanoeuvred him. Unfortunately Pilot's gun jammed after firing the first few shots and his machine got into an uncontrollable spinning nose dive, falling about 2,000 feet. Pilot, after turning off his engine, succeeded in righting his machine. Fortunately a Fighter machine, which was close by, succeeded in driving the enemy off.

Pilot then regained his height and dropped his bombs on the objective. This Pilot distinctly saw smoke rising from several of the sheds.

A large enemy biplane of the L.V.G. type endeavoured to cut this machine off after he had released his bombs. The hostile machine was about 1,500 feet below and held its own both in climb and speed. The enemy fired several drums into our machine from below, but turned back 5 or 6 miles E. of the lines. Machine was hit several times by machine gun bullets and splinters from anti-aircraft fire. Fortunately the Pilot escaped any injuries.

The anti-aircraft fire experienced was very severe, several machines being hit. One machine only was seriously shot about, but in spite of this, a successful landing was made. All machines returned safely.

FIGHTER PATROLS:-

Nine Fighting machines acted as escort to the above bombing machines on their return journey.

The Fighters also confirmed the fact that a good deal of smoke was seen rising from the AERODROME.

During the morning hostile aeroplanes were very busy spotting. On all occasions they were driven back but were difficult to attack, as they were at too low an altitude and kept on their own side of the lines.

Wintry operations by Sopwith
1½ Strutters of 5 Wing RNAS at
Coudekerque in 1916.

NOS. 9 & 11 KITE BALLOON SECTIONS:-

No ascents were made during the day, owing to the unfavourable weather conditions.

[Signed]
Lieutenant, R.N.V.R.,
for WING CAPTAIN.

0084

ROYAL NAVAL AIR SERVICE.

DAILY SUMMARY.

September 9th. 1916.

(Midnight to Midnight.)

RECONNAISSANCES:-

No Seaplane or Coastal reconnaissances were carried out during the day, owing to the unfavourable weather conditions.

BOMBING RAIDS:-

During the early hours of the morning a bombing raid was carried out on the Aerodromes at GHISTELLES and HANDZAEME. Owing to the misty visibility the results could not be observed by the bombers, but one of the Fighter patrols, who was the last to leave, observed the result of some of the bombs which fell on the GHISTELLES Aerodrome and the railway line alongside the sheds. The same difficulty was experienced whilst attacking the HANDZAEME Aerodrome and results were very difficult to observe. Some bombs, however, were observed to have fallen in the middle of a cluster of sheds on the Aerodrome.

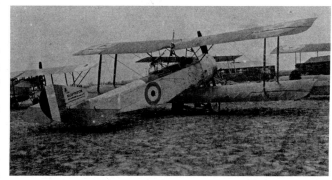

A third raid was carried out on the LICHTERVELDE AMMUNITION DUMPS in the afternoon. Bombs were observed to fall on the railway siding and one of the Fighter patrols observed a certain amount of smoke rising from this vicinity.

The machines from all three raids all returned safely and none of the bombers were [*sic*] attacked by any hostile machines. The visibility on all three raids rendered accurate shooting difficult and detail observations of results practicality impossible, as the mist over the objectives was very low.

This 5 Wing Sopwith 1½ Strutter has no fixed forward-firing Vickers gun, but it has two moveable Lewis guns; one on the rear cockpit mounting and another affixed to the rear of the upper wing in the central cut-out. Note the Caudron G.IV and Breguet Z in the background. (Bruce/Leslie)

FIGHTER PATROLS:-

Fighter Patrols escorted machines on the three bombing raids and the only important observations were made during the morning:-

One pilot observed a good deal of train activity between 5.30 a.m. and 6.15 a.m -

Three trains with steam up on the line between HANDZAEME and ZARREN, headed towards the junction at CORTEMARCK.

One train steaming from CORTEMARCK to STADEN.

One train steaming from THOUROUT towards GHISTELLES.

The usual patrols were carried out over the DIXMUDE-NIEUPORT-OSTEND area.

One hostile light-coloured biplane was observed between MARIAKERKE and MIDDELKERKE at 10,000 feet, proceeding towards . . . [Report ends here; no second page in Diary. Ed.]

0086

REPORT OF ATTACK ON HOSTILE KITE BALLOON ABOUT 1 MILE S.E. OF STEENE, BY A NIEUPORT.

7.9.1916 [pencilled. Ed.]

Time started 2.30 p.m. Time returned 3.45 p.m.

A signal was received at 2.10 p.m. from No. 11 Kite Balloon Section, saying Hostile Balloon was up at WILSKERKE.

The weather conditions seeming moderately favourable, pilot consequently proceeded, and on reaching NIEUPORT at 11,000 feet no balloon was visible. Pilot hung out to sea for 10 minutes and proceeded over WILSKERKE and saw balloon arriving at its position E. of STEENE being towed. Pilot proceeded out to sea again till the balloon had reached a considerable altitude and came in over OSTEND, throttled down at 16,000 feet. Pilot manoeuvred for position and commenced diving from 14,200 feet. The sky in this neighbourhood was cloudless and the wind about 50 m.p.h. at 16,000 feet.

The dive shaped well, but the force of the wind caused machine to drift back continually, so pilot flattened out at about 7,000 feet, ran his engine and dived again very steeply at the "head end" of the balloon (speed about 200 m.p.h.).

On reaching the balloon, pilot aimed on 1/5th. of the balloon's length from its "head end", fired, and evaded the balloon, which was at 2,000 feet.

The engine entirely failed to pick up for 10 seconds, then fired and stopped again, but fired immediately after closing the throttle and gradually opening out again. Meanwhile pilot had turned to the right and was at about 1,600 feet.

He looked round and saw the balloon with at least three, if not more, flaming points amidships.

The second time pilot looked round balloon was on fire at the "head end", the third time she was half on fire, falling and leaving a trail of smoke above her, and the third time she was falling fast, a mass of flame with a large column of smoke above.

She fell in I.17.B.7.4. Pilot returned over PERVYSE and experienced exceptionally heavy A.A. gunfire and machine gun fire.

Aerial photograph of German kite balloon near Steene. The balloon is near the centre of the picture.

An enlargement of the area with the kite balloon in the previous photograph.

0088

Coast Batteries and Inland Batteries of importance.

0089

"PREDICKBOOM".

Belgian Photograph of 15″ gun which bombarded DUNKERQUE on four occasions.

Photograph shows the destroyed empty gun emplacement and the subterranean tunnel laid bare.

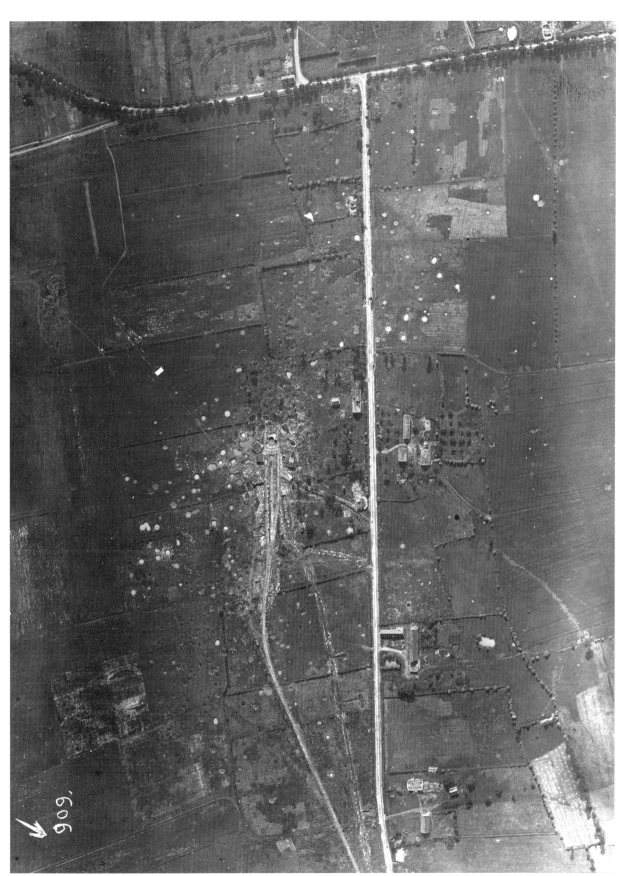

0091

"PREDICKBOOM".
Enlargement of the destroyed 15" gun.

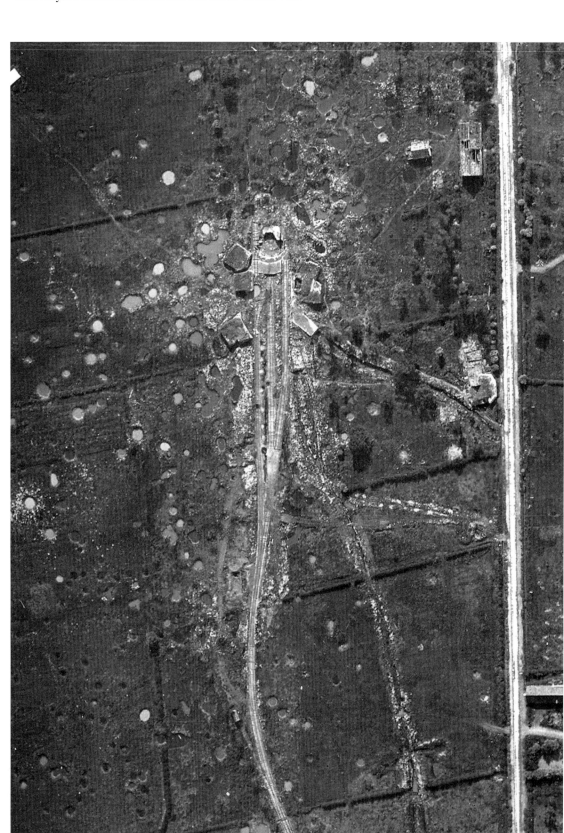

0093

(2).

Last photograph taken of the PREDICKBOOM gun, showing the gun in its emplacement and the subterranean tunnels.

0095

(2a).

Enlargement of (2) – PREDICKBOOM GUN.

0096

0097

BATTERY AACHEN.

4 – 6″ guns.

French Photograph.

Date:- August 9th. 1916.

Height:- 10,000 feet.

Time:- 3.00 p.m.

0098

0099

BATTERY CECILIA.

4 – 4.2" guns.

French Photograph.

Height:- 12,000 feet.

Time:- 3.00 p.m.

0100

0101

<u>HINDENBURG BATTERY – OSTEND.</u>
Date:- August 1st. 1916
Time:- 5.15. p.m.
Height:- 12.000 feet.
Camera:- R.N.A.S. No. 1.
Machine:- Sopwith.
Pilot:- Lieut. Fowler.
Observer:- Lieut. Gow.

0102

0103

KNOCKE BATTERY.
Date:- July 31st. 1916.
Time:- 4.10 p.m.
Height:- 10,000 feet.
Machine:- Sopwith.
Camera:- R.N.A.S. No.l.
Pilot:- Lieut. Fowler.
Observer:- Lieut. Gow.

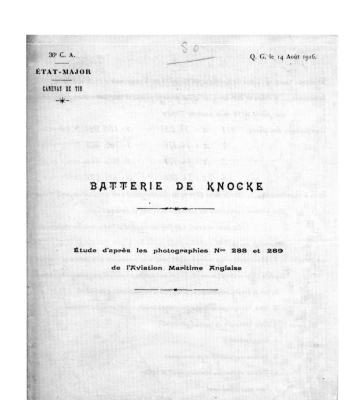

Situation.... Ouest de l'Église de Knocke à 300^m environ au N. de la route d'Heyst à Knocke.

Armement.... 4 Pièces de 305. long, sur affût protégé pivotant disposées d'une façon analogue
aux pièces de 28 de la batterie Tirpitz

Coordonnées des pièces: N° 1   x = 74.231   y = 105.684 _ N. 10. d. 0.6 _ 5.3

          „   2   x = 74.176   y = 105.665 _ N. 10. c. 9.4 _ 4.9

          „   3   x = 74.121   y = 105.645 _ N. 10. c. 8.2 _ 4.5

          „   4   x = 74.066   y = 105.626 _ N. 10. c. 7.0 _ 4.1

Poste d'observation .... Sur la dune 23 près de Duinbergen il a été construit un poste d'observation bétonné, comportant un télémètre de 12 mètres de long.

          La dune en avant a été fixée au moyen d'un filet à mailles en forme de losan-
ge, constitué par de fortes tresses de paille posées sur le sable. Photo R.N.A.S. N° 287. 1er Août 1916

Légende: A. Chemin de fer, à voie normale ayant servi à la construction de la batterie et rejoignant à
Heyst la ligne existante (la voie des épis passant par chaque pièce a été presque complètement enlevée)

          B. Voie de 1 mètre. actuellement en service pour le ravitaillement de la batterie

          a. Abris bétonnés (dépôts de munitions) reliés à la batterie par un couloir bétonné

          b Abris recouverts de gazon (personnel)

          c Baraquements

          d Maisons paraissant déjà anciennes

          e Maisons servant de chantier, dépôt et atelier

          f Abri pour travailleurs

          g Moulin à vent.   Coordonnées: x = 74.457   N. 10. d. 5.3 _ 0.5
                                          y = 105.461

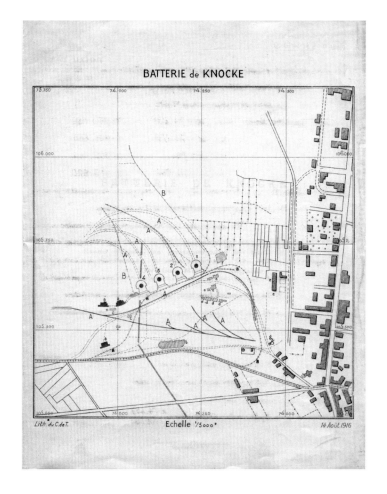

BATTERIE de KNOCKE

0106

<u>INDIVIDUAL PHOTOGRAPHS OF INTEREST.</u>

0107

<u>Combined English and French Aerodrome at St. Pol.</u>

0109

Top W. corner of the French and English Aerodrome at ST. POL, showing the DOCKERAY WORKING CAMP

0119
(2) WEST SIDE OF DIXMUDE.
REFERENCE H.12.a & b. – Showing the NIEUPORT-DIXMUDE Road with destroyed Bridge. Reference H.12.a.3.7

0121

(3). SOUTH-WEST CORNER of DIXMUDE.

Showing the destroyed Railway Bridge over the YSER

Reference:- H.12.c.2.8

Also the destroyed Bridge over the NIEUPORT-DIXMUDE Road.

Reference:- H.12.a.3.7.

0123

(4). RAILWAY DEPOT SOUTH-EAST of DIXMUDE TOWN.

Reference:- I.7.a.

0125

TOWN OF FURNES.

Belgian Photograph.

0127

Presentation of the "CROIX DE GUERRE" with the Palm to Sub-Lieutenants DALLAS, GERARD and IRWING by General ROQUEROL on July 24th, 1916.

His Majesty inspects officers of the R.N.A.S.

During his visit to the front the King presented decorations—the and the Military Cross—to Belgian officers and men, while Queen the recipient of a medal. She has worked hard at hospitals and

Beginnings: 1

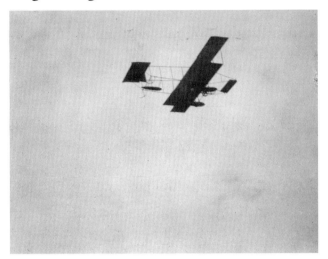 

Very early days. Taken on December 1, 1911, this sequence depicts Lt Arthur Longmore conducting "water landing trials" on the Short S.38 after it had been fitted with three streamlined airbags. Following a successful descent on the River Medway off the Isle of Grain, the aircraft was towed ashore by a naval picket boat. After allowing a short time for drying-out, Longmore took off from the beach and flew back to Eastchurch. This aircraft, piloted by Lt C.R. Samson, later made the first take-off from one of HM ships (HMS *Africa* on January 10, 1912) and the first take-off from one of HM ships under way (HMS *Hibernia* on May 2, 1912).

Beginnings: 2

A nice series of shots showing Borel seaplane No 85 being launched and taxying. Ordered through agents DelaCombe & Maréchal, this aircraft had an 80 hp Gnome rotary engine. It was delivered to Cromarty on July 23, 1913, and took part in that year's fleet manoeuvres. Early in October that year it carried Winston Churchill on a passenger flight. In September 1914 it was fitted with a land undercarriage, and after serving at Eastchurch and Hendon in this form it was deleted on December 9, 1914. Although the location and date of these pictures is unknown, the same four names are listed on the reverse of each print: Col G.F. Mackenzie; Lt Oliver, RN; Lt Crosbie, 93rd ?????; and Capt D. Wanand.

RNAS Tresco

A graphic portrayal of life at the RNAS seaplane base at Tresco, on the Isles of Scilly, in 1917–18. The "x" on the general view of the base marks the canteen and recreation room, the inside of which is shown in the second picture. The third photograph depicts two solid-tyred lorries used for anti-aircraft work, one carrying a gun and the other a searchlight. The searchlight vehicle is prominently marked "OHMS" fore and aft, and both bear the initials "RNAAS", presumably standing for Royal Naval Anti-Aircraft Service, along their sides. The next three views show both vehicles, the third being taken over the roof of the searchlight lorry's cab, looking into the gun carrier.

Camel recovery

Sopwith 2F.1 Ship's Camel N6648 was built in Sopwith's Kingston-upon-Thames factory and delivered to the RNAS Central Supply Depot at White City, London, on the weekend of 26 January 1918. After a brief period in HMS *Nairana* it was taken aboard the battleship HMS *Tiger* during the week ending 11 July. This undated sequence shows it shortly after ditching. First, the whaler from the V&W class destroyer HMS *Vimiera* rescues the unfortunate pilot; next, the Camel is hoisted aboard *Vimiera* and made fast on deck; finally we see a close-up of the aircraft's 150 hp Bentley B.R.1 rotary engine. The impact with the sea has shattered the propeller, torn off the cowling and dislocated the Lewis gun on the fuselage top-decking. Apparently N6648 was not written off, as it is recorded as going to Turnhouse during the week ending 19 September 1918.

A significant event

These three pictures depicting Flt Cdr Frederick J. Rutland making the first flight from a fixed platform on HMS *Yarmouth*, while the ship was under way in the Firth of Forth on 28 June 1917, are something of a revelation. The lower picture, depicting the actual take-off, is well known, and the aircraft has always been identified as Sopwith Pup 9901, a Beardmore-built machine. The second picture in this sequence, however, clearly reveals that the aircraft flown by Rutland for this proving test of the prototype of all of the fixed platforms installed in RN cruisers was another Beardmore-built machine, N6431. The misidentification of the aircraft was almost certainly due to the Admiralty's quaint practice of designating specific aircraft types using the serial number of a typical machine. The Admiralty designation for the Pup was Sopwith Type 9901, and the original caption to the take-off picture probably described the machine thus, leading subsequent chroniclers to assume that 9901 was the actual machine used.

Seaplane recovery

Two sets of pictures showing how seaplanes with leaking floats were rescued. The port float of the Short 184 in the first two pictures (top) is taking in water, so a crew member is standing on the starboard float to keep the port wingtip clear of the water. Two bombs are still attached to the carrier between the float struts. Then, with the bombs removed and another man standing by the front innermost interplane strut on the lower starboard wing, the seaplane taxies up to the seaplane carrier, believed to be HMS *Riviera*, for recovery.

The second sequence depicts a Short 310 in dire straits with a holed starboard float. The engine cowlings have been removed. Three men have clambered out to the port wingtip in an effort to right the aircraft; then a tender arrives and attaches a towline, and one of the "wingmen" returns to the cockpit. The final view, taken from the tender, shows the seaplane, still carrying three bombs, safely under tow with two men seated nonchalantly on the port lower wingtip and another in the rear cockpit looking anxiously over the side. The port aileron is down to compensate for the extra drag of the partly submerged starboard float and keep the aircraft straight.

HMS *Riviera* and its Aircraft

The second fast cross-Channel steamer to be converted to a torpedo seaplane carrier was the 22-knot *Riviera*, originally launched in 1911 and converted at Chatham Dockyard during August 1914. After 1915 it was fitted with a large hangar aft, complete with two jib cranes for lifting its charges on to and out of the water. In 1917, now obsolete, *Riviera* was attached to the Dover Force. These photographs, taken at various locations according to the minimal notes pencilled on them, were taken during the vessel's later life.

Three studies of HMS *Riviera*. The first two were taken in the Downs off Deal, and a single Short 184 (Improved) is on the aft deck. The third shows it on the River Dart in Devon, with a Blackburn-built Sopwith Baby on the aft deck.

Three more views on the Dart. In the first, a Short 184 is on the aft deck and Blackburn-built Sopwith Baby N1124 is suspended from the starboard jib crane. The second view shows one Short on the deck and two, bombed up, on the jib cranes. The third picture, probably taken at the same time as the previous one, shows Short 184 (Improved) N1622, built by S.E. Saunders Ltd, on the starboard crane. This aircraft joined *Riviera* on 26 November 1917 and went to Newlyn on 27 February 1918.

An unusual view from the rear of the hangar, looking out, with one Short 184 on the aft deck and two in the hangar.

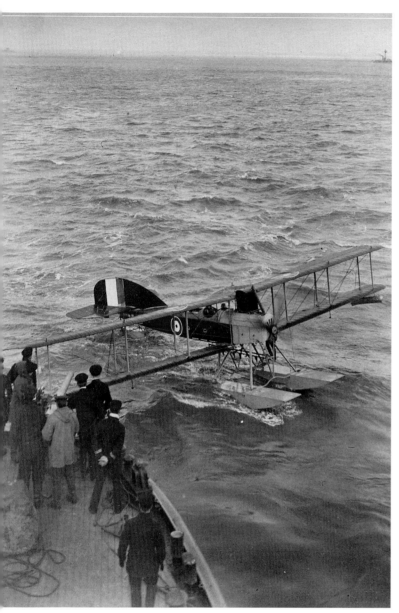

A folded Short seaplane on the starboard jib crane in Dover harbour.

A short 184 taxies past a monitor in the Downs.

Another Short taxies out for take-off in the Downs. Note the conspicuous pale triangles of fabric in the upper wing root trailing edges where the wings folded back for stowage.

Above: A bomb-laden Short 184 taxies past in Devonport.

Left: Another of *Riviera*'s Short 184s was N1678, built by the Brush Electrical Engineering Co Ltd and delivered to the ship on 26 November 1917. Seen here on the Dart, it dropped two 100lb bombs on a U-boat on 3 December 1917, with Flt Sub-Lt N.I. Larter and Obs Sub-Lt C.S.A. Sivil in its cockpits. On 9 December, however, it failed to return from an antisubmarine patrol, Larter and CPO wireless telegraphy operator Robbins being drowned.

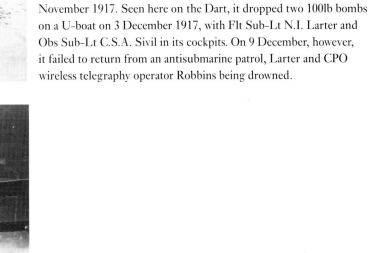

A splendid study of a bombed-up Short 184 "going off on patrol from skiff" at Dartmouth.

A Short 184 taxies up for retrieval in the Downs off Deal after a patrol, its bomb racks empty.

Riviera retrieves a Short 184 with a collapsed main undercarriage in the Downs.

A nice side view of a taxying Short 184.

A sequence depicting the retrieval of Short 184 number 847
(the Short Brothers c/n S.136 is discernible in two views) after
capsizing off Deal. This seaplane joined *Riviera* on 29 July
1915. Records state that Flt Lt E.I.M. Bird was in this machine
when it overturned in the sea on 4 October 1915, and that it was
towed back to Dover and dismantled the following day. As these
pictures testify, it was retrieved aboard *Riviera* and righted;
perhaps it was then lowered overboard for towing to Dover.

Hydrovanes and Flotation Gear

Ditching a landplane, with its wheeled undercarriage, was a risky business. There was a good chance that, when the undercarriage structure hit the water, the aircraft's fuselage would nose down sharply, turning the machine over and causing it to sink rapidly. At Grain experiments were conducted with two devices to lessen the risk, flotation bags and hydrovanes. Initially, air bags were installed in the rear fuselage. Although this arrangement kept the machine afloat, the cockpit could still become submerged, endangering the pilot's life. The alternative arrangement had deflated flotation bags mounted externally on either side of the forward fuselage. These inflated automatically upon the machine entering the water and kept the fuselage on the surface. To prevent the machine nosing over on impact, small flat or aerofoil-section metal hydrovanes were added to the undercarriage struts. These lifted the aircraft's nose in the water, allowing it to settle in a level attitude. Sometimes a small hydrovane was also attached to the tailskid. Although internally stowed flotation bags became standard equipment in naval aeroplanes in subsequent years, hydrovanes never gained popularity, probably because they must have caused a great increase in aerodynamic drag.

This A-serialled Sopwith 1½ Strutter is fitted with a skid undercarriage and has flotation bags attached beneath wooden boards fitted on either side of the forward fuselage.

Another 1½ Strutter, this time with a biplane hydrovane arrangement in addition to the flotation bags, which are seen deployed but not inflated. The oxygen bottle to inflate them can be seen attached to the upper fuselage longeron alongside the forward cockpit.

One of the drawbacks of being a designer of the Grain flotation gear was that you were expected to be aboard the aeroplane during the first trial ditchings. Howard Earl, who designed the gear for this 1½ Strutter, was accordingly on board when it was ditched. It is seen here shortly after recovery.

The larger, twin-engine Caudron G.IV was a different proposition. This one has flotation bags housed in fabric pockets beneath the leading edge of the lower mainplane, seen here deployed but not inflated. The tail structure was supported by twin floats, and single flat sheet-steel hydrovanes with dihedral were mounted forward of the twin-wheel main undercarriage units.

Grain Griffin N50 with a biplane hydrovane arrangement in front of its undercarriage.

Airco D.H.4 A7457, powered by an R.A.F.3A engine, displays its underwing stabilising floats, stowed flotation gear and biplane hydrovanes. The wheels could be jettisoned by means of compressed air before the aircraft alighted.

Westland-built Airco D.H.4 D1769, with a Siddeley Puma engine, has biplane hydrovanes, underwing floats and provision for flotation gear.

The Parnall N.2A Panther two-seat fleet reconnaissance and spotting aircraft appeared too late to see wartime service, but did go into production for postwar use. The third prototype, N93, is here seen at Grain with biplane hydrovanes and Grain flotation gear. Note the hinged trailing edge of the upper wing centre-section, which enabled the pilot to climb over the rear spar and then descend through the hole in the forward centre-section to enter his cockpit.

The sixth and final Panther prototype, N96, displays the type's folding rear fuselage, which helped conserve precious hangar space in a carrier. Also visible is the flotation bag in the rear fuselage, supplementing the Grain flotation gear attached to the undercarriage legs. The aeroplane is not miraculously balanced in this position; a supporting trestle has been artfully retouched out.

By the time Hanriot HD.3.C2 two-seat shipboard fighter No 2003 arrived there, in September 1918, the Isle of Grain was an RAF station. When this picture was taken the aircraft, which never had a British Service identity, had already undergone one ditching, fitted with a combined wheel-and-skid undercarriage, Grain flotation gear and jettisonable wheels. This was unsuccessful owing to the failure to fit a tailskid hydrovane, but the Hanriot was recovered and tested again, this time fitted out as seen here, with a shorter-span front hydrovane, a small one with negative incidence on its tailskid, and Grain flotation gear. Although a ditching on 4 December 1918 was successful, the French need for the type had all but passed.

This view displays the Panther's inflated Grain flotation gear and hydrovanes to good advantage, and also the cut-out in the upper-wing centre section.

Deck landing

One of the early experiments at Grain concerning deck landing entailed the construction of an "artificial hill" in the form of a steeply inclined wire rope-way. On a ship, the cables would have been anchored near the stern, rising in a catenary curve to a bridge some 30ft above deck level, about 100ft further forward. The idea was that an aeroplane with metal claws attached to its undercarriage would run into the cables, be secured to them by the claws, and be slowed to a halt by the uphill run. Consequently the personnel at Grain, who believed they had escaped the chore of digging trenches, ended up digging trenches to take tall posts to support a crossbar. From this, steel hawsers spaced at about 6in intervals ran down to the ground. These two pictures show this structure in the course of erection.

To test the "uphill landing" device, this Royal Aircraft Factory B.E.2C had a bar fitted with a row of metal claws attached to the tail ends of its undercarriage skids. When landed on the cable ramp, however, it became jammed, and the experiment was deemed a complete failure.

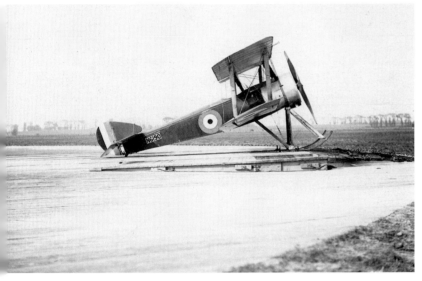

Sopwith Pup N6190 was allocated to the Experimental Constructive and Armament Department at Grain in March 1918 for deck-landing experiments, and was tested with both skid and wheel undercarriages. It is seen at Grain with a skid undercarriage, sitting on a shallow wooden ramp fitted with a multitude of longitudinal arrester cables running back off the picture to the left. Steel claws protruding above the skids have engaged these cables, holding the aircraft down and, with the help of the ramp, bringing it to a halt.

A movie still of Beardmore-built Sopwith Pup 9922 during trials at Grain of a tall skid undercarriage and a large but rather frail-looking arrester hook attached to the apex of an inverted pyramid of tubes beneath the forward fuselage.

This Beardmore-built Pup (right and below right) might well be 9922 again, as it has the same arrester hook as shown in the previous picture. However, the skids are not attached rigidly to the struts. Instead, they are strut-braced to the vees of the aircraft's normal land undercarriage, the rear pair of inverted vee struts being attached to the original bungee-sprung split axles to provide suspension.

Sopwith-built Pup 9497 was modified by Beardmore and fitted with an experimental arrester hook and a tubular steel propeller guard. Late in 1916 it was tested on a dummy deck at Grain, as seen here.

Shipboard trials in HMS *Furious*

Commissioned in July 1917, *Furious* initially had only a 228ft-long forward flying deck, but the need to avoid forcing pilots to land by manoeuvring their aircraft round the ship's funnel led to the provision of a 284ft-long flying-on deck aft of the superstructure. Incorporated in this deck was an arrester system comprising longitudinal wires to be engaged by hooks on the aeroplanes' undercarriages, coupled with a ramp to help kill their speed, transverse ropes weighted with sandbags, and a crash barrier of hanging ropes to safeguard the superstructure against overshooting aircraft. As the following collection of pictures shows, even this seemingly thorough system proved unsatisfactory, largely owing to the disturbing eddies caused by the ship's superstructure and funnel. The problem was resolved after the war by fitting a flush deck running from bow to stern. This portrait shows *Furious* with the separate flying decks fore and aft and the central superstructure.

Pups

Watched by a gaggle of seemingly fearless "goofers", Beardmore-built Pup 9949 runs off the end of the ramp and into the hanging rope barrier.

Having come to rest, the Pup displays its badly damaged engine cowling and broken propeller and skid undercarriage.

Another view of the unfortunate 9949.

A three-quarter rear view of the aftermath. Note that the Admiralty tripod mounting for an upward-firing machine-gun is still fitted immediately in front of the cockpit.

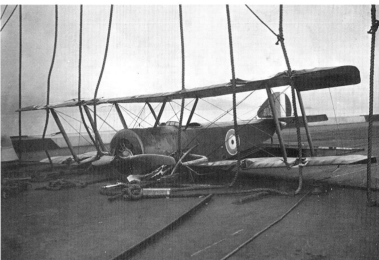

Pup N6438, bearing the legend "Excuse me!" below the cockpit, after a rough touchdown on 16 April 1918, its undercarriage having collapsed completely. The damage caused to the upper wing by the rope barrier is evident.

Both upper and lower wings of Pup C214, built in Coventry by the Standard Motor Co Ltd, suffered severely when it ran into the barrier during skid undercarriage tests on 20 March 1918. Its pilot was Wg Cdr H.R. Busteed.

A heavy landing has smashed the undercarriage and propeller of this Pup before it has even reached the ramp. This picture is dated 20 March 1918.

An unusual study of Sqn Cdr Frederick Rutland "on finals" in a skid-equipped Sopwith Pup on 29 March 1918. The longitudinal arrester wires, raised above the deck of *Furious* by small individual supports, stretch away from the camera.

Helpers run towards a skid-equipped Pup as it careers into the low sidewall along the deck edge, in a vain attempt to prevent it going over the side.

Seconds later the Pup has gone over, but has become caught in some structure on the carrier's side. Personnel set about rescuing the unfortunate pilot from his precarious perch.

Dated 5 April 1918, this study shows an experimental arrester hook affixed to Beardmore-built Pup N6446.

A Pup approaches the ramp after a successful if somewhat askew touchdown on 15 April 1918.

This fine close-up of the skid undercarriage of a Pup shows the claws sticking up from the rear ends of the skids and another pointing down at the centre of the spreader bar, ready to snare the longitudinal deck wires if the aircraft exhibits a tendency to lift.

A closer study of a Pup landing on *Furious*. This aircraft has three claws on its undercarriage spreader bar.

Lieutenant Acland in the process of landing a Pup on 19 April 1918.

Acland's Pup approaches the end of the ramp and the dreaded rope barrier.

A close-up of the undercarriage of Acland's Pup after it had successfully halted at the top of the ramp. Three cables have been snagged by claws on the spreader bar, and their restraining sandbags are visible to the rear on the right.

A less successful landing on the same day, by a Beardmore-built Pup, which has overshot the ramp and broken its undercarriage in the ensuing fall. The half-roundel on the fuselage side testifies to previous repairs to the fabric.

A four-picture sequence depicting the retrieval of a Beardmore-built Pup, almost certainly N6456, after ditching on 22 March 1918. First, a whaler rescues the pilot; then a tender tows the aeroplane tail-first to *Furious* and comes alongside. Finally a line from one of the carrier's jib cranes is made fast to the Pup's nose and the aircraft is hoisted aboard.

Ship Strutters

Lieutenant Jackson, flying Ship Strutter "DJ3", about to touch down on the deck of *Furious* on 8 May 1918. The supports for the longitudinal arrester wires and the sandbags for the transverse cables are clearly visible.

Although he appears to have caught some transverse cables, Jackson's aeroplane careers on to the ramp.

Having been brought abruptly to a halt at the far end of the ramp, DJ3 ends up on its nose with its propeller, cowling and skid undercarriage smashed. Visible here is the underfuselage arrester hook, which seems to have failed to perform as hoped.

Another angle on DJ3 after its ignominious landing.

A final close-up of DJ3 provides an unusual view of the forward fuselage of the Ship Strutter.

Jackson's machine was obviously repaired, as here it is on 4 June 1918, piloted by Lt McCleary, taking off for "experimental flying on to deck".

Royal Flying Corps 1½ Strutter A6987 was converted to a Ship Strutter at Grain, and went to *Furious* on the weekend of 15 August 1918. Taken on 7 November that year, this study depicts its retrieval after a ditching. It has a wheeled undercarriage and was probably fitted with hydrovanes, as a small one set at a negative angle is attached to the tailskid.

A fine take-off study of Lt McCleary in a Sopwith 1½ Strutter with wheeled undercarriage, taken during "experimental flying on to deck" on 5 June 1918. Note the smoke streaming back from the bows, indicating the wind direction over the deck.

Another take-off by McCleary, taken on the same day.

Camels

Lieutenant Thynne, flying a Sopwith 2F.1 Camel fitted with a Lewis gun on an Admiralty top plane mounting, takes off from *Furious* on 5 June 1918 during "experimental flying on to deck".

Sopwith-built 2F.1 Camel N6602 comes alongside *Furious* in two parts aboard a launch on 6 April 1918. The series of white crosses along the rear fuselage were continued on the last fabric panel on the forward fuselage, as the subsequent pictures in this sequence reveal.

The wings and forward fuselage on the launch, waiting to be hoisted on to the carrier. The last of the fuselage crosses is seen, plus the fuel tank immediately aft of the cockpit.

The front half of N6602, complete with a Lewis gun on its top plane mounting, suspended from one of *Furious*'s jib cranes.

A nice study of N6602 as it comes aboard *Furious*, with the Vickers and Lewis guns and the pump impeller on the rear starboard centre-section strut clearly visible.

Beardmore-built 2F.1 Camel N6779 is towed alongside on 15 July 1918 after ditching.

As N6779 is hoisted aboard *Furious*, it appears that it has suffered far less damage than the previous picture might lead one to believe. It was evidently repaired, as it was not finally written off until 12 September 1918.

Disposition of Aircraft, 24th February 1917

Before and during the war the RNAS issued periodical listings giving the disposition and status of the aircraft in its charge. Despite the instruction at the top of the first page, which stated: "This list is to be destroyed immediately on receipt of the new list which supersedes it", several of these listings have survived, though they are quite scarce. This one was found among the files of the late Owen Thetford, author of *British Naval Aircraft since 1912* (Putnam, 1958, and several subsequent editions), and is reproduced in facsimile, with illustrations added. It covers an interesting period, when many new and hardier types, more suited to the rigours of warfare, had largely replaced the somewhat less capable aircraft of the earlier war years. A study of the listings, however, shows that quite a number of the earlier machines were still soldiering on, including the odd Blériot monoplane. Also of interest is the generous number of experimental types, many of which had outlived their usefulness.

This wash painting by Leonard Bridgman depicts Bristol Scout Type C number 1255, the first landplane to be launched from the deck of a naval vessel specifically equipped for the purpose, HMS *Vindex*, on 3 November 1915.

DISPOSITION OF AIRCRAFT.

Corrected to 6 p.m., 23rd February, 1917.

ORGANIZATION OF ACTIVE SERVICE UNITS.

1 Wing	=	2 or more Squadrons.
1 Squadron	=	3 Flights.

		AEROPLANES.	SEAPLANES.	LARGE FLYING BOATS.
1 Flight	=	6 machines ready.	4 machines ready.	2 machines ready.
		4 machines spare.	2 machines spare.	1 machine spare.

NAVAL AIR STATIONS, GREAT BRITAIN.

No.	Condition.	Total.	Type.	H.p.	Engine.	Duties.

Aldeburgh Night Landing Ground.
See under Yarmouth.

Bacton Night Landing Ground.
See under Yarmouth.

Bembridge Naval Air Sub-Station.
See under Calshot.

Burgh Castle Night Landing Ground.
See under Yarmouth.

Calshot Naval Air Station.

WITH SUB-STATIONS AT BEMBRIDGE, PORTLAND, AND QUARTERS AT WARSASH.

Wing Commander A. W. Bigsworth, D.S.O., in Command.

Telegrams : AEROPLANES, WARSASH.

POLICY.

Duty.	Flights.	In No.	Present aim.	Type.
Seaplanes—				
War Flight—				
Patrol	{ 1	3	3	Large America.
	1	6	6	Short 184.
Portland		6	6	Short 184.
Bembridge	1	6	6	Short 184.
		10		F.B.A.
Training Machines	40 {	5		Short 184.
		15		Short 827.
		10		Baby.

SEAPLANES, PORTLAND AND BEMBRIDGE PATROL.

No.	Condition.	Total	Type.	H.p.	Engine.	Duties.
8651	Ready ..		Large America	2–250	R.R. ..	Patrol.
8655	Ready ..	2	Large America	2–250	R.R. ..	Patrol.
8024	Engine out		Short 184 ..	240	Sunbeam ..	Bembridge.
8352	Ready ..	2	Short 184 ..	225	Sunbeam ..	Portland.
3327	Ready ..		Short 827 ..	150	Sunbeam ..	Portland.
3329	Ready ..	2	Short 827 ..	150	Sunbeam ..	Portland.

SEAPLANES, TRAINING SCHOOL.

No.	Condition.	Total	Type.	H.p.	Engine.	Duties.
130	Ready ..	1	Avro Tractor..	150	Sunbeam ..	
3637	Ready ..		F.B.A. F. Boat	100	Mono ..	
3644	Ready ..		F.B.A. F. Boat	100	Mono ..	
3652	Repairs ..		F.B.A. F. Boat	100	Mono ..	
3654	Repairs ..		F.B.A. F. Boat	100	Mono ..	
3655	Ready ..		F.B.A. F. Boat	100	Mono ..	Training.
9602	Ready ..		F.B.A. F. Boat	100	Mono ..	
9603	Ready ..		F.B.A. F. Boat	100	Mono ..	
9607	Ready ..		F.B.A. F. Boat	100	Mono ..	
9609	Repairs ..		F.B.A. F. Boat	100	Mono ..	
N1040	Erected ..	10	F.B.A. F. Boat	100	Mono ..	
3065	Repairs ..		Short 827 W.T.	150	Sunbeam ..	
3325	Repairs ..		Short 827 ..	150	Sunbeam ..	
8225	Eng. repair		Short 827 Duel	150	Sunbeam ..	
8228	Repairs ..		Short 827 Duel	150	Sunbeam ..	
8229	Fitting engine.		Short 827 Duel	150	Sunbeam ..	
8255	Ready ..		Short 827 ..	150	Sunbeam ..	
8550	Ready ..		Short 827 W.T.	150	Sunbeam ..	
8551	Engine repairs.		Short 827 ..	150	Sunbeam ..	
8552	Eng. repair		Short 827 ..	150	Sunbeam ..	
8553	Ready ..		Short 827 ..	150	Sunbeam ..	
8555	Waiting eng.		Short 827 ..	150	Sunbeam ..	
8559	Ready ..	12	Short 827 ..	150	Sunbeam ..	
8002	Ready ..		Short 184 ..	225	Sunbeam ..	

No.	Condition.	Total.	Type.	H.p.	Engine.	Duties.

CALSHOT (WARSASH) NAVAL AIR STATION—*continued.*

No.	Condition.	Total	Type.	H.p.	Engine.	Duties.
8010	New engine		Short 184 ..	225	Sunbeam ..	
8011	Waiting eng.		Short 184 ..	225	Sunbeam ..	
8027	Ready		Short 184 ..	240	Sunbeam ..	Patrol.
8092	New engine		Short 184 ..	225	Sunbeam ..	
8344	Eng. repair		Short 184 ..	225	Sunbeam ..	
8348	Eng. trouble		Short 184 ..	225	Sunbeam ..	Patrol
8356	New engine		Short 184 ..	225	Sunbeam ..	
8362	Eng. repair		Short 184 ..	225	Sunbeam ..	
8363	Wait'g eng.		Short 184 ..	225	Sunbeam ..	
8365	Ready ..		Short 184 ..	225	Sunbeam ..	
8367	Ready ..		Short 184 ..	225	Sunbeam ..	Patrol.
8377	Ready ..		Short 184 ..	225	Sunbeam ..	Patrol.
9044	Ready ..	14	Short 184 ..	225	Sunbeam ..	Patrol.
9089	Altering ..		Short 184 Imp.	225	Sunbeam ..	
9094	Repairs ..	2	Short 184 Imp.	225	Sunbeam ..	Bembridge.
9756	Ready ..		Short 166 ..	200	C. Unne ..	
9767	Ready ..		Short 166 ..	200	C. Unne ..	Patrol.
9768	Ready ..	3	Short 166 ..	200	C. Unne ..	Patrol
8170	Engine out		Sopwith Baby	..	None ..	
8210	Ready ..		Sopwith Baby	100	Gnome ..	
8211	Engine out		Sopwith Baby	100	Gnome ..	
8212	Ready ..		Sopwith Baby	100	Gnome ..	
8213	Ready ..	5	Sopwith Baby	100	Gnome ..	
3726	Ready ..		Sopwith Schndr.	100	Mono ..	
3734	New floats	2	Sopwith Schndr.	100	Mono ..	
1195	Overhaul..		W.&T. F. Boat	120	Beardmore	
3807	Ready ..		W.&T. F. Boat	120	Beardmore	
3808	Ready ..	3	W.&T. F. Dual	120	Beardmore	

ALLOCATED.

No.	Condition.	Total	Type.	H.p.	Engine.	Duties.
8657	Felixstowe		Large America	2–250	R.R. ..	Patrol.
8659	Felixstowe	2	Large America	2–250	R.R. ..	
8338	Thompson	1	S.Am. Thompsn.	2–140	Hispano ..	School.
9608	N.Th'mps'n		F.B.A. F. Boat	100	Mono ..	
N1043	N.Th'mps'n		F.B.A. F. Boat	100	Mono ..	
N1044	N.Th'mps'n	3	F.B.A. F. Boat	100	Mono ..	
8347	Transit +..		Short 184 ..	225	Sunbeam ..	
N1081	Grain ..		Short 184 Imp.	220	Renault ..	
N1082	Grain ..		Short 184 Imp.	220	Renault ..	Patrol.
N1083	Short ..		Short 184 Imp.	220	Renault ..	Patrol.
N1084	Short ..		Short 184 Imp.	220	Renault ..	Patrol.
N1085	Short ..	6	Short 184 Imp.	220	Renault ..	
3323	Windermere		Short 827 ..	150	Sunbeam ..	
8237	Brush ..		Short 827 ..	150	Sunbeam ..	Patrol.
8561	Fairey ..		Short 827 ..	150	Sunbeam ..	
8638*	Dover ..		Short 827 W.T.	150	Sunbeam ..	
8648*	Dover ..	5	Short 827 W.T.	150	Sunbeam ..	
9782	K., Grain	1	Short 830 ..	140	C. Unne ..	
N1039	Blackburn	1	Sopwith Baby	110	Clerget ..	
3781	Windermere	1	Sopwith Schndr.	100	Mono ..	

FOR OTHER STATIONS.

No.	Condition.	Total	Type.	H.p.	Engine.	Duties.
8321	Ready ..	1	Wight School	100	Mono ..	K

FOR DELETION.

No.	Condition.	Total	Type.	H.p.	Engine.	Duties.
8012	Missing ..		Short 184 ..	225	Sunbeam ..	Patrol.
8071	Survey ..		Short 184 ..	225	Sunbeam ..	Portland.

* Wrecked at Dover.   † Repair at Ramsgate.

No.	Condition.	Total.	Type	H.p.	Engine.	Duties.

Chingford Naval Air Station.

WITH LANDING GROUND AT FAIRLOP.
SUB-STATION TO CRANWELL.

Wing Captain E. L. Gerrard, D.S.O., in Command.

Telegrams : NAVYAIR, CHING., LONDON.

POLICY.

Duty.	No.	Present aim.	Type.
School	20 {	10	M.F. Longhorn
		10	G. White
Advanced School (1) ..	30 {	15	Avro
		15	J.N.
Advanced School (2) ..	(7 dual) 20	20	B.E. 2 C.
Fast types	(6 dual) 4	14	Various

AEROPLANES

No.	Condition.	Total.	Type	H.p.	Engine.	Duties.
939	No engine	1	Avro Tractor..	50	Gnome ..	School.
876	Ready ..		Avro 179 ..	80	Gnome ..	Adv. School.
1002	Ready ..		Avro 179 ..	80	Gnome ..	Adv. School.
1019	Ready ..		Avro 179 ..	80	Gnome ..	Adv. School.
1046	Overhaul..		Avro 179 Dual	80	Gnome ..	Dual Tractor.
4823	For erection		Avro 179 Dual	75	Gnome ..	Dual Tractor.
9825	Ready ..		Avro 179 Dual	80	Gnome ..	Dual Tractor.
9826	Overhaul..		Avro 179 Dual	80	Gnome ..	Dual Tractor.
9877	Repairs ..		Avro 179 Dual	80	Gnome ..	Dual Tractor.
9878	Ready ..		Avro 179 Dual	80	Gnome ..	Dual Tractor.
9888	Ready ..		Avro 179 Dual	80	Gnome ..	School.
N6133	Ready ..		Avro 179 Dual	80	Gnome ..	School.
N6134	Ready ..		Avro 179 Dual	80	Gnome ..	School.
N6135	Ready ..		Avro 179 Dual	80	Gnome ..	School.
N6136	Ready ..		Avro 179 Dual	80	Gnome ..	School.
N6137	Ready ..	15	Avro 179 Dual	80	Gnome ..	School.
3313	Repairs ..		Avro Scout ..	80	Gnome ..	Adv. School.
3314	Ready ..		Avro Scout ..	80	Gnome ..	Adv. School.
8589	Ready .		Avro Scout ..	80	Gnome ..	Adv. School.
8590	Repairs ..		Avro Scout ..	80	Gnome ..	Adv. Sch.
8593	Ready ..	5	Avro Scout ..	80	Gnome ..	Adv. Sch.
9277	Ready ..		Avro Scout ..	100	Mono ..	Adv. Sch.
9279	Ready ..		Avro Scout ..	100	Mono ..	Adv. Sch.
9280	Engine out		Avro Scout ..	100	Mono ..	Adv. School.
9283	Ready ..		Avro Scout ..	100	Mono ..	Adv. Sch.
9284	Ready ..		Avro Scout ..	100	Mono ..	Adv. Sch.
9285	Ready ..	6	Avro Scout ..	100	Mono ..	Adv. Sch.
980	Ready ..		B.E. 2 C ..	70	Renault ..	Adv. Sch.
983	Ready ..		B.E. 2 C ..	70	Renault ..	Adv. Sch.
986	Repairs ..		B.E. 2 C ..	70	Renault ..	Adv. Sch.
1114	Repairs ..		B.E. 2 C ..	70	Renault ..	Adv. Sch.
1115	Repairs ..		B.E. 2 C ..	70	Renault ..	Adv. Sch.
1116	Ready ..		B.E. 2 C ..	70	Renault ..	Adv. Sch.
1121	Overhaul		B.E. 2 C ..	80	Renault ..	Adv. School.
1122	Repairs ..		B.E. 2 C ..	70	Renault ..	Adv. School.
1124	Ready ..		B.E. 2 C ..	70	Renault ..	Adv. Sch.
1151	Ready ..		B.E. 2 C ..	75	Renault ..	Adv. Sch.
1155	Ready ..		B.E. 2 C ..	75	Renault ..	Adv. School.
1165	Ready ..		B.E. 2 C ..	75	Renault ..	Adv. School.
1168	Ready ..		B.E. 2 C ..	75	Renault ..	Adv. Sch.
1170	Ready ..	14	B.E. 2 C ..	75	Renault ..	Adv. Sch.
8299	Waiting cyl.		B.E. 2 C ..	90	R.A.F. ..	Adv. Sch.
8300	Ready ..		B.E. 2 C ..	90	R.A.F. ..	Adv. Sch.
8409	Ready ..		B.E. 2 C ..	90	R.A.F. ..	Fin. training.
9456	Ready ..	4	B.E. 2 C ..	90	Curtiss ..	Adv. Sch.
1247	Ready ..		Bristol Scout..	80	Gnome ..	Adv. School.
1265	Repairs ..		Bristol Scout..	80	Gnome ..	Adv. School.
1266	Ready ..		Bristol Scout..	80	Gnome ..	Adv. Sch.
3013	Ready ..		Bristol Scout..	80	Gnome ..	Adv. School.
3047	Ready ..		Bristol Scout..	80	Gnome ..	Adv. School.
3051	Ready ..		Bristol Scout..	80	Gnome ..	Adv. School.
3053	Ready ..		Bristol Scout .	80	Gnome ..	Adv. School.
3054	Ready ..		Bristol Scout	80	Gnome ..	Adv. School.
N5402	Repairs ..		Bristol Scout..	80	Gnome ..	Adv. School.
N5407	Repairs ..		Bristol Scout..	80	Gnome ..	Adv. School.
N5408	Ready ..		Bristol Scout..	80	Gnome ..	Adv. School.
N5417	Ready ..		Bristol Scout..	80	Gnome ..	Adv. School.
N5418	Ready ..		Bristol Scout .	80	Gnome ..	Adv. School.
N5419	Ready ..	14	Bristol Scout..	80	Gnome ..	Adv. School.
8987	Waiting bear'r supps.		Bristol Scout..	100	Mono ..	Adv. School.
8988	Waiting bear'r supps.		Bristol Scout .	100	Mono ..	Adv. School.
N5397	Erected ..	3	Bristol Scout..	100	Mono ..	Adv. School.

CHINGFORD NAVAL AIR STATION—*continued.*

No.	Condition.	Total.	Type	H.p.	Engine.	Duties.
3610	Ready ..		G.W. 1600 ..	60	Gnome ..	School.
3611	Ready ..		G.W. 1600 ..	60	Gnome ..	School.
3612	Ready ..		G.W. 1600 ..	60	Gnome .	School.
8312	Ready ..		G.W. 1600 ..	60	Gnome ..	School.
8314	Repairs ..		G.W. 1600 ..	60	Rhone ..	School.
8315	Ready ..		G.W. 1600 ..	60	Rhone ..	School.
8760	Repairs ..		G.W. 1600 ..	60	Rhone ..	School.
8769	Ready ..		G.W. 1600 ..	60	Rhone ..	School.
8770	Ready ..		G.W. 1600 ..	60	Gnome ..	School.
8774	Ready ..		G.W. 1600 ..	60	Gnome ..	School.
8775	Ready ..		G.W. 1600 ..	60	Gnome ..	School.
8779	Changing engine.		G.W. 1600 ..	60	Gnome ..	School.
8780	Ready ..		G.W. 1600 ..	60	Gnome ..	School.
8783	Ready ..		G.W. 1600 ..	60	Rhone ..	School.
8784	Ready ..		G.W. 1600 ..	60	Rhone ..	School.
8785	Ready ..		G.W. 1600 ..	80	Gnome ..	School.
8786	Ready ..		G.W. 1600 ..	80	Gnome ..	School.
8787	Ready ..	18	G.W. 1600 ..	80	Gnome ..	School.
1525	Ready ..		H. Farman ..	80	Gnome ..	School.
1528	No engine	2	H. Farman ..	80	Gnome ..	School.
67	Engine overhaul.		M Farman L.	70	Renault ..	School.
3006	Ready ..		M. Farman L.	70	Renault ..	School.
3010	Ready ..		M. Farman L.	80	Renault ..	School.
8921	Ready ..		M. Farman L.	80	Renault ..	School.
8924	Ready ..		M. Farman L.	80	Renault ..	School.
8928	Ready ..		M. Farman L.	80	Renault ..	School.
N5001	Ready ..		M. Farman L.	75	R.R. ..	School.
N5034	Ready ..		M. Farman L.	80	Renault .	School.
N5039	Ready ..		M. Farman L.	80	Renault ..	School.
N5040	Changing engine.		M. Farman L.	80	Renault ..	School.
N5331	Erected ..		M. Farman L.	75	R.R. ..	School.
N5050	Ready ..	12	M. Farman L.	80	Renault ..	School.
N5060	Ready ..	1	M. Farman S.	80	Renault ..	School.
9233	Repairs ..		Nieuport ..	110	Clerget ..	Fin. training.
9243	Ready ..		Nieuport ..	110	Clerget ..	Fin. training.
9244	Ready ..	3	Nieuport ..	110	Clerget ..	Fin. training.

ALLOCATED.

No.	Condition.	Total.	Type	H.p.	Engine.	Duties.
1014	At S.C.A., R.		Avro 179 ..	80	Gnome ..	Adv. School.
1041	Parnall R.		Avro 179 Dual		No engine..	School.
9822	Eastbourne	3	Avro 179 Dual	80	Gnome ..	Dual Tractor.
988	Eastchurch	1	B.E. 2 C ..	70	Renault ..	Adv. School.
9458	Oakley's R.	1	B.E. 2 C ..	75	R.R. ..	Experiment.
N3215	France ..		F. 40 ..	160	Renault ..	Adv. School.
N3216	France ..		F. 40 ..	160	Renault ..	Adv. School.
N3217	France ..		F. 40 ..	160	Renault ..	Adv. School.
N3218	C.S.D. ..		F. 40 ..	160	Renault ..	Adv. School.
N3219	France ..	5	F. 40 ..	160	Renault ..	Adv. School.
9241	Beardmore	1	Nieuport ..	110	Clerget ..	Adv. School.

FOR OTHER STATIONS—TRIALS.

No.	Condition.	Total.	Type	H.p.	Engine.	Duties.
N5399	Repairs ..		Bristol Scout..	100	Mono ..	Allocated to Cranwell.

FOR DELETION.

Covehithe Night Landing Ground.

See under Yarmouth.

French-built FBA Model B flying boat 9607 was with the Seaplane Training School at Calshot at the time of this census. Here it is seen being launched from the Norman Thompson slipway at Middleton-on-Sea, Sussex, after the company had modified it to NT5 standard.

Sopwith Baby 8210, powered by a 100 hp Gome rotary, was "ready" at Calshot (Warsash) Naval Air Station. It was deleted as wrecked on 3 December 1917.

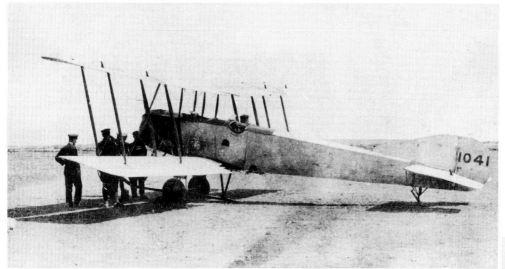

By the time of this census, Avro 504B (Admiralty Type 179 Dual) 1041, seen here at Imbros earlier in its life, was under repair by Parnall and allocated to Chingford RNAS as a school aircraft. By February 1917 it was one of the few survivors from this early batch; it was finally deleted on 23 July.

Royal Aircraft Factory B.E.2C 8433, the last of a 24-aircraft batch built by Hewlett & Blondeau, was with D Flight at Cranwell on 25 October 1916, and was still there at the time of the census. As can be seen here, it acquired an erroneous "N" prefix to its serial number.

Another of Cranwell's B.E.2Cs was 8722, a Beardmore-built example, here being dismantled after an encounter with a ditch. Note its removed 90 hp R.A.F.1A engine on the extreme left. Based at Frieston, it was used as a nightfighter; hence the rocket rails attached to its outer interplane struts. At the time of the census it was being overhauled.

Probably photographed at Cranwell, Avro 504C ("Avro Scout") single-seater 330? was one of a batch of 20 built by the Brush Electrical Engineering Co, serialled 3301-3320.

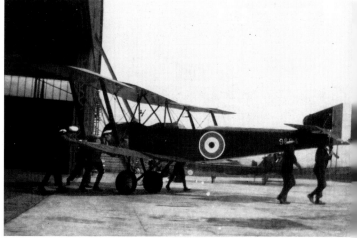

Another of the Brush-built Avro 504Cs, 3315, is seen here shortly after completion. It was ready for use as a school machine when the census was compiled.

Sopwith 1½ Strutter (Admiralty Type 9400S) two-seat fighter 9894 was at Cranwell RNAS Training Establishment as a final training aircraft, and was undergoing overhaul. It met its end while flying from Turnhouse on 4 September 1918, when it collided with Pup B8012 over the Firth of Forth, both of its crew being killed.

Cranwell R.N.A.S. Training Establishment.

WITH AEROPLANE STATION AT CHINGFORD, SEAPLANE STATION AT WINDERMERE AND LANDING GROUND AT FRIESTON.

Commodore J. Luce, C.B., R.N., in Command.

Telegrams : AVION, SLEAFORD.

POLICY.

Duty.	No.	Present aim.	Type.
School	5	5	M.F. Longhorn
Advanced School (1)	25	15	Avro
		10	Curtiss J. N. 4.
Advanced School (2)	20	20	B.E. 2 C.
		10	Sopwith 9400 S.
Fast types	50	10	Bristol Scout
		10	Nieuport
		20	Other types
Gunnery training, Freiston.	..	5	M. Farman S.

No.	Condition.	Total.	Type.	H.p.	Engine.	Duties.
1028	Ready		Avro 179 Dual	80	Gnome	School.
1031	Ready		Avro 179 Dual	80	Gnome	School.
1048	Ready		Avro 179 Dual	80	Gnome	School.
9821	Ready		Avro 179 Dual	80	Gnome	School.
9829	Ready		Avro 179 Dual	80	Gnome	School.
9830	Ready		Avro 179 Dual	80	Gnome	School.
9862	Ready		Avro 179 Dual	86	Gnome	School.
9863	Overhaul..		Avro 179 Dual	80	Gnome	School.
9870	Ready		Avro 179 Dual	80	Gnome	School.
N5252	Ready		Avro 179 Dual	80	Gnome	School.
N5253	Ready		Avro 179 Dual	80	Gnome	School.
N5254	Ready		Avro 179 Dual	80	Gnome	School.
N5255	Erecting..		Avro 179 Dual	80	Gnome Gun	School.
N5271	Ready	14	Avro 179 Dual	80	Gnome	School.
1478	Ready		Avro Scout	80	Gnome	School.
1492	Wrecked..		Avro Scout	80	Gnome	School.
1493	Engine overhaul.		Avro Scout	80	Gnome	School.
1494	Ready		Avro Scout	80	Gnome	School.
1495	Wrecked..		Avro Scout	80	Gnome	School.
1496	For erection		Avro Scout	80	Gnome	School.
3301	For erection		Avro Scout		None	School.
3302	Ready		Avro Scout		None	School.
3303	Wrecked..		Avro Scout	80	Gnome	School.
3315	Ready		Avro Scout	86	Gnome	School.
3316	Overhaul.		Avro Scout	80	Gnome	School.
3317	Ready		Avro Scout	80	Gnome	School.
3318	Ready		Avro Scout	80	Gnome	School.
3319	Ready		Avro Scout	80	Gnome	School.
3320	Ready		Avro Scout	80	Gnome	School.
8585	Ready	16	Avro Scout	80	Gnome	School.
9278	Ready	1	Avro Scout	100	Mono	School.
1738	Ready		B.E. 2 C	90	Curtiss	School.
4337	Overhaul..		B.E. 2 C	90	Curtiss	School.
4426	Ready		B.E. 2 C Dual	90	Curtiss	School.
4524	Ready		B.E. 2 C	90	Curtiss	School.
4525	Engine overhaul.		B.E. 2 C	75	Renault	School.
4526	Ready		B.E. 2 C Dual	80	Renault	School.
4570	Repairs		B.E. 2 C	90	Curtiss	School.
4571	Ready		B.E. 2 C Dual	75	Renault	School.
4572	Ready		B.E. 2 C	90	Curtiss	Night.
9462	Erected		B.E. 2 C	90	Curtiss	School.
9464	Not flying	11	B.E. 2 C	90	Curtiss	School.
2735	Ready		B.E. 2 C	90	R.A.F.	School.
2737	Ready		B.E. 2 C	90	R.A.F.	Night.
8302	Repairs		BE. 2 C	90	R.A.F.	School.
8404	Ready		B.E. 2 C	90	R.A.F.	School.
8406	Ready		B.E. 2 C	90	R.A.F.	School.
8422	Overhaul..		B.E. 2 C	90	R.A.F.	School.
8423	Wrecked..		B.E. 2 C	90	R.A.F.	Freiston.
8433	Ready		B.E. 2 C	90	R.A.F.	Freiston.
8620	Overhaul..		B.E. 2 C	90	R.A.F.	School.
8621	Ready		B.E. 2 C	90	R.A.F.	School.
8623	Overhaul..		B.E. 2 C	90	R.A.F.	School.
8722	Overhaul..	12	B.E. 2 C	90	R.A.F.	Freiston.
6259	Ready		B.E. 2 E	75	R.R.	Night flying.
6324	Ready		B.E. 2 E	75	R.R.	Night flying.
6325	Ready	3	B.E. 2 E	75	R.R.	Night flying.

CRANWELL R.N.A.S. TRAINING ESTABLISHMENT—continued.

No.	Condition.	Total.	Type.	H.p.	Engine.	Duties.
1256	Repairs		Bristol Scout	80	Gnome	Fin. training.
3019	Wrecked..		Bristol Scout	80	Gnome	Freiston
3020	Overhaul..		Bristol Scout	80	Gnome	Fin. training.
3021	Ready		Bristol Scout	80	Gnome	Fin. training.
3022	Ready		Bristol Scout	80	Gnome	Fin. training
3031	Ready		Bristol Scout	80	Gnome	Fin. training.
3032	Repairs		Bristol Scout	80	Gnome	Fin. training.
3034	Repairs		Bristol Scout	80	Gnome	Fin. training.
5565	Repairs		Bristol Scout	80	Gnome	Fin. training.
N5410	Ready		Bristol Scout	80	Gnome	Fin. training.
A1769	Repairs		Bristol Scout	80	Gnome	Fin. training.
A1771	Repairs		Bristol Scout	80	Gnome	Fin. training.
A1772	Repairs		Bristol Scout	80	Gnome	Fin. training.
A1790	Repairs		Bristol Scout	89	Gnome	Fin. training.
A1791	Ready	15	Bristol Scout	80	Gnome	Fin. training.
8981	For erection		Bristol Scout	100	Mono	Fin. training.
8982	Ready		Bristol Scout	100	Mono	Fin. training
8983	Ready		Bristol Scout	100	Mono	Fin. training.
8984	Ready	4	Bristol Scout	100	Mono	Fin. training.
3425	Ready		J N 4 Dual	90	Curtiss	School.
8844	Ready		J N 4 Dual	90	Curtiss	School.
8846	Ready		J N 4 Dual	90	Curtiss	School.
8848	Ready		J N 4 Dual	90	Curtiss	School.
8862	Ready		J N 4 Dual	90	Curtiss	School.
8864	Ready	6	J N 4 Dual	90	Curtiss	School.
3390	Repairs		J N 3 Imp.	90	Curtiss	School.
3428	Ready		J N 4	90	Curtiss	School.
3433	For repair		J N 4	90	Curtiss	School.
3435	Ready		J N 4	90	Curtiss	School.
3437	Ready		J N 4	90	Curtiss	School.
3439	Ready		J N 4	90	Curtiss	School.
3441	Ready		J N 4	90	Curtiss	School.
8841	Repairs		J N 4	90	Curtiss	School.
8843	Repairs		J N 4	90	Curtiss	School.
8855	Overhaul..		J N 4	90	Curtiss	School.
8865	Ready		J N 4 Imp.	90	Curtiss	School.
8867	Ready	12	J N 4 Imp.	90	Curtiss	School.
3452	Ready		Curtiss R. 2	160	Curtiss	School.
3463	Ready	2	Curtiss R. 2	160	Curtiss	School.
3011	Ready		M. Farman L.	80	Renault	School.
8922	Ready		M. Farman L.	80	Renault	School.
8934	Ready		M. Farman L.	80	Renault	School.
8939	Ready		M. Farman L.	80	Renault	School.
N5000	Wait'g nut		M. Farman L.	75	R.R.	School.
N5032	Repairs		M. Farman L.	80	Renault	School.
N5033	Ready		M. Farman L.	80	Renault	School.
N5042	Ready		M. Farman L.	80	Renault	School.
N5043	Ready		M. Farman L.	80	Renault	School.
N5046	Ready	10	M. Farman L.	80	Renault	School.
A334	Ready		M. Farman S.	80	Renault	School.
A354	Ready		M. Farman S.	80	Renault	School.
7385	Engine overhaul.	3	M. Farman S.	80	Renault	Gun training.
9161	Overhaul..	1	Fmn F. 40 W.T.	150	Renault	Fin. training.
N3170	Ready		Nieuport	110	Clerget	Fin. training.
N3171	Ready		Nieuport	110	Clerget	Fin. training.
3924	For erection		Nieuport	110	Clerget	Fin. training.
8713	For erection		Nieuport	110	Clerget	Fin. training.
8732	Ready		Nieuport	110	Clerget	Fin. training.
8741	Ready		Nieuport	110	Clerget	Fin. training.
8743	Repairs		Nieuport	110	Clerget	Fin. training.
8915	For erection		Nieuport W.T.	110	Clerget	Fin. training.
9201	Ready		Nieuport	110	Clerget	Fin. training.
9207	Ready		Nieuport	110	Clerget	Fin. training.
9211	Repairs		Nieuport	110	Clerget	Fin. training.
9234	Repairs		Nieuport	110	Clerget	Fin. training.
9235	Ready		Nieuport	110	Clerget	Fin. training.
9236	Repairs		Nieuport	110	Clerget	Fin. training.
9245	Ready		Nieuport	110	Clerget	Fin. training.
9246	Ready	16	Nieuport	110	Clerget	Fin. training.
2201	For overhaul		R.E. 7	120	A. Daimler	Fin. training.
2362	Ready	2	R.E. 7	120	A. Daimler	Fin. training.
N5280	Testing	1	Sage School	75	R.R.	School.
9398	Engine overhaul.		Sopwith 9400 S.	110	Clerget	Fin. training.
9399	Ready		Sopwith 9400 S.	110	Clerget	Fin. training.
9893	Overhaul		Sopwith 9400 S.	110	Clerget	Fin. training.
9894	Overhaul..	4	Sopwith 9400 S.	110	Clerget	Fin. training.
N5166	Wrecked..	1	Sopwith 9700		None	Fin. training
9902	Ready		Sopwith 9901	80	Clerget	Fin. training.
9903	Ready		Sopwith 9901	80	Clerget	Fin. training.
9908	Overhaul..		Sopwith 9901	80	Clerget	Fin. training.
9909	Ready	4	Sopwith 9901	80	Clerget	Fin. training.

FOR OTHER STATIONS.

No.	Condition.	Total.	Type.	H.p.	Engine.	Duties.

CRANWELL R.N.A.S. TRAINING ESTABLISHMENT—*continued.*

ALLOCATED.

No.	Condition.	Total.	Type.	H.p.	Engine.	Duties.
9889	Killingholme	1	Avro 179 Dual	80	Gnome ..	(Gun) School.
9951	Blackburn	1	B.E. 2 C ..	90	Curtiss ..	Fin. training.
2324	R.F.C. ..	1	B.E. 2 E ..	75	R.R. ..	School.
9426	Hendon	1	Breguet Conc.	250	R.R. ..	Fin. training.
N5399	Chingford	1	Bristol Scout..	100	Mono ..	Fin. training.
N3220	France ..		F. 40	160	Renault ..	Fin. training.
N3221	France ..		F. 40	160	Renault ..	Fin. training.
N3222	France ..		F. 40	160	Renault ..	Fin. training.
N3223	France ..		F. 40 ..	160	Renault ..	Fin. training.
N3224	France ..	5	F. 40	160	Renault ..	Fin. training.
9251	Brush		H. Farman .	140	C. Unne ..	Fin. training.
9252	Brush ..	2	H. Farman ..	140	C. Unne ..	Gun training.
N5065	Eastbourne Av. Co.		M. Farman S.	80	Renault ..	Gun training.
N5069	Eastbourne Av. Co.	2	M. Farman S.	80	Renault ..	Gun training.
3348	Hendon ..	1	J N 3 Imp. ..	90	Curtiss ..	School.
9239	Beardmore		Nieuport ..	110	Clerget ..	Fin. training.
9240	Beardmore		Nieuport ..	110	Clerget ..	Fin. training.
9248	Beardmore		Nieuport ..	110	Clerget ..	Fin. training.
9249	Beardmore		Nieuport ..	110	Clerget ..	Fin. training.
9250	Beardmore	5	Nieuport ..	110	Clerget ..	Fin. training.
2260	Sunbeam R.	1	R.E. 7 ..	200	Sunbeam ..	Experiments.
N5281	Sage ..	1	Sage School ..	75	R.R. ..	Fin. training.
N5230	Mann, R.	1	Sopwith 9400 S.	110	Clerget ..	Fin. training.
N5605	Westland		Sopwith 9700	None	..	School.
N5606	Westland	2	Sopwith 9700	None	..	School.
9907	Westgate		Sopwith 9901	80	Clerget ..	Fin. training.
9923	Beardmore		Sopwith 9901	80	Rhone ..	School.
9924	Beardmore		Sopwith 9901	80	Rhone ..	School.
9925	Beardmore	4	Sopwith 9901	80	Rhone ..	School.

FOR DELETION.

No.	Condition.	Total.	Type.	H.p.	Engine.	Duties.
8429	For survey		B.E. 2 C ..	90	R.A.F. ..	Fin. training.

AT NORTHERN AIRCRAFT SCHOOL, WINDERMERE.

(To be Closed).

Flight Commander J. M. R. Cripps in Command.

Telegrams : SEAPLANES, WINDERMERE.

SEAPLANES.

ALLOCATED.

FOR OTHER STATIONS.

No.	Condition.	Total.	Type.	H.p.	Engine.	Duties.
3323	Dismantled	1	Short 827 ..	150	Sunbeam ..	Calshot.
3781	Dismantled	1	Sopwith Schndr.	100	Mono ..	Calshot.

FOR DELETION.

Detling Naval Air Sub-Station.

See under Manstone.

Dover Naval Aeroplane Station.

See Dunkirk.

Dover Seaplane Station.

See Dunkirk.

Dundee Naval Air Station.

Flight Commander T. W. Elsdon, in Command

Telegrams : AEROPLANES, DUNDEE.

POLICY.

Duty.	Flights.	In No.	Present aim.	Type.
Seaplanes—				
War Flight .. .. {	1	6	6	Short 184.
	½	3	3	Baby 110 Clerget.

No.	Condition.	Total.	Type.	H.p.	Engine.	Duties.
SEAPLANES.						
8256	Ready ..		Short 827 ..	150	Sunbeam ..	Patrol.
8257	Alter'g gear		Short 827 ..	150	Sunbeam ..	Patrol.
8645	Ready ..		Short 827 W.T.	150	Sunbeam ..	Patrol.
8646	Ready ..	4	Short 827 W.T.	150	Sunbeam ..	Patrol.
ALLOCATED.						
8236	Brush	1	Short 827 ..	150	Sunbeam ..	Patrol.
9783	Grain ..		Short 830 ..	140	C. Unne ..	Patrol.
9784	Grain ..		Short 830 ..	140	C. Unne ..	Patrol.
9785	Grain ..		Short 830 ..	140	C. Unne ..	Patrol.
9786	Grain ..	4	Short 830 ..	140	C. Unne ..	Patrol.
FOR OTHER STATIONS.						Allocated—
9053	Dismantled		Short 184 ..	240	Sunbeam ..	Otranto.
9070	Dismantled		Short 184 ..	225	Sunbeam ..	Otranto.
9071	Dismantled		Short 184 ..	225	Sunbeam ..	Otranto.
9072	Dismantled		Short 184 ..	240	Sunbeam ..	Otranto.
9087	Dismantled		Short 184 Imp.	225	Sunbeam ..	Otranto.
9091	Dismantled	6	Short 184 Imp.	225	Sunbeam ..	Otranto.

FOR DELETION.

French-built Nieuport 12 two-seater 3924, powered by a 110 hp Clerget 9Z rotary, was awaiting erection at Cranwell, having previously been in France, where this picture of it in unfortunate circumstances was probably taken. It was nearing the end of its life, however. After being surveyed on 15 October 1917 it was written off as damaged beyond repair on the 26th of that month.

Another Cranwell-based trainer was Beardmore-built Nieuport 12 two-seater 9211, which was under repair. It survived until late February 1918.

Sage Type 3 primary trainer N5280, seen here under construction in the manufacturer's Peterborough factory, was under test at Cranwell, but was condemned and relegated to ground training. Deleted on 17 January 1918, it was crashed and rebuilt. The second and last of the type to be built, N5281, had been allocated to Cranwell, but the contract was cancelled.

Short-lived Parnall-built Avro 504B (Type 179) 9889 was delivered to Cranwell on 17 February 1917, the census stating that it had been allocated from Killingholme as a gun school machine. This picture was probably taken at Vendome in France. The aircraft was deleted on 19 May 1917.

Pemberton-Billing P.B.25 pusher scout 9002, powered by a 100 hp Gnome Monosoupape, at Eastchurch NAS in September 1916. Produced at the Supermarine Company's Woolston works, the 20 examples of this unlovely and unloved aeroplane that were built survived for a remarkably long time, considering that they were probably very little flown. This one was "ready" by 11 September 1916, went first to Eastchurch's War Flight and then its Design Flight and Gunnery School Flights, and was not deleted until 31 August 1918.

Another of the Eastchurch P.B.25s was 9003, again photographed in September 1916. Five were at this station at the time of the census, and another 14 were at Killingholme, whence they had been delivered without engines. The odd man out, 9004, went to Dover and was earmarked "for deletion" at the time of the census. Despite this it survived until 2 October 1917, when it was recorded as damaged beyond repair.

The first Brush-built Maurice Farman M.F.7 Longhorn, 3001, seen in factory-fresh state, was ready for use by the Eastchurch Flying School. Powered by an 80 hp Renault engine, it spent its entire working life at Eastbourne, being delivered there on 27 October 1915 and surviving until its deletion on 26 April 1917.

Another nightmare to emerge from the Supermarine works was the P.B.31E Nighthawk anti-airship quadruplane, powered by a pair of 100/125 hp Anzani radial engines. Two were ordered, 1388 and 1389, but only the first was completed. The type appears at least three times in this census. On page 6, 1388 is listed in the Design Flight at Eastchurch, and it also appears on page 26 under "machines for trial and experiment"; on page 35, 1389 is listed in the proposed cancellations. Shortly after the census date, on 3 March, 1388 was deleted.

No.	Condition.	Total.	Type.	H.p.	Engine.	Duties.

Eastbourne Naval Flying School.
Care and Maintenance Party.
Sub-Lieutenant R. Spickernell, R.N.V.R., in Charge.
Telegrams : AEROPLANES, EASTBOURNE.

POLICY.

Duty.			No.	Present aim.	Type.
School	..	..	15	..	} Temporarily
Fin. Training	..	..	15	..	} closed.

AEROPLANES

3892	Dismantled		Blériot Tractor	80	Gnome	.. Adv. School.
3893	Ready ..		Blériot Tractor	80	Gnome	.. Adv. School.
3948	Dismantled		Blériot Tractor	80	Gnome	.. Adv. School.
3949	Dismantled		Blériot Tractor	80	Gnome	.. Adv. School.
3952	Dismantled	5	Blériot Tractor	80	Gnome	..
1216	Ready ..	1	Bristol Tractor	80	Gnome	.. Adv. School.

FOR OTHER STATIONS.

9822	Ready ..	1	Avro 179 Dual	80	Gnome	.. Chingford.
8810	Dismantled		J N 4 Dual ..		None	.. Vendome.
8850	Dismantled	2	J N 4 Dual ..		None	.. Vendome.
8930	Repairs ..	1	M. Farman L.	80	Renault	.. Eastchurch Flying Sch.

SEAPLANES.

FOR DELETION.

3237	Surveyed..		Blériot	..	80	Gnome ..

Eastchurch Naval Air Station.
in Command.
WITH SUB-STATION AT LEYSDOWN.
Observers' School.
Flight Commander K. S. Savory in Charge.
Telegrams : AEROPLANES, EASTCHURCH.

POLICY (M. 010977).

Duty.	No	Present aim.	Type.

AEROPLANES

N5259	Ready ..		Avro 179 Dual	80	Gnome	.. Gun Tractor.
N5260	Ready ..	2	Avro 179 Dual	80	Gnome	.. Gun Tractor.
8294	Ready ..		B.E. 2 C	90	R.A.F.	.. Night.
8336	Repairs ..		B.E. 2 C	90	R.A.F.	.. Night.
8405	Repairs ..		B.E. 2 C	90	R.A.F.	.. Gun Tractor.
8408	Repairs ..		B.E. 2 C	90	R.A.F.	.. Night.
8426	Repairs ..		B.E. 2 C	90	R.A.F.	.. Gun Tractor.
8495	Ready ..		B.E. 2 C	90	R.A.F.	.. Night.
8610	Ready ..		B.E. 2 C	90	R.A.F.	.. Night.
8624	Ready ..		B.E. 2 C	90	R.A.F.	.. Night.
9465	Erecting ..	9	B.E. 2 C	90	Curtiss	.. Night.
9156	For re-covering.		Farman F. 40	150	Renault	..
9165	For re-covering.		Farman F. 40	150	Renault	..
9172	For re-covering.	3	Farman F. 40	150	Renault	..
8837	Repairs ..	1	J N 4 ..	90	Curtiss	.. Gun Tractor.
9237	Ready ..		Nieuport	110	Clerget	.. Obs. Tr'ning.
9238	Repairs ..	2	Nieuport	110	Clerget	.. Obs. Tr'ning.
3686	Ready ..	1	Sopwith 9400 S.	110	Clerget	.. Type tr'n'ng.
8521	Crushed ..	1	Voisin		150	C. Unne ..

ALLOCATED.

N5273	Sunbeam..	1	Avro 179 Dual	80	Gnome	.. Gun Tractor.
8328	Dunkirk..		B.E. 2 C	90	R.A.F.	.. Night.
8494	Dover ..		B.E. 2 C	90	R.A.F.	.. Night.
8617	Dunkirk ..	3	B.E. 2 C	90	R.A.F.	.. Night.
9169	Grain (G.)		Farman F. 40	150	Renault	..
N3211	France		Farman F. 40	160	Renault	..
N3212	France ..		Farman F. 40	160	Renault	..
N3213	France ..	4	Farman F. 40	160	Renault	..

No.	Condition.	Total.	Type.	H.p.	Engine.	Duties.

EASTCHURCH NAVAL AIR STATION—*continued.*

Gunnery School.
Squadron Commander A. C. Barnby in Charge.

POLICY.

Duty.			No.	Present aim.	Type.
1-str. fighters	..	..	10 {	5	P.B. Scout
				5	Bristol Scout
2-str. tractors	..	..	10 {	5	J.N.
				5	B.E. 2 C
Pusher types	..	..	15 {	10	M.F. Shorthorn
				5	Other types

AEROPLANES

N5257	Eng. repair	1	Avro 179 Dual	80	Gnome	.. Dual Tractor
3059	Ready ..		Bristol Scout..	80	Gnome	.. F. and G.T.
N5392	Ready ..		Bristol Scout..	100	Mono	.. F. and G.T.
N5395	Ready ..	3	Bristol Scout..	100	Mono	.. F. and G.T.
N3210	Erected ..		Farman F. 40	160	Renault	..
N3214	Erected ..		Farman F. 40	160	Renault	..
9170	Ready ..	3	Farman F 40	150	Renault	.. Gun Pusher.
8108	Ready ..		M. Farman S.	80	Renault	.. Gun Pusher.
8109	Ready ..		M. Farman S.	80	Renault	.. Gun Pusher.
8111	Ready ..		M. Farman S.	70	Renault	.. Gun Pusher.
8466	Repairs ..		M. Farman S.	80	Renault	.. Gun Pusher.
8468	Repairs ..		M. Farman S.	75	Renault	.. Gun Pusher.
8470	Ready ..		M. Farman S.	75	R.R.	.. Gun Pusher.
8471	Ready ..		M. Farman S.	75	Renault	.. Gun Pusher.
8472	Ready ..		M. Farman S.	75	Renault	.. Gun Pusher.
8473	Ready ..		M. Farman S.	80	Renault	.. Gun Pusher.
N5062	Ready ..		M. Farman S.	80	Renault	.. Gun Pusher.
N5063	Repairs ..		M. Farman S.	80	Renault	.. Gun Pusher.
N5064	Ready ..	12	M. Farman S.	80	Renault	.. Gun Pusher.
N5332	Erecting ..		M. Farman L.	75	R.R.	.. Gun Pusher.
N5333	Erecting ..	2	M. Farman L.	75	R.R.	.. Gun Pusher.
9001	For test ..		P.B. Scout	100	Mono	..
9002	Ready ..		P.B. Scout ..	100	Mono	.. F. and G.T.
9003	Repairs ..		P.B. Scout ..	100	Mono	.. F. and G.T.
9005	Ready ..		P.B. Scout ..	100	Mono	.. F. and G.T.
9006	Ready ..	5	P.B. Scout ..	100	Mono	.. F. and G.T.
8509	Ready ..	1	Voisin	..	150	C. Unne ..

ALLOCATED.

N5066	E. A. Co...		M. Farman S.	80	Renault	.. Gun Pusher.
N5067	E. A. Co...		M. Farman S.	80	Renault	.. Gun Pusher.
N5068	E. A. Co...	3	M. Farman S.	80	Renault	.. Gun Pusher.

EASTCHURCH NAVAL AIR STATION—continued.

Flying School.

Squadron Commander C. E. Maude in Charge.

POLICY.

Duty.	No.	Present aim.	Type.
School	10	10	M.F. Longhorn
Advanced School (1) ..	10	6	Avro
		4	J.N.
Advanced School (2) ..	10	4	B.E. 2 C
Fast types	4	2	Bristol Scout

AEROPLANES

No.	Condition.	Total.	Type.	H.p.	Engine.	Duties.
1011	Ready		Avro 179	80	Gnome	Adv. School.
1012	Repairs		Avro 179	80	Gnome	Adv. School.
9827	Ready		Avro 179 Dual	80	Gnome	Dual Tractor
9868	Ready		Avro 179 Dual	80	Gnome	Dual Tractor
9871	Ready		Avro 179 Dual	80	Gnome	Dual Tractor
9872	Ready		Avro 179 Dual	80	Gnome	Dual Tractor
N5251	Ready		Avro 179 Dual	80	Gnome	Dual Tractor
N5258	Ready	8	Avro 179 Dual	80	Gnome	Dual Tractor
8574	Damaged		Avro Scout	80	Gnome	Adv. School.
8575	Ready		Avro Scout	80	Gnome	Adv. School.
8577	Ready		Avro Scout	80	Gnome	Adv. School.
8586	Overhaul		Avro Scout	80	Gnome	Gun Tractor.
8582	Overhaul		Avro Scout	80	Gnome	Adv. School.
8583	Repairs	6	Avro Scout	80	Gnome	Adv. School.
992	Ready		B.E. 2 C	70	Renault	Adv. School.
1142	Repairs		B.E. 2 C	75	Renault	Adv. School.
1167	Ready		B.E. 2 C	75	Renault	Adv. School.
1191	Repairs	4	B.E. 2 C Dual	75	Renault	Adv. School.
9463	Erecting	1	B.E. 2 C	90	Curtiss	Adv. School.
3014	Repairs		Bristol Scout	80	Gnome	Adv. School.
3042	Ready		Bristol Scout	80	Gnome	F. and G.T.
N5409	Ready	3	Bristol Scout	80	Gnome	Adv. School.
3444	Ready		J N 4 Dual	90	Curtiss	Dual Tractor
8804	Ready		J N 4 Dual	90	Curtiss	Dual Tractor
8828	Ready		J N 4 Dual	90	Curtiss	Dual Tractor
8830	Ready		J N 4 Dual	90	Curtiss	Dual Tractor
8834	Ready	5	J N 4 Dual	90	Curtiss	Dual Tractor
3381	Ready		J N 3 Og. Imp.	90	Curtiss	Gun Tractor.
3394	Ready		J N 3 Og. Imp.	90	Curtiss	Gun Tractor.
3397	Ready		J N 3 Og. Imp.	90	Curtiss	Gun Tractor.
8807	Ready		J N 4	90	Curtiss	Adv. School.
8809	Ready		J N 4	90	Curtiss	Adv. School.
8849	Repairs		J N 4 Imp.	90	Curtiss	Adv. School.
8861	Instructional	7	J N 4 Imp.	90	Curtiss	Adv. School.
3001	Ready		M. Farman L.	80	Renault	School.
3005	Repairs		M. Farman L.	80	Renault	School.
8926	Ready		M. Farman L.	80	Renault	School.
8927	Ready		M. Farman L.	80	Renault	School.
8929	Repairs		M. Farman L.	80	Renault	School.
8935	Repairs		M. Farman L.	80	Renault	School.
8936	Repairs		M. Farman L.	80	Renault	School.
8937	Repairs		M. Farman L.	80	Renault	School.
N5030	Ready		M. Farman L.	80	Renault	School.
N5031	Ready		M. Farman L.	80	Renault	School.
N5041	Repairs		M. Farman L.	80	Renault	School.
N5044	Ready		M. Farman L.	80	Renault	School.
N5045	Fan broken		M. Farman L.	80	Renault	School.
N5053	Ready		M. Farman L.	80	Renault	School.
N5330 g	?	15	M. Farman L.	75	R.R.	School.

ALLOCATED.

No.	Condition.	Total.	Type.	H.p.	Engine.	Duties.
N6147	Sunbeam	1	Avro 179 Dual	80	Gnome	School.
8930	Eastbourne	1	M. Farman L.	80	Renault	School.

EASTCHURCH NAVAL AIR STATION—continued.

Design Flight.

Squadron Commander H. R. Busteed in Charge.

AEROPLANES

No.	Condition.	Total.	Type.	H.p.	Engine.	Duties.
8803	Ready	1	J N 4	150	Renault	K.
9901	Repairs		Sopwith 9901	80	Clerget	K.
9950	Ready	2	Sopwith 9901	80	Rhone	K.
9377	Ready		Sopwith 9400 S.	110	Clerget	K.
9390	Repairs	2	Sopwith 9400 S.	110	Clerget	E.
1388	E ?	1	S'marine Q'plne	2-125	Anzani	K.
9842	Ready	1	Wight Land	250	R.R.	K.

SEAPLANES.

No.	Condition.	Total.	Type.	H.p.	Engine.	Duties.
8134	Repairs	1	Sopwith Baby	110	Clerget	K.

FOR OTHER STATIONS.

No.	Condition.	Total.	Type.	H.p.	Engine.	Duties.
988	Repairs		B.E. 2 C	70	Renault	Allocated to Chingford.
3451	Repairs	1	Curtiss R 2	160	Curtiss	G.
9306	Engine out		Short Bomber	250	R.R. Mk. II	
9307	Engine out		Short Bomber	250	R.R. Mk. II	
9313	Engine out		Short Bomber	250	R.R. Mk. I	
9317	Engine out		Short Bomber	250	R.R. Mk. III	
9322	Engine out		Short Bomber	250	R.R. Mk. III	
9340	Ready		Short Bomber	250	R.R. Mk. IV	E.
9356	Remov'g eng.		Short Bomber	240	Sunbeam	
9357	Remov'g eng.		Short Bomber	250	Sunbeam	
9358	Remov'g eng.		Short Bomber	240	Sunbeam	
9360	Remov'g eng.		Short Bomber	240	Sunbeam	
9361	Remov'g eng.		Short Bomber	240	Sunbeam	
9362	Remov'g eng.		Short Bomber	240	Sunbeam	
9363	Remov'g eng.		Short Bomber	240	Sunbeam	
9365	Remov'g eng.		Short Bomber	240	Sunbeam	
9367	Remov'g eng.		Short Bomber	240	Sunbeam	
9486	Engine out		Short Bomber			
9492	Ready		Short Bomber	250	R.R. Mk. IV	
9493	Ready		Short Bomber	250	R.R. Mk. IV	
9494	Ready	19	Short Bomber	250	R.R. Mk. IV	
N5525	Ready	1	Sopwith 9700	110	Clerget	Dunkirk.
N5350	Ready	1	Sopwith T'plane	130	Clerget	Dunkirk.

ALLOCATED.

No.	Condition.	Total.	Type.	H.p.	Engine.	Duties.
*9318	Burnt		Short Bomber	250	R.R. Mk. I	
9495	Mann, E.	2	Short Bomber	250	R.R. Mk. IV	
9841	White		Wight Land m/c	250	R.R.	
9843	White		Wight Land m/c	250	R.R.	
9844	White		Wight Land m/c	250	R.R.	
9845	White		Wight Land m/c	250	R.R.	
9846	White	5	Wight Land m/c	250	R.R.	

FOR DELETION.

No.	Condition.	Total.	Type.	H.p.	Engine.	Duties.
8441	For survey		Avro Bomber	200	Sunbeam	K.
1482	Survey		Avro Scout	80	Gnome	Gun Tractor.
987	Surveyed		B.E. 2 C	70	Renault	Night.
1102	Surveyed		B.E. 2 C	70	Renault	Experiment.
1105	Surveyed		B.E. 2 C	70	Renault	Gun Tractor.
1164	Surveyed		B.E. 2 C	75	Renault	Gun Tractor.
8327	Surveyed		B.E. 2 C	90	R.A.F.	Gun Tractor.
3058	Survey		Bristol Scout	80	Gnome	F. and G.T.
3339	Survey		Caudron Twin	2-100	Anzani	G.
9145	Survey		H. Farman	160	C. Unne	G. (Grain).
8757	Survey		G.W. 1600	60	Rhone	School.
8758	Survey		G.W. 1600	60	Rhone	School.
8766	Survey		G.W. 1600	60	Rhone	School.
8771	Survey		G.W. 1600	60	Rhone	School.
8772	Survey		G.W. 1600	60	Rhone	School.
8773	Survey		G.W. 1600	60	Rhone	School.
3361	Surveyed		J N 3 Og. Imp.	90	Curtiss	Gun Tractor.
3376	Survey		J N 3 Imp.	90	Curtiss	
3384	Survey		J N 3 Imp.	90	Curtiss	Adv. School.
3386	Survey		J N 3 Imp.	90	Curtiss	Adv. School.
8818	Surveyed		J N 4 Dual	90	Curtiss	Dual Tractor
N5423	Lost		Sopwith T'plane	130	Clerget	

* Down at Dunmow.

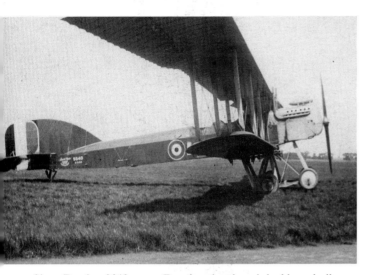

Short Bomber 9340 was at Eastchurch, where it had been built, "ready" to go to another station, at the time of the census. It was destined to spend its life with the Testing Squadron at Martlesham Heath and at Grain.

At the time of the census, Deperdussin monoplane 1378 was at Felixstowe, earmarked for deletion. On 4 November 1915, piloted by Flt Lt R.J.J. Hope-Vere, it had taken off from a fixed forecastle ramp on HMS *Aurora* in an effort to find a means of countering Zeppelin reconnaissance of the Grand Fleet's movements in the North Sea, but it was not up to the task.

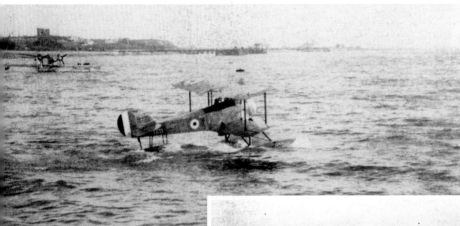

Sopwith Baby 8166 taxies out. This machine was listed as one of the "Nore War Flight Seaplanes" under RNAS Felixstowe. Delivered to Killingholme on 6 September 1917, it crashed on arrival and was written off.

Awaiting deletion at Felixstowe at the time of the census, Wight Admiralty Type187 Improved Twin Seaplane 1451 had been deemed unsafe for further use in November 1916, but was not finally written off until 25 April 1917.

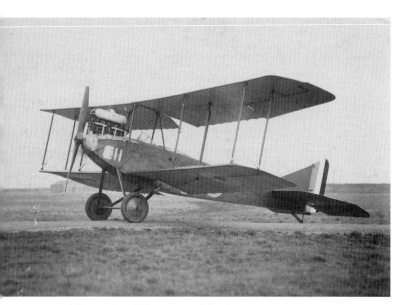

Albatros B.II 890 was one of Grain's oldest residents, having been impressed into service at the outbreak of war, when it had been flying at Hendon. Used for station defence among other things, it survived until April 1918.

Sopwith 9901 Pup 9922, a Beardmore-built machine, was allocated to Grain for deck flying experiments, and is seen in this movie still with a skid undercarriage and an experimental arrester hook beneath the forward fuselage.

This Voisin LA Canon Pusher Biplane at Grain is almost certainly 9154, which was initially used for gunnery experiments and was fitted with a 12lb Davis gun. Here, named *Wild Duck*, it is fitted with underwing flotation bags and a tail float, the bags being seen inflated in the second view, in which the aircraft lacks rudder stripes. It was powered by a 150 hp Canton Unné radial engine.

No.	Condition.	Total	Type.	H.p.	Engine.	Duties.

East Fortune Naval Air Sub-Station.

Squadron Commander J. W. O. Dalgleish in Command.

Telegrams : AEROPLANES, ATHELSTANEFORD.

POLICY.

Duty.	Flights.	In No.	Present aim.	Type.
Aeroplanes—				
Patrol	1	10	10	Various

No.	Condition		Type.	H.p.	Engine.	Duties.
AEROPLANES						
1473	Repairs ..		Avro Scout ..	80	Gnome ..	C.P. and F.T.
3308	Ready ..		Avro Scout ..	80	Gnome ..	C.P. and F.T.
3309	Ready ..		Avro Scout ..	80	Gnome ..	C.P. and F.T.
3310	Waiting fittings.	4	Avro Scout ..	80	Gnome ..	C.P. and F.T.
8407	Ready ..		B.E. 2 C ..	90	R.A.F. ..	Night.
8717	Ready ..		B.E. 2 C ..	90	R.A.F. ..	Night.
8719	Repairs ..		B.E. 2 C ..	90	R.A.F. ..	Night.
8720	Ready ..		B.E. 2 C ..	90	R.A.F. ..	Night.
8724	Ready ..	5	B.E. 2 C ..	90	R.A.F. ..	Night.
8991	Waiting spares.		Bristol Scout..	100	Mono ..	C.P. & F.T.
8992	Ready ..		Bristol Scout..	100	Mono ..	C.P. & F.T.
N5394	Dismantled	3	Bristol Scout..	100	Mono ..	C.P. & F.T.
N5400	Ready ..		Bristol Scout..	80	Gnome ..	C.P. & F.T.
N5401	Ready ..	2	Bristol Scout..	80	Gnome ..	C.P. & F.T.
8805	Ready ..		J N 4	90	Curtiss ..	C.P. and F.T.
8821	Repairs ..	2	J N 4	90	Curtiss ..	C.P. and F.T.
8814	Ready ..		J N 4 Dual ..	90	Curtiss ..	C.P. and F.T.
8822	Ready ..	2	J N 4 Dual ..	90	Curtiss ..	C.P. and F.T.

ALLOCATED.

FOR OTHER STATIONS.

No.	Condition		Type.	H.p.	Engine.	Duties.
9913	For erection		Sopwith 9901	80	Rhone ..	Allocated to H.M.S. "Manxman."
9914	For erection		Sopwith 9901	80	Rhone ..	H.M.S. "Manxman."
9917	Ready ..		Sopwith 9901	80	Rhone ..	Fleet use.
9918	Ready ..		Sopwith 9901	80	Rhone ..	Fleet use.
9919	Ready ..		Sopwith 9901	80	Rhone ..	Fleet use.
9920	Ready ..	4	Sopwith 9901	80	Rhone ..	Fleet use.

FOR DELETION.

Fairlop Landing Ground.

See under Chingford.

Felixstowe Naval Air Station.

Wing Commander J. C. Porte in Command.

WITH NIGHT LANDING GROUND AT TRIMLEY.

Telegrams : AEROPLANES, FELIXSTOWE.

POLICY.

Duty.	Flights.	In No.	Present aim.	Type.
Seaplanes—	1	3	3	Large America
War Flight ..	2	6	6	Porte F. Boat
(N.B.—Torpedo Flight will be transferred to Scapa	½	3	3	Short 184
	½	3	3	Baby 110 Clerget
	1	6	6	Short Torpedo
Nore War Flight ..	1	3	3	Large America
	½		3	Short 184
	½	3	3	Baby 110 Clerget
Training		20	20	Small America

No.	Condition		Type.	H.p.	Engine.	Duties.
AEROPLANES						
ALLOCATED.						
N5203	Mann, E.		Sopwith 9700		None ..	
N5601	Westland		Sopwith 9700		None ..	
N5602	Westland		Sopwith 9700		None ..	
N5603	Westland		Sopwith 9700		None ..	
N5604	Westland		Sopwith 9700		None ..	
N5607	Westland		Sopwith 9700		None ..	
N5608	Westland	7	Sopwith 9700		None ..	
FOR OTHER STATIONS.						
FOR DELETION.						
1595	Surveyed..		Caudron ..	100	Anzani ..	
1378	Surveyed..		Deperdussin ..	100	Mono ..	
1379	Surveyed..		Deperdussin ..	100	Mono ..	
SEAPLANES.						
3073	Repairs ..	1	Curtiss Tripl..	4-240	Renault ..	
3546	Dismantled		Small America	2-100	Mono ..	School.
3547	Ready ..		Small America	2-100	Anzani ..	School.
3548	Ready ..		Small America	2-100	Anzani ..	School.
3549	Erecting ..		Small America	2-100	Anzani ..	School.
3554	Ready ..		Small America	2-100	Anzani ..	School.
3569	Dismantled		Small America	2-100	Anzani ..	School.
3570	Dismantled		Small America	2-100	Anzani ..	School.
3580	Ready ..		Small America	2-100	Anzani ..	School.
3581	Repairs ..		Small America	2-100	Anzani ..	
3582	Repairs ..		Small America	2-100	Anzani ..	
3583	Ready ..		Small America	2-100	Anzani ..	School.
3584	Erecting..		Small America	2-100	Anzani ..	School.
3585	Erecting ..	13	Small America	2-100	Anzani ..	School.
	Not unpacked	12	Small America			
8652	Ready ..		Large America	2-250	R.R. ..	Patrol.
8654	Ready ..		Large America	2-250	R.R. ..	Patrol.
8656	For test ..		Large America	2-250	R.R. ..	Patrol.
8658	Erecting ..		Large America	2-250	R.R. ..	Patrol.
8661	Erecting ..		Large America	2-250	R.R. ..	
8662	Erecting ..		Large America	2-250	R.R. ..	
8663	Erecting ..		Large America	2-250	R.R. ..	
8664	Erecting ..		Large America	2-250	R.R. ..	
8665	Erecting ..		Large America	2-250	R.R. ..	
8666	For erection		Large America	2-250	R.R. ..	
8667	For erection		Large America	2-250	R.R. ..	
8668	For erection		Large America	2-250	R.R. ..	
8669	For erection		Large America	2-250	R.R. ..	
8670	For erection		Large America	2-250	R.R. ..	
8671	For erection		Large America	2-250	R.R. ..	
8672	For erection		Large America	2-250	R.R. ..	
8673	For erection	17	Large America	2-250	R.R. ..	
9800	Waiting propellers.		Porte F. Boat	3-250	R.R. ..	Scouting.
9802	Erecting..		Porte F. Boat	3-250	R.R. ..	Scouting.
9803	Erecting..		Porte F. Boat	3-250	R.R. ..	Scouting.
9804	Erecting..	4	Porte F. Boat	3-250	R.R. ..	Scouting.
8005	Float repairs		Short 184 ..	225	Sunbeam ..	Patrol.
9068	Ready ..	2	Short 184 ..	225	Sunbeam ..	Patrol.
3730	Ready ..		Sopwith Schndr.	100	Mono ..	Fighter.
3747	Ready ..	2	Sopwith Schndr.	100	Mono ..	Fighter.
8198	Ready ..		Sopwith Baby	100	Mono ..	Fighter.
8199	Ready ..	2	Sopwith Baby	100	Mono ..	Fighter.

No.	Condition.	Total.	Type.	H.p.	Engine.	Duties.

FELIXSTOWE NAVAL AIR STATION—*continued.*

ALLOCATED.

No.	Condition.	Total.	Type.	H.p.	Engine.	Duties.
9810	Aircraft Co.	1	Porte F. Boat	3-250	R.R.	.. Patrol.
8320	Short ..	1	Sht. N. Sea W.T.	310	Sunbeam	.. Patrol.
ℵ5609	Westlands		Sopwith 9400 S.		None	..
ℵ5610	Westlands		Sopwith 9400 S.		None	..
ℵ5611	Westlands	3	Sopwith 9400 S.		None	..
ℵ1036	Blackburn		Sopwith Baby	110	Clerget	.. Fighter.
1000	J. S. White		Wight 1000 ..	3-450	Sunbeam	..

NORE WAR FLIGHT SEAPLANES.

No.	Condition.	Total.	Type.	H.p.	Engine.	Duties.
8009	Ready ..		Short 184	225	Sunbeam	.. Nore Flight.
8063	Ready ..		Short 184 ..	225	Sunbeam	.. Nore Flight.
9085	Ready ..	3	Short 184	225	Sunbeam	.. Nore Flight.
3330	Ready ..		Short 827 W.T.	150	Sunbeam	.. Nore Flight.
8630	Testing ..		Short 827 ..	150	Sunbeam	.. Nore Flight.
8631	Ready ..		Short 827 ..	150	Sunbeam	.. Nore Flight.
8634	Ready ..	4	Short 827 W.T.	150	Sunbeam	.. Nore Flight.
8137	Ready ..		Sopwith Baby	110	Clerget	.. Nore Flight.
8166	Ready ..	2	Sopwith Baby	110	Clerget	.. Nore Flight.
8187	Repairs ..	1	Sopwith Baby	100	Mono	.. Nore Flight.
3746	Ready ..		Sopwith Schndr.	100	Mono	.. Nore Flight.
3794	Ready		Sopwith Schndr.	100	Mono	.. Nore Flight.
3803	Ready ..	3	Sopwith Schndr.	100	Mono	.. Nore Flight.

ALLOCATED.

No.	Condition.	Total.	Type.	H.p.	Engine.	Duties.
ℵ1037	Blackburn	1	Sopwith Baby	110	Clerget	.. Nore Flight.

FOR DELETION.

No.	Condition.	Total.	Type.	H.p.	Engine.	Duties.
3577	For survey		Small America	2-100	Anzani	.. School.
3578	Survey ..		Small America	2-100	Anzani	..
1451	Survey ..		Wight 187 ..	2-200	C. Unne	.. T.

FOR OTHER STATIONS AND TRIALS.

No.	Condition.	Total.	Type.	H.p.	Engine.	Duties.
1358	Ready ..		A.D. 1000	3-310	Sunbeam	.. K.
8653	Ready ..		Large America	2-250	R.R.	.. Yarmouth.
8657	For test ..		Large America	2-250	R.R.	.. Calshot.
8659	Erecting..		Large America	2-250	R.R.	.. Calshot.
8660	Erecting..		Large America	2-250	R.R.	.. Yarmouth.
8353	Dismantling		Short 184 ..	225	Sunbeam	.. Malta.
9801	Repairs ..		Porte F. Boat	3-250	R.R.	.. K.

Fishguard Naval Air Station.

SEAPLANES.

ALLOCATED.

No.	Condition.	Total.	Type.	H.p.	Engine.	Duties.
9086	Grain ..		Short 184 Imp.	225	Sunbeam	.. Patrol.
9090	K'holme ..	2	Short 184 Imp.	225	Sunbeam	.. Patrol.
ℵ1029	Blackburn		Sopwith Baby	110	Clerget	.. Patrol.
ℵ1030	Blackburn	2	Sopwith Baby	110	Clerget	.. Patrol.

Frieston Landing Ground.

See under Cranwell.

Grain Island Naval Air Station.

Wing Commander C. E Risk in Command.

Telegrams : AEROPLANES, ISLE OF GRAIN.

POLICY.

Duty.	Flights.	In No.	Present aim.	Type.
Aeroplanes	1	10	5	B.E. 2 C
			5	Bristol Scout
Seaplanes—				
Nore War Flight ..	1	6	6	Short 184
	1	6	6	Baby 110 Clerget
Experimental gunnery		4	3	Short 184
			1	Short 827

AEROPLANES

No.	Condition.	Total.	Type.	H.p.	Engine.	Duties.
890	Ready ..	1	Albatross ..	100	Mercedes ..	
1163	Repairs ..	1	B.E. 2 C	75	Renault	.. Night flying.
1484	Repairs ..	1	Avro Scout ..	80	Gnome	.. Night flying.
8296	Ready ..		B.E. 2 C	90	R.A.F.	.. Night flying.
8297	Ready ..		B.E. 2 C	90	R.A.F.	.. Night flying.
8430	Ready ..		B.E. 2 C	90	R.A.F.	.. Night flying.
8619	Ready ..		B.E. 2 C	90	R.A.F.	.. Night flying.
8629	Ready ..		B.E. 2 C	90	R.A.F.	.. Night flying.
9459	Ready ..	6	B.E. 2 C ..	90	R.A.F.	.. Night flying.
3046	Ready ..	1	Bristol Scout ..	80	Gnome	.. Fighter.
8958	Ready ..		Bristol Scout .	100	Mono	.. Fighter.;
8985	Ready ..		Bristol Scout ..	100	Mono	.. Fighter.
8986	Ready ..		Bristol Scout..	100	Mono	.. Fighter.
ℵ5390	Ready ..		Bristol Scout..	100	Mono	.. Fighter.
ℵ5391	Repairs ..	5	Bristol Scout..	100	Mono	.. Fighter.
3430	Ready ..		J N 4..	90	Curtiss	.. Patrol & F.T.
8823	Repairs ..		J N 4..	90	Curtiss	.. Patrol & F.T.
8829	Repairs ..		J N 4..	90	Curtiss	.. Patrol & F.T.
8831	Ready ..	4	J N 4 ..	90	Curtiss	.. Patrol & F.T
3432	Ready ..		J N 4 Dual	90	Curtiss	.. Patrol & F.T.
8826	Ready ..	2	J N 4 Dual ..	90	Curtiss	.. Patrol & F.T.

ALLOCATED.

No.	Condition.	Total.	Type.	H.p.	Engine.	Duties.
3885	P. Victoria	1	Breguet de Ch.	225	Sunbeam	..
9922	Beardmore	1	Sopwith 9901	80	Rhone	.. Deck flying.

FOR OTHER STATIONS AND TRIALS.

No.	Condition.	Total.	Type.	H.p.	Engine.	Duties.
9276	Ready ..		Avro Scout ..	100	Mono	.. G.
8628	Ready ..		B.E. 2 C	90	R.A.F.	.. Manstone.
8432	Engine overhaul.		B.E. 2 C	90	R.A.F.	.. G.
9461	Ready ..		B.E. 2 C	90	R.A.F.	.. G.
9470	Ready ..		B.E. 2 C	90	R.A.F.	.. G.
3449	Ready ..		Curtiss R 2	160	Curtiss	.. G., then No. 3 Wing.
3687	Ready ..		Dyott Fighter	2-120	A. Daimler	.. G., then Dunkirk.
9359	Ready ..		Short Bomber	240	Sunbeam	.. G.
9489	Ready ..		Short Bomber	250	R.R. Mk. IV	.. Dunkirk.
9380	Waiting engine spares.		Sopwith 9400 S	110	Clerget	.. G.
9154	Ready ..		Voisin ..	150	C. Unne	.. G.

FOR DELETION.

No.	Condition.	Total.	Type.	H.p.	Engine.	Duties.
1243	Surveyed..		Bristol Scout..	80	Gnome	.. Fighter.
9169	Surveyed..		Farman F. 40	150	Renault	.. G., then Eastchurch.

No.	Condition.	Total.	Type.	H.p.	Engine.	Duties.

GRAIN ISLAND NAVAL AIR STATION—continued.

SEAPLANES.

No.	Condition.	Total.	Type.	H.p.	Engine.	Duties.
3063	Ready ..		Short 827 W.T.	150	Sunbeam ..	Fin. training.
3103	Ready ..	2	Short 827 ..	150	Sunbeam ..	Fin. training.
9789	Erected ..	1	Short 830	140	C. Unne ..	
8053	Repairs ..		Short 184 Single	240	Sunbeam ..	
8070	For altera-tion.		Short 184 W.T. Imp.	225	Sunbeam ..	Fin. training.
8387	Ready ..	3	Short 184 Dual	225	Sunbeam ..	Fin. training.
8118	Ready ..	1	Sopwith Baby	100	Mono	Nore Flight.
3754	Ready ..		Sopwith Schndr.	100	Mono ..	Fin. training.
3757	Ready ..	2	Sopwith Schndr.	100	Mono ..	Fin. training.

ALLOCATED.

9790	Short ..	1	Short 830 ..	140	C. Unne ..	

NORE WAR FLIGHT SEAPLANES.

8251	Ready ..	1	Short 827 W.T.	150	Sunbeam ..	Nore Flight.
8006	Eng. repair		Short 184	225	Sunbeam ..	Nore Flight.
8364	Ready ..		Short 184	225	Sunbeam ..	Nore Flight.
9093	Ready ..	3	Short 184 Imp.	225	Sunbeam ..	Nore Flight.
8119	Ready ..	1	Sopwith Baby	100	Mono ..	Nore Flight.
8160	Ready ..		Sopwith Baby	110	Clerget ..	Nore Flight.
8168	Overhaul..	2	Sopwith Baby	110	Clerget ..	Nore Flight.
3804	Ready ..	1	Sopwith Schndr.	100	Mono ..	Nore Flight.

ALLOCATED.

FOR DELETION.

3753	Survey ..		Sopwith Schndr.	100	Mono	..	Fin. training.

DESIGN FLIGHT.

Squadron Commander H. M. Cave-Brown-Cave, in Charge.

AEROPLANES

3603	Trials ..	1	Avro Scout ..	75	R.R.	..	K. then G.

SEAPLANES.

No.	Condition.	Total.	Type.	H.p.	Engine.	Duties.
1415	Ready ..	1	Blackburn Twin	2–160	Sunbeam ..	K.
N1000	Trials ..	1	Campania W.T.	250	R.R. ..	K.
3326	Repairs ..	1	Short 827 ..	150	Sunbeam ..	G.
8052	Repairs ..	1	Short 184 ..	225	Sunbeam ..	G.
8104	Repairs ..	1	Short 184 ..	250	R.R. ..	K.
N1080 E	?	1	Short 184 Imp.	220	Renault ..	K.
9782	Trials ..	1	Short 830 ..	140	C. Unne ..	K. then Calshot.
8123	Ready ..		Sopwith Baby	110	Clerget ..	G.
N1010	Trials ..		Sopwith Baby	110	Clerget ..	K. then Car-riers, P. Said.
N1019	Altering ..	3	Sopwith Baby	130	Clerget ..	K.
9098	Alterations	1	Wight Baby ..	100	Mono ..	K. then Yarmouth.

FOR DELETION.

3102	For survey		Short 827 ..	150	Sunbeam ..	Nore Flight.
3106	Surveyed..		Short 827 ..	150	Sunbeam ..	Fin. training.

FOR OTHER STATIONS AND TRIALS.

						Allocated to
3332	Ready ..		Short 827 ..	150	Sunbeam ..	Cape.
8232	E		Short 827 ..	150	Sunbeam ..	Otranto.
8233	E ?		Short 827 ..	150	Sunbeam ..	Otranto.
8234	E		Short 827 ..	150	Sunbeam ..	Otranto.
8640	E ?	5	Short 827 W.T.	150	Sunbeam ..	Cape.
9781	E ?		Short 830 ..	140	C. Unne ..	K. then Dunkirk.
9783	Ready ..		Short 830 ..	140	C. Unne ..	Dundee.
9784	Ready ..		Short 830 ..	140	C. Unne ..	Dundee.
9785	E ?		Short 830 ..	140	C. Unne ..	Dundee.
9786	Ready ..		Short 830 ..	140	C. Unne ..	Dundee.
9787	Ready ..		Short 830 ..	140	C. Unne ..	S. Shields.
9788	Ready ..	7	Short 830 ..	140	C. Unne ..	S. Shields.
8317	Ready ..	1	Short Torpedo	310	Sunbeam ..	White City.
9086	Ready ..		Short 184 Imp.	225	Sunbeam ..	Fishguard.
N1081	E		Short 184 Imp.	220	Renault ..	Calshot.
N1082	E ?	3	Short 184 Imp.	220	Renault ..	Calshot.

Grain Repair Depot.

See Port Victoria.

Hendon Erecting Station.

Flight Commander T. D. Hallam, D.S.C., in Command.

Telegrams : NAVYPLANE, HYDE, LONDON.

AEROPLANES

No.	Condition.	Total.	Type.	H.p.	Engine.	Duties.
9864	For test ..		Avro 179 Dual	80	Gnome ..	
9869	Ready ..	2	Avro 179 Dual	80	Gnome .	
1192	Ready ..	1	B.E. 2 C	75	Renault ..	
3025	Ready ..		Bristol Scout .	80	Gnome ..	
N5416	Repairs ..	2	Bristol Scout..	80	Gnome ..	
8840	Ready ..		J N 4 Dual ..	90	Curtiss ..	
8866	Repairs ..	2	J N 4 Dual ..	90	Curtiss ..	Spec. serv.

FOR OTHER STATIONS.

						Allocated to
9426	Repairs ..	1	Breguet Conc.	250	R.R. ..	Cranwell.
3348	Ready ..	1	J N 3 Imp. ..	90	Curtiss ..	Cranwell.
8869	Packing ..		J N 4 . ..	90	Curtiss ..	Vendome.
8871	Packing ..		J N 4 . ..	90	Curtiss ..	Vendome.
8874	Packing ..		J N 4 Dual ..	90	Curtiss ..	Vendome.
8876	Testing ..	4	J N 4 Dual ..	90	Curtiss ..	Vendome.
3446	Dismantled		Curtiss R 2 dual	160	Sunbeam ..	
3450	Dismantled		Curtiss R 2 ..	160	Curtiss ..	
3453	E ?		Curtiss R 2 ..	200	Sunbeam ..	For alteration
3454	Dismantled		Curtiss R 2 ..	160	Curtiss ..	
3455	Packing ..		Curtiss R 2 ..	200	Sunbeam ..	Luxeuil.
3456	Packing .		Curtiss R 2 ..	200	Sunbeam ..	No. 3 Wing.
3460	E ?		Curtiss R 2 ..	200	Sunbeam ..	
3461	E ?		Curtiss R 2 ..	200	Sunbeam ..	No. 3 Wing.
3462	E ?		Curtiss R 2 ..	200	Sunbeam ..	
3464	E ?		Curtiss R 2 ..	200	Sunbeam ..	No. 3 Wing.
3466	E ?		Curtiss R 2 ..	200	Sunbeam ..	
3467	E ?		Curtiss R 2 ..	200	Sunbeam ..	
3468	E ?		Curtiss R 2 .	200	Sunbeam ..	
3469	E ?		Curtiss R 2 ..	200	Sunbeam ..	
3470	E ?		Curtiss R 2 ..	200	Sunbeam ..	
3471	E ?		Curtiss R 2 ..	200	Sunbeam ..	
3472	E ?		Curtiss R 2 ..	200	Sunbeam ..	
3473	E ?		Curtiss R 2 ..	200	Sunbeam ..	
3474	E ?	19	Curtiss R 2 ..	200	Sunbeam ..	
3115	Ready ..		Handley Page	2–250	R.R. ..	Dunkirk.
3119	Ready ..		Handley Page	2–250	R.R. ..	Dunkirk.
3120	Testing ..	3	Handley Page	2–250	R.R. ..	Dunkirk.
N6173	Repairs ..		Sopwith 9901	80	Rhone ..	Dunkirk.
N6209	Ready ..	2	Sopwith 9901	08	Rhone ..	Dunkirk.

ALLOCATED.

N3229	France ..	1	F. 40 ..	160	Renault ..	
3701	Fairey ..	1	Sloane ..	130	Hall Scott..	
9931	Beardmore		Sopwith 9901	80	Rhone ..	Launching experiments.
9932	Beardmore	2	Sopwith 9901	80	Rhone ..	Launching experiments.

FOR DELETION.

Holt Night Landing Ground.

See under Yarmouth.

C

No.	Condition.	Total.	Type.	H.p.	Engine.	Duties.

Killingholme Naval Air Station.

Squadron Commander C. R. Finch Noyes in Command.

Telegrams : AEROPLANES, SOUTH KILLINGHOLME.

POLICY.

Duty.	Flights.	In No.	Present num.	Type.
Seaplanes—				
War Flight	2	3	3	Large America
	2	3	3	Porte F. Boat
	1	6	6	Short 184
	1	6	6	Baby 110 Clerget
Training		20	20	Small America

AEROPLANES

No.	Condition.	Total.	Type.	H.p.	Engine.	Duties.
9873	Ready ..		Avro 179 Dual	80	Gnome	.. Fin. training.
9874	Ready ..	2	Avro 179 Dual	80	Gnome	.. Fin. training.

ALLOCATED.

No.	Condition.	Total.	Type.	H.p.	Engine.	Duties.
9890	Parnall ..		Avro 179 Dual	80	Gnome	..
N5267	Sunbeam..		Avro 179 Dual	80	Gnome(gun)	
N5278	Sunbeam..		Avro 179 Dual	80	Gnome(gun)	
N5279	Sunbeam..		Avro 179 Dual	80	Gnome(gun)	
N6010	Parnall ..		Avro 179 Dual	80	Gnome(gun)	
N6011	Parnall ..		Avro 179 Dual	80	Gnome(gun)	
N6012	Parnall ..		Avro 179 Dual	80	Gnome(gun)	
N6013	Parnall ..		Avro 179 Dual	80	Gnome(gun)	
N6014	Parnall ..		Avro 179 Dual	80	Gnome	..
N6138	Sunbeam ..		Avro 179 Dual	80	Gnome	..
N6139	Sunbeam .		Avro 179 Dual	80	Gnome	..
N6140	Sunbeam..		Avro 179 Dual	80	Gnome	..
N6145	Sunbeam .		Avro 179 Dual	80	Gnome	..
N6146	Sunbeam .		Avro 179 Dual	80	Gnome	..
N6150	Sunbeam..		Avro 179 Dual	80	Gnome	..
N6151	Sunbeam..		Avro 179 Dual	80	Gnome	..
N6152	Sunbeam..	18	Avro 179 Dual	80	Gnome	..
9427	G.W. Co.		Breguet Conc.	250	R.R.	..
9428	G.W. Co.		Breguet Conc.	250	R.R.	..
9429	G.W. Co.		Breguet Conc.	250	R.R.	..
9430	G.W. Co.		Breguet Conc.	250	R.R.	..
9431	G.W. Co.		Breguet Conc.	250	R.R.	..
9432	G.W. Co.		Breguet Conc.	250	R.R.	..
9433	G.W. Co.		Breguet Conc.	250	R.R.	..
9434	G.W. Co.		Breguet Conc.	250	R.R.	..
9435	G.W. Co.	9	Breguet Conc.	250	R.R.	..
3123	Handley P.	1	Handley Page	2-250	R.R.	..
N5006	Robey ..		M. Farman L.	75	R.R.	..
N5007	Robey ..		M. Farman L.	75	R.R.	..
N5008	Robey ..		M. Farman L.	75	R.R.	..
N5009	Robey ..		M. Farman L.	75	R.R.	..
N5058	Brush ..		M. Farman L.	80	Renault	..
N5059	Brush ..		M. Farman L.	80	Renault	
N5339	Phœnix ..		M. Farman L.	75	R.R.	..
N5342	Phœnix ..		M. Farman L.	75	R.R.	..
N5344	Phœnix ..		M. Farman L.	75	R.R.	..
N5345	Phœnix ..		M. Farman L.	75	R.R.	..
N5346	Phœnix ..		M. Farman L.	75	R.R.	..
N5347	Phœnix ..		M. Farman L.	75	R.R.	..
N5348	Phœnix ..		M. Farman L.	75	R.R.	..
N5349	Phœnix ..		M. Farman L.	75	R.R.	..
N5750	Phœnix ..		M. Farman L.	75	R.R.	..
N5751	Phœnix ..		M. Farman L.	75	R.R.	..
N5752	Phœnix ..		M. Farman L.	75	R.R.	..
N5753	Phœnix ..		M. Farman L.	75	R.R.	..
N5720	Brush ..		M. Farman L.	80	Renault	..
N5721	Brush ..		M. Farman L.	80	Renault.	
N5722	Brush ..		M. Farman L.	80	Renault	..
N5723	Brush ..		M. Farman L.	80	Renault	,,
N5724	Brush ..	23	M. Farman L.	80	Renault	..
N5070	E.A. Co...		M. Farman S.	80	Renault	..
N5071	E.A. Co...	2	M. Farman S.	80	Renault	..
9007	Supermarine		P.B. Scout ..	100	Mono	..
9008	Supermarine		P.B. Scout ..	100	Mono	..
9009	Supermarine		P.B. Scout ..	100	Mono	..
9010	Supermarine		P.B. Scout ..	100	Mono	..
9011	Supermarine		P.B. Scout ..	100	Mono	..
9012	Supermarine		P.B. Scout ..	100	Mono	..
9013	Supermarine		P.B. Scout ..	100	Mono	..
9014	Supermarine		P.B. Scout ..	100	Mono	..
9015	Supermarine		P.B. Scout ..	100	Mono	..
9016	Supermarine		P.B. Scout ..	100	Mono	..
9017	Supermarine		P.B. Scout ..	100	Mono	..

No.	Condition.	Total.	Type.	H.p.	Engine.	Duties.
9018	Supermarine		P.B. Scout ..	100	Mono	..
9019	Supermarine		P.B. Scout ..	100	Mono	..
9020	Supermarine	14	P.B. Scout ..	100	Mono	..
9930	Beardmore		Sopwith 9901	80	Rhone	.. Fleet use.
9933	Beardmore		Sopwith 9901	80	Rhone	.. Fleet use.
9934	Beardmore		Sopwith 9901	80	Rhone	.. Fleet use.
9935	Beardmore		Sopwith 9901	80	Rhone	.. Fleet use.
9936	Beardmore	5	Sopwith 9901	80	Rhone	.. Fleet use.

FOR OTHER STATIONS.

No.	Condition.	Total.	Type.	H.p.	Engine.	Duties.
9875	Ready ..		Avro 179 Dual	80	Gnome	..
9876	Ready ..		Avro 179 Dual	80	Gnome	..
9879	Ready ..		Avro 179 Dual	80	Gnome	..
9880	Ready ..		Avro 179 Dual	80	Gnome	..
9881	Erecting ..		Avro 179 Dual	80	Gnome	..
9882	Erecting ..		Avro 179 Dual	80	Gnome	..
9883	Erecting ..		Avro 179 Dual	80	Gnome	..
9884	For erection		Avro 179 Dual	80	Gnome	..
9887	Erected ..		Avro 179 Dual	80	Gnome	..
N9889	Erected ..		Avro 179 Dual	80	Gnome	.. Cranwell.
N5262	Erected ..		Avro 179 Dual	80	Gnome	.. Redcar.
N5263	Erecting ..		Avro 179 Dual	80	Gnome	..
N5264	Erecting ..		Avro 179 Dual	80	Gnome	..
N5265	Erecting ..		Avro 179 Dual	80	Gnome	..
N5266	Erecting ..		Avro 179 Dual	80	Gnome	..
N5268	Erecting ..		Avro 179 Dual	80	Gnome	..
N5272	Erecting ..		Avro 179 Dual	80	Gnome	..
N5274	For erection		Avro 179 Dual	80	Gnome	..
N5277	Erecting ..		Avro 179 Dual	80	Gnome	..
N6130	Erecting ..		Avro 179 Dual	80	Gnome	..
N6131	Erecting ..		Avro 179 Dual	80	Gnome	..
N6132	Erecting ..		Avro 179 Dual	80	Gnome	..
N6141	Erecting..		Avro 179 Dual	80	Gnome	..
N6142	For erection		Avro 179 Dual	80	Gnome	..
N6143	For erection		Avro 179 Dual	80	Gnome	..
N6144	For erection	25	Avro 179 Dual	80	Gnome	..
N5002	Erecting ..		M. Farman L.	75	R.R.	..
N5003	Erecting ..		M. Farman L.	75	R.R.	..
N5004	Erecting ..		M. Farman L.	75	R.R.	..
N5005	Erecting ..		M. Farman L.	75	R.R.	..
N5051	Ready ..		M. Farman L.	80	Renault	..
N5054	Ready ..		M. Farman L.	80	Renault	..
N5055	Ready ..		M. Farman L.	80	Renault	..
N5056	Ready ..		M. Farman L.	80	Renault	..
N5057	Ready ..		M. Farman L.	80	Renault	..
N5334	Ready ..		M. Farman L.	75	R.R.	..
N5335	For erection		M. Farman L.	75	R.R.	..
N5336	Erecting ..		M. Farman L.	75	R.R.	..
N5337	Ready ..		M. Farman L.	75	R.R.	..
N5338	Erecting ..		M. Farman L.	75	R.R.	..
N5340	Ready ..		M. Farman L.	75	R.R.	..
N5341	Ready ..		M. Farman L.	75	R.R.	..
N5343	For erection	17	M. Farman L.	75	R.R.	..

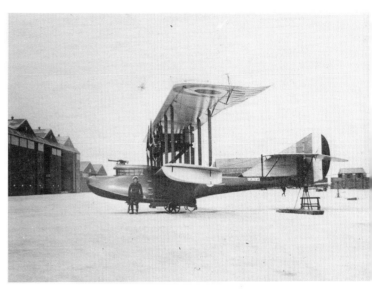

New-York-built Sloane-Day H.1 tractor biplane 3701, powered by a 130 hp Hall-Scott engine, was delivered to Hendon and tested by Sidney Pickles, but on 14 January 1916 it crashed into a parked Grahame-White Boxkite on take-off and was badly damaged. It went to Fairey for repair and was there at the time of the census, allocated to Hendon, but was scrapped at Fairey's on 26 February 1917.

Ordered from the Aircraft Manufacturing Co Ltd, Curtiss H.4 Small America 1232, powered by a pair of 100 hp Anzani radials, served as a trainer at Killingholme. It was deleted on the week ending 20 April 1918.

Another Killingholme trainer was Curtiss H.4 1234, which crashed on 23 July 1917 and was deleted a month later.

The census recorded three Porte F.B.2 Baby flying boats at Killingholme, plus another three allocated. Built by May, Harden & May, they had three engines, two mounted as tractors and one as a pusher. Seen here is 9805, which had two 250 hp Rolls-Royce Eagle IIIs as its tractor power, and a single 260 hp Green pushing. It was being erected at the time of the survey.

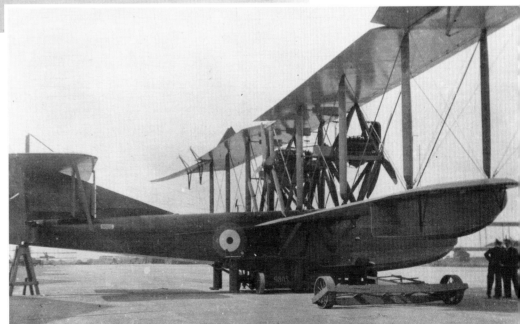

Breguet de Chasse 3885, powered by a 200/225 h.p. Sunbeam engine, appears under Grain on page 8 of the Disposition as 'allocated to Port Victoria', and is listed again on page 12 as 'for deletion'. It is seen here with a recoilless Davis gun mounted on its nose, undergoing examination by curious officers and ratings. The unconventional rudder markings are noteworthy.

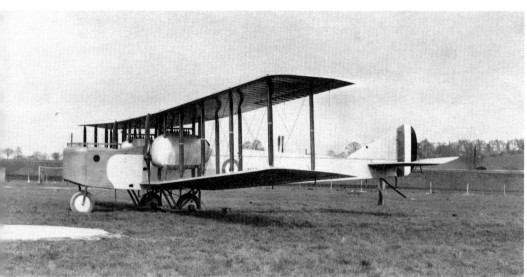

Dyott Bomber 3687, seen here in its original form with its 120 h.p. Austro-Daimler engines fully cowled, makes several appearances in the Disposition, being described as 'ready' at Grain on page 8. Confusingly, it is also identified as the 'Dyott Fighter'.

At the time this Disposition was in hand, Royal Aircraft Factory R.E.7 2260, fitted with a 225 h.p. Sunbeam Mohawk, was at Cranwell for 'experiments'.

No.	Condition.	Total.	Type.	H.p.	Engine.	Duties.	No.	Condition.	Total.	Type.	H.p.	Engine.	Duties.
	KILLINGHOLME NAVAL AIR STATION—*continued.*							KILLINGHOLME NAVAL AIR STATION—*continued.*					
SEAPLANES.							**ALLOCATED.**						
1232	Ready ..		Small America	2–100	Anzani ..	Training.	9612	France ..		F.B.A. ..		None ..	
1233	Repairs ..		Small America	2–100	Anzani ..	Training.	9613	France ..		F.B.A. ..		None .	
1234	Erecting ..		Small America	2–100	Anzani ..	Training.	9614	France ..		F.B.A. ..		None ..	
1235	Erecting ..		Small America	2–100	Anzani ..	Training.	9615	France ..		F.B.A. ..		None ..	
8339	Erecting ..		Small America		None ..		9616	France ..		F.B.A. ..		None ..	
8340	Erecting ..		Small America		None ..		9617	France ..		F.B.A. ..		None ..	
8341	Erecting ..	7	Small America		None ..		9618	France ..		F.B.A. ..		None ..	
3643	Damaged..	1	F.B.A. F. Boat	100	Mono ..	Training.	9619	France ..		F.B.A. ..		None ..	
9805	Erecting ..		Porte F. Boat	3–250	R.R. ..	Erection and trials.	9620	France ..		F.B.A. ..		None ..	
9806	Erecting ..		Porte F. Boat	3–250	R.R. ..	Erection and trials.	9621	France ..		F.B.A. ..		None ..	
9807	For erection	3	Porte F. Boat	3–250	R.R. ..	Scouting.	9622	France ..		F.B.A. ..		None ..	
8226	**Ready** ..		Short 827 Dual	150	Sunbeam ..	Training.	9623	France ..	12	F.B.A. ..		None	
8227	**Ready** ..	2	Short 827 Dual	150	Sunbeam ..	Training.	ℵ1041	Thompson		F.B.A. F. Boat	100	Mono ..	Training.
8068	Repairs ..		Short 184 W.T.	225	Sunbeam ..	Patrol.	ℵ1042	Thompson		F.B.A. F. Boat	100	Mono ..	Training.
8371	Repairs ..		Short 184 ..	225	Sunbeam ..	Patrol.	ℵ1045	Thompson		F.B.A. F. Boat	100	Mono ..	Training.
8375	Repairs ..		Short 184 ..	225	Sunbeam ..	Patrol.	ℵ1046	Thompson	4	F.B.A. F. Boat	100	Mono ..	Training.
8386	Engine overhaul.		Short 184 Dual	225	Sunbeam ..	Patrol.	9808	Aircraft ..		Porte F. Boat	3–250	R.R. ..	Scouting.
8390	**Ready** ..		Short 184 ..	225	Sunbeam ..	Patrol.	9809	Aircraft ..		Porte F. Boat	3–250	R.R. ..	Scouting.
8391	True up ..	6	Short 184 ..	225	Sunbeam ..	Patrol.	9811	Aircraft ..	3	Porte F. Boat	3–250	R.R. ..	Patrol.
8130	**Ready** ..		Sopwith Baby	110	Clerget ..	Pad. Swprs.	8055	Sage, R.		Short 184 ..	225	Sunbeam ..	Patrol.
8141	Eng. seized		Sopwith Baby	110	Clerget ..	Pad. Swprs.	8069	Yarmouth	2	Short 184 ..	225	Sunbeam ..	Patrol.
8148	Engine overhaul.		Sopwith Baby	110	Clerget ..	Pad. Swprs.							
8161	Overhaul..	4	Sopwith Baby	110	Clerget ..	Pad. Swprs.	**FOR OTHER STATIONS.**						
8207	**Ready** ..	1	Sopwith Baby	100	Mono ..	Pad. Swprs.	9059	**Ready** ..		Short 184 W.T.	240	Sunbeam ..	Carriers P.S.
3769	**Ready** ..		Sopwith Schndr.	100	Mono ..	Pad. Swprs.	9060	Erected ..		Short 184 W.T.	240	Sunbeam ..	Carriers P.S.
3800	**Ready** ..		Sopwith Schndr.	100	Mono ..	Pad. Swprs.	9090	Repairs ..		Short 184 Imp.	225	Sunbeam ..	Fishguard.
3801	**Ready** ..	3	Sopwith Schndr.	100	Mono ..	Pad. Swprs.	8190	Erecting..		Sopwith Baby	110	Clerget ..	"Campania."
							8191	Erecting..		Sopwith Baby	110	Clerget ..	"Campania."
							8192	Erecting..	3	Sopwith Baby	110	Clerget ..	"Campania."
							FOR DELETION.						

No.	Condition.	Total.	Type.	H.p.	Engine.	Duties.	No.	Condition.	Total.	Type.	H.p.	Engine.	Duties.

At Killingholme, for Rear-Admiral, East Coast.

FLEET MESSENGER 59 (P.S. KILLINGHOLME.)

WITH SEAPLANES FROM KILLINGHOLME.

(TO BE PAID OFF.)

Leysdown Naval Air Sub-station.

See under Eastchurch.

Manstone Naval Air Station.

See under Westgate.

Newlyn Naval Air Station.

Flight Commander E. de C. Hallifax in Command.

POLICY.

Duty.	Flights.	In No.	Present aim.	Type.
Seaplanes— War Flight	1	6	4	Short 184

SEAPLANES.

No.	Condition.	Total.	Type.	H.p.	Engine.	Duties.
8049	Ready ..		Short 184 ..	225	Sunbeam ..	Patrol.
8350	Repairs ..	2	Short 184 ..	225	Sunbeam ..	Patrol.

ALLOCATED.

N1191	Parnall ..		Hamble Baby	130	Clerget ..	Patrol.
N1192	Parnall ..	2	Hamble Baby	130	Clerget ..	Patrol.
8025	Saunders		Short 184 ..	240	Sunbeam ..	Patrol.
8076	Short R...	2	Short 184 Davis	225	Sunbeam ..	Patrol.

FOR OTHER STATIONS.

| 8355 | Minor repair | | Short 184 | .. | 225 | Sunbeam .. | Scilly. |

Northern Aircraft School, Windermere.

See under Cranwell.

Paris Naval Air Station.

Wing Commander I. T. Courtney in Command.

AEROPLANES ALLOCATED.

| N3228 | France .. | 1 | Farman F. 40 | 160 | Renault | .. |

Port Victoria Repair Station.

Wing Commander G. W. S. Aldwell in Command.

Telegrams : AIR-REPAIR, PORT VICTORIA.

AEROPLANES

No.	Condition.	Total.	Type.	H.p.	Engine.	Allocated to—
1485	Ready ..	1	Avro Scout ..	80	Gnome ..	K.
3026	Ready ..	1	Bristol Scout..	80	Gnome ..	K.
N5061	Altering ..	1	M. Farman S.	None	..	For fitting 125 h.p. engine.
9912	Ready ..	1	Sopwith 9901	80	Rhone ..	K.
8487	Altering ..	1	P.B. Scout ..	80	Rhone ..	K.
9497	Repairs ..	1	Sopwith 9901	80	Rhone ..	K.

SEAPLANES.

N1	Altering ..	1	P.V. 2 ..	100	Mono ..	K.
852	Altering ..	1	Sopwith 860 ..	225	Sunbeam ..	K.
3742	Trials ..	1	Sopwith Schndr.	100	Mono ..	

FOR DELETION.

| 3885 | Surveyed.. | 1 | Breguet de Ch. | 225 | Sunbeam .. | Grain. |

Plymouth Naval Air Station.

in Command.

ALLOCATED.

8042	S. Shields		Short 184 W.T.	240	Sunbeam ..	
9051	S. Shields		Short 184 ..	225	Sunbeam ..	
9084	S. Shields		Short 184 ..	225	Sunbeam ..	

The first task undertaken by the team at Grain was to fit Sopwith Schneider 3742 with new wings having a high-lift section developed by the National Physical Laboratory. The resulting aircraft, dubbed the P.V.1, had a fair degree of wing stagger and enlarged floats. This is the only known photograph of this machine, which was undergoing trials at the time of the census.

At the time of the census the Port Victoria P.V.2 seaplane scout N1 was undergoing alteration at Port Victoria. In its first form, as tested in the second half of 1916, its upper wing was attached directly to the fuselage upper longerons and it had slab-sided floats.

After modification as the P.V.2bis the seaplane emerged with the upper wing raised above the fuselage and curvaceous Linton-Hope main floats, though the boxy tail float was retained. It was deleted on 27 August 1918.

The old Sopwith Admiralty Type 860 seaplane number 852, which had served in the carriers *Ben-my-Chree* and *Engadine* in 1915, was used for a number of Grain's earliest experimental trials. The first of these three pictures shows it fitted with the Admiralty Air Department's experimental "aileron Propeller", which had a moveable flap, operated from the cockpit, attached to the blade trailing edges to enable its pitch to be varied. It is reported to have flown apart on test. The second experiment was to fit 852 with new high-lift wings designed at Grain, as shown below. These were entirely successful, enabling the seaplane to lift a 500lb bomb, seen suspended between the main floats in the middle picture.

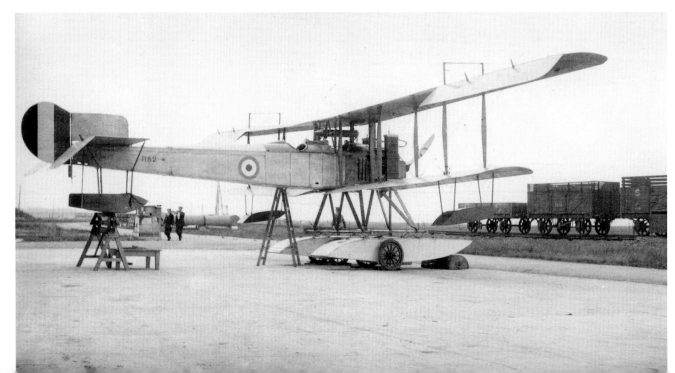

Avro 504C 1485, built by Brush, was modified at Port Victoria Repair Station for landing trials on a dummy deck. The arrester hook fitted beneath its rear fuselage has engaged lateral wires with sandbags affixed to their ends, successfully retarding the aeroplane.

Avro 504C 1487 was at RNAS Redcar for the census, as part of the advanced flying school. It spent its whole life there, from its delivery on 13 March 1916 to its deletion on 23 February 1918.

Blackburn-built B.E.2C 1139 did not survive at Redcar to be recorded by the census. On 1 April 1916 Flt Sub Lt B.P.H. de Roeper suffered engine failure during an anti-Zeppelin patrol and forced-landed with the result shown. Although 1139 was deleted two weeks later, two sister machines from the same batch were still on strength at Redcar for the census.

Beardmore-built B.E.2C 1109, which was used for night-flying training at Redcar and had earlier flown some anti-Zeppelin patrols, was active at the time of the census, but after being transferred to Cranwell late in May 1917 it was deleted on the week ending 2 November that year.

Transferred engineless from the RFC to the RNAS, B.E.2C 9469 had a 90 hp Curtiss OX-5 engine installed by its maker, Frederick Sage & Co Ltd of Peterborough, where it is seen shortly after completion. It was delivered by rail to Redcar on 25 January 1917, but survived only until 25 June.

Right: A close-up of the Curtiss OX-5 installation in B.E.2C 9469.

Below: Another Blackburn-built B.E.2C, 1145 was "ready" at Redcar when recorded in the census, but earlier, on the night of 2/3 May 1916, Flt Lt B.P.H de Roeper hit a searchlight while landing after an anti-Zeppelin patrol, with this result. It survived until 2 November 1917, by which time it was at Cranwell.

No.	Condition.	Total.	Type.	H.p.	Engine.	Duties.

Redcar Naval Air Station.

Squadron Commander C. F. Kilner, D.S.O., in Command.

Telegrams: AEROPLANES, REDCAR.

POLICY.

Duty.	Flights.	In No.	Present aim.	Type.
Aeroplanes—				
War Flight	½	5	5	Bristol Scout
Training		30	10	Caudron or M. Farman L.
			10	Avro
			10	B.E. 2 C Renault

AEROPLANES

No.	Condition.	Total.	Type.	H.p.	Engine.		Duties.
1477	Ready ..		Avro Scout ..	80	Gnome	..	Adv. School.
1487	Ready ..		Avro Scout ..	80	Gnome	..	Adv. School.
3304	Ready ..		Avro Scout ..	80	Gnome	..	Adv. School.
3306	Ready ..		Avro Scout ..	80	Gnome	..	Adv. School.
8594	Repairs ..		Avro Scout ..	80	Gnome	..	Adv. School.
8600	Repairs ..	6	Avro Scout ..	80	Gnome	..	Adv. School.
2929	Ready ..		Avro 179 Dual	80	Gnome	..	Dual Tractor
2933	Repairs ..		Avro 179 Dual	80	Gnome	..	Dual Tractor
2934	Ready ..		Avro 179 Dual	80	Gnome	..	Dual Tractor
9865	Repairs ..		Avro 179 Dual	80	Gnome	..	Dual Tractor
9866	Ready ..		Avro 179 Dual	80	Gnome	..	Dual Tractor
9867	Wrecked ..		Avro 179 Dual	80	Gnome	..	Dual Tractor
N5256	Repairs ..	7	Avro 179 Dual	80	Gnome	..	Dual Tractor
1109	Ready ..		B.E. 2 C ..	70	Renault	..	Night tr'ng.
1118	Ready ..		B.E. 2 C ..	70	Renault	..	Night tr'ng.
1119	Redoping		B.E. 2 C ..	70	Renault	..	Night tr'ng.
1144	Ready ..		B.E. 2 C ..	75	Renault	..	Night tr'ng.
1145	Ready ..	5	B.E. 2 C ..	75	Renault	..	Night tr'ng.
9469	Erected ..	1	B.E. 2 C ..	90	Curtiss	..	Night tr'ng.
3231	Ready ..		Blériot Tractor	80	Gnome	..	Adv. School.
3947	Ready ..	2	Blériot Tractor	80	Gnome	..	Adv. School.
1250	Ready ..		Bristol Scout..	80	Gnome	..	Fighter.
3030	Ready ..		Bristol Scout..	80	Gnome	..	Fighter.
3041	Ready ..		Bristol Scout..	80	Gnome	..	Fighter.
N5403	Repairs ..		Bristol Scout ..	80	Gnome	..	Fighter.
N5404	Repairs ..		Bristol Scout..	80	Gnome	..	Fighter.
N5405	Repairs ..		Bristol Scout..	80	Gnome	..	Fighter.
N5406	Ready ..		Bristol Scout .	80	Gnome	..	Fighter.
N5414	Test ..		Bristol Scout..	80	Gnome	..	Fighter.
N5415	Test ..	9	Bristol Scout ..	80	Gnome	..	Fighter.
8993	Fitting eng.		Bristol Scout..	100	Mono	..	Fighter.
9000	Ready ..	2	Bristol Scout .	100	Mono	..	Fighter.
3274	Ready ..		Caudron ..	80	Gnome	..	School.
8943	Ready ..		Caudron ..	80	Gnome	..	School.
8949	Ready ..	3	Caudron ..	80	Gnome	..	School.
3347	Repairs ..		J N 3 Imp. ..	90	Curtiss	..	Adv. School.
8392	Ready ..		J N 3 Imp. ..	90	Curtiss	..	Adv. School.
8402	Ready ..	3	J N 3 Imp. ..	90	Curtiss	..	Adv. School.
3440	Engine overhaul		J N 4 Dual ..	90	Curtiss	..	Dual Tractor
3442	Ready ..		J N 4 Dual ..	90	Curtiss	..	Dual Tractor
8820	Overhaul..	3	J N 4 Dual ..		Curtiss	..	Dual Tractor
3443	Pipe changing.		J N 4	90	Curtiss	..	Adv. School.
8845	Engine overhaul.		J N 4	90	Curtiss	..	Adv. School.
8847	Engine out	3	J N 4	90	Curtiss	..	Adv. School.
8932	Repairs ..		M. Farman L.	80	Renault	..	G'nn'ry tr'ng
8940	Ready ..		M. Farman L.	80	Renault	..	G'nn'ry tr'ng
N5035	Ready ..		M. Farman L.	80	Renault	..	G'nn'ry tr'ng
N5036	Ready ..		M. Farman L.	80	Renault	..	G'nn'ry tr'ng
N5037	Ready ..	5	M. Farman L.	80	Renault	..	G'nn'ry tr'ng

REDCAR NAVAL AIR STATION—*continued*.

ALLOCATED.

No.	Condition.	Total.	Type.	H.p.	Engine.		Duties.
N5262	K'holme ..		Avro 179 Dual	80	Gnome	..	Dual Tractor School.
N6148	Sunbeam..		Avro 179 Dual	80	Gnome	..	School.
N6149	Sunbeam..	3	Avro 179 Dual	80	Gnome	..	School.
9468	Sage ..	1	B.E. 2 C ..	150	Hispano	..	Night tr'ng.

FOR DELETION.

Scapa Flow Naval Air Sub-station.

See under "Campania."

Scilly Isles Naval Air Station.

POLICY.

Duty.	Flights.	In No.	Present aim.	Type.
Seaplanes—				
War Flight	1	6	4	Short 184

SEAPLANES.

ALLOCATED.

No.	Condition.	Total.	Type.	H.p.	Engine.		Duties.
8355	Newlyn ..		Short 184	225	Sunbeam	..	Patrol.
*9092	Penzance	2	Short 184	225	Sunbeam	..	Patrol.

*Stored at Trinity House, Penzance

D

No.	Condition.	Total.	Type.	H.p.	Engine.	Duties.

South Shields Naval Air Station.

Squadron Commander J. T. Cull, D.S.O., in Command.

POLICY.

Duty.	Flights.	In No.	Present aim.	Type.
Seaplanes..	1	6	6	Short 184

SEAPLANES.

No.	Condition	Total	Type	H.p.	Engine	Duties
8007	Overhaul	1	Short 184	.. 225	Sunbeam ..	

ALLOCATED.

| 9787 | Grain .. | | Short 830 | .. 140 | C. Unne .. | Patrol. |
| 9788 | Grain .. | 2 | Short 830 | .. 140 | C. Unne .. | Patrol. |

FOR OTHER STATIONS.

9051	Dismantling		Short 184	.. 225	Sunbeam ..	Plymouth.
8042	Dismantling		Short 184 W.T.	240	Sunbeam ..	Plymouth.
9084	Dismantling		Short 184	.. 225	Sunbeam ..	Plymouth.

Trimley Night Landing Ground.

See under Felixstowe.

Westgate Naval Air Station

WITH SUB-STATIONS AT DETLING AND MANSTONE.

Wing Commander R. P. Ross in Command.

Telegrams: AEROPLANES, WESTGATE-ON-SEA.

POLICY.

Duty.	Flights.	In No.	Present aim.	Type.
Aeroplanes—				
Westgate War Flight ..	1	10	10	Bristol Scout
Detling War Flight ..	½	5	5	Bristol Scout
Seaplanes—	1	6	6	Short 184
War Flight	1	6	6	Short 184 Single Bomber.
	1	6	6	Baby 110 Clerget

AEROPLANES

No.	Condition	Total	Type	H.p.	Engine	Duties
1483	Ready ..	1	Avro Scout	80	Gnome ..	
1159	Changing engine.		B.E. 2 C	75	Renault ..	Night flying.
1188	Ready ..	2	B.E. 2 C	75	Renault ..	Night flying.
8298	Ready ..		B.E. 2 C	90	R.A.F. ..	Night flying.
8413	Ready ..		B.E. 2 C	90	R.A.F. ..	Night flying.
8496	New engine.		B.E. 2 C	90	R.A.F. ..	Night flying.
8497	Ready ..	4	B.E. 2 C	90	R.A.F. ..	Night flying.
3049	Ready ..		Bristol Scout..	80	Gnome ..	Fin. training.
3055	Ready ..	2	Bristol Scout	80	Gnome ..	Fin. training.
8951	Ready ..		Bristol Scout..	100	Mono ..	Fighter.
8956	Ready ..		Bristol Scout..	100	Mono ..	Fighter.
8957	Repairs ..		Bristol Scout..	100	Mono ..	Fighter.
8960	Ready ..		Bristol Scout .	100	Mono ..	Fighter.
8363	Ready ..		Bristol Scout .	100	Mono ..	Fighter.
8965	Ready ..		Bristol Scout..	100	Mono ..	Detling.
8969	Repairs ..		Bristol Scout..	100	Mono ..	Detling.
8970	Ready ..		Bristol Scout..	100	Mono ..	Detling.
8972	Ready ..		Bristol Scout..	100	Mono ..	Detling.
8973	Ready ..		Bristol Scout..	100	Mono ..	Detling.
8977	Ready ..		Bristol Scout..	100	Mono ..	Detling.
8978	Repairs ..		Bristol Scout..	100	Mono ..	Detling.
8989	Ready ..		Bristol Scout..	100	Mono ..	Detling.
8990	Ready ..		Bristol Scout..	100	Mono ..	Detling.
N5398	Repairs ..15		Bristol Scout..	100	Mono ..	
N509	Ready ..		Sopwith T'plane	150	Hispano ..	School.
N5424	Ready ..	2	Sopwith T'plane	130	Clerget ..	Fighting.

ALLOCATED.

No.	Condition	Total	Type	H.p.	Engine	Duties
8628	Grain ..	1	B.E. 2 C ..	90	R.A.F. ..	Night flying.

FOR OTHER STATIONS.

9364	Engine out		Short Bomber	240	Sunbeam ..	
9366	Engine out		Short Bomber	240	Sunbeam	
9368	Engine out		Short Bomber	240	Sunbeam ..	
9369	Engine out		Short Bomber	240	Sunbeam ..	
9370	Removing engine.		Short Bomber	240	Sunbeam ..	
9491	Ready ..		Short Bomber	250	R.R. Mk. IV	Dunkirk.
9775	Ready ..		Short Bomber	250	R.R. Mk. IV	Dunkirk.
9831	Repairs ..		Short Bomber	250	R.R. Mk. IV	
9836	Ready ..	9	Short Bomber	250	R.R. Mk. IV	Dunkirk.
9907	Ready ..	1	Sopwith 9901	80	Clerget ..	Cranwell.

FOR DELETION.

8962	Survey ..		Bristol Scout..	100	Mono ..	Fighter.
9316	Surveyed..		Short Bomber		None.	
9480	Surveyed..		Short Bomber		None.	
9481	Surveyed..		Short Bomber		None.	

SEAPLANES.

3068	Re-doping		Short 827 W.T.	150	Sunbeam ..	Nore flight.
3072	Repairs ..		Short 827 W.T.	160	Sunbeam ..	Nore flight.
3111	Ready ..		Short 827 W.T.	150	Sunbeam ..	Nore flight
3331	Repairs ..		Short 827 W.T.	150	Sunbeam ..	Nore flight.
8252	Repairs ..		Short 827 W.T.	150	Sunbeam ..	Nore flight.
8633	Fitting eng.	6	Short 827 ..	150	Sunbeam ..	Nore flight.
9058	Ready ..	1	Short 184 ..	240	Sunbeam ..	Nore flight.
8094	Ready ..		Short 184 ..	225	Sunbeam ..	Nore flight.
9088	Waiting spares.	2	Short 184 ..	225	Sunbeam ..	Nore flight.
3760	Repairs ..		Sopwith Schndr.	100	Mono ..	Nore flight.
3766	Ready ..	2	Sopwith Schndr.	100	Mono ..	Nore flight.
8146	Ready ..		Sopwith Baby	110	Clerget ..	Nore flight.
8186	Ready ..	2	Sopwith Baby	110	Clerget] ..	Nore flight.

ALLOCATED.

| N1025 | Blackburn | | Sopwith Baby | 110 | Clerget .. | Nore flight. |

FOR DELETION.

| 9054 | Wrecked .. | | Short 184 W.T. | 240 | Sunbeam .. | Nore flight. |

Handley-Page Squadron.

Flight Commander G. L. Thomson, D.S.C., in Command.

AEROPLANES

No.	Condition	Total	Type	H.p.	Engine	Duties
8500	True up ..	1	B.E. 2 C ..	90	R.A.F. ..	Night flying.
1456	New engines.		Handley Page	2-250	R.R. ..	Training.
1458	New engines.	2	H.P. Sol. Lngn.	2-250	R.R. ..	Training.

FOR OTHER STATIONS.

1466	Ready ..		Handley Page	2-250	R.R. ..	Dunkirk.
1465	Engine overhaul.		Handley Page	2-250	R.R. ..	Dunkirk.
3116	Ready ..		Handley Page	2-250	R.R. ..	Dunkirk.
3118	Ready ..	4	Handley Page	2-250	R.R. ..	French Govt.

FOR DELETION.

ALLOCATED.

| 3122 | H. Page .. | 1 | Handley Page | 2-250 | R.R. .. | Training. |

Redcar still had two 80 hp Gnome-engined Blériot XI-2 two-seat monoplanes on strength for the census, but this one, 3229, was written off on 18 February 1916 when it nosedived into the ground, severely injuring its pilot, Flt Sub Lt T.C. Angus.

Bristol Scout C number 1250 enjoyed a long life. Delivered to Eastbourne on 24 June 1915, it served at Yarmouth, Hornsea, Redcar and Cranwell, becoming 201/2 at Cranwell Training Depot Station on 1 April 1918. At the time of this census it was "ready" at Redcar.

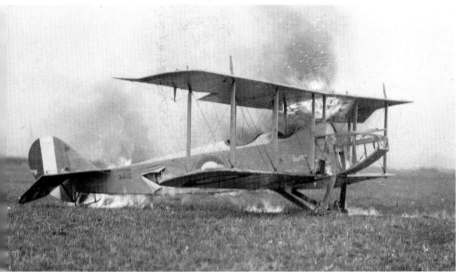

Built in Toronto, Curtiss J.N.3 number 3416 was delivered to Hendon in October 1915 and was received at Redcar on the 31st of that month. It was deleted on 7 May 1916 and, after useful parts such as the engine and wheels had been removed, it was burnt. A few of its sisters were listed on the census.

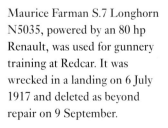

Maurice Farman S.7 Longhorn N5035, powered by an 80 hp Renault, was used for gunnery training at Redcar. It was wrecked in a landing on 6 July 1917 and deleted as beyond repair on 9 September.

Another Longhorn listed as "ready" on the census
was N5036, seen here in a Redcar hangar surrounded
by several others of its kind and, in the background, a
Caudron G.III. By coincidence, this aircraft was also
damaged in a landing on the same day as N5035, being
deleted on the day before that machine. Did they collide?

Bristol Scout Type D number 8956, used principally
for home defence, was initially delivered to Westgate on
1 May 1916, and was still there at the time of this census.
It later served at Manston, Walmer and Dover, finally
being deleted on 23 November 1917. Here it is seen at
Walmer, with sister aircraft 8958 for company.

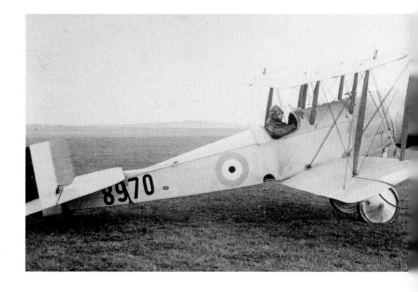

Another Bristol Scout D on Westgate's inventory was
8970, which had been delivered to Eastchurch War
Flight on 20 June 1916 and had then served at Detling
and Manston, where it crashed on 21 May 1917 and was
deleted on 14 June.

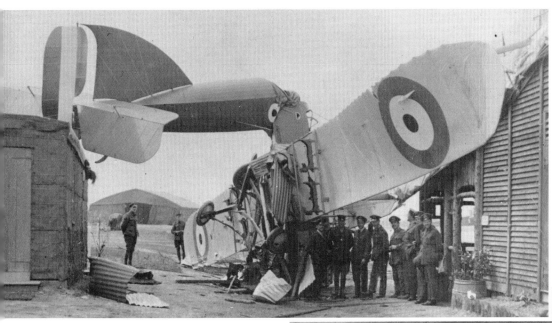

Short Bomber 9491, built by Mann, Egerton & Co Ltd, was "ready" at Westgate, destined for the Aeroplane Depot Dunkirk (St Pol), where it arrived on 17 March 1917, being allotted to 7 Sqn. However, it was wrecked on 29 April when Flt Sub Lt L.A. Sands crashed on the roof of the office belonging to 5 Wing's CO. Deletion followed shortly thereafter.

Handley Page O/100 1458 served as a training machine at Manston for much of its life, and was there at the time of the census, though it is listed under Westgate, because "Manstone" was a sub-station of that base. In 1918 the bomber moved to Stonehenge, where it was written off in a crash.

Ready for night-flying duties on Yarmouth's inventory was Blackburn-built Royal Aircraft Factory B.E.2c 8626, with a 90 hp RAF engine. This aircraft, which spent its time at Yarmouth and the night landing grounds at Bacton and Burgh Castle, was flown by Flt Lt E. Cadbury in an attack on a Zeppelin on the night of 2/3 September 1916, and Flt Sub-Lt E.L. Pulling was awarded the DSO when he flew it to bring down the Zeppelin L21 on 28 November 1916. Unfortunately it broke up while performing a loop on 2 March 1917, killing Pulling and Flt Sub-Lt J.E. Northrop. Pulling is believed to be in the cockpit in this picture.

Used for home defence against night raiders, Farman F.40 (otherwise Type LVI) number 9162, which was listed on the strength of Yarmouth NAS, had its serial painted in stylish fashion on the white section of its rudder stripes. Conspicuous here are the rocket rails attached to its outer interplane struts.

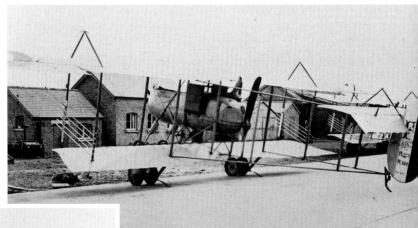

Short 827 serial 8636 forsakes horsepower for manpower while serving on Yarmouth's War Flight. Delivered by road on 23 April 1916, it was deleted on the week ending 8 September 1917.

Yarmouth Naval Air Station.

Squadron Commander D. A. Oliver, D.S.O., in Command.

(WITH NIGHT LANDING GROUNDS AT BACTON, BURGH CASTLE, COVEHITHE, HOLT AND ALDEBURGH.)

Telegrams: AEROPLANES, GREAT YARMOUTH.

POLICY.

Duty.	Flights.	In No.	Present aim.	Type.
Aeroplanes—				
War Flight	2	20	15	B.E. 2 C or F. 40
			5	Bristol Scout
Seaplanes—	1	3	3	Large America
War Flight	2	12	12	Short 184
	1	6	6	Baby 110 Clerget

AEROPLANES

No.	Condition.	Total.	Type.	H.p.	Engine.	Duties.
9281	Repairs ..		Avro Scout ..	100	Mono ..	Fin. training.
9282	Ready	2	Avro Scout ..	100	Mono ..	Fin. training.
977	Eng. trouble		B.E. 2 C ..	70	Renault ..	Night flying.
8301	Ready ..		B.E. 2 C ..	90	R.A.F. ..	Night flying.
8326	Ready .		B.E. 2 C ..	90	R.A.F. ..	Night flying.
8411	Ready ..		B.E. 2 C ..	90	R.A.F. ..	Night flying.
8417	Ready ..		B.E. 2 C ..	90	R.A.F. ..	Night flying.
8419	Repairs ..		B.E. 2 C ..	90	R.A.F. ..	Night flying.
8420	Ready ..		B.E. 2 C ..	90	R.A.F. ..	Night flying.
8492	Ready ..		B.E. 2 C ..	90	R.A.F. ..	Night flying.
8493	Ready ..		B.E. 2 C ..	90	R.A.F. ..	Night flying.
8498	Ready ..		B.E. 2 C ..	90	R.A.F. ..	Night flying.
8499	Ready ..		B.E. 2 C ..	90	R.A.F. ..	Night flying.
8607	Ready ..		B.E. 2 C ..	90	R.A.F. ..	Night flying.
8608	Ready ..		B.E. 2 C ..	90	R.A.F. ..	Night flying.
8625	Ready ..		B.E. 2 C ..	90	R.A.F. ..	Night flying.
8626	Ready ..	15	B.E. 2 C ..	90	R.A.F. ..	Night flying.
1252	Repairs ..		Bristol Scout	80	Gnome ..	Fighter.
1257	Ready		Bristol Scout	80	Gnome ..	Fighter.
5056	Repairs ..	3	Bristol Scout..	80	Gnome ..	Fighter.
8959	Repairs ..		Bristol Scout..	100	Mono ..	Fighter.
8961	Ready ..	2	Bristol Scout..	100	Mono ..	Fighter.
9158	Repairs ..		F. 40 ..	150	Renault ..	Night.
9160	Ready ..		F. 40 ..	150	Renault ..	Night.
9162	Altering ..		F. 40 ..	150	Renault ..	Night.
9163	Waiting propr.	4	F. 40 ..	150	Renault ..	Night.
9904	Repairs ..		Sopwith 9901	80	Clerget ..	Fighter.
9905	Ready ..	2	Sopwith 9901	80	Clerget ..	Fighter.

ALLOCATED.

No.	Condition.	Total.	Type.	H.p.	Engine.	Duties.
9466	Sage ..	1	B.E. 2 C ..	90	Curtiss ..	Night flying.

FOR OTHER STATIONS.

FOR DELETION.

YARMOUTH NAVAL AIR STATION—*continued.*

SEAPLANES.

No.	Condition.	Total.	Type.	H.p.	Engine.	Duties.
8222	Ready ..		Short 827 ..	150	Sunbeam ..	War flight
8223	Rad'r defect		Short 827 ..	160	Sunbeam ..	War flight.
8636	Ready ..	3	Short 827 W.T.	150	Sunbeam ..	War flight.
8062	Ready ..		Short 184 W.T.	225	Sunbeam ..	War flight.
8066	Repairs ..		Short 184 W.T.	225	Sunbeam ..	War flight.
8074	Repairs ..		Short 184 W.T.	225	Sunbeam ..	War flight.
8105	Ready ..		Short 184 High	225	Sunbeam ..	War flight.
8368	Repairs ..		Short 184 ..	225	Sunbeam ..	War flight.
8369	Repairs ..		Short 184 ..	225	Sunbeam ..	War flight.
8370	Repairs ..		Short 184 ..	225	Sunbeam ..	War flight.
8378	Repairs ..		Short 184 ..	225	Sunbeam ..	War flight.
8389	Ready ..		Short 184 Dual	225	Sunbeam ..	War flight.
9056	Ready ..	10	Short 184 W.T.	240	Sunbeam ..	War flight.
8133	Ready ..		Sopwith Baby	110	Clerget ..	Pad. Swprs.
8149	Repairs ..		Sopwith Baby	110	Clerget ..	Pad. Swprs.
8150	Ready ..	3	Sopwith Baby	110	Clerget ..	Pad. Swprs.
3716	Ready ..		Sopwith Schndr.	100	Mono ..	Pad. Swprs.
3736	Ready ..		Sopwith Schndr.	100	Mono ..	Pad. Swprs.
3737	Ready ..		Sopwith Schndr.	100	Mono ..	Pad. Swprs.
3738	Ready ..		Sopwith Schndr.	100	Mono ..	Pad. Swprs.
3791	Ready ..	5	Sopwith Schndr.	100	Mono ..	Pad. Swprs.

ALLOCATED.

No.	Condition.	Total.	Type.	H.p.	Engine.	Duties.
8653	Felixstowe		Large America	2-250	R.R. ..	Patrol.
8660	Felixstowe	2	Large America	2-250	R.R. ..	Patrol.
N1061	Blackburn	1	Sopwith Baby	110	Clerget ..	Patrol.
9098	K. (Grain)	1	Wight Baby ..	100	Mono ..	

FOR OTHER STATIONS.

No.	Condition.	Total.	Type.	H.p.	Engine.	Duties.
8069	Ready ..		Short 184 ..	225	Sunbeam ..	Allocated to Killingholme.

FOR DELETION.

No.	Condition.	Total.	Type.	H.p.	Engine.	Duties.
8120	Surveyed..		Sopwith Baby	100	Mono ..	
3776	Surveyed..		Sopwith Schndr.	100	Mono ..	Pad. Swprs.

At Yarmouth, for Commodore-in-Charge, Lowestoft.

FLEET MESSENGER 60 (P.S. BROCKLESBY).

WITH SEAPLANES FROM YARMOUTH.

No.	Condition.	Total.	Type.	H.p.	Engine.	Duties.

H.M.S. "Campania."

WITH SHORE BASE, SCAPA FLOW.
Wing Captain O. Schwann in Command.
Corrected by latest weekly report.

POLICY.

Duty.	Flights.	In No.	Present aim.	Type.
Seaplanes— War Flight	1	3	3	Large America
	2	12	12	Short 184
	2	12	12	Baby 110 Clerget
Instruction of observers		4	4	Short 184
Instructional— Flying from deck		6	6	Baby 110 Clerget
Gunnery practice				

SEAPLANES.

No.	Condition	Total	Type	H.p.	Engine	
823	Repairs		Short 827	150	Sunbeam	
3070	Repairs	2	Short 827	150	Sunbeam	
8060	Repairs		Short 184 W.T.	225	Sunbeam	
8354	Ready		Short 184	225	Sunbeam	
8361	Ready		Short 184	225	Sunbeam	
9043	Ready		Short 184	225	Sunbeam	
9077	Repairs		Short 184	240	Sunbeam	
9078	Ready	6	Short 184	240	Sunbeam	
8127	Ready		Sopwith Baby	110	Clerget	
8172	Waiting spares.		Sopwith Baby	110	Clerget	
8183	Ready		Sopwith Baby	110	Clerget	
8184	Repairs	4	Sopwith Baby	110	Clerget	
3796	Ready	1	Sopwith Baby	100	Mono	
836	Repairs		Wight 840	225	Sunbeam	
839	Overhaul	2	Wight 840	225	Sunbeam	

ALLOCATED.

No.	Condition	Total	Type	H.p.	Engine	
N1901	Faireys	1	Campania	250	R.R.	
845	Sage		Short 184	225	Sunbeam	
8026	Saunders		Short 184	240	Sunbeam	
8028	Saunders		Short 184	240	Sunbeam	
8030	Saunders		Short 184	240	Sunbeam	
8056	Sage	5	Short 184	225	Sunbeam	
8230	Brush		Short 827 W.T.	150	Sunbeam	
8231	Brush	2	Short 827 W.T.	150	Sunbeam	
N300	Blackburn		Sopwith Baby	110	Clerget	
8190	Killingh'lme		Sopwith Baby	110	Clerget	
8191	Killingh'lme		Sopwith Baby	110	Clerget	
8192	Killingh'lme		Sopwith Baby	110	Clerget	
N1026	Blackburn		Sopwith Baby	110	Clerget	
N1027	Blackburn	6	Sopwith Baby	110	Clerget	

FOR DELETION.

H.M.S. "Engadine."

MACHINES ASHORE AT PORT LAING ARE SHOWN HERE.
Commander P. W. Waterer, R.N., in Command.

POLICY.

Duty.	Flights.	In No.	Present aim.	Type.
Seaplanes	1	6	6	Short 184
	½	3	3	Baby 110 Clerget

SEAPLANES.

No.	Condition		Type	H.p.	Engine	
8064	Ready		Short 184 W.T.	225	Sunbeam	For 240 h.p. engine.
8065	Dismantled		Short 184 W.T.	225	Sunbeam	
8079	Ready		Short 184	240	Sunbeam	
8359	Ready		Short 184	240	Sunbeam	
9074	Ready	5	Short 184	240	Sunbeam	
8175	Ready		Sopwith Baby	110	Clerget	
8176	Ready		Sopwith Baby	110	Clerget	
8180	Repairs		Sopwith Baby	110	Clerget	
8182	Ready	4	Sopwith Baby	110	Clerget	

ALLOCATED.

8029	Saunders	1	Short 184	240	Sunbeam	

FOR OTHER STATIONS.

FOR DELETION.

H.M.S. "Manxman."

Commander C. G. Robinson, R.N., in Command.

POLICY.

Duty.	Flights.	In No.	Present aim.	Type.
Aeroplanes			4	Sopwith 9901
Seaplanes	1	6	6	Short 184
	½	3	3	Baby 110 Clerget

AEROPLANES — ALLOCATED.

No.	Condition	Total	Type	H.p.	Engine	
9913	East Fortune.		Sopwith 9901	80	Rhone	
9914	East Fortune.	2	Sopwith 9901	80	Rhone	

SEAPLANES.

9052	Ready		Short 184 W.T.	240	Sunbeam	
9055	Ready		Short 184 W.T.	240	Sunbeam	
9076	Ready		Short 184	240	Sunbeam	
9083	Ready	4	Short 184	225	Sunbeam	
N1021	Ready		Sopwith Baby	110	Clerget	
N1022	Ready	2	Sopwith Baby	110	Clerget	

SEAPLANES— ALLOCATED.

9073	Sage	1	Short 184	240	Sunbeam	

For Fleet Use.

POLICY.

Duty.	Flights.	In No.	Present aim.	Type.
Aeroplanes			6	Sopwith 9901
Seaplanes			3	Baby 110 Clerget

AEROPLANES *

SEAPLANES.

ALLOCATED.

* *See machines at East Fortune and Killingholme.*

H.M.S. "Riviera."

Under V.A., Dover.

Lieut.-Commander A. S. Elwell-Sutton, R.N., in Command.

MACHINES SHOWN UNDER DOVER AND DUNKIRK.

Based at Yarmouth was the PS *Brocklesby*, alias Fleet Messenger 60, a double-ended paddle steamer built in 1912 as a New-Holland-Hull ferry and commissioned into the Royal Navy as a paddle minesweeper early in 1916. Described as a "very unhandy ship", it operated in the North Sea, carrying two Sopwith Schneiders or Babies for anti-Zeppelin patrols. One of its charges was Sopwith Schneider 3736, delivered to Yarmouth by road on 17 June 1916 and deleted on 1 May 1917.

Ungainly Wight Baby seaplane 9098, seen here at Grain, was allocated for Yarmouth at the time of the census, but in fact spent all of its life at Grain undergoing modification and test. It had a 100 hp Gnome Monosoupape rotary engine.

Another machine allocated to Yarmouth was Curtiss H.8 Large America 8660, which first arrived there on 13 April 1917. It was used in attacks on the Zeppelin L46 and German U-boats, wrecked on 6 November 1917, rebuilt with a Felixstowe F.2A hull, and met its end when it alighted owing to engine trouble on 30 May 1918 and was attacked by enemy seaplanes.

Sopwith Baby 8182, belonging to the seaplane carrier HMS *Engadine*, was ashore at Port Laing (Fife) and "ready" at the time of the census. It had been delivered to the carrier on 24 April 1916.

Sopwith 1½ Strutter Type 9400S N5114, powered by a 130 hp Clerget, was "ready" with 5 Wing at Coudekerque, but crashed and overturned on 27 February 1917 and was deleted on 24 March.

Nieuport 12 two-seater 9209, seen here at Beardmore's Dalmuir Airfield shortly after completion, was held in reserve at Dunkirk Repair Depot at the time of the census. Powered by a 110 hp Clerget 9Z rotary, it had been delivered to Dover on 20 June 1916 for erection, and was written off on 27 June 1917 owing to "general fatigue".

Held in reserve at Dunkirk Repair Depot, Sopwith Type 9700 N5152 was destined to go to 5(N) Squadron on 30 March 1917. It was wrecked by Flt Sub Lt N.S. Wright on 13 July and deleted three days later.

The census caught Sopwith Triplane N5451, powered by a 130hp Clerget rotary, in reserve at Dunkirk Repair Depot. It subsequently served with Nos 1 and 9 Sqns, RNAS, and, while with the latter unit, brought down an Albatros D.III out of control over Dixmunde on 8 June 1917. Unfortunately the Triplane's starboard rudder controls had been shot away and its wounded pilot, Flt Sub Lt H.F. Stackard, crashed while making a forced landing. After return to Dunkirk, N5451 was written off.

No.	Condition.	Total.	Type.	H.p.	Engine.	Duties.	No.	Condition.	Total.	Type.	H.p.	Engine.	Duties.

H.M.S. "Vindex."

MACHINES ASHORE AT FELIXSTOWE ARE SHOWN HERE.

Lieut.-Commander G. Ducat, R.N., in Command.

POLICY.

Duty.	Flights.	In No.	Present aim.	Type.
Aeroplanes	..	..	4	Sopwith 9901
Seaplanes.. .. .. {	1	6	6	Short 184
	½	3	3	Baby 110 Clerget

AEROPLANES

No.	Condition	Total	Type	H.p.	Engine	Duties
3028	Repairs ..	1	Bristol Scout..	80	Gnome	..
8954	For erection		Bristol Scout..	100	Mono	..
8955	Ready ..		Bristol Scout..	100	Mono	..
8979	Ready ..		Bristol Scout..	100	Mono	..
8980	Repairs ..	4	Bristol Scout..	100	Mono	..
9910	Ready ..		Sopwith 9901	80	Clerget	..
9911	Ready ..	2	Sopwith 9901	80	Rhone	..

ALLOCATED.

No.	Condition	Total	Type	H.p.	Engine	Duties
9921	Beardmore	1	Sopwith 9901	80	Rhone	..
9926	Beardmore		Sopwith 9901	80	Rhone	..
9927	Beardmore	2	Sopwith 9901	80	Rhone	..

SEAPLANES.

No.	Condition	Total	Type	H.p.	Engine	Duties
9751	Repairs ..		Short 166 ..	200	C. Unne	..
9753	Ready ..		Short 166 ..	200	C. Unne	..
9760	Ready ..		Short 166 ..	200	C. Unne	..
9761	Ready ..	4	Short 166 ..	200	C. Unne	..
9079	Ready ..		Short 184 ..	240	Sunbeam	..
9081	Ready ..	2	Short 184 ..	240	Sunbeam	..
3755	Repairs ..	1	Sopwith Schndr.	100	Mono	..

ALLOCATED.

FOR OTHER STATIONS.

FOR DELETION.

No.	Condition	Total	Type	H.p.	Engine	Duties
3748	For survey		Sopwith Schndr.	100	Mono	..

H.M.S. "Ark Royal."

Acting Commander C. B. Hampshire, R.N., in Command.

For machines *see* Eastern Mediterranean.

H.M.S. "Empress."

Lieut.-Commander E. D. Drury, R.N.R., in Command.

For machines *see* Eastern Mediterranean.

Seaplane Carriers, Port Said.

Wing Commander C. R. Samson, D.S.O., in Command.

H.M.S. "Ann," "Raven II."

POLICY.

Duty.	Flights.	In No.	Present aim.	Type.
Seaplanes .. .. {	2	12	12	Short 184
	1	6	6	Baby 110 Clerget

Telegraphic Report dated 18th February, 1917.

Ready—Short 184 Type	3
Sopwith Schneider	2
	5

*SEAPLANES.

No.	Condition	Total	Type	H.p.	Engine	Duties
8004			Short 184 ..	225	Sunbeam ..	
8075			Short 184 ..	225	Sunbeam ..	
8080			Short 184 ..	225	Sunbeam ..	
8085			Short 184 ..	225	Sunbeam ..	
8090		5	Short 184 ..	225	Sunbeam ..	
3721			Sopwith Schndr.	100	Mono ..	} Clerget
3770			Sopwith Schndr.	100	Mono	engines
3774			Sopwith Schndr.	100	Mono	shipped for
3778	Damaged..		Sopwith Schndr.	100	Mono ..	four of
3786			Sopwith Schndr.	100	Mono ..	these,
3789			Sopwith Schndr.	100	Mono ..	30. 6. 16.
3790		7	Sopwith Schndr.	100	Mono ..	
8188			Sopwith Baby	100	Mono ..	
8189		2	Sopwith Baby	100	Mono ..	

IN TRANSIT.

No.	Condition	Total	Type	H.p.	Engine	Shipped
8018			Short 184 Single	240	Sunbeam ..	13. 1. 17.
8019			Short 184 Single	240	Sunbeam ..	13. 1. 17.
8020			Short 184 Single	240	Sunbeam ..	13. 1. 17.
8021			Short 184 ..	240	Sunbeam ..	13. 1. 17.
8022		5	Short 184 Single	240	Sunbeam ..	13. 1. 17.
N1012			Sopwith Baby	110	Clerget ..	16. 12. 16.
N1014			Sopwith Baby	110	Clerget ..	15. 12. 16.
N1016		3	Sopwith Baby	110	Clerget ..	15. 12. 16.

ALLOCATED.

No.	Condition	Total	Type	H.p.	Engine	Duties
N1010	Grain, K.		Sopwith Baby	110	Clerget ..	
N1028	Blackburn		Sopwith Baby	110	Clerget ..	
N1038	Blackburn		Sopwith Baby	110	Clerget ..	
N1060	Blackburn	4	Sopwith Baby	110	Clerget ..	
9059	K'holme ..		Short 184 W.T.	240	Sunbeam ..	
9060	K'holme ..	2	Short 184 W.T.	240	Sunbeam ..	

FOR DELETION.

No.	Condition	Total	Type	H.p.	Engine	Duties
859			Short 184 ..	225	Sunbeam ..	
8045			Short 184 ..	225	Sunbeam ..	
8054			Short 184 ..	225	Sunbeam ..	
8091			Short 184 ..	225	Sunbeam ..	
3772	Surveyed..		Sopwith Schndr.	100	Mono ..	

RETURNING.

No.	Condition	Total	Type	H.p.	Engine	Shipped
9045			Short 184 Single	225	Sunbeam ..	? 9. 1. 17;

* 2 Short's and 4 Sopwith's destroyed.

Force "D."

SEAPLANES, DISPOSAL NOT YET REPORTED.

No.	Condition.	Total.	Type.	H.p.	Engine.	Duties.	No.	Condition.	Total.	Type.	H.p.	Engine.	Duties.

Dover Command—Dunkirk.
Wing Captain C. L. Lambe in Command.

Aeroplane Units.
Telegrams: SEAIR, DOVER.

POLICY.

Duty.	Flights.	In No.	Present aim.	Type.
Aeroplanes—				
4 Fighting Squadrons ..	12	120	120	} Various types
1 Reconnaissance Squadron	3	30	30	
2 Bombing Squadrons ..	6	60	60	
Handley-Page Flight ..	1	10	10	Handley Page
5 Fighting Squadrons with R.F.C.	15	150	150	Various types

No. 1 WING—ST. POL.
Wing Commander E. T. R. Chambers in Command.

No.	Condition.	Total.	Type.	H.p.	Engine.	Duties.
9173	Repairs ..	1	Farman F. 40	150	Renault	..
3956	Ready ..		Nieuport Single	80	Rhone	..
3958	Ready ..		Nieuport Single	80	Rhone	..
3965	Ready ..		Nieuport 2-str.	80	Rhone	..
3986	Repairs ..		Nieuport Single	80	Rhone	..
3992	Ready ..		Nieuport Single	80	Rhone	..
8750	Ready ..		Nieuport Single	80	Rhone	..
8751	Ready ..	7	Nieuport Single	80	Rhone	..
3923	Ready ..		Nprt.2-str.W.T.	110	Clerget	..
8728	Ready ..	2	Nieuport 2-str.	110	Clerget	..
9915	Repairs ..		Sopwith 9901	80	Rhone	..
9916	Repairs ..		Sopwith 9901	80	Rhone	..
N6164	Ready ..		Sopwith 9901	80	Rhone	..
N6167	Repairs ..		Sopwith 9901	80	Rhone	..
N6168	Ready ..	5	Sopwith 9901	80	Rhone	..
9417	Ready ..		Sopwith 9400 S.	110	Clerget	..
9419	Ready ..		Sopwith 9400 S.	110	Clerget	..
9422	Ready ..		Sopwith 9400 S.	110	Clerget	..
9425	Ready ..		Sopwith 9400 S.	110	Clerget	..
9897	Ready ..		Sopwith 9400 S.	110	Clerget	..
N5080	Repairs ..		Sopwith 9400 S.	110	Clerget	..
N5105	Ready ..		Sopwith 9400 S.	110	Clerget	..
N5172	Ready ..	8	Sopwith 9400 S.	110	Clerget	..
N500	Ready ..		Sopwith T'plane	110	Clerget	..
N504	Ready ..		Sopwith T'plane	130	Clerget	..
N5421	Ready ..		Sopwith T'plane	130	Clerget	..
N5429	Ready ..		Sopwith T'plane	130	Clerget	..
N5442	Ready ..		Sopwith T'plane	130	Clerget	..
N5447	Ready ..	6	Sopwith T'plane	130	Clerget	..

No. 4 WING—PETITE SYNTHE.
Wing Commander C. L. Courtney in Command.

No.	Condition.	Total.	Type.	H.p.	Engine.	Duties.
N3184	Ready ..	1	Nieuport Single	130	Clerget	..
3981	Ready ..		Nieuport Single	80	Rhone	..
3185	Crashed .		Nieuport 2 str.	80	Rhone	..
3962	Ready ..		Nieuport 2-str.	80	Rhone	..
3987	Ready ..		Nieuport Single	80	Rhone	..
3988	Crashed ..		Nieuport Single	80	Rhone	..
3989	Ready ..		Nieuport Single	80	Rhone	..
3994	Ready ..		Nieuport Single	80	Rhone	..
8746	Ready ..		Nieuport Single	80	Rhone	..
8747	Ready ..	9	Nieuport Single	80	Rhone	..
8512	Repairs ..		Nieuport 2-str.	110	Clerget	..
8712	Ready ..		Nieuport 2-str.	110	Clerget	..
8726	Ready ..		Nieuport 2-str.	110	Clerget	..
8734	Ready ..		Nieuport 2-str.	110	Clerget	..
9205	Ready ..		Nieuport 2-str.	110	Clerget	..
9206	Ready ..	6	Nieuport 2-str.	110	Clerget	..
9385	Repairs ..		Short Bomber	250	R.R. Mk. IV	..
9336	Ready ..		Short Bomber	250	R.R. Mk. IV	..
9337	Crashed ..		Short Bomber	250	R.R. Mk. IV	..
9338	Ready ..		Short Bomber	250	R.R. Mk. IV	..
9339	Repairs ..		Short Bomber	250	R.R. Mk. IV	..
9490	Repairs ..		Short Bomber	250	R.R. Mk. IV	..
9776	Ready ..	7	Short Bomber	250	R.R. Mk. IV	..
N5153	Ready ..		Sopwith 9700	110	Clerget	..
N5504	Ready ..	2	Sopwith 9700	110	Clerget	..
N5509	Ready ..		Sopwith 9700	130	Clerget	..
N5519	Repairs ..		Sopwith 9700	130	Clerget	..
N5520	Ready ..		Sopwith 9700	130	Clerget	..
N5528	Ready ..	4	Sopwith 9700	130	Clerget	..

DUNKIRK NAVAL AIR STATION—continued.
No. 5 WING—COUDEKERKE.
Wing Commander S. D. A. Grey, D.S.O., in Command,

No.	Condition.	Total.	Type.	H.p.	Engine.	Duties.
9376	Ready ..		Sopwith 9400 S.	110	Clerget	..
9379	Ready ..		Sopwith 9400 S.	110	Clerget	..
9382	Repairs ..		Sopwith 9400 S.	110	Clerget	..
9385	Repairs ..		Sopwith 9400 S.	110	Clerget	.
9394	Ready ..		Sopwith 9400 S.	110	Clerget	..
9395	Ready ..		Sopwith 9400 S.	110	Clerget	..
9672	Ready ..		Sopwith 9400 L.	130	Clerget	..
N5082	Ready ..		Sopwith 9400 S.	110	Clerget	..
N5093	Ready ..		Sopwith 9400 S.	110	Clerget	..
N5096	Ready ..		Sopwith 9400 S.	110	Clerget	..
N5114	Ready ..		Sopwith 9400 S.	130	Clerget	..
N5221	Ready ..		Sopwith 9400 S.	110	Clerget	..
N5222	Ready ..	13	Sopwith 9400 S.	110	Clerget	..

No. 1 SQUADRON.
(ATTACHED TO No. 14 WING, R.F.C.)
Squadron Commander P. V. Harkin, D.S.C., in Charge.

No.	Condition.	Total.	Type.	H.p.	Engine.	Duties.
N5422	Ready ..		Sopwith T'plane	130	Clerget	..
N5425	Ready ..		Sopwith T'plane	130	Clerget	..
N5426	Ready ..		Sopwith T'plane	130	Clerget	..
N5427	Ready ..		Sopwith T'plane	130	Clerget	..
N5432	Ready ..		Sopwith T'plane	130	Clerget	..
N5434	Ready ..		Sopwith T'plane	130	Clerget	..
N5435	Ready ..		Sopwith T'plane	130	Clerget	..
N5436	Repairs ..		Sopwith T'plane	130	Clerget	..
N5437	Ready ..		Sopwith T'plane	130	Clerget	..
N5440	Ready ..		Sopwith T'plane	130	Clerget	..
N5441	Ready ..		Sopwith T'plane	130	Clerget	..
N5443	Ready ..		Sopwith T'plane	130	Clerget	..
N5444	Ready ..		Sopwith T'plane	130	Clerget	..
N5446	Ready ..		Sopwith T'plane	130	Clerget	..
N5448	Ready ..		Sopwith T'plane	130	Clerget	..
N5484	Ready ..	16	Sopwith T'plane	130	Clerget	..

No. 8 SQUADRON.
(ATTACHED TO No. 22 WING, R.F.C.)
Squadron Commander G. R. Bromet in Charge.

No.	Condition.	Total.	Type.	H.p.	Engine.	Duties.
9898	Ready ..		Sopwith 9901	80	Rhone	..
9899	Ready ..		Sopwith 9901	80	Rhone	..
9900	Ready ..		Sopwith 9901	80	Rhone	..
N5181	Repairs ..		Sopwith 9901	80	Rhone	..
N5183	Repairs ..		Sopwith 9901	80	Rhone	..
N5185	Repairs ..		Sopwith 9901	80	Rhone	..
N5186	Ready ..		Sopwith 9901	80	Rhone	..
N5188	Ready ..		Sopwith 9901	80	Rhone	..
N5194	Ready ..		Sopwith 9901	80	Rhone	..
N5196	Ready ..		Sopwith 9901	80	Rhone	..
N5197	Ready ..		Sopwith 9901	80	Rhone	..
N5199	Ready ..		Sopwith 9901	80	Rhone	..
N6160	Ready ..		Sopwith 9901	80	Rhone	..
N6166	Ready ..		Sopwith 9901	80	Rhone	..
N6169	Ready ..		Sopwith 9901	80	Rhone	..
N6172	Ready ..		Sopwith 9901	80	Rhone	..
N6174	Ready ..		Sopwith 9901	80	Rhone	..
N6175	Ready ..		Sopwith 9901	80	Rhone	..
N6178	Ready ..		Sopwith 9901	80	Rhone	..
N6179	Ready ..	20	Sopwith 9901	80	Rhone	..

Taken in 1916, this study shows Bristol Scouts, Nieuport 10 two-seaters and B.E.2s of the War Flight at Dover Naval Air Station. The nearest machine, Bristol Scout C number 3044, was under repair at the time of the census, but Nieuport 10 number 3165, second in line, which had flown hostile aircraft patrols in February and April 1916, had been deleted on 30 October that year.

French-built Nieuport 10 two-seater 3967, powered by an 80 hp Le Rhone rotary, was "ready" at Dover Naval Air Station. Delivered to Dunkirk, it was with 1 Wing at St Pol by October 1915, then went to 5 Wing at Dover on 11 November. It was used for a number of hostile aircraft patrols from Dover until its deletion on 30 April 1917.

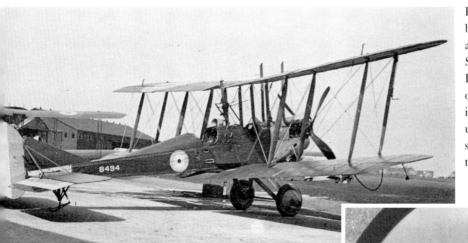

Beardmore-built B.E.2c 8494, which had been in France in 1916, was at Dover NAS, awaiting delivery to Eastchurch Observers School, but apparently never went there. It is seen here at Dover, equipped for night operations, with Holt flare brackets beneath its lower wingtips and a mounting for an upward-firing Lewis gun. After being surveyed on 16 October 1917 it was deleted three days later owing to wear and tear.

Canton-Unné engined Short 830 number 1340 was based at Dover and "ready" for use. Dover's aircraft were listed under "Dover Command – Dunkirk", under the subheading "Seaplane Units".

Another Dover-based Short 830 for *Riviera* was 1346, which well portrays the single-acting ailerons of the type, both ailerons hanging down when the aircraft was stationary, and being held level by the airflow when the aeroplane was in flight.

Squadron Commander J.T. Babington and Flt Sub Lt J.F. Jones depart Manston for Luxeuil-les-Bains on 26 October 1916 in Handley Page O/100 1460. Unfortunately it forced landed shortly after this picture was taken, and was some weeks under repair on site before it departed. At the time the census information was gathered, this machine was at Auxerre "in transit" to 3 Wing at Luxeuil, where it arrived on 24 December 1916.

Above: Bristol Scout Type D serial N5393 was in transit to Mudros, having been shipped on 20 January 1917. There it joined 2 Wing, serving at various bases. Notable here are the makeshift means employed when rigging machines in remote locations, and the gun mounting on the upper wing centre section.

Below: Bristol Scout Type C number 3060 arrived at the RNAS Training Establishment at Vendome, France, on Christmas Day 1916. This picture, showing it as the nearest aircraft in a line-up with Sopwith Pup B1820 *Johnny Walker* and six Parnall-built Avro 504Js, including B8634, was taken in 1918.

DUNKIRK NAVAL AIR STATION—*continued.*
DUNKIRK REPAIR DEPÔT.

No.	Condition.	Total.	Type.	H.p.	Engine.	Duties.
1491	Reserve	1	Avro Scout	80	Rhone	
3688	Reserve	1	Dyott Fighter	2-120	A.D.	
9155	Repairs		Farman F. 40	150	Renault	
9157	Repairs		Farman F. 40	150	Renault	
9166	Reserve	3	Farman F. 40	150	Renault	
3176	Repairs		Nieuport, 2 Str.	80	Rhone	
3963	Repairs		Nieuport Single	80	Rhone	
3991	Repairs		Nieuport Single	80	Rhone	
3993	Reserve	4	Nieuport Single	80	Rhone	
8711	Repairs		Nieuport 2-str.	110	Clerget	
8727	Repairs		Nieuport 2-str.	110	Clerget	
8733	Repairs		Nieuport 2-str.	110	Clerget	
8737	Reserve		Nieuport 2-str.	110	Clerget	
8740	Repairs		Nieuport 2-str.	110	Clerget	
9209	Reserve	6	Nieuport 2-str.	110	Clerget	
3691	Repairs		Sopwith 9901	80	Rhone	
N5182	Repairs		Sopwith 9901	80	Rhone	
N5184	Repairs		Sopwith 9901	80	Rhone	
N5187	Repairs		Sopwith 9901	80	Rhone	
N5189	Repairs		Sopwith 9901	80	Rhone	
N5195	Repairs		Sopwith 9901	80	Rhone	
N6163	Repairs		Sopwith 9901	80	Rhone	
N6165	Reserve		Sopwith 9901	80	Rhone	
N6170	Reserve		Sopwith 9901	80	Rhone	
N6171	Reserve	10	Sopwith 9901	80	Rhone	
9378	Repairs		Sopwith 9400 S.	110	Clerget	
9423	Repairs		Sopwith 9400 S.	130	Clerget	
9663	Reserve		Sopwith 9400 L.	110	Clerget	
9896	Repairs		Sopwith 9400 S.	110	Clerget	
N5081	Repairs		Sopwith 9400 S.	110	Clerget	
N5090	Repairs		Sopwith 9400 S.	110	Clerget	
N5220	Repairs	7	Sopwith 9400 S.	110	Clerget	
N5152	Reserve		Sopwith 9700	110	Clerget	
N5154	Reserve		Sopwith 9700	110	Clerget	
N5156	Reserve		Sopwith 9700	110	Clerget	
N5508	Repairs		Sopwith 9700	110	Clerget	
N5521	Crashed	5	Sopwith 9700	110	Clerget	
N5351	Reserve		Sopwith T'plane	130	Clerget	
N5352	Repairs		Sopwith T'plane	130	Clerget	
N5439	Repairs		Sopwith T'plane	130	Clerget	
N5450	Reserve		Sopwith T'plane	130	Clerget	
N5451	Reserve		Sopwith T'plane	130	Clerget	
N5454	Ready		Sopwith T'plane	130	Clerget	
N5455	Ready	7	Sopwith T'plane	130	Clerget	

DOVER NAVAL AIR STATION.
Squadron Commander E. Osmond in Command.

No.	Condition.	Total.	Type.	H.p.	Engine.	Duties.
1489	Repairs		Avro Scout	80	Rhone	
1490	Ready		Avro Scout	80	Rhone	
8598	Ready	3	Avro Scout	80	Gnome	
997	Repairs		B.E. 2 C	70	Renault	
998	Repairs		B.E. 2 C	70	Renault	
8335	Ready		B.E. 2 C	90	R.A.F.	
8337	Ready		B.E. 2 C	90	R.A.F.	
8616	Ready	5	B.E. 2 C	90	R.A.F.	
1249	Ready		Bristol Scout	80	Gnome	
1254	Ready		Bristol Scout	80	Gnome	
3039	Ready		Bristol Scout	80	Gnome	
3043	Repairs		Bristol Scout	80	Gnome	
3044	Repairs	5	Bristol Scout	80	Gnome	
3035	Ready		Bristol Scout	100	Mono	
8966	Ready		Bristol Scout	100	Mono	
8967	Repairs		Bristol Scout	100	Mono	
8971	Ready	4	Bristol Scout	100	Mono	
9174	Ready	1	Farman F. 40	150	Renault	
8824	Ready		J N 4 Dual	90	Curtiss	
8833	Repairs		J N 4	90	Curtiss	
8835	Ready		J N 4	90	Curtiss	
8859	Ready		J N 4 Imp	90	Curtiss	
8863	Ready	5	J N 4 Imp	90	Curtiss	
3966	Ready		Nieuport 2-str.	80	Rhone	
3967	Ready	2	Nieuport 2-str.	80	Rhone	
3928	Repairs		Nieuport 2-str.	110	Clerget	
8510	Ready		Nieuport 2-str.	110	Clerget	
8528	Repairs		Nieuport 2-str.	110	Clerget	
8710	Ready		Nieuport 2-str.	110	Clerget	
8742	Ready		Nieuport 2-str.	110	Clerget	
8744	Ready		Nieuport 2-str.	110	Clerget	
8902	Ready		Nieuport 2-str.	110	Clerget	
8908	Ready		Nieuport 2-str.	110	Clerget	
8918	Ready		Nprt. 2-str. W.T.	110	Clerget	

DUNKIRK NAVAL AIR STATION—*continued.*

No.	Condition.	Total.	Type.	H.p.	Engine.	Duties.
9210	Repairs		Nieuport	110	Clerget	
9212	Repairs		Nieuport	110	Clerget	
9242	Ready	12	Nieuport	110	Clerget	
N5150	Ready		Sopwith 9700	110	Clerget	
N5151	Wrecked		Sopwith 9700		None	
N5155	Ready		Sopwith 9700	110	Clerget	
N5164	For erection		Sopwith 9700		None	
N5165	Erecting		Sopwith 9700		None	
N5167	For erection	6	Sopwith 9700		None	
N5449	Ready	1	Sopwith T'plane	130	Clerget	

ALLOCATED.

No.	Condition.	Total.	Type.	H.p.	Engine.	Duties.
3696	Aircraft Co.	1	De Havilland 4	250	R.R.	
3687	Grain (G)	1	Dyott Fighter	2-120	A.D.	
N3225	France		F. 40	160	Renault	
N3226	France		F. 40	160	Renault	
N3227	France	3	F. 40	160	Renault	
*1464	Transit		Handley Page	2-250	R.R.	
1465	Manstone		Handley Page	2-250	R.R.	
1466	Manstone		Handley Page	2-250	R.R.	
3115	Hendon		Handley Page	2-250	R.R.	
3116	Manstone		Handley Page	2-250	R.R.	
3117	H. Page		Handley Page	2-250	R.R.	
3119	Hendon		Handley Page	2-250	R.R.	
3120	Hendon		Handley Page	2-250	R.R.	
3121	H. Page	9	Handley Page	2-250	R.R.	
N5860	N'port Eng. then K.		Nieuport Single	130	Clurget	
N5861	N'port Eng.	2	Nieuport Single	130	Clerget	
?	France	28	Nieuport Single	130	Clerget	Whole output
9489	Grain		Short Bomber	250	R.R. Mk. IV	
9491	Manstone		Short Bomber	250	R.R. Mk. IV	
9775	Manstone		Short Bomber	250	R.R. Mk. IV	
9836	Manstone	4	Short Bomber	250	R.R. Mk. IV	
N5244	Mann, E.		Sopwith 9400 S.	110	Clerget	
N5245	Mann, E.		Sopwith 9400 S.	110	Clerget	
N5207	Mann, E.		Sopwith 9700	110	Clerget	
N5208	Mann, E.		Sopwith 9700	110	Clerget	
N5214	Mann, E.		Sopwith 9700	110	Clerget	
N5215	Mann, E.		Sopwith 9700	110	Clerget	
N5525	Eastchurch	7	Sopwith 9700	110	Clerget	
9928	Beardmore		Sopwith 9901	80	Rhone	
9929	Beardmore		Sopwith 9901	80	Rhone	
N6173	Hendon		Sopwith 9901	80	Rhone	
N6176	Sopwith		Sopwith 9901	80	Rhone	
N6177	Sopwith		Sopwith 9901	80	Rohne	
N6180	Sopwith		Sopwith 9901	80	Rhone	
N6181	Sopwith		Sopwith 9901	80	Rhone	
N6182	Sopwith		Sopwith 9901	80	Rhone	
N6183	Sopwith		Sopwith 9901	80	Rhone	
N6184	Sopwith		Sopwith 9901	80	Rhone	
N6186	Sopwith		Sopwith 9901	80	Rhone	
N6187	Sopwith		Sopwith 9901	80	Rhone	
N6188	Sopwith		Sopwith 9901	80	Rhone	
N6189	Sopwith		Sopwith 9901	80	Rhone	
N6207	Hendon	15	Sopwith 9901	80	Rhone	
N5350	Eastchurch		Sopwith T'plane	130	Clerget	
N5438	Sopwith		Sopwith T'plane	130	Clerget	
N5452	Sopwith		Sopwith T'plane	130	Clerget	
N5453	Sopwith		Sopwith T'plane	130	Clerget	
N5456	Sopwith		Sopwith T'plane	130	Clerget	
N5457	Sopwith		Sopwith T'plane	130	Clerget	
N5458	Sopwith		Sopwith T'plane	130	Clerget	
N5459	Sopwith		Sopwith T'plane	130	Clerget	
N5460	Sopwith		Sopwith T'plane	130	Clerget	
N5461	Sopwith		Sopwith T'plane	130	Clerget	
N5462	Sopwith		Sopwith T'plane	130	Clerget	
N5463	Sopwith		Sopwith T'plane	130	Clerget	
N5464	Sopwith		Sopwith T'plane	130	Clerget	
N5465	Sopwith	14	Sopwith T'plane	130	Clerget	

FOR OTHER STATIONS.

No.	Condition.	Total.	Type.	H.p.	Engine.	Duties.
8328	Ready		B.E. 2 C	90	R.A.F.	E'ch Obs. Sch.
8494	Ready		B.E. 2 C	90	R.A.F.	E'ch Obs. Sch.
8617	Reserve		B.E. 2 C	90	R.A.F.	E'ch Obs. Sch.

FOR DELETION.

No.	Condition.	Total.	Type.	H.p.	Engine.	Duties.
3300	Survey		Caudron Twin	2-100	Anzani	
9113	Surveyed		Caudron Twin	2-100	Anzani	
9119	Survey		Caudron Twin	2-100	Anzani	
9120	Survey		Caudron Twin	2-100	Anzani	
9121	Survey		Caudron Twin	2-100	Anzani	
9123	Survey		Caudron Twin	2-100	Anzani	
9130	Survey		Caudron Twin	2-100	Anzani	
9131	Survey		Caudron Twin	2-100	Anzani	
8729	Survey		Nieuport 2-str.	110	Clerget	
9208	Survey		Nieuport 2-str.	110	Clerget	
9004	Survey		P.B. Scout	100	Mono	
N5191	Missing		Sopwith 9901	80	Rhone	
N5505	Survey		Sopwith 9700	110	Clerget	
9383	Survey		Sopwith 9400 S.	110	Clerget	
9405	Lost		Sopwith 9400 S.	110	Clerget	
N5102	Missing		Sopwith 9400 S.	110	Clerget	

* Wrecked near Boulogne.

No.	Condition.	Total.	Type.	H.p.	Engine.	Duties.

DUNKIRK NAVAL AIR STATION—*continued.*

Seaplane Units.

DUNKIRK SEAPLANE STATION.
Squadron Commander F. E. T. Hewlett in Command.

DOVER SEAPLANE STATION.
Squadron Commander V. G. Blackburn, D.S.O., in Command.
Telegrams : SEAPLANES, DOVER.

H.M.S. "RIVIERA."
POLICY.

Duty.	Flights.	In No.	Present aim.	Type.
Seaplanes—				
Dunkirk, with "Riviera" {	1	6	6	Short 184
	2	12	12	Short 184 Single
	2	12	12	Baby 110 Clerget
Dover	1	6	6 {	Short 184
				Baby 110 Clerget

No.	Condition.	Total.	Type.	H.p.	Engine.	Duties.
1337	Repairs ..		Short 830 ..		None ..	
1340	**Ready** ..		Short 830 ..	140	C. Unne ..	
1341	**Ready** ..		Short 830 W.T.	140	C. Unne ..	
1342	**Ready** ..		Short 830 ..	140	C. Unne ..	
1343	Overhaul..		Short 830 ..	140	C. Unne ..	
1344	Repairs ..		Short 830 ..	140	C. Unne ..	
1346	Repairs ..	7	Short 830 ..	140	C. Unne ..	
8015	Repairs ..		Short 184 Single	225	Sunbeam ..	
8017	**Ready** ..		Short 184 Single	240	Sunbeam ..	
8098	**Ready** ..		Short 184 Single	225	Sunbeam ..	
8099	**Ready** ..		Short 184 Single	225	Sunbeam ..	
8100	**Ready** ..		Short 184 Single	225	Sunbeam ..	
8101	**Ready** ..		Short 184 Single	225	Sunbeam ..	
8102	**Ready** ..		Short 184 Single	240	Sunbeam ..	
9046	**Ready** ..		Short 184 Single	240	Sunbeam ..	
9047	Repairs ..		Short 184 ..	240	Sunbeam ..	
9048	**Ready** ..		Short 184 Single	240	Sunbeam ..	
9050	Repairs ..		Short 184 Single	240	Sunbeam ..	
9057	Repairs ..		Short 184 W.T.	240	Sunbeam ..	
8067	**Ready** ..	13	Short 184 W.T.	240	Sunbeam ..	"Riviera."
8003	**Ready** ..		Short 184 ..	225	Sunbeam ..	"Riviera."
8013	Repairs ..		Short 184 ..	225	Sunbeam ..	
8048	Rebuilding		Short 184 ..	240	Sunbeam ..	
8357	**Ready** ..		Short 184 ..	220	Mercedes ..	
8382	Repairs ..		Short 184 ..	225	Sunbeam ..	
9042	Overhaul..		Short 184 ..	240	Sunbeam ..	
9065	Repairs ..	7	Short 184 ..	225	Sunbeam ..	
9766	Eng. repairs	1	Short 166 ..	200	C. Unne ..	
8145	**Ready** ..		Sopwith Baby	110	Clerget ..	
8157	**Ready** ..		Sopwith Baby	110	Clerget ..	
8171	Repairs ..		Sopwith Baby	110	Clerget ..	
N1011	Wrecked..		Sopwith Baby	110	Clerget ..	
N1017	Overhaul..	5	Sopwith Baby	110	Clerget ..	

ALLOCATED.

No.	Condition.	Total.	Type.	H.p.	Engine.	Duties.
9781	Grain, K.	1	Short 830 ..	140	C. Unne ..	
N1015	Blackburn		Sopwith Baby	110	Clerget ..	
N1024	Blackburn		Sopwith Baby	110	Clerget ..	
N1031	Blackburn	3	Sopwith Baby	110	Clerget ..	

FOR OTHER STATIONS.

FOR DELETION.

No.	Condition.	Total.	Type.	H.p.	Engine.	Duties.
9049	Wrecked..		Short 184 Single	240	Sunbeam ..	
8638	Wrecked..		Short 827 W.T.	150	Sunbeam ..	Calshot.
8648	Wrecked..		Short 827 W.T.	150	Sunbeam ..	Calshot.
9765	Lost ..		Short 166 ..	200	C. Unne ..	

No. 3 Wing (Luxeuil).

Acting Wing Captain W. L. Elder (Captain, R.N.) in Command.

POLICY.

Duty.	Flights.	In No.	Present aim.	Type.
Aeroplanes—				
1 Fighting Squadron ..	3	30	30	Sopwith 9400
3 Bombing Squadrons ..	9	90	90	Sopwith 9700
(to be increased to 4).				
Handley Page Flight ..	1	10	19	Handley Page

AEROPLANES

No.	Condition.	Total.	Type.	H.p.	Engine.	Duties.
1459	**Ready** ..	1	Handley Page	2-250	R.R. ..	
3393	For test ..	1	J N 3 Imp	90	Curtiss ..	
8852	Repairs ..		J N 4 Dual ..		None ..	
8856	**Ready** ..		J N 4 Dual ..	90	Curtiss ..	
8858	**Ready** ..	3	J N 4 Dual ..	90	Curtiss ..	
9496	**Ready** ..	1	Sopwith 9901	80	Clerget ..	
9400	Repairs ..		Sopwith 9400 S.	130	Clerget ..	
9401	No engine		Sopwith 9400 S.	110	Clerget ..	
9407	**Ready** ..		Sopwith 9400 S.	130	Clerget ..	
9408	**Ready** ..		Sopwith 9400 S.	110	Clerget ..	
9410	Repairs ..		Sopwith 9400 S.	110	Clerget ..	
9414	Repairs ..		Sopwith 9400 S.	130	Clerget ..	
9654	Repairs ..		Sopwith 9400 S.	130	Clerget ..	
9667	Repairs ..		Sopwith 9400 S.	130	Clerget ..	
9708	Repairs ..		Sopwith 9400 S.	110	Clerget ..	
9722	**Ready** ..		Sopwith 9400 L.	130	Clerget ..	
9730	**Ready** ..		Sopwith 9400 L.	110	Clerget ..	
9735	Repairs ..		Sopwith 9400 L.	110	Clerget ..	
9739	**Ready** ..		Sopwith 9400 L.	130	Clerget ..	
9744	Repairs ..		Sopwith 9400 L.	110	Clerget ..	
N5117	Repairs ..		Sopwith 9400 S.	110	Clerget ..	
N5170	**Ready** ..		Sopwith 9400 S.	130	Clerget ..	
N5171	**Ready** ..		Sopwith 9400 S.	130	Clerget ..	
N5173	**Ready** ..		Sopwith 9400 S.	130	Clerget ..	
N5174	**Ready** ..	19	Sopwith 9400 S.	130	Clerget ..	
9651	**Ready** ..		Sopwith 9700	110	Clerget ..	
9652	**Ready** ..		Sopwith 9700	110	Clerget ..	
9655	Repairs ..		Sopwith 9700	110	Clerget ..	
9657	**Ready** ..		Sopwith 9700	110	Clerget ..	
9661	Repairs ..		Sopwith 9700	110	Clerget ..	
9664	**Ready** ..		Sopwith 9700	110	Clerget ..	
9666	Repairs ..		Sopwith 9700	110	Clerget ..	
9669	Repairs ..		Sopwith 9700	110	Clerget ..	
9670	Repairs ..		Sopwith 9700	130	Clerget ..	
9673	Repairs ..		Sopwith 9700	110	Clerget ..	
9700	Repairs ..		Sopwith 9700	110	Clerget ..	
9706	Repairs ..		Sopwith 9700	110	Clerget ..	
9709	**Ready** ..		Sopwith 9700	110	Clerget ..	
9711	Repairs ..		Sopwith 9700	110	Clerget ..	
9714	**Ready** ..		Sopwith 9700	110	Clerget ..	
9720	**Ready** ..		Sopwith 9700	110	Clerget ..	
9723	**Ready** ..		Sopwith 9700	110	Clerget ..	
9724	**Ready** ..		Sopwith 9700	110	Clerget ..	
9733	**Ready** ..		Sopwith 9700	110	Clerget ..	
9736	**Ready** ..		Sopwith 9700	110	Clerget ..	
9738	Repairs ..		Sopwith 9700	110	Clerget ..	
9741	**Ready** ..		Sopwith 9700	110	Clerget ..	
9742	**Ready** ..		Sopwith 9700	110	Clerget ..	
9745	**Ready** ..		Sopwith 9700	110	Clerget ..	
N5088	**Ready** ..		Sopwith 9700	110	Clerget ..	
N5089	Repairs ..		Sopwith 9700	110	Clerget ..	
N5091	**Ready** ..		Sopwith 9700	110	Clerget ..	
N5092	**Ready** ..		Sopwith 9700	110	Clerget ..	
N5094	Repairs ..		Sopwith 9700	110	Clerget ..	
N5095	**Ready** ..		Sopwith 9700	110	Clerget ..	
N5098	Repairs ..		Sopwith 9700	110	Clerget ..	
N5100	**Ready** ..		Sopwith 9700	110	Clerget ..	
N5104	Repairs ..		Sopwith 9700	110	Clerget ..	
N5106	**Ready** ..		Sopwith 9700	110	Clerget ..	
N5107	Repairs ..		Sopwith 9700	110	Clerget ..	
N5109	Repairs ..		Sopwith 9700	110	Clerget ..	
N5112	For erection		Sopwith 9700	110	Clerget ..	
N5113	**Ready** ..		Sopwith 9700	110	Clerget ..	
N5115	**Ready** ..		Sopwith 9700	110	Clerget ..	
N5116	**Ready** ..		Sopwith 9700	110	Clerget ..	
N5120	**Ready** ..		Sopwith 9700	110	Clerget ..	
N5121	Wrecked..		Sopwith 9700	110	Clerget ..	
N5122	Repairs ..		Sopwith 9700	110	Clerget ..	

No.	Condition.	Total.	Type.	H.p.	Engine.	Duties.	No.	Condition.	Total.	Type.	H.p.	Engine.	Duties.
			No. 3 WING (LUXEUIL)—*continued.*							**No. 3 WING (LUXEUIL)**—*continued.*			
N5123	Ready ..		Sopwith 9700	110	Clerget ..		**ALLOCATED.**						
N5124	Repairs ..		Sopwith 9700	110	Clerget ..		3449	Grain (G.)	1	Curtiss R 2 ..	160	Curtiss ..	
N5125	No engine		Sopwith 9700		None		3455	Hendon ..		Curtiss R 2 ..	200	Sunbeam ..	
N5126	Repairs ..		Sopwith 9700	110	Clerget ..		3456	Hendon ..		Curtiss R 2 ..	200	Sunbeam ..	
N5128	Ready ..		Sopwith 9700		None		3461	Hendon ..		Curtiss R 2 ..	200	Sunbeam ..	
N5138	For erection		Sopwith 9700	110	Clerget ..		3464	Hendon ..	4	Curtiss R 2 ..	200	Sunbeam ..	
N5144	For erection		Sopwith 9700		None ..								
N5145	For erection		Sopwith 9700		None								
N5146	For erection		Sopwith 9700		None ..		**FOR DELETION.**						
N5147	For erection		Sopwith 9700	110	Clerget ..								
N5148	For erection		Sopwith 9700	110	Clerget ..								
N5149	For erection		Sopwith 9700	130	Clerget ..								
N5157	For erection		Sopwith 9700		None ..								
N5158	For erection		Sopwith 9700		None								
N5159	For erection		Sopwith 9700	130	Clerget ..								
N5160	For erection		Sopwith 9700		None								
N5501	Ready ..		Sopwith 9700	110	Clerget ..								
N5502	Ready ..		Sopwith 9700	130	Clerget ..								
N5503	Ready ..		Sopwith 9700	110	Clerget ..								
N5507	Ready ..		Sopwith 9700	110	Clerget ..								
N5510	Ready .		Sopwith 9700	110	Clerget ..								
N5511	Ready ..		Sopwith 9700	130	Clerget ..								
N5512	For erection		Sopwith 9700	110	Clerget ..								
N5513	For erection		Sopwith 9700	130	Clerget ..								
N5514	For erection		Sopwith 9700	130	Clerget ..								
N5515	For erection		Sopwith 9700	110	Clerget ..								
N5516	For erection		Sopwith 9700	130	Clerget ..								
N5518	For erection		Sopwith 9700	110	Clerget ..								
N5522	For erection		Sopwith 9700	110	Clerget ..								
N5526	For erection	73	Sopwith 9700	130	Clerget ..								
IN TRANSIT.													
3345			J N 3 Imp ..	90	Curtiss ..	10.2.17.							
8403		2	J N 3 Imp ..	90	Curtiss .	25.1.17							
3457			Curtiss R 2 ..	200	Sunbeam ..	17.2.17.							
3458			Curtiss R 2 ..	200	Sunbeam ..	9.2.17							
3459			Curtiss R 2 ..	200	Sunbeam ..	12.2.17.							
3465		4	Curtiss R 2 ..	200	Sunbeam ..	19.2.17.							
1460			Handley Page	2–250	R.R. ..	Auxerre.							
1461			Handley Page	2–250	R.R. ..	Paris.							
1462		3	Handley Page	2–250	R.R. ..	Paris.							
9906		1	Sopwith 9901	80	Clerget ..	Paris.							
N5161			Sopwith 9700		None ..	29.1.17.							
N5162			Sopwith 9700		None ..	29.1.17.							
N5163			Sopwith 9700		None ..	29.1.17.							
N5168			Sopwith 9700		None ..	13.2.17.							
N5169			Sopwith 9700		None ..	17.2.17.							
N5517			Sopwith 9700	130	Clerget ..	8.1.17.							
N5523			Sopwith 9700	110	Clerget ..	16.1.17.							
N5524			Sopwith 9700	110	Clerget ..	17.1.17.							
N5529			Sopwith 9700	110	Clerget ..	25.1.17.							
N5530			Sopwith 9700	110	Clerget ..	23.1.17.							
N5531			Sopwith 9700	110	Clerget ..	24.1.17.							
N5600		12	Sopwith 9700		None ..	20.2.17.							

Mudros and Bases in Ægean.

Wing Captain F. R. Scarlett in Command.

Telegrams : Navalwings.

No. 2 WING.

Thasos (A., S.).	Mudros Repair Base.
Thermi (A.).	H.M.S. "Ark Royal" (S.).
Imbros (A.).	H.M.S. "Empress" (S.).
Stavros (A.).	

POLICY.

Duty.	Flights	In No.	Present aim.	Type.
Aeroplanes—				
1 Bombing Squadron ..	3	30	30	}
Fighting and Observation ..	2	20	20	} Various types
Single-seater Fighters ..	1	10	10	}

Report, 17th February, 1917.

AEROPLANES.

	Ready.	Under repair.	Not erected.	Beyond repair.	Total.
B.E. 2 C. 90-h.p.	4	1	1	..	6
Bristol Scout 80-h.p. ..	2	1	.	..	3
Bristol Scout 100-h.p. ..	2	2	1	..	5
H. Farman ..	8	5	9	1	23
Nieuport 110-h.p. ..	14	4	3	1	22
Nieuport 80-h.p. single ..	..	..	..	1	1
Nieuport 80-h.p. double ..	..	..	..	..	..
Short 166 Land Chassis..	..	2	..	..	2
Sopwith 9400 S... .. } Sopwith 9700 .. }	8	2	8	1	19
	38	16	23	4	81
Previous week	40	11	18	2	71

State as reported 1st January, 1917.

AEROPLANES

No.	Condition.	Total.	Type.	H.p.	Engine.	Duties.
8304	Unerected		B.E. 2 C ..	90	R.A.F. ..	
8332	Ready ..		B.E. 2 C ..	90	R.A.F. ..	Observation.
8333	Ready ..		B.E. 2 C ..	90	R.A.F. ..	Observation.
8414	Ready ..		B.E. 2 C ..	90	R.A.F. ..	Observation.
8490	Unerected		B.E. 2 C ..	90	R.A.F. ..	Observation.
8611	Ready ..	6	B.E. 2 C	90	R.A.F. ..	Observation.
3036	Ready ..		Bristol Scout .	80	Rhone ..	Fighter.
3037	Repairs		Bristol Scout..	80	Rhone ..	Fighter.
3040	Repairs ..	3	Bristol Scout..	80	Rhone ..	Fighter.
8995	Repairs ..		Bristol Scout..	100	Mono ..	Fighter.
8996	Ready ..		Bristol Scout..	100	Mono ..	Fighter.
8997	Repairs ..		Bristol Scout..	100	Mono ..	Fighter.
8998	Repairs ..		Bristol Scout..	100	Mono ..	Fighter.
8999	Ready ..	5	Bristol Scout..	100	Mono ..	Fighter.
3908	Repairs ..		H. Farman ..	150	C. Unne ..	Observation.
3915	Repairs ..		H. Farman ..	150	C. Unne ..	Observation.
3918	Repairs ..		H. Farman .	150	C. Unne ..	Observation.
3919	Ready ..	4	H. Farman ..	150	C. Unne ..	Observation.
9137	Repairs ..		H. Farman ..	160	C. Unne ..	Observation.
9138	Ready ..		H. Farman ..	160	C. Unne ..	Observation.
9139	Erecting ..		H. Farman ..	160	C. Unne ..	Observation.
9140	Ready ..		H. Farman ..	160	C. Unne ..	Observation.
9141	Ready ..	5	H. Farman ..	160	C. Unne ..	Observation.
9135	Unerected		H Farman Trop.	160	C. Unne ..	
9146	Erecting ..		H.Farman. Trop.	160	C. Unne ..	
9147	Unerected		H.Farman Trop.	160	C. Unne ..	
9149	Erecting ..		H.Farman Trop.	160	C. Unne ..	
9150	Unerected		H.Farman Trop.	160	C. Unne ..	
N3001	Ready ..		H.Farman Trop.	160	C. Unne ..	Observation.
N3003	Ready ..		H.Farman Trop.	160	C. Unne ..	Observation.
N3004	Unerected		H.Farman Trop.	160	C. Unne ..	Roumania.
N3007	Ready ..		H.Farman Trop.	160	C. Unne ..	Roumania.
N3008	Unerected		H.Farman Trop.	160	C. Unne ..	Roumania.
N3010	Erecting ..		H.Farman Trop.	160	C. Unne ..	Observation.
N3012			H.Farman Trop.	160	C. Unne ..	
N3013			H.Farman Trop.	160	C. Unne ..	

No.	Condition.	Total.	Type.	H.p.	Engine.	Duties.
N3014	Unerected		H.Farman Trop.	160	C. Unne ..	
N3015			H.Farman Trop.	160	C. Unne ..	
N3016			H.Farman Trop.	160	C. Unne ..	
N3017	Unerected		H.Farman Trop.	160	C. Unne ..	
N3018			H.Farman Trop.	160	C. Unne ..	
N3019	Ready ..		H.Farman Trop.	160	C. Unne ..	
N3020	For erection		H.Farman Trop.	160	C. Unne ..	
N3021	For erection		H.Farman Trop.	160	C. Unne ..	
N3022	For erection		H.Farman Trop.	160	C. Unne ..	
N3023	For erection		H.Farman Trop.	160	C. Unne ..	
N3024	For erection	30	H.Farman Trop.	160	C. Unne ..	
3168	Ready ..	1	Nieuport 2-str.	80	Rhone ..	Fighting.
3975	Ready ..		Nieuport Single	80	Rhone ..	Fighting.
3978	Ready ..	2	Nieuport Single	80	Rhone ..	Roumania.
3925	Ready ..		Nieuport ..	110	Clerget ..	Fighting.
3929	Ready ..		Nieuport ..	110	Clerget ..	Fighting.
8513	Ready ..		Nieuport ..	110	Clerget ..	Roumania.
8514	Unerected		Nieuport ..	110	Clerget ..	Roumania.
8515	Repairs ..		Nieuport ..	110	Clerget ..	Fighting.
8524	Unerected		Nieuport ..	110	Clerget ..	Roumania.
8525	Unerected		Nieuport ..	110	Clerget ..	Roumania.
8529	Repairs ..		Nieuport ..	110	Clerget ..	Fighting.
8708	Ready ..		Nieuport ..	110	Clerget ..	Fighting.
8730	Repairs ..		Nieuport ..	110	Clerget ..	Fighting.
8731	Ready ..		Nieuport ..	110	Clerget ..	Roumania.
8735	Repairs ..		Nieuport ..	110	Clerget ..	Fighting.
8736	Ready ..		Nieuport ..	110	Clerget ..	Fighting.
8903	Ready ..		Nieuport ..	110	Clerget ..	Fighting.
8905	Repairs ..		Nieuport ..	110	Clerget ..	Fighting.
8912	Repairs ..		Nieuport ..	110	Clerget ..	Fighting.
9203	Repairs ..		Nieuport ..	110	Clerget ..	Fighting.
N3173	Ready ..		Nieuport ..	110	Clerget ..	
N3174	Unerected		Nieuport ..	110	Clerget ..	
N3175	Unerected		Nieuport 2-str.	130	Clerget ..	
N3176	Unerected		Nieuport 2-str.	130	Clerget ..	
N3177	Unerected		Nieuport 2-str.	130	Clerget ..	
N3178	Unerected		Nieuport 2-str.	130	Clerget ..	
N3179	For erection		Nieuport 2-str.	130	Clerget ..	
N3180	For erection		Nieuport 2-str.	130	Clerget ..	
N3181	For erection	26	Nieuport 2-str.	130	Clerget ..	
163	Testing ..		Short 166 Land	200	C. Unne ..	
9754	Ready ..	2	Short 166	200	C. Unne ..	
9748	For erection		Sopwith 9400 S.	110	Clerget ..	
9750	For erection		Sopwith 9400 S.	110	Clerget ..	
N5083	Ready ..		Sopwith 9400 S.	110	Clerget ..	
N5086	Ready ..		Sopwith 9400 S.	110	Clerget ..	
N5087	Ready ..		Sopwith 9400 S.	110	Clerget ..	
N5099			Sopwith 9400 S.	110	Clerget ..	
N5108			Sopwith 9400 S.	130	Clerget ..	
N5111			Sopwith 9400 S.	110	Clerget ..	
N5176	For erection		Sopwith 9400 S.	130	Clerget ..	
N5177	For erection		Sopwith 9400 S.	130	Clerget ..	
N5178			Sopwith 9400 S.	110	Clerget ..	
N5179	For erection		Sopwith 9400 S.	130	Clerget ..	
N5223	For erection	13	Sopwith 9400 S.	110	Clerget ..	
9715	For erection		Sopwith 9700	110	Clerget ..	
9718	For erection		Sopwith 9700	110	Clerget ..	
9727	For erection		Sopwith 9700	130	Clerget ..	
N5110	Ready ..		Sopwith 9700	110	Clerget ..	
N5119			Sopwith 9700	130	Clerget ..	
N5506	For erection	6	Sopwith 9700	110	Clerget ..	

IN TRANSIT.

No.	Condition.	Total.	Type.	H.p.	Engine.	Shipped.
N5393			Bristol Scout..	100	Mono ..	20.1.17.
N5396		2	Bristol Scout..	100	Mono ..	20.1.17.
9134			H.Farman Trop.	160	C. Unne ..	Mar.15.11.16
9136			H.Farman Trop.	160	C. Unne ..	Mar.29.11.16
9142			H.Farman Trop.	160	C. Unne ..	Mar.15.11.16
9143			H.Farman Trop.	160	C. Unne ..	Mar.15.11.16
9144			H.Farman Trop.	160	C. Unne ..	Mar.15.11.16
9148			H.Farman Trop.	160	C. Unne ..	Mar.15.11.16
9151			H.Farman Trop.	160	C. Unne ..	Mar.29.11.16
9153			H.Farman Trop.	160	C. Unne ..	Mar.29.11.16
N3009			H.Farman Trop.	160	C. Unne ..	18.12.16.
N3011		10	H.Farman Trop.	160	C. Unne ..	18.12.16.
N3182			Nieuport 2-str.	130	Clerget ..	Mar.27.1.17
N3183		2	Nieuport 2-str.	130	Clerget ..	Mar.27.1.17
N5224			Sopwith 9400 S.	110	Clerget ..	19.1.17.
N5225			Sopwith 9400 S.	110	Clerget ..	2.2.17.
N5226			Sopwith 9400 S.	110	Clerget ..	2.2.17.
N5227			Sopwith 9400 S.	110	Clerget ..	2.2.17.
N5228		5	Sopwith 9400 S.	110	Clerget ..	2.2.17.
N5590		1	Sopwith 9700	130	Clerget ..	6.1.17.
N5532		1	Sopwith 9700	110	Clerget ..	22.2.17.
N5431		1	Sopwith T'plane	130	Clerget ..	6.1.17.

MUDROS AND BASES IN ÆGEAN—*continued.*

No.	Condition.	Total.	Type.	H.p.	Engine.	Duties.
ALLOCATED.						
?	France ..	?	H. Farman ..	160	C. Unne ..	1 per week.
?	France ..	3	Nieuport 2-str.	130	Clerget ..	
N5229	Mann, E...		Sopwith 9400 S.	110	Clerget ..	
N5233	White City		Sopwith 9400 S.	110	Clerget ..	
N5231	Mann, E.		Sopwith 9400 S.	110	Clerget ..	
N5232	Mann, E.		Sopwith 9400 S.	110	Clerget ..	
N5243	Mann, E.		Sopwith 9400 S	110	Clerget ..	
9717	Oakley's ..	6	Sopwith 9400 L.	110	Clerget ..	
N5200	Mann, E...		Sopwith 9700	110	Clerget ..	
N5201	Mann, E...		Sopwith 9700	110	Clerget ..	
N5202	Mann, E...		Sopwith 9700	110	Clerget ..	
N5204	Mann, E.		Sopwith 9700	110	Clerget ..	
N5205	Mann, E.		Sopwith 9700	110	Clerget ..	
N5206	Mann, E.		Sopwith 9700	110	Clerget ..	
N5209	Mann, E.		Sopwith 9700	110	Clerget ..	
N5210	Mann, E.		Sopwith 9700	110	Clerget ..	
N5211	Mann, E.		Sopwith 9700	110	Clerget ..	
N5212	Mann, E.		Sopwith 9700	.10	Clerget ..	
N5213	Mann, E.		Sopwith 9700	110	Clerget ..	
N5216	Mann, E.		Sopwith 9700	110	Clerget ..	
N5217	Mann, E.		Sopwith 9700	110	Clerget ..	
N5218	Mann, E.		Sopwith 9700	110	Clerget ..	
N5219	Mann, E.		Sopwith 9700	110	Clerget ..	
N5527	White City		Sopwith 9700	130	Clerget ..	
N5533	Sopwith		Sopwith 9700	110	Clerget ..	
N5534	Sopwith ..		Sopwith 9700	110	Clerget ..	
N5535	Sopwith		Sopwith 9700	110	Clerget ..	
N5536	Sopwith ..		Sopwith 9700	110	Clerget ..	
N5537	Sopwith ..	21	Sopwith 9700	110	Clerget ..	
RETURNING TO ENGLAND.						
1391			Breguet de Ch.	200	C. Unne ..	
3877			Caudron Tract'r	80	Gnome ..	
3878			Caudron Tract'r	80	Gnome ..	
FOR DELETION.						
N3002 R.D.	..		H.Farman Trop.	160	C. Unne ..	Observation.

SEAPLANES.

(Including machines in "Ark Royal" and "Empress.")

POLICY.

Duty.	Flights.	In No.	Present aim.	Type.
Seaplanes	2	12	12	Short 184
	1	6	6	Baby 110 Clerget

Report 17th February, 1917.

	Ready.	Under repair.	Not erected.	Beyond repair.	Total.
Short Tractor 200 C.U... ..	5	1	2	1	9
Short 184, 225 Sunbeam ..	4	1	..	..	5
Sopwith-Schneider ..	8	2	1	..	11
F.F. (German machine) ..	..	1	..	..	1
	17	5	3	1	26
Previous week	15	7	3	2	27

State as reported 1st January, and "Ark Royal," 2nd February, 1917.

SEAPLANES.

No.	Condition.	Total.	Type.	H.p.	Engine.
165	Ready ..		Short 166 ..	200	C. Unne ..
166	Repairs ..		Short 166 Land	200	C. Unne ..
9752	Ready ..		Short 166 ..	200	C. Unne ..
9755	Ready ..		Short 166 ..	200	C. Unne ..
9758	Ready ..		Short 166 ..	200	C. Unne ..
9759	Damaged in transit.		Short 166 ..	200	C. Unne ..
9762	For erection		Short 166 ..	200	C. Unne ..
9763	Ready		Short 166 ..	200	C. Unne ..
9764	Ready ..	9	Short 166 ..	200	C. Unne ..
8077	Ready ..		Short 184 ..	225	Sunbeam ..
8078	For test ..		Short 184 ..	225	Sunbeam ..
8095	Ready ..		Short 184 ..	225	Sunbeam ..
8360	Repairs ..		Short 184 ..	225	Sunbeam ..
8381	Ready ..	5	Short 184 ..	225	Sunbeam ..

MUDROS AND BASES IN ÆGEAN—*continued.*

No.	Condition.	Total.	Type.	H.p.	Engine.	Duties.
3772	Repairs ..		Sopwith Schndr.	100	Mono ..	
3782	Ready ..		Sopwith Schndr.	100	Mono ..	
3783	Ready ..		Sopwith Schndr.	100	Mono ..	
3784	Ready ..		Sopwith Schndr.	100	Mono ..	
3787	Ready ..		Sopwith Schndr.	100	Mono ..	
3788	Ready ..		Sopwith Schndr.	100	Mono ..	
3792	Ready ..		Sopwith Schndr.	100	Mono ..	
3793	Repairs ..	8	Sopwith Schndr.	100	Mono ..	
8202	Ready ..		Sopwith Baby	100	Mono ..	
8203	Ready ..	2	Sopwith Baby	100	Mono ..	
536	Repairs ..	1	German F.F.	150	Benz ..	
IN TRANSIT.						Shipped.
8088		1	Short 184 ..	225	Sunbeam ..	24.5.16.
N1018		1	Sopwith Baby	110	Clerget ..	2.1.17.
ALLOCATED.						
N1193	Parnall ..	1	Hamble Baby	130	Clerget ..	
N1033	Blackburn	1	Sopwith Baby	110	Clerget ..	
RETURNING TO ENGLAND.						Shipped
820			Short 830 Type	135	C. Unne ..	25.3.16.
821		2	Short 830 Type	135	C. Unne ..	25.3.16
1566		1	Sopwith Schndr.		None ..	27.11.16.
FOR DELETION.						

Gibraltar Naval Air Station.

Squadron Commander A. B. Gaskell in Command.

POLICY.

Duty.	Flights.	In No.	Present aim.	Type.
Seaplanes..	1	6	6	Small America

Report 12th February, 1917.

Seaplanes—					
Ready ..	..	..	..	..	1
Under repair ..	..	..	..	1
Not erected ..	..	..	..	2
					4

SEAPLANES.

No.	Condition	Total	Type.	H.p.	Engine.
3551			Small America	2-100	Anzani ..
3552			Small America	2-100	Anzani ..
3556			Small America	2-100	Anzani ..
3558		4	Small America	2-100	Anzani ..

IN TRANSIT.   Shipped.

ALLOCATED.

No.	Condition.	Total.	Type.	H.p.	Engine.	Duties.	No.	Condition.	Total.	Type.	H.p.	Engine.	Duties.

Malta Naval Air Station.

Flight Commander J. D. Maude in Command.

POLICY.

Duty.	Flights.	In No.	Present aim.	Type.
Seaplanes	1	6	6	Small America
Torpedo School .. .. {	..	4	..	240 h.p. Short
	..	2	..	310 h.p. Short

Report 9th February, 1917.

Seaplanes—Ready	3
Under repair	
Beyond repair	
Spares	1
	4

SEAPLANES.

No.		Total	Type.	H.p.	Engine.	
3561			Small America	2–100	Anzani	..
3563			Small America	2–100	Anzani	..
3566		3	Small America	2–100	Anzani	..

IN TRANSIT.

ALLOCATED.

8353	Felixstowe	1	Short 184	..	225	Sunbeam	..

FOR DELETION.

3559		1	Small America	2–100	Anzani	..

Otranto Naval Air Station.

Squadron Commander C. H. K. Edmonds, D.S.O., in Command.

POLICY.

Duty.	No.	Type.
Seaplanes—		
Torpedo and bombing	12	310 h.p. Short
Barrage	6	Sopwith Baby
Barrage	6	2-seater
Aeroplanes—		
Escort	6	2-seater

SEAPLANES.

ALLOCATED.

No.		Total	Type.		H.p.	Engine.	
9053	Dundee ..		Short 184	..	240	Sunbeam	..
9070	Dundee ..		Short 184	..	225	Sunbeam	..
9071	Dundee ..		Short 184	..	225	Sunbeam	..
9072	Dundee ..		Short 184	..	240	Sunbeam	..
9087	Dundee ..		Short 184 Imp.		225	Sunbeam	..
9091	Dundee ..	6	Short 184 Imp.		225	Sunbeam	..
8232	Grain ..		Short 827	..	150	Sunbeam	..
8233	Grain ..		Short 827	..	150	Sunbeam	..
8234	Grain ..		Short 827	..	150	Sunbeam	..
8235	Brush ..	4	Short 827	..	150	Sunbeam	..
N1032	Blackburn ..		Sopwith Baby		110	Clerget	..
N1034	Blackburn ..		Sopwith Baby		110	Clerget	..
N1035	Blackburn ..	3	Sopwith Baby		110	Clerget	..

East African Field Force (No. 7 Squadron).

Squadron Commander F. W. Bowhill in Command.

Under orders to return to England, A.O. 305, 14th December, 1916.

Report, 17th February, 1917.

		With R.F.C.	Zanzibar.
Aeroplanes—Ready		5	..
Damaged beyond local repair	..	..	..
Under repair	..	1	..
Not yet erected	..	..	3
		6	3

AEROPLANES

No.		Total	Type.		H.p.	Engine.	
8424			B.E. 2 C	..	90	R.A.F.	..
8425			B.E. 2 C	..	90	R.A.F.	..
8427			B.E. 2 C	..	90	R.A.F.	..
8428			B.E. 2 C	..	90	R.A.F.	..
8715			B.E. 2 C	..	90	R.A.F.	..
8716		6	B.E. 2 C	..	90	R.A.F.	..
8522			Voisin	..	150	C. Unne	..
8700			Voisin	..	150	C. Unne	..
8703		3	Voisin	..	150	C. Unne	..

IN TRANSIT.   Shipped.

RETURNING TO ENGLAND.

3875			Caudron Tract'r	80	Gnome	..
3876		2	Caudron Tract'r	80	Gnome	..

FOR DELETION.

No.		Total	Type.		H.p.	Engine.	
8489			B.E. 2 C	..	90	R.A.F.	..
3268			Caudron	..	80	Gnome	..
3269			Caudron	..	80	Gnome	..
3873			Caudron	..	80	Gnome	..
3880			Caudron	..	80	Gnome	..
3881			Caudron	..	80	Gnome	..
8702	Wrecked..		Voisin	..	150	C. Unne	..
8707			Voisin	..	150	C. Unne	..

Cape Station (No. 8 Squadron).

Squadron Commander E. R. C. Nanson in Command.

POLICY.

Duty.	Flights.	In No.	Present aim.	Type.
Seaplanes..	1	6	6	Short 827

Zanzibar Report, 17th February, 1917.

Seaplanes—Ready	3
Under repair	3
Beyond repair	
Not yet erected	
	6

SEAPLANES.

No.		Total	Type.		H.p.	Engine.	
3096	Overhaul..		Short 827	..	150	Sunbeam	..
3097	Overhaul..		Short 827	..	150	Sunbeam	..
3098	Overhaul..		Short 827	..	150	Sunbeam	..
8253			Short 827	..	150	Sunbeam	..
8641			Short 827 W.T.		150	Sunbeam	..
8642		6	Short 827 W.T.		150	Sunbeam	..

IN TRANSIT.

ALLOCATED.

3332	Grain ..		Short 827	..	150	Sunbeam	..
8649	Grain ..	2	Short 827 W.T.		150	Sunbeam	..

FOR DELETION.

8254	Lost ..		Short 827	..	150	Sunbeam	..

Mechanics dismantle Vendome-based two-seat Caudron G.III N3067 after a forced landing. At the time of the census the G.III with its 100 hp Anzani radial engine was the mainstay of this school, no fewer than 59 being on strength. This aircraft was wrecked twice and overturned once before Probationary Flying Officer W.J. Allen nosedived it from 250ft into a nearby field and wrecked it completely on 16 March 1918.

The French-built Caudrons at Vendome were delivered with incorrectly-applied serials that seem not to have been amended. They should have had N prefixes, but the Caudron company followed French military practice and applied the prefix C, standing for Caudron. This example, N3082, is seen after a collision with another of its kind. It survived several accidents before it was wrecked on 22 October 1918.

Caudron G.IIIs ranged in front of the A and B Flight hangars at Vendome. Nearest is N3098, which was delivered new to the station by road on 14 January 1917 and was still there in November 1918.

Another Caudron line-up at Vendome, with N3253 nearest. This machine, which was in reserve at the time of the census, had been delivered on 31 January 1917, survived several accidents, but was earmarked for deletion by 30 March 1918.

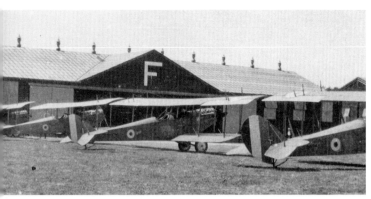

The other prolific type at Vendome was the Curtiss J.N.4, powered by the 90 h.p Curtiss OX-2 in-line engine, four of which are seen in front of the F Flight hangar. The nearest, 8874, survived to be transferred to the 2nd Aviation Centre of the American Air Service at Tours on 18 August 1918.

A hangar-full of J.N.4s at Vendome, with the tail of 8811 in the foreground. Like all of these Canadian-built aircraft, it was initially delivered to Hendon, where it was erected and flown before going to its first appointed station.

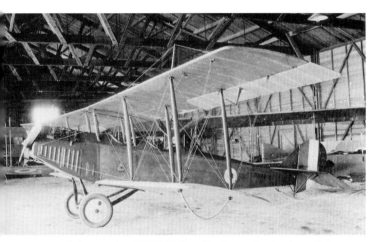

A fine study of J.N.4 8876 at Vendome. At the time of the census this machine was still at Hendon pending delivery. It eventually joined the US forces in 1918.

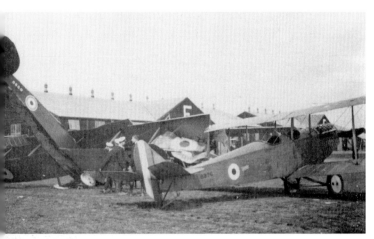

It is recorded that 8876 had its wings damaged on 21 May 1917, and this is probably the incident concerned. Sister J.N.4 8869 (with its serial in white, rather than black) has run into the J.N.4s parked in front of F Flight hangar.

Sopwith Admiralty Type 9901 (Pup) N6189, seen here in unhappy circumstances, was under construction at Sopwith's Kingston-upon-Thames factory at the time of the census, and destined for the Aeroplane Depot at Dunkirk, where it arrived on 15 March 1917. It served with 9 Sqn, the Dover War Flight and the War School at Manston, surviving until the end of March 1918.

Vendome Royal Naval Air Service. Training Establishment.

Wing Commander H. D. Briggs in Command.

Telegrams: Aviation Britannique Vendome.

POLICY.

Duty.	Flights.	In No.	Present aim.	Type.
Aeroplanes—Training	50	{ 40 / 10 }		Caudron / M. Farman L.

AEROPLANES

No.	Condition.	Total.	Type.	H.p.	Engine.	Duties. (Forwarded.)
9885	Transit ..		Avro 179 Dual	80	Gnome ..	26.1.17.
9886	Transit ..		Avro 179 Dual	80	Gnome ..	2.2.17.
N5275	Transit		Avro 179 Dual	80	Gnome (gun)	18.2.17.
N5276	Transit ..	4	Avro 179 Dual	80	Gnome ,.	18.2.17.
3060	Ready ..		Bristol Scout	80	Gnome ..	
3061	Ready ..		Bristol Scout	80	Gnome ..	
N5411	Ready ..		Bristol Scout	80	Gnome ..	
N5412	Ready ..		Bristol Scout	80	Gnome ..	
N5413	Ready ..	5	Bristol Scout	80	Gnome ..	
N3050	Ready ..		Caudron ..	100	Anzani ..	
N3051	Ready ..		Caudron ..	100	Anzani ..	
N3052	Ready ..		Caudron ..	100	Anzani ..	
N3053	Ready ..		Caudron ..	100	Anzani ..	
N3054	Ready ..		Caudron ..	100	Anzani ..	
N3055	Repair		Caudron ..	100	Anzani ..	
N3056	Ready ..		Caudron ..	100	Anzani ..	
N3057	Ready ..		Caudron ..	100	Anzani ..	
N3058	Repairs		Caudron ..	100	Anzani ..	
N3059	Repairs		Caudron ..	100	Anzani ..	
N3060	Repairs		Caudron ..	100	Anzani ..	
N3062	Repairs		Caudron ..	100	Anzani ..	
N3063	Ready ..		Caudron ..	100	Anzani ..	
N3065	Ready ..		Caudron ..	100	Anzani ..	
N3066	Repairs		Caudron ..	100	Anzani ..	
N3067	Ready ..		Caudron ..	100	Anzani ..	
N3068	Ready ..		Caudron ..	100	Anzani ..	
N3069	Ready ..		Caudron ..	100	Anzani ..	
N3072	Ready		Caudron ..	100	Anzani ..	
N3073	Ready ..		Caudron ..	100	Anzani ..	
N3074	Repairs		Caudron ..	100	Anzani ..	
N3076	Repairs ..		Caudron ..	100	Anzani ..	
N3077	Repairs ..		Caudron ..	100	Anzani ..	
N3078	Ready ..		Caudron ..	100	Anzani ..	
N3081	Reserve..		Caudron ..	100	Anzani ..	
N3082	Repairs ..		Caudron ..	100	Anzani ..	
N3083	Repair		Caudron ..	100	Anzani ..	
N3085	Ready ..		Caudron ..	100	Anzani ..	
N3086	Reserve..		Caudron ..	100	Anzani ..	
N3087	Ready ..		Caudron ..	100	Anzani ..	
N3088	Ready ..		Caudron ..	100	Anzani ..	
N3089	Ready ..		Caudron ..	100	Anzani ..	
N3090	Ready ..		Caudron ..	100	Anzani ..	
N3091	Ready ..		Caudron ..	100	Anzani ..	
N3092	Repairs		Caudron ..	100	Anzani ..	
N3093	Ready ..		Caudron ..	100	Anzani ..	
N3094	Ready ..		Caudron ..	100	Anzani ..	
N3095	Reserve .		Caudron ..	100	Anzani ..	
N3096	Reserve..		Caudron ..	100	Anzani ..	
N3097	Reserve..		Caudron ..	100	Anzani ..	
N3098	Reserve..		Caudron ..	100	Anzani ..	
N3099	Reserve..		Caudron ..	100	Anzani ..	
N3240	Repairs ..		Caudron ..	100	Anzani ..	
N3241	Ready ..		Caudron ..	100	Anzani ..	
N3242	Repairs ..		Caudron ..	100	Anzani ..	
N3243	Reserve..		Caudron ..	100	Anzani ..	
N3244	Reserve..		Caudron ..	100	Anzani ..	
N3246	Reserve..		Caudron ..	100	Anzani ..	
N3247	Reserve..		Caudron ..	100	Anzani ..	
N3248	Reserve..		Caudron ..	100	Anzani ..	
N3249	Reserve..		Caudron ..	100	Anzani ..	
N3250	Reserve..		Caudron ..	100	Anzani ..	
N3253	Reserve..		Caudron ..	100	Anzani ..	
N3254	Reserve..		Caudron ..	100	Anzani ..	
N3256	Reserve..		Caudron ..	100	Anzani ..	
N3257	Repairs ..		Caudron ..	100	Anzani ..	
N5259	Erecting..		Caudron ..	100	Anzani ..	
N5261	Erecting..		Caudron ..	100	Anzani ..	
N5262	Erecting..	59	Caudron ..	100	Anzani ..	

VENDOME—TRAINING ESTABLISHMENT—continued.

No.	Condition.	Total.	Type.	H.p.	Engine.	Duties.
3436	Ready ..		J N 4 Dual ..	90	Curtiss ..	
3438	Repairs ..		J N 4 Dual ..	90	Curtiss ..	
8812	Ready ..		J N 4 Dual ..	90	Curtiss ..	
8816	Ready ..		J N 4 Dual ..	90	Curtiss ..	
8836	Ready ..		J N 4 Dual ..	90	Curtiss ..	
8838	Ready ..		J N 4 Dual ..	90	Curtiss ..	
8860	Ready ..		J N 4 Dual ..	90	Curtiss ..	
8870	Ready ..		J N 4 Dual ..	90	Curtiss ..	
8872	Ready ..	9	J N 4 Dual ..	90	Curtiss ..	
8811	Ready ..		J N 4.. ..	90	Curtiss ..	
8813	Ready ..		J N 4.. ..	90	Curtiss ..	
8815	Ready ..		J N 4.. ..	90	Curtiss ..	
8817	Ready ..		J N 4.. ..	90	Curtiss ..	
8839	Repairs	5	J N 4.. ..	90	Curtiss ..	
N5047	Erecting..		M. Farman L.	80	Renault ..	
N5048	Transit ..		M. Farman L.	80	Renault ..	8.2.17.
N5049	Erecting..		M. Farman L.	80	Renault ..	
N5052	Transit ..	4	M. Farman L.	80	Renault ..	4.2.17.
A4144	Reserve..		M. Farman L.		None ..	
A4145	Reserve .		M. Farman L.		None ..	
A4146	Reserve..	3	M. Farman L.		None ..	
A7043	Reserve..		M. Farman L.	70	Renault ..	5.1.17.
A7044	Reserve..		M. Farman L.		None ..	
A7045	Reserve..		M. Farman L.		None ..	
A7046	Reserve..		M. Farman L.	70	Renault ..	10.1.17.
A7047	Transit ..		M. Farman L.	70	Renault ..	9.1.17.
A7048	Reserve..		M. Farman L.		None ..	
A7049	Transit ..		M. Farman L.	70	Renault ..	10.1.17.
A7050	Transit ..	8	M. Farman L.	70	Renault ..	13.1.17.

ALLOCATED.

No.	Condition.	Total.	Type.	H.p.	Engine.	Duties.
3410	Fairey, R.	1	J N 3 Imp. ..	90	Curtiss ..	
8810	Eastbourne		J N 4 Dual ..	90	Curtiss ..	
8850	Eastbourne	2	J N 4 Dual ..	90	Curtiss ..	
8869	Hendon ..		J N 4.. ..	90	Curtiss ..	
8871	Hendon ..		J N 4.. ..	90	Curtiss ..	
8874	Hendon ..		J N 4.. ..	90	Curtiss ..	
8876	Hendon ..	4	J N 4.. ..	90	Curtiss ..	

FOR DELETION.

No.	Now at.	Type.	H.p.	Engine.	Nature of trials. Duties.	Place of trials.	Date allocated.	Date arrived.	Date release expected.	Second allocation.	Remarks.
B SECTION. Seaplanes.											
8193	Fairey ..	Sopwith Baby	100	Mono ..	Packing trial..	Fairey ..	15.10.16	6.11.16			
8169	Armstrong	Sopwith Baby		None ..	..	Armstrong	23.8.16				
E SECTION. Aeroplanes.											
9340	Eastchurch	Short Bomber	250	R.R. Mk. IV.	Dynamometer experiments	E'church..	23.11.16	21.12.16			
9390	Eastchurch	Sopwith 9400 S.	110	Clerget ..	Carburetter ..	E'church..					
Allocated.											
9247	Beardmore	Nieuport ..	110	Clerget ..	Trials of A.R. 1	Daimler ..	24.1.17				
G SECTION. Aeroplanes.											
9276	Grain ..	Avro Scout ..	100	Gnome ..	Gun	Grain ..	9.6.16	20.6.16			
8432	Grain ..	B.E. 2 C ..	90	R.A.F. ..	Gun ..	Grain ..	12.9.16	15.9.16			
9461	Grain ..	B.E. 2 C ..	90	R.A.F. ..	Gun ..	Grain ..	15.1.17	15.1.17			
9470	Grain .	B.E. 2 C ..		None ..	Gun ..	Grain ..	29.9.16	25.10.16			
3339	Eastchurch	Caudron Twin	2-100	Anzani ..	Bomb ..	E'church..	1.7.16	6.7.16			
3449	Grain ..	Curtiss R 2 ..	160	Curtiss ..	Bomb ..	Grain ..	24.10.16	1.11.16	..	No.3 Wing.	
3451	Eastchurch	Curtiss R 2 ..	160	Curtiss ..	Bomb ..	E'church..	3.10.16	9.9.16			
3687	Grain ..	Dyott Fighter	2-120	A. Daimler ..	Gun	Grain ..	19.8.16	6.10.16	..	Dunkirk..	
9169	Grain ..	F. 40	150	Renault ..	Gun	Grain ..	4.9.16	28.9.16	..	E'church	
9145	Eastchurch	H. Farman ..	160	C. Unne ..	Gun	Grain ..	22.9.16				
9498	Robey, then K	Robey-Davis..	250	R.R... ..	Gun	Grain ..	11.9.16	12.9.16			
9359	Grain ..	Short Bomber	250	Sunbeam ..	Gun	Grain ..	9.1.17	9.1.17			
9380	Grain ..	Sopwith 9400 S.	110	Clerget ..	Gun	Grain ..	30.3.16				
9154	Grain ..	Voisin ..	150	C. Unne ..	Gun	Grain ..	13.6.16	13.6.16			
8603	K. (P. Vict.)	Avro Scout ..	75	R.R. ..	Gun	Grain ..	28.9.16	22.8.16			
Allocated.											
N6162	Sopwith ..	Sopwith 9901	80	Rhone ..	Fitting Vickers guns.	Grain ..	15.12.16				
N5445	Sopwith ..	Sopwith T'plane	110	Clerget ..	Fitting Vickers guns.	Grain ..	15.12.16				
8123	Grain ..	Sopwith Baby	110	Clerget ..	Experiment ..	Grain ..	15.1.17	15.1.17			
Seaplanes.											
8052	Grain ..	Short 184 ..	225	Sunbeam ..	Gun	Grain ..	..	6.6.16			
3326	Grain ..	Short 827 ..	150	Sunbeam ..	Experiment ..	Grain ..	15.1.17	15.1.17			
8144	Battersea	Sopwith Baby	110	Clerget ..	Experiment ..	Battersea	28.7.16				
I SECTION. Aeroplanes.											
9611	Mann, E.	Spad Scout ..	150	Hispano ..	Examination..	Mann, E.	1.1.17	11.1.17			
Allocated.											
Seaplanes.											
3765	Blackburn	Sopwith Schndr.	100	Mono ..	Examination..	Blackburn	..	6.8.16			
8194	Parnall ..	Sopwith Baby	100	Mono ..	Examination..	Parnall's..	22.1.17				
K SECTION. Aeroplanes.											
8441	Eastchurch	Avro Bomber	200	Sunbeam ..	Design ..	E'church..	9.8.16	23.12.16			
8603	Grain ..	Avro Scout ..	75	R.R. ..	Experiment ..	Grain ..	28.9.16	22.8.16	..	G Section	
3026	P. Victoria	Bristol Scout..	80	Gnome ..	Landing trials	Grain ..	25.10.16	25.10.16			
8803	Eastchurch	J N 4 ..	150	Renault ..	Service ..	E'church..	31.8.16	5.9.16			
9901	Eastchurch	Sopwith 9901	80	Clerget ..	Air Bag ..	E'church..	..	6.11.16			
9912	P. Victoria	Sopwith 9901	80	Clerget ..	Landing trials	Grain ..	23.11.16	23.1.17			
9497	P. Victoria	Sopwith 9901	80	Clerget ..	Landing trials	Grain ..	4.9.16	27.10.16			
9950	Eastchurch	Sopwith 9901	80	Rhone ..	Design ..	E'church..	30.12.16	3.2.17			
9377	Eastchurch	Sopwith 9400 S.	110	Clerget ..	Experiment ..	E'church..	3.9.16	20.10.16			
1388	Eastchurch	S'marine Quad.	2-125	Anzani ..	Design ..	E'church..	..	9.8.16			
9842	Eastchurch	Wight Land m/c	250	R.R. ..	Design ..	E'church..	20.9.16	22.11.16			

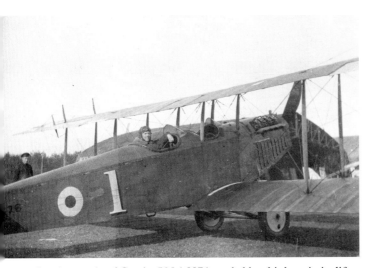

Another study of Curtiss J.N.4 8876, probably a bit later in its life, after it had acquired the individual identity "1" on its fuselage sides.

Only two examples of the Avro 519 single-seat bomber, with its 200 hp Sunbeam engine, were built. At the time of the census the second, 8441, was with the Design Flight at Eastchurch and was therefore listed under "Machines for Trial and Experiment". This picture, taken at Eastchurch in September 1916, depicts sister aircraft 8440, which had been deleted on 8 February 1917.

Two studies of Short 320 torpedo carrier 8317 with the Torpedo School at Malta in mid-1917. Previously, this aircraft had spent most of its time at Grain following delivery there on 26 July 1916. Although the constructor's number S.299 has recently been quoted as the correct manufacturer's identity for 8317, the number S.399 is clearly visible in the stationary side view. The aircraft was crashed and written off during trials on 11 June 1917. In the census it appears under "Central Supply Depot, White City and Crystal Palace", allocated to Grain.

Seen here during trials at Grain in 1916, the Blackburn TB ("Blackburn Twin") was a twin-fuselage biplane designed to meet an Admiralty requirement for a long-range Zeppelin interceptor. Only nine were built, 1510 being the second prototype. Four, including 1510, were with the RNAS Central Supply Depot, White City, at the time of the census, minus their engines, and another three at Blackburn's had been allocated there.

Two Robey-Peters Davis Gun Carriers, serialled 9498 and 9499, were on order and listed under experimental aircraft in the summary, but even at this early stage in their existence the second machine, wrongly listed as "9949", was already among the proposed cancellations on page 35. The pilot was seated not far forward of the tail surfaces, and the two gunners were to be housed in nacelles in the upper wings. In the first machine the port gunner was to have a Lewis machine-gun with 300 rounds, while the starboard gunner was to have a Davis recoilless gun with ten rounds. This aircraft, which had shorter-span lower wings, crashed in September 1917. Despite the Admiralty's cancellation of the second aircraft, it was completed, and is seen here. It had equal-span wings and a fin was added, and was to have two Davis guns. Unfortunately it stalled on take-off on its maiden flight, on 8 April 1917.

A mysterious entry under the "experimental" heading in the summary (p. 34) is the "Parnall Night Flyer". This can only refer to the Parnall Scout, two of which were ordered as N505 and N506. Although an unspecified 200 hp Sunbeam engine is attributed in the census, the only example built, N505, had a 260 hp Sunbeam Maori. The Scout might never have flown. When it was sent to Upavon for testing, its factors of safety proved so slow that it was condemned as unsafe, and the manufacturer broke it up and burned it.

Short 830 9790, powered by a 140 hp Canton Unné radial, was "ready" at Rochester and allocated to Grain, whence it was delivered on 19 February 1917. It was short-lived, being deleted on 11 July.

No.	Now at.	Type.	H.p.	Engine.	Nature of trials. Duties.	Place of trials.	Date allocated.	Date arrived.	Date release expected.	Second allocation.	Remarks.
K SECTION—	*continued.*										
Allocated.											
N511	Phœnix ..	A.W. Quad. ..	130	Clerget	.. Design ..	E'church..	18. 1. 17				
N513	Armstrong	Armstr'g B'pl'e	200	Sunbeam	.. Design ..	E'church..	23. 12. 16				
3694	Roe ..	A.D. Fighter..	2–190	R.R.	.. Design ..	E'church..	4. 4. 16				
3695	Roe ..	A.D. Fighter..	2–190	R.R.	.. Design ..	E'church..	4. 4. 16				
9467	Sage ..	B.E. 2 C	150	Hispano	.. Design ..	E'church	12. 1. 17				
N502	Blackburn	Bl'kb'rn T'plane	100	Mono	.. Performance ..	E'church..	23. 8. 16				
3697	Aircraft Co.	De Haviland 4	250	R.R...	.. Design ..	E'church	31. 1. 17				
3704	Fairey ..	Fairey Fighter	2–190	R.R...	.. Performance ..	E'church..	30. 11. 16				
N5860	N'port Eng.	Nieuport Single	130	Clerget	.. Design ..	E'church..	18. 1. 17	..	..	Dunkirk..	
?	France ..	Nieuport 1-str.	130	Clerget	.. Design ..	E'church..					
9498	Robey	Robey-Davis ..	250	R.R.	.. Design ..	E'church..	12. 9. 16	..	..	G Section	
9712	Sopwith ..	Sopwith 9400 L.	140	Smith	.. Performance ..	E'church.	6. 8. 16				
N5234	Mann, E.	Sopwith 9400 S.	110	Clerget	.. Design ..	Grain	24. 1. 17				
N6210	Mann, E.	Spad	150	Hispano	.. Performance ..	E'church..	5. 2. 17				
N6230	Mann, E.	Spad	150	Hispano	.. Performance ..	E'church..	5. 2. 17				
Seaplanes.											
1358	Felixstowe	A.D. 1000 ..	3–310	Sunbeam	.. Design ..	Felixstowe	15. 5. 16	8. 6. 16			
1415	Grain ..	Bl'ckb'rn Twin	2–160	Sunbeam	.. Design ..	Grain ..	..	8. 12. 16			
N1000	Grain ..	Campania W.T.	250	R.R. ..	.. Design ..	Grain ..	25. 10. 16	18. 1. 17			
9801	Felixstowe	Porte F. Boat	3–250	R.R. .	.. Design ..	Felixstowe	31. 5. 16	1. 8. 16			
N1	P. Victoria	P.V. 2 ..	100	Mono	.. Design ..	Grain ..	4. 8. 16	29. 6. 16			
8104	Grain ..	Short 184	250	R.R...	.. Performance ..	Grain ..	..	14. 12. 16			
852	P. Victoria	Sopwith 860 ..	225	Sunbeam	.. Wing ..	Grain ..	..	14. 12. 15			
9781	Grain ..	Short 830 ..	140	C. Unne	.. Performance ..	Grain ..	23. 8. 16	6. 11. 16	..	Dunkirk..	
9782	Grain ..	Short 830 ..	140	C. Unne	.. Performance ..	Grain ..	16. 11. 16	16. 11. 16	..	Calshot ..	
N1080	Grain ..	Short 184 Imp.	220	Renault	.. Design ..	Grain ..	20. 12. 16	1. 2. 17			
8134	Eastchurch	Sopwith Baby	110	Clerget	.. Experiment ..	E'church..	14. 4. 16	22. 1. 17			
N1010	Grain ..	Sopwith Baby	110	Clerget	.. Type	Grain ..	1. 11. 16	24. 11. 16	..	Carriers..	
N1019	Grain ..	Sopwith Baby	130	Clerget	.. Performance ..	Grain ..	6. 11. 16	10. 1. 17	..		
9098	Grain ..	Wight Baby ..	100	Mono	.. Design ..	Grain ..	17. 8. 16	8. 12. 16	..	Yarmouth	
8321	Calshot ..	Wight School	100	Mono	.. Design ..	Calshot ..	..	5. 2. 17			
Allocated.											
1513	Blackburn	Blackburn Twin		? ..	.. Design ..	Grain ..	3. 8. 16				
N1190	Parnall .	Hamble Baby	130	Clerget	.. Design ..	Grain ..	7. 2. 17				
N1320	Fairey ..	Hamble Baby	110	Clerget	.. Design ..	Grain ..	21. 2. 17				
N1180	N. Thomp'n	N.T. 2 B. F.B.	120	A D...	.. Design ..	Grain ..	14. 2. 17				
N1260	Robey	Short 184 Imp.	225	Sunbeam	.. Design ..	Grain ..	12. 1. 17				
8318	Short ..	Short Torpedo	310	Sunbeam	.. Design ..	Grain ..	23. 8. 16				
8319	Short ..	Sht. N. Sea W.T.	310	Sunbeam	.. Design ..	Grain ..	3. 8. 16	5. 10. 16			
N1023	Blackburn	Sopwith Baby	110	Clerget	.. Deck trials ..	Fairey Co.	23. 11. 16				
N9	Fairey ..	Type III ..	190	R.R...	.. Design ..	Grain ..	31. 1. 17				
8322	J. S. White	Wight School	100	Anzani	.. F'ti'g 100 Mono	J. S. White	7. 12. 16				
T SECTION.											
Seaplanes.											
1451	Felixstowe	Wight 187 ..	2–200	C. Unne	.. Torpedo ..	Felixstowe	..	28. 6. 16			
Allocated.											

Captain N. Grant, C.B., R.N., Captain-Superintendent.

No.	Condition.	Total.	Type.	H.p.	Engine.	Duties.
AEROPLANES						Allocated to—
9828		1	Avro 179 Dual	80	Gnome	.. French Sch'l.
9471			B.E. 2 C ..		None	..
9472			B.E. 2 C ..		None	..
9473			B.E. 2 C ..		None	..
9474			B.E. 2 C ..		None	..
9475		5	B.E. 2 C ..		None	..
8948		1	Caudron ..	80	Gnome	.. Schools.
None	Packed ..	27	Curtiss R 2 ..		None	..
None	Packed ..	6	Curtiss R 2 ..	160	Curtiss	..
None	Packed ..	5	J N 3 ..	90	Curtiss	..
3388	Packed ..		J N 3 Imp. ..	90	Curtiss	..
3422	Packed ..		J N 3 Imp. ..	90	Curtiss	..
8399	Packed ..	3	J N 3 Imp. ..	90	Curtiss	..
None	F'sel'ge only	1	J N 4..		None	..
None		2	J N 4..	90	Curtiss	..
N3218		1	Farman F 40	160	Renault	.. Chingford.
8788			G.W. 1600 ..		None	.. Schools.
8789			G.W. 1600 ..		None	.. Schools.
8790			G.W. 1600 ..		None	.. Schools.
8791			G.W. 1600 ..		None	.. Schools.
8792			G.W. 1600 ..		None	.. Schools.
8793			G.W. 1600 ..		None	..
8794			G.W. 1600 ..		None	..
8795			G.W. 1600 ..		None	.. Schools.
8796			G.W. 1600 ..		None	.. Schools.
8797			G.W. 1600 ..		None	..
8798			G.W. 1600 ..		None	..
8799			G.W. 1600 ..		None	..
8800			G.W. 1600 ..		None	..
8801		14	G.W. 1600 ..		None	..
N5233		1	Sopwith 9400 S.	110	Clerget	.. Mudros.
N5527		1	Sopwith 9700	130	Clerget	.. Mudros.
ALLOCATED.						
	R.F.C. ..	11	B.E. 2 C ..	90	R.A.F.	..
6326	R.F.C. ..		B.E. 2 E ..		None	..
6327	R.F.C. ..		B.E. 2 E ..		None	..
3374	Fairey ..		J N 3 Imp. ..	90	Curtiss	..
3379	Fairey ..		J N 3 Imp. ..	90	Curtiss	..
3412	Fairey ..		J N 3 Imp. ..	90	Curtiss	..
3383	Fairey ..		J N 3 Imp. ..	90	Curtiss	..
3385	Fairey ..		J N 3 Imp. ..	90	Curtiss	..
3389	Fairey ..		J N 3 Imp. ..	90	Curtiss	..
3391	Fairey ..		J N 3 Imp. ..	90	Curtiss	..
3411	Fairey ..		J N 3 Imp. ..	90	Curtiss	..
3413	Fairey ..		J N 3 Imp. ..	90	Curtiss	..
FOR DELETION.						
3851	Packed ..	1	Sopwith 806..	150	Sunbeam	..

No.	Condition.	Total.	Type.	H.p.	Engine.	Duties.
SEAPLANES.						Allocated to—
1509	Packed ..		Blackburn Twin		None	..
1510	Packed ..		Blackburn Twin		None	..
1511			Blackburn Twin		None	..
1512		4	Blackburn Twin		None	..
9769	P20.11.16		Short 166 ..	200	C. Unne	..
9770	A 8.12.16	2	Short 166 ..	200	C. Unne	..
8216			Sopwith Baby	100	Gnome G.D.	
8217		2	Sopwith Baby	100	Gnome G...	
ALLOCATED.						
1514	Blackburn		Blackburn Twin		?	
1515	Blackburn		Blackburn Twin		?	
1517	Blackburn	3	Blackburn Twin		None	..
N1150	Short ..		Short Torpedo	310	Sunbeam	..
N1151	Short ..		Short Torpedo	310	Sunbeam	..
8317	Grain ..	3	Short Torpedo	310	Sunbeam	..

Survey Section.

AEROPLANES.

FOR SURVEY (NOT YET DELETED).

ALLOCATED.

DELETED, BUT TO BE KEPT.

No.	Condition.	Total.	Type.	H.p.	Engine.	Duties.
3253*			Morane ..		None	.. Lt. Warneford's m/c.

SEAPLANES.

FOR SURVEY (NOT YET DELETED).

At Crystal Palace.

For instructional purposes.

Wing Commander J. W. L. Hunt in Command.

No.	Condition.	Total.	Type.	H.p.	Engine.	Duties.
AEROPLANES						
8947			Caudron ..	80	Gnome	..

SEAPLANES.

Battersea (R.N.A.S. Experimental Workshop).

No.	Condition.	Total.	Type.	H.p.	Engine.	Duties.
SEAPLANES.						
8144			Sopwith Baby	110	Clerget	.. G.

NOTE.—Only machines expected within the next few weeks are included.

Date prefixed by letter A = date accepted.
Date prefixed by letter E = date expected ready for trial.
Date prefixed by letter P = date passed trial.

Date prefixed by letter s = date sent for repair.
Date prefixed by letter T = in transit from maker to station.

No.	Expected for trials.	Type.	H.p.	Engine.	Allocation.	No.	Expected for trials.	Type.	H.p.	Engine.	Allocation.

Aircraft Co.

AEROPLANES (NEW).

| 3696 | E 24.2.17 | De Haviland 4 | 250 | R.R... | .. Dunkirk. |
| 3697 | E 24.2.17 | De Haviland 4 | 190 | R.R... | .. E'church (K). |

SEAPLANES (NEW).

9808	T 17.3.17	Porte F.B.	3-250	R.R...	.. Killingholme.
9809	E 24.3.17	Porte F.B.	3-250	R.R...	.. Killingholme.
9810	E 3.3.17	Porte F.B.	3-250	R.R...	.. Felixstowe.
9811	E 10.3.17	Porte F.B.	3-250	R.R...	.. Killingholme.

Approximate deliveries 1 per week.

Armstrong, Whitworth Co.

AEROPLANES

| N513 | | A. W. Biplane | 200 | Sunbeam | .. K. |

SEAPLANES.

| 8169 | s 25.7.16 | Sopwith Baby | | None | .. B Section. |

W. Beardmore & Co., Ltd.

AEROPLANES (NEW).

9239	E ?	Nieuport	..	110	Clerget	.. Cranwell.
9240	E ?	Nieuport	..	110	Clerget	.. Cranwell.
9241	E ?	Nieuport	..	110	Clerget	.. Chingford.
9247	A 1.2.17	Nieuport	..	110	Clerget	.. E. (Daimler).
9248	E 24.2.17	Nieuport	..	110	Clerget	.. Cranwell.
9249	E 10.3.17	Nieuport	..	110	Clerget	.. Cranwell.
9250	E ?	Nieuport	..	110	Clerget	.. Cranwell.

Approximate deliveries 1 per week.

9921	A 19.2.17	Sopwith 9901	80	Rhone	.. "Vindex."
9922	A 19.2.17	Sopwith 9901	80	Rhone	.. Grain.
9923	A 19.2.17	Sopwith 9901	80	Rhone	.. Cranwell.
9924	A 19.2.17	Sopwith 9901	80	Rhone	.. Cranwell.
9925	E 24.2.17	Sopwith 9901	80	Rhone	.. Cranwell.
9926	E 24.2.17	Sopwith 9901	80	Rhone	.. "Vindex."
9927	E 24.2.17	Sopwith 9901	80	Rhone	.. "Vindex."
9928	E 3.3.17	Sopwith 9901	80	Rhone	.. Dunkirk.
9929	E 3.3.17	Sopwith 9901	80	Rhone	.. Dunkirk.
9930	E 3.3.17	Sopwith 9901	80	Rhone	.. Killingholme.
9931	E 10.3.17	Sopwith 9901	80	Rhone	.. Hendon.
9932	E 10.3.17	Sopwith 9901	80	Rhone	.. Hendon.
9933	E 10.3.17	Sopwith 9901	80	Rhone	.. Killingholme.
9934	E 17.3.17	Sopwith 9001	80	Rhone	.. Killingholme.
9935	E 17.3.17	Sopwith 9901	80	Rhone	.. Killingholme.
9936	E 17.3.17	Sopwith 9901	80	Rhone	.. Killingholme.

Approximate deliveries 2-3 per week.

ALLOCATED.

Blackburn & Co.

AEROPLANES (NEW).

| N502 | E ? | Triplane | .. | 100 | Mono | .. K. (E'church). |
| 9951 | E 3.3.17 | B.E. 2 C | .. | 90 | Curtiss | .. Cranwell. |

Approximate deliveries 1-2 per week.

ALLOCATED.

SEAPLANES (NEW).

1513	⎫	Bl'ckb'rn Twin		?	..	.. K. (P. Vict.).
1514	⎬ Waiting	Bl'ckb'rn Twin		?	..	.. C.S. Depôt.
1515	engines.	Bl'ckb'rn Twin		?	..	.. C.S. Depôt.
1516	⎭	Bl'ckb'rn Twin		?	..	..
1517	E ?	Bl'ckb'rn Twin		None	..	.. White City.

Approximate deliveries uncertain.

N 300	T 10.2.17	Sopwith Baby	110	Clerget	.. "Campania."
N1015	Wrecked..	Sopwith Baby	110	Clerget	.. Dunkirk.
N1023	Ready	Sopwith Baby	110	Clerget	.. K. (Faireys).
N1024	Ready ..	Sopwith Baby	110	Clerget	.. Dunkirk.
N1025	Ready ..	Sopwith Baby	110	Clerget	.. Westgate.
N1026	T 10.2.17	Sopwith Baby	110	Clerget	.. "Campania."
N1027	T 17.2.17	Sopwith Baby	110	Clerget	.. "Campania."
N1028	E 24.2.17	Sopwith Baby	110	Clerget	.. Carriers, P S.
N1029	E 24.2.17	Sopwith Baby	110	Clerget	.. Fishguard.
N1030	E 3.3.17	Sopwith Baby	110	Clerget	.. Fishguard.
N1031	E 3.3.17	Sopwith Baby	110	Clerget	.. Dover.
N1032	E 3.3.17	Sopwith Baby	110	Clerget	.. Otranto.
N1033	E 3.3.17	Sopwith Baby	110	Clerget	.. Mudros.
N1034	E 10.3.17	Sopwith Baby	110	Clerget	.. Otranto.
N1035	E 10.3.17	Sopwith Baby	110	Clerget	.. Otranto.
N1036	E 10.3.17	Sopwith Baby	110	Clerget	.. Felixstowe.
N1037	E 10.3.17	Sopwith Baby	110	Clerget	.. Felixst'we, N.F.
N1038	E 17.3.17	Sopwith Baby	110	Clerget	.. Carriers, P.S.
N1039	E 17.3.17	Sopwith Baby	110	Clerget	.. Calshot.
N1060	E 17.3.17	Sopwith Baby	110	Clerget	.. Carriers, P.S.
N1061	E 17.3.17	Sopwith Baby	110	Clerget	.. Yarmouth.

Approximate deliveries 4 per week.

SEAPLANES (REPAIR).

3806		Sopwith Baby	100	Mono	.. ⎫
8125		Sopwith Baby	110	Clerget	.. ⎪
8197		Sopwith Baby	110	Clerget	.. ⎪ For fitting
8204		Sopwith Baby	110	Clerget	.. ⎬ Clerget
8205		Sopwith Baby	110	Clerget	.. ⎪ engines.
8208		Sopwith Baby	110	Clerget	.. ⎪
8209		Sopwith Baby	110	Clerget	.. ⎭
3707		Sopwith Schndr.	100	Mono	..
3709	s 30.8.16	Sopwith Schndr.	100	Mono	..
3765		Sopwith Schndr.	100	Mono	.. I Section.

ALLOCATED.

Bristol Co.

AEROPLANES (NEW).

AEROPLANES (REPAIR).

Brush Electrical Engineering Co.

AEROPLANES (NEW).

No.	Expected for trials.	Type.	H.p.	Engine.		Allocation.
9251	E 24.2.17	H. Farman All steel.	140	C. Unne	..	Cranwell.
9252	E 3.3.17	H. Farman All steel.	140	C. Unne	..	Cranwell.
Approximate		deliveries	un	certain.		
N5058	T 10.2.17	M. Farman L.	80	Renault	..	Killingholme.
N5059	T 10.2.17	M. Farman L.	80	Renault	..	Killingholme.
N5720	E 24.2.17	M. Farman L.	80	Renault	..	Killingholme.
N5721	E 3.3.17	M. Farman L.	80	Renault	..	Killingholme.
N5722	E 3.3.17	M. Farman L.	80	Renault	..	Killingholme.
N5723	E 10.3.17	M. Farman L.	80	Renault	..	Killingholme.
N5724	E 10.3.17	M. Farman L.	80	Renault	..	Killingholme.
Approximate		deliveries	2	per week.		

SEAPLANES (NEW).

No.	Expected for trials.	Type.	H.p.	Engine.		Allocation.
8230	T 17.2.17	Short 827 W.T.	150	Sunbeam	..	"Campania."
8231	T 17.2.17	Short 827 W.T.	150	Sunbeam	..	"Campania."
8235	E 24.2.17	Short 827 ..	150	Sunbeam	..	Otranto.
8236	E 24.2.17	Short 827 ..	150	Sunbeam	..	Dundee.
8237	E 3.3.17	Short 827 ..	150	Sunbeam	..	Calshot.

Caudron (British) Co.

AEROPLANES (NEW).

Clayton & Shuttleworth.

AEROPLANES (NEW).

Approximate	deliveries	1-3	per week.

Eastbourne Aviation Co.

No.	Expected for trials.	Type.	H.p.	Engine.		Allocation.
N5065	A 8.2.17	M. Farman S.	80	Renault	..	Cranwell.
N5066	A 14.2.17	M. Farman S.	80	Renault	..	E'church, Gun.
N5067	E 24.2.17	M. Farman S.	80	Renault	..	E'church, Gun.
N5068	E 24.2.17	M. Farman S.	80	Renault	..	E'church, Gun.
N5069	Waiting engine.	M. Farman S.	80	Renault	..	Cranwell.
N5070	Waiting engine.	M. Farman S.	80	Renault	..	Killingholme.
N5071	Waiting engine.	M. Farman S.	80	Renault	..	Killingholme.
Approximate		deliveries	1	per week.		

Fairey Aviation Co.

AEROPLANES (NEW).

No.	Expected for trials.	Type.	H.p.	Engine.		Allocation.
3704	Ready ..	Fighter ..	2-190	R.R.		K (E'church).

AEROPLANES (REPAIR).

No.	Expected for trials.	Type.	H.p.	Engine.		Allocation.
3374	S 16.6.16	J N 3 Imp. ..	90	Curtiss	..	C.S.D.
3379	E 3.3.17	J N 3 Imp. ..	90	Curtiss	..	C.S.D.
3383	E 3.3.17	J N 3 Imp. ..	90	Curtiss	..	C.S.D.
3385	S 11.7.16	J N 3 Imp. ..	90	Curtiss	..	C.S.D.
3389	S 11.7.16	J N 3 Imp. ..	90	Curtiss	..	C.S.D.
3391	S 12.7.16	J N 3 Imp. ..	90	Curtiss	..	C.S.D.
3410	S 28.8.16	J N 3 Imp. ..	90	Curtiss	..	Vendome.
3411	S 12.7.16	J N 3 Imp. ..	90	Curtiss	..	C.S.D.
3412	S 11.7.16	J N 3 Imp. ..	90	Curtiss	..	C.S.D.
3413	E 28.2.17	J N 3 Imp. ..	90	Curtiss	..	C.S.D.
3701	E 28.2.17	Sloane ..	130	Hall Scott	..	Hendon.

ALLOCATED.

SEAPLANES (NEW).

No.	Expected for trials.	Type.	H.p.	Engine.		Allocation.
N1320	E 17.3.17	Hamble Baby	110	Clerget	..	K. (Grain).
8561	T 17.2.17	Short 827 ..	150	Sunbeam	..	Calshot.
N9	E 17.3.17	Type III. ..	190	R.R.	..	K. (Grain).
N1001	E 10.3.17	"Campania"..	250	R.R...	..	"Campania."

SEAPLANES (REPAIR).

No.	Expected for trials.	Type.	H.p.	Engine.		Allocation.
8193		Sopwith Baby	100	Mono G.D...		B.

Grahame White Aviation Co.

AEROPLANES (NEW).

No.	Expected for trials.	Type.	H.p.	Engine.		Allocation.
9427	E ?	Breguet Conc.		None	..	Killingholme.
9428	E ?	Breguet Conc.		None	..	Killingholme.
9429	E ?	Breguet Conc.		None	..	Killingholme.
9430	E ?	Breguet Conc.		None	..	Killingholme.
9431	E ?	Breguet Conc.		None	..	Killingholme.
9432	E ?	Breguet Conc.		None	..	Killingholme.
9433	E ?	Breguet Conc.		None	..	Killingholme.
9434	E ?	Breguet Conc.		None	..	Killingholme.
9435	E ?	Breguet Conc.		None	..	Killingholme.
Approximate		deliveries	2	per week.		

AEROPLANES (REPAIRS).

Handley Page & Co.

AEROPLANES (NEW).

No.	Expected for trials.	Type.	H.p.	Engine.		Allocation.
3117	E 10.3.17	Handley Page	2-320	Sunbeam	..	Dunkirk.
3121	E 24.2.17	Handley Page	2-250	R.R...	..	Dunkirk.
3122	E 3.3.17	Handley Page	2-250	R.R...	..	Manstone.
3123	E 10.3.17	Handley Page	2-250	R.R...	..	Killingholme.
Approximate		deliveries	1	per week.		

ALLOCATED.

AEROPLANES (REPAIRS).

No.	Expected for trials.	Type.	H.p.	Engine.		Allocation.
1455		Handley Page	2-250	R.R...	..	

Hewlett & Blondeau.

AEROPLANES (NEW).

No.	Expected for trials.	Type.	H.p.	Engine.	Allocation.

Mann, Egerton & Co.

AEROPLANES (NEW).

No.	Expected for trials.	Type.	H.p.	Engine.	Allocation.
9495	A 17. 2. 17	Short Bomber	250	R.R.	Eastchurch.
Approximate		deliveries	1	per week.	
N5229	A 22. 12. 16	Sopwith 9400 S.	110	Clerget	Mudros.
N5230	A 30. 1. 17	Sopwith 9400 S.	110	Clerget	Cranwell.
N5231	A 30. 1. 17	Sopwith 9400 S.	110	Clerget	Mudros.
N5232	A 30. 1. 17	Sopwith 9400 S.	110	Clerget	Mudros.
N5234	A 6. 2. 17	Sopwith 9400 S.	110	Clerget	K.
N5235	Ready	Sopwith 9400 S.		None	Belgian Govt.
N5236	Ready	Sopwith 9400 S.		None	Belgian Govt.
N5237	Ready	Sopwith 9400 S.		None	Belgian Govt.
N5238	Ready	Sopwith 9400 S.		None	Belgian Govt.
N5239	Ready	Sopwith 9700 S.		None	Belgian Govt.
N5240	E 10. 3. 17	Sopwith 9400 S.		None	Belgian Govt.
N5241	E 10. 3. 17	Sopwith 9400 S.		None	Belgian Govt.
N5242	E 10. 3. 17	Sopwith 9400 S.		None	Belgian Govt.
N5243	E 17. 3. 17	Sopwith 9400 S.	110	Clerget	Mudros.
N5244	E 17. 3. 17	Sopwith 9400 S.	110	Clerget	Dunkirk.
N5245	E 17. 3. 17	Sopwith 9400 S.	110	Clerget	Dunkirk.
Approximate		deliveries	8	per month.	
N5200	A 15. 1. 17	Sopwith 9700	110	Clerget	Mudros.
N5201	A 15. 1. 17	Sopwith 9700	110	Clerget	Mudros.
N5202	A 15. 1. 17	Sopwith 9700	110	Clerget	Mudros.
N5203	A 15. 1. 17	Sopwith 9700		None	Felixstowe.
N5204	A 6. 1. 17	Sopwith 9700	110	Clerget	Mudros.
N5205	A 18. 1. 17	Sopwith 9700	110	Clerget	Mudros.
N5206	A 18. 1. 17	Sopwith 9700	110	Clerget	Mudros.
N5207	A 30. 1. 17	Sopwith 9700	110	Clerget	Dunkirk.
N5208	A 30. 1. 17	Sopwith 9700	110	Clerget	Dunkirk.
N5209	A 17. 2. 17	Sopwith 9700	110	Clerget	Mudros.
N5210	A 17. 2. 17	Sopwith 9700	110	Clerget	Mudros.
N5211	Ready	Sopwith 9700	110	Clerget	Mudros.
N5212	Ready	Sopwith 9700	110	Clerget	Mudros.
N5213	Ready	Sopwith 9700	110	Clerget	Mudros.
N5214	E 24. 2. 17	Sopwith 9700	110	Clerget	Dunkirk.
N5215	E 24. 2. 17	Sopwith 9700	110	Clerget	Dunkirk.
N5216	E 24. 2. 17	Sopwith 9700	110	Clerget	Mudros.
N5217	E 3. 3. 17	Sopwith 9700	110	Clerget	Mudros.
N5218	E 3. 3. 17	Sopwith 9700	110	Clerget	Mudros.
N5219	E 3. 3. 17	Sopwith 9700	110	Clerget	Mudros.
N6210	E 3. 3. 17	Spad	150	Hispano	K.
N6211	E 10. 3. 17	Spad	150	Hispano	K.
Approximate		deliveries	8	per month.	

ALLOCATED.

AEROPLANES (REPAIR).

No.	Expected for trials.	Type.	H.p.	Engine.	Allocation.
9611	S 8. 1. 17	Spad Scout	150	Hispano	I.

SEAPLANES (NEW).

Nieuport and General Aircraft Co.

AEROPLANES (NEW).

No.	Expected for trials.	Type.	H.p.	Engine.	Allocation.
N5860	E ?	Nieuport Single	130	Clerget	K., then Dunkirk.
N5861	E ?	Nieuport Single	130	Clerget	Dunkirk.
Approximate		deliveries	1	per week.	

Oakley.

AEROPLANES (REPAIRS).

No.	Expected for trials.	Type.	H.p.	Engine.	Allocation.
8415		B.E. 2 C		None	
8416		B.E. 2 C		None	
9458		B.E. 2 C	75	R.R.	Chingford.
9460		B.E. 2 C		None	
9717		Sopwith 9400 L	80	Clerget	Mudros.

ALLOCATED.

Parnall & Sons.

AEROPLANES (NEW).

No.	Expected for trials.	Type.	H.p.	Engine.	Allocation.
9890	T 3. 2. 17	Avro 179 Dual	80	Gnome	Killingholme.
N6010	T 17. 2. 17	Avro 179 Dual	80	Gnome (gun)	Killingholme.
N6011	E 24. 2. 17	Avro 179 Dual	80	Gnome (gun)	Killingholme.
N6012	E 24. 2. 17	Avro 179 Dual	80	Gnome (gun)	Killingholme.
N6013	E 3. 3. 17	Avro 179 Dual	80	Gnome (gun)	Killingholme.
N6014	E 3. 3. 17	Avro 179 Dual	80	Gnome	Killingholme.
N6015	E 10. 3. 17	Avro 179 Dual	80	Gnome	R.F.C.
N6016	E 10. 3. 17	Avro 179 Dual	80	Gnome	R.F.C.
N6017	E 17. 3. 17	Avro 179 Dual	80	Gnome	R.F.C.
N6018	E 17. 3. 17	Avro 179 Dual	80	Gnome	R.F.C.
N6019	E 24. 3. 17	Avro 179 Dual	80	Gnome	R.F.C.
N6020	E 24. 3. 17	Avro 179 Dual	80	Gnome	R.F.C.
Approximate		deliveries	3	per week.	

AEROPLANES (REPAIR).

No.	Expected for trials.	Type.	H.p.	Engine.	Allocation.
1041	E 17. 2. 17	Avro 179 type		None	Chingford.

SEAPLANES (NEW).

No.	Expected for trials.	Type.	H.p.	Engine.	Allocation.
N1190	E 3. 3. 17	Hamble Baby	130	Clerget	K Section.
N1191	E 10. 3. 17	Hamble Baby	130	Clerget	Newlyn.
N1192	E 17. 3. 17	Hamble Baby	130	Clerget	Newlyn.
N1193	E 17. 3. 17	Hamble Baby	130	Clerget	Mudros.

SEAPLANES (REPAIR).

No.	Expected for trials.	Type.	H.p.	Engine.	Allocation.
8033	S 20. 1. 17	Short 184	240	Sunbeam	
9066	S 5. 2. 17	Short 184	225	Sunbeam	
8194	S 27. 1. 17	Sopwith Baby	100	Gnome	I Section.

ALLOCATED.

Phoenix Co.

AEROPLANES (NEW).

No.	Expected for trials.	Type.	H.p.	Engine.	Allocation.
N 511	E 10. 3. 17	A.W. Quad.	130	Clerget	K. (E'church).
N5339	T 3. 2. 17	M. Farman L.	75	R.R.	Killingholme.
N5342	Ready	M. Farman L.	75	R.R.	Killingholme.
N5344	T 24. 2. 17	M. Farman L.	75	R.R.	Killingholme.
N5345	T 24. 2. 17	M. Farman L.	75	R.R.	Killingholme.
N5346	E 24. 2. 17	M. Farman L.	75	R.R.	Killingholme.
N5347	E 24. 2. 17	M. Farman L.	75	R.R.	Killingholme.
N5348	E 3. 3. 17	M. Farman L.	75	R.R.	Killingholme.
N5349	E 3. 3. 17	M. Farman L.	75	R.R.	Killingholme.
N5750	E 10. 3. 17	M. Farman L.	75	R.R.	
N5751	E 10. 3. 17	M. Farman L.	75	R.R.	
N5752	E 17. 3. 17	M. Farman L.	75	R.R.	
N5753	E 17. 3. 17	M. Farman L.	75	R.R.	
Approximate		deliveries	2	per week.	

Robey.

AEROPLANES (NEW).

No.	Expected for trials.	Type.	H.p.	Engine.	Allocation.
9498	E ?	Robey Davis	250	R.R.	K. (E'church), then G.
N5006	Ready	M. Farman L.	75	R.R.	Killingholme.
N5007	T 17. 2. 17	M. Farman L.	75	R.R.	Killingholme.
N5008	E 24. 2. 17	M. Farman L.	75	R.R.	Killingholme.
N5009	E 24. 2. 17	M. Farman L.	75	R.R.	Killingholme.
N5010	E 3. 3. 17	M. Farman L.	75	R.R.	
N5011	E 3. 3. 17	M. Farman L.	75	R.R.	
Approximate		deliveries	1-2	per week.	

SEAPLANES (NEW).

No.	Expected for trials.	Type.	H.p.	Engine.	Allocation.
N1260	E 3. 3. 17	Short 184 Imp.	225	Sunbeam	K. (Grain).
Approximate		deliveries	1	per week.	

SEAPLANES (REPAIR).

No.	Expected for trials.	Type.	H.p.	Engine.	Allocation.

A. V. Roe.

AEROPLANES (NEW).

No.	Expected for trials.	Type.	H.p.	Engine.	Allocation.
3694	E 3.3.17	A.D. Fighter..	2–190	R.R... ..	K. (P. Vict.).
3695	Waiting engine.	A.D. Fighter..	2–190	R.R... ..	K. (P. Vict.).

AEROPLANES (REPAIR).

ALLOCATED.

No.	Expected for trials.	Type.	H.p.	Engine.	Allocation.
N5261	Sunbeam ..	Avro 179 Dual	80	Gnome ..	Spec. alteration
N5269	Sunbeam ..	Avro 179 Dual	80	Gnome ..	Spec. alteration
N5270	Sunbeam ..	Avro 179 Dual	80	Gnome ..	Spec. alteration

Sage.

AEROPLANES (NEW).

No.	Expected for trials.	Type.	H.p.	Engine.	Allocation.
None		Fighting Scout	100	Mono ..	
N5251	E ?	School ..	75	R.R... ..	Cranwell.

AEROPLANES (REPAIR)

No.	Expected for trials.	Type.	H.p.	Engine.	Allocation.
9466		B.E. 2 C ..	90	Curtiss ..	Yarmouth.
9467		B.E. 2 C ..	150	Hispano-Suiza	K. (E'church).
9468		B.E. 2 C ..	150	Hispano-Suiza	Redcar.
A2564	S20.12.16	B.E. 2 E ..	150	Hispano ..	

ALLOCATED.

SEAPLANES (NEW).

No.	Expected for trials.	Type.	H.p.	Engine.	Allocation.
9080	Waiting engine.	Short 184 ..	240	Sunbeam ..	Wrecked.
Approximate	deliveries	1	per week.		

SEAPLANES (REPAIR).

No.	Expected for trials.	Type.	H.p.	Engine.	Allocation.
845	T 10.2.17	Short 184 ..	225	Sunbeam ..	"Campania."
8055	E 24.2.17	Short 184 ..	225	Sunbeam ..	Killingholme.
8056	T 10.2.17	Short 184 ..	225	Sunbeam ..	"Campania."
9073	Waiting engine.	Short 184 ..	240	Sunbeam ..	"Manxman."

ALLOCATED.

S. E. Saunders, Ltd.

SEAPLANES (NEW).

No.	Expected for trials.	Type.	H.p.	Engine.	Allocation.
8025	A 16.2.17	Short 184 ..	240	Sunbeam ..	Newlyn.
8026	A 16.2.17	Short 184 ..	240	Sunbeam ..	"Campania."
8028	A 16.2.17	Short 184 ..	240	Sunbeam ..	"Campania."
8029	E 19.2.17	Short 184 ..	240	Sunbeam ..	"Engadine."
803C	E 26.2.17	Short 184 ..	240	Sunbeam ..	"Campania."
Approximate	deliveries	1	per week.		

SEAPLANES (REPAIR).

Short Bros.

AEROPLANES (NEW).

ALLOCATED.

SEAPLANES (NEW).

No.	Expected for trials.	Type.	H.p.	Engine.	Allocation.
8318	E ?	Short Torpedo	310	Sunbeam ..	K. (P. Vict.)
8319	E 3.3.17	Short North Sea W.T.	310	Sunbeam .	K. (P. Vict.).
8320	E ?	Short North Sea W.T.	310	Sunbeam ..	Felixstowe.
N1150	Ready ..	Short Torpedo	310	Sunbeam ..	White City.
N1151	E 24.2.17	Short Torpedo	310	Sunbeam ..	White City
9790	Ready ..	Short 830 ..	140	C. Unne ..	Grain.
N1083	E 3.3.17	Short 184 Imp.	220	Renault ..	Calshot.
N1084	E 10.3.17	Short 184 Imp.	220	Renault ..	Calshot.
N1085	E 17.3.17	Short 184 Imp.	220	Renault ..	Calshot.
Approximate	deliveries	1	per week.		

SEAPLANES (REPAIR).

No.	Expected for trials.	Type.	H.p.	Engine.	Allocation.
8076	Repairs ..	Short 184 Davis	225	Sunbeam ..	Newlyn.

Sopwith Aviation Co.

	Approximate	deliveries	12	per week	(all types).

AEROPLANES (NEW).

No.	Expected for trials.	Type.	H.p.	Engine.	Allocation.
9712	Waiting engine.	Sopwith 9400 L.	140	Smith ..	K. (E'church).
N6162	E ?	Sopwith 9901	80	Rhone ..	G. (E'church).
N6176	T 10.2.17	Sopwith 9901	80	Rhone ..	Dunkirk.
N6177	E 24.2.17	Sopwith 9901	80	Rhone ..	Dunkirk.
N6180	E 24.2.17	Sopwith 9901	80	Rhone ..	Dunkirk.
N6181	E 24.2.17	Sopwith 9901	80	Rhone ..	Dunkirk.
N6182	E 24.2.17	Sopwith 9901	80	Rhone ..	Dunkirk.
N6183	E 24.2.17	Sopwith 9901	80	Rhone ..	Dunkirk.
N6184	E 3.3.17	Sopwith 9901	80	Rhone ..	Dunkirk.
N6186	E 3.3.17	Sopwith 9901	80	Rhone ..	Dunkirk.
N6187	E 3.3.17	Sopwith 9901	80	Rhone ..	Dunkirk.
N6188	E 24.2.17	Sopwith 9901	80	Rhone ..	Dunkirk.
N6189	E 3.3.17	Sopwith 9901	80	Rhone ..	Dunkirk.
N5438	E 24.2.17	Sopwith T'plane	130	Clerget ..	Dunkirk.
N5445	E ?	Sopwith T'plane	130	Clerget ..	G. (E'church).
N5452	A 17.2.17	Sopwith T'plane	130	Clerget ..	Dunkirk.
N5453	E 24.2.17	Sopwith T'plane	130	Clerget ..	Dunkirk.
N5456	E 24.2.17	Sopwith T'plane	130	Clerget ..	Dunkirk.
N5457	E 24.2.17	Sopwith T'plane	130	Clerget ..	Dunkirk.
N5458	E 24.2.17	Sopwith T'plane	130	Clerget ..	Dunkirk.
N5459	E 24.2.17	Sopwith T'plane	130	Clerget ..	Dunkirk.
N5460	E 24.2.17	Sopwith T'plane	130	Clerget ..	Dunkirk.
N5461	E 24.2.17	Sopwith T'plane	13C	Clerget ..	Dunkirk.
N5462	E 3.3.17	Sopwith T'plane	130	Clerget ..	Dunkirk.
N5463	E 3.3.17	Sopwith T'plane	130	Clerget ..	Dunkirk.
N5464	E 3.3.17	Sopwith T'plane	130	C'erget ..	Dunkirk.
N5465	E 3.3.17	Sopwith T'plane	130	Clerget ..	Dunkirk.
N5533	E 24.2.17	Sopwith 9700	110	Clerget ..	Mudros.
N5534	E 3.3.17	Sopwith 9700	110	Clerget ..	Mudros.
N5535	E 3.3.17	Sopwith 9700	110	Clerget ..	Mudros.
N5536	E 10.3.17	Sopwith 97C0	110	Clerget ..	Mudros.
N5537	E 10.3.17	Sopwith 97C0	110	Clerget ..	Mudros.

SEAPLANES (NEW).

SEAPLANES (REPAIRS).

No.	Expected for trials.	Type.	H.p.	Engine.	Allocation.
854		Sopwith 860 ..			
858		Sopwith 860 ..			
931		Sopwith 860 ..			
932		Sopwith 860 ..			
933		Sopwith 860 ..			
938		Sopwith 860 ..			

South Coast Aircraft Works.

AEROPLANES (REPAIR).

No.	Expected for trials.	Type.	H.p.	Engine.	Allocation.
1014 E	?	Avro 179	80	Gnome	Chingford.

Sunbeam Co.

AEROPLANES (NEW).

No.	Expected for trials.	Type.	H.p.	Engine.	Allocation.
N5261 A	8.1.17	Avro 179 Dual	80	Gnome	A. V. Roe.
N5267 E	3.3.17	Avro 179 Dual	80	Gnome	Killingholme.
N5269 A	8.1.17	Avro 179 Dual	80	Gnome	A. V. Roe.
N5270 A	8.1.17	Avro 179 Dual	80	Gnome	A. V. Roe.
N5273 E	10.3.17	Avro 179 Dual	80	Gnome	East'ch Ob. Sch.
N5278 E	10.3.17	Avro 179 Dual	80	Gnome (Gun)	Killingh lme.
N5279 E	17.3.17	Avro 179 Dual	80	Gnome (Gun)	Killingholme.
N6138 T	10.2.17	Avro 179 Dual	80	Gnome	Killingholme.
N6139 T	10.2.17	Avro 179 Dual	80	Gnome	Killingholme.
N6140 T	10.2.17	Avro 179 Dual	80	Gnome	Killingholme.
N6145 E	24.2.17	Avro 179 Dual	80	Gnome	Killingholme.
N6146 E	24.2.17	Avro 179 Dual	80	Gnome	Killingholme.
N6147 E	24.2.17	Avro 179 Dual	80	Gnome	E'church F.S.
N6148 E	24.2.17	Avro 179 Dual	80	Gnome	Redcar.
N6149 E	24.2.17	Avro 179 Dual	80	Gnome	Redcar.
N6150 E	3.3.17	Avro 179 Dual	80	Gnome	Killingholme.
N6151 E	3.3.17	Avro 179 Dual	80	Gnome	Killingholme.
N6152 E	10.3.17	Avro 179 Dual	80	Gnome	Killingholme.
Approximate	deliveries	4	per week.		

AEROPLANES (REPAIR).

No.	Expected for trials.	Type.	H.p.	Engine.	Allocation.
2260	s14.11.16	R.E. 7	200	Sunbeam	Cranwell.

Supermarine Co.

AEROPLANES (NEW).

No.	Expected for trials.	Type.	H.p.	Engine.	Allocation.
9007 T		P.B. Scout		None	Killingholme.
9008 T		P.B. Scout		None	Killingholme.
9009 T		P.B. Scout		None	Killingholme.
9010 T		P.B. Scout		None	Killingholme.
9011 T		P.B. Scout		None	Killingholme.
9012 T		P.B. Scout		None	Killingholme.
9013 T		P.B. Scout		None	Killingholme.
9014 T		P.B. Scout		None	Killingholme.
9015 T		P.B. Scout		None	Killingholme.
9016 T		P.B. Scout		None	Killingholme.
9017 E	24.2.17	P.B. Scout		None	Killingholme.
9018 E	24.2.17	P.B. Scout		None	Killingholme.
9019 E	24.2.17	P.B. Scout		None	Killingholme.
9020 E	3.3.17	P.B. Scout		None	Killingholme.
Approximate	deliveries	1	per week.		

ALLOCATED.

SEAPLANES (REPAIR).

N. Thompson Flight Co.

SEAPLANES (NEW).

No.	Expected for trials.	Type.	H.p.	Engine.	Allocation.
8338	Altering	Sm. America	2-140	Hispano Suiza	Calshot.
9608 E	24.2.17	F.B.A.F. Boat	100	Mono	Calshot.
N1041 E	24.2.17	F.B.A.F. Boat	100	Mono	Killingholme.
N1042 E	24.2.17	F.B.A.F. Boat	100	Mono	Killingholme.
N1043 E	26.2.17	F.B.A.F. Boat	100	Mono	Calshot.
N1044 E	3.3.17	F.B.A.F. Boat	100	Mono	Calshot.
N1045 E	10.3.17	F.B.A.F. Boat	100	Mono	Killingholme.
N1046 E	17.3.17	F.B.A.F. Boat	100	Mono	Killingholme.
N1180 E	24.3.17	N.T. 2 B. F.B.	120	A.D...	K. Grain.
Approximate	deliveries	1	per week.		

SEAPLANES (REPAIR).

No.	Expected for trials.	Type.	H.p.	Engine.	Allocation.
3201		F.B.A.F. Boat	100	Mono	
3206		F.B.A.F. Boat	100	Mono	

ALLOCATED.

Westland.

AEROPLANES

No.	Expected for trials.	Type.	H.p.	Engine.	Allocation.
N5601 E	24.2.17	Sopwith 9700		None	Felixstowe.
N5602 E	24.2.17	Sopwith 9700		None	Felixstowe.
N5603 E	24.2.17	Sopwith 9700		None	Felixstowe.
N5604 E	24.2.17	Sopwith 9700		None	Felixstowe.
N5605 E	24.2.17	Sopwith 9400 S.		None	Cranwell.
N5606 E	24.2.17	Sopwith 9400 S.		None	Cranwell.
N5607 E	24.2.17	Sopwith 9400 S.		None	Felixstowe.
N5608 E	24.2.17	Sopwith 9400 S.		None	Felixstowe.
N5609 E	3.3.17	Sopwith 9400 S.		None	Felixstowe.
N5610 E	3.3.17	Sopwith 9400 S.		None	Felixstowe.
N5611 E	3.3.17	Sopwith 9400 S.		None	Felixstowe.
Approximate	deliveries	4-5	per week.		

SEAPLANES (NEW).

ALLOCATED (REPAIR).

J. S. White & Co.

AEROPLANES (NEW).

No.	Expected for trials.	Type.	H.p.	Engine.	Allocation.
9841 E	?	Wight Land	250	R.R.	Eastchurch (storage).
9843	Ready	Wight Land	250	R.R.	Eastchurch (storage).
9844	Ready	Wight Land	250	R.R.	Eastchurch (storage).
9845	Ready	Wight Land	250	R.R.	Eastchurch (storage).
8322 E	17.3.17	Wight School	100	Anzani	K.

SEAPLANES.

No.	Expected for trials.	Type.	H.p.	Engine.	Allocation.
1000	Engine repairs.	1000 Type	3-450	Sunbeam	Felixstowe.
9846 E	10.3.17	Converted to seaplane.	250	R.R.	Eastchurch (storage).

ALLOCATED.

French Machines.

AEROPLANES

No.	Expected for trials.	Type.	H.p.	Engine.	Allocation.
N3211	T26.12.16	Farman F. 40	160	Renault	E'church Gun.
N3212		Farman F. 40	160	Renault	E'church Gun.
N3213		Farman F. 40	160	Renault	E'church Gun.
N3215	T 5.1.17	Farman F. 40	160	Renault	Chingford.
N3216	T 5.1.17	Farman F. 40	160	Renault	Chingford.
N3217	T11.1.17	Farman F. 40	160	Renault	Chingford.
N3219	T16.1.17	Farman F. 40	160	Renault	Chingford.
N3220	T17.1.17	Farman F. 40	160	Renault	Cranwell.
N3221		Farman F. 40	160	Renault	Cranwell.
N3222	T22.1.17	Farman F. 40	160	Renault	Cranwell.
N3223	T24.1.17	Farman F. 40	160	Renault	Cranwell.
N3224	T26.1.17	Farman F. 40	160	Renault	Cranwell.
N3225		Farman F. 40	160	Renault	Dover.
N3226		Farman F. 40	160	Renault	Dover.
N3227		Farman F. 40	160	Renault	Dover.
N3228		Farman F. 40	160	Renault	Paris.
N3229		Farman F. 40	160	Renault	Hendon.

FUTURE ALLOCATION.

No.	Expected for trials.	Type.	H.p.	Engine.	Allocation.
10 in No.		H. Fmn Trop.	160	C. Unne	Roumania.
16 in No.		H. Fmn. L. Tank	160	C. Unne	Roumania.
1 per week		H. Fmn. S. Tank	160	C. Unne	Mudros.
1 in No.		Nieuport Single	130	Clerget	K. (E'church).
28 in No.		Nieuport Single	130	Clerget	Dunkirk.
3 in No.		Nieuport 2-str.	130	Clerget	Mudros.

SEAPLANES.

No.	Expected for trials.	Type.	H.p.	Engine.	Allocation.
9612		F.B.A.F. Boat		None	Killingholme.
9613		F.B.A.F. Boat		None	Killingholme.
9614		F.B.A.F. Boat		None	Killingholme.
9615		F.B.A.F. Boat		None	Killingholme.
9616		F.B.A.F. Boat		None	Killingholme.
9617		F.B.A.F. Boat		None	Killingholme.
9618		F.B.A.F. Boat		None	Killingholme.
9619		F.B.A.F. Boat		None	Killingholme.
9620		F.B.A.F. Boat		None	Killingholme.
9621		F.B.A.F. Boat		None	Killingholme.
9622		F.B.A.F. Boat		None	Killingholme.
9623		F.B.A.F. Boat		None	Killingholme.

SUMMARY.

NOTE.—These figures include machines wrecked and machines in store.

AEROPLANES.

Type.	H.p.	Engine.	Total, 28.1.17.	Add acceptances since.	Deduct deletions and transfers.	Present total.	Total, 28.1.17.	Add orders placed.	Deduct acceptances & orders cancelled	Present total.
WAR MACHINES. Class I.										
De Havilland 4	190	R.R.	..			..	51			51
De Havilland 4	250	R.R.	..			..	52			52
Farman F. 40	150	Renault	19	8		27	26		8	18
Handley Page	2–250	Rolls-Royce	12	1		13	26		1	25
Nieuport 1-seater	80	Rhone	19		1	18	..			..
Nieuport 2-seater	130	Clerget	7	2		9	3		2	1
Nieuport Single	130	Clerget	..	1		1	125		1	124
S.E. 5	200	Hispano	..			..	50	50*		..
Sopwith 9901	80	Rhone or Clerget.	37	21	4	54	187		21	166
Sopwith 9400 S	110	Clerget	65	5	1	69	63		5	58
Sopwith 9400 L	110	Clerget	11			11	1			1
Sopwith 9700	110	Clerget	88	18	3	103	88		18	70
Sopwith Single	130	Clerget	..			..	50			50
Sopwith Triplane	110	Clerget	22	15		37	100		15	85
Spad	150	Hispano	1			1	100	50		150
Total	..	..	281	71	9	343	922	50	121	851
WAR MACHINES. Class II.										
B.E. 2 C.	90	R.A.F.	84		2	82	..			..
B.E. 2 E.	75	R.R.	4			4	3			3
Breguet Concours	250	R.R.	2	2	1	3	11		2	9
Breguet Concours	250	Renault	..	11	8	3	11	11		..
Bristol Scout	80	Gnome	65	1		64	46		1	45
Bristol Scout	100	Mono	48	1		49	3		1	2
Caudron Twin	2–100	Anzani	17			17	20			20
H. Farman	135–160	C. Unne	50		2	48	37			37
Nieuport 2-seater	110	Clerget	71	1	4	68	8		1	7
Short Bomber	240	Sunbeam	10	3		13	5		3	2
Short Bomber	250	Rolls-Royce	24	2	1	25	7		2	5
Total	..	..	375	21	20	376	151		21	130
SCHOOL MACHINES.										
Avro Scout	80	Gnome	51		4	47	..			..
Avro Scout	100	Gnome	10			10	..			..
Avro 179 Type	80	Gnome	44	21	3	62	168		21	147
B.E. 2 C.	70–75	Renault	38			38	..			..
B.E. 2 C.	90	Curtiss	22		1	23	50			50
Caudron School	90	Anzani	47	14	5	56	29		14	15
Curtiss J.N. 3	90	Curtiss	28			28	..			..
Curtiss J.N. 4	90	Curtiss	74	3	3	74	30		3	27
Curtiss J.N. 4 Imp.	100	Curtiss	..			..	50			50
M. Farman Long.	70–80	Renault	54	14	2	66	118		14	104
M. Farman Short.	70–80	Renault	17	2		19	15		2	13
G.W. 1600 Type	60	Rhone	41		3	38	..			..
Sage School			..			..	30			30
Total	..	..	426	54	21	459	490		54	436
EXPERIMENTAL.										
A.W. Biplane	200	Sunbeam	1			1	..			..
A.W. Quad.	110	Clerget	..			..	3			3
Avro Fighter	2–190	Rolls-Royce	..			..	2			2
Blackburn T'plane	100	Mono	..			..	1			1
Curtiss R. 2	160	Curtiss	5	5		10	92		5	87
Dyott Fighter	2–120	A. Daimler	2			2	..			..
Fairey Fighter	2–190	R.R.	..			..	2			2
Parnall N't Flyer	200	Sunbeam	..			..	2			2
Robey Davis Gun	250	R.R.	..			..	2			2
Sopwith Triplane	150	Hispano	..			..	1			1
Sunbeam Type 7			..			..	2			2
Supermarine Quadruplane.	2–125	Anzani	..			..	2			2
Voisin Canon	150	C. Unne	1			1	..			..
Total	..	..	9	5		14	109		5	104
MISCELLANEOUS. For details *see* Monthly List.	..	..	64		2	62	36			36
Grand total	..	..	1155	151	56	1250	1708	50	201	1557

SEAPLANES.

Type.	H p.	Engine.	Total, 28.1.17.	Add acceptances since.	Deduct acetions and transfers.	Present total.	Total, 28.1.17.	Add orders placed.	Deduct acceptances.	Present total.
WAR MACHINES. Class I.										
A.D. F. Boat	190	R.R.	..			..	10			10
M. Farman	140	Hispano	..			..	50			50
Hamble Baby	130	Clerget	..			..	80			80
Large America	2–250	R.R.	1			1	83	10*		73
Porte F.B.	3–250	R.R.	1			1	20			20
Short 184—										
14-inch Torpedo	225	Sunbeam ⎫	89	1	7	83	1		1	..
14-inch Torpedo	240	Sunbeam ⎪	26	4	1	29	9		4	5
Single Bomber	225	Sunbeam ⎪	6			6	..			..
Single Bomber	240	Sunbeam ⎬	11			11	..			..
Improved	225	Sunbeam ⎪	8	1		9	43	1		42
Improved	240	Sunbeam ⎪	..			..	20			20
Improved	240	Renault ⎪	..			..	70			70
Experimental	..	Various ⎭	1			1	..			..
Short North Sea	310	Sunbeam	..			..	72			72
Short Torpedo	310	Sunbeam	1			1	36			36
Sopwith Baby	110	Clerget	42		3	39	99			99
Total	..	..	186	6	11	181	593		16	577
WAR MACHINES. Class II.										
Short S 827	150	Sunbeam	51	1	5	47	15		1	14
Short S 166	200	C. Unne	22			22	..			..
Short S 830	135–140	C. Unne	9	7		16	10		7	3
Sopwith Baby	100	Mono	28			28	..			..
Sopwith Schndr	100	Mono	54		7	47	..			..
Total	..	..	164	8	12	160	25		8	17
SCHOOL MACHINES.										
Avro Tractor	150	Sunbeam	5	4	1	..				..
Small America	2–100	Various	21	3	18	31				31
F.B.A. F. Boat	100	Mono	17	4	13	32				32
Sopwith 2-str.	100	Mono	..			..	20			20
W. & T. F. Boat	120	A. Daimler	3			3	16			10
Total	..	..	46	11	35	93				93
EXPERIMENTAL.										
A.D. 1,000 Type	3–450	Sunbeam	1			1	7			7
A.D. F. Boat	160	Sunbeam	..			..	2			2
A.D. Navyplane	140	Smith	..			..	7			7
Blackburn Twin	2–140	Smith	2			2	7			7
Blackburn Twin	2–160	Sunbeam	..			..	1			1
Blackburn Twin	2–190	R.R.	..			..	1			1
Cruiser	2–310	Sunbeam	..			..	2			2
Fairey Campania	250	R.R.	..			..	10			10
Fairey Type 3	190	R.R.	..			..	2			2
Mann Type 4	130	Clerget	..			..	1			1
P.V. 2	100	Mono	1			1	..			..
P.V. 4	150	Smith	..			..	1			1
Sopwith Imp. Baby	130	Clerget	..			..	2			2
Submarine Patrol	200	Sunbeam	..			..	6			6
Westland Type 4	130	Clerget	..			..	2			2
White Type 4	130	Clerget	..			..	2			2
Wight Baby	100	Mono	1			1	..			..
Wight School	100	Anzani	2			2	..			..
Total	..	..	7			7	53			53
MISCELLANEOUS. For details *see* Monthly List.	..	..	9			9	8			8
Grand total	..	..	412	14	34	392	772		24	748

* Order cancelled.

Proposed Orders

NOT IN CURRENT MONTHLY LIST.

Agenda No.	Numbers.	In No.	Type.	H.p.	Engine.	Maker.	Whether order placed.	Whether order cancelled.	Remarks.
AEROPLANES.									
203	N519, N520	2	H. Page Triplane	320	Sunbeam	Handley Page	No.		
209		4	Sopwith F. 1	130	Clerget	Sopwith	No.		
SEAPLANES.									
174		100	Flying Boats	140	Hispano		No.		
198		50	Fairey "Campania"	250	R.R.	Fairey	No.		
198		25	Short 184 Single	240	Renault		No.		
198		30	Short Torpedo	310	Sunbeam	Short	No.		
201		30	Large America	2–310	Sunbeam		No.		
205	N6030–N6079	50	Spad	150	Hispano	Nieuport E.	YES.		
206		1	A.B.F. Boat	190	R.R.	Supermarine	No.		

Proposed Cancellations

OF ORDERS IN CURRENT MONTHLY LIST.

Agenda No.	Numbers.	In No.	Type.	H.p.	Engine.	Maker.	Whether order placed.	Whether order cancelled.	Remarks.
AEROPLANES.									
	9286–9305	20	Caudron Twin	2–100	Anzani	British Caudron		No.	? to be delivered as spares.
174	9841–9860	20	Wight Land m/c	250	R.R.	J. S. White		No.	? to be converted to seaplanes.
193	9949	1	Robey-Davis	250	R.R.	Robey		No.	
193	1389	1	Supermarine Quad	2–125	Anzani	Supermarine Co.		No.	
193	N502	1	Blackburn Triplane	100	Mono	Blackburn		No.	
193	N511, N512	2	A.W. Quad	110	Clerget	Phœnix		No.	
200	N513	1	A.W. Biplane	200	Sunbeam	A.W. Co.		No.	
205	N6030–N6079	50	S.E. 5	200	Hispano	Nieuport E.		YES.	Changed to Spad.
SEAPLANES.									
198	N1360–N1389	30	Short North Sea	310	Sunbeam	Sunbeam		No.	
201	N1520–N1529	10	Large America	2–250	R.R.	Aircraft Co.		YES.	
201	9811–9820	10	Porte F. Boat	3–250	R.R.	Aircraft Co.		No.	

Number	Type.	Engine.	Ready.	Number	Type.	Engine.	Ready.

ANGLESEY NAVAL AIRSHIP STATION.
Flight Commander G. H. Scott in Command.
Telegrams : AIRSHIPS, LLANGEFNI.

Number	Type.	Engine.	Ready.
22	SS Type (B.E. 2 C)	75 hp. Renault ...	No.
24	SS Type (B.E. 2 C)	75 hp. Renault ...	**YES.**
25	SS Type (B.E. 2 C)	75 hp. Renault ...	**YES.**
33	SS Type (M.F.) ...	75 hp. Renault ...	No.

BARROW NAVAL AIRSHIP STATION.
Squadron Commander T. K. Elmsley in Command.
Telegrams : AIRSHIPS, BARROW-IN-FURNESS.

Number	Type.	Engine.	Ready.
34	SS Type (M.F.) ...	75 hp. Renault ...	No.
9	Rigid	4–180 hp. Maybach	No.

CRANWELL NAVAL AIR STATION.
Commodore J. Luce, C.B., R.N., in Command.
Telegrams : AVION, SLEAFORD.

Number	Type.	Engine.	Ready.
13	Coastal Type ...	2–150 hp. Sunbeam	**YES.**
31	SS Type (M.F.) ...	75 hp. Renault ...	**YES.**
39	SS Type (M.F.) ...	75 hp. Renault ...	No.

EAST FORTUNE NAVAL AIRSHIP STATION.
Squadron Commander J. W. O. Dalgleish in Command.
Telegrams : AIRSHIPS, ATHELSTANEFORD.

Number	Type.	Engine.	Ready.
15	Coastal Type ...	2–150 hp. Sunbeam	**YES.**
20	Coastal Type ...	2–150 hp. Sunbeam	**YES.**
24	Coastal Type ...	2–150 hp. Sunbeam	**YES.**
25	Coastal Type ...	2–150 hp. Sunbeam	No.

FOLKESTONE, NAVAL AIRSHIP STATION.
(with sub-station at St. Pol).
Flight Commander Hon. R. Coke in Command.
Telegrams : AIRSHIPS, DOVER.

Number	Type.	Engine.	Ready.
0	SS Type Pusher ...	80 hp. R.R. ...	**YES.**
4	SS Type (B.E. 2 C)	75 hp. Renault ...	**YES.**
10B	SS Type (B.E. 2 C).	75 hp. Renault ...	No.
11	SS Type (B.E. 2 C)	75 hp. Renault ...	No.
12	SS Type (B.E. 2 C)	75 hp. Renault ...	**YES.**
29	SS Type (M.F.) ...	75 hp. Renault ...	**YES.**
23	Coastal Type ...	2–150 hp. Sunbeam	**YES.**

AIRSHIP DETACHMENT No 2—FOREIGN SERVICE.

Number	Type.	Engine.	Ready.
3	SS Type (B.E. 2 C)	75 hp. Renault ...	
7	SS Type (B.E. 2 C)	75 hp. Renault ...	
8	SS Type (B.E. 2 C)	75 hp. Renault ...	
17	SS Type (B.E. 2 C)	75 hp. Renault ...	
19	SS Type (B.E. 2 C)	75 hp. Renault ...	

HOWDEN NAVAL AIRSHIP STATION.
Wing Commander F. L. M. Boothby in Command.
Telegrams : AIRSHIPS, HOWDEN.

Number	Type.	Engine.	Ready.
4	Coastal Type ...	2–150 hp. Sunbeam	**YES.**
11	Coastal Type	1–150 hp. Sunbeam / 1–220 Renault ...	**YES.**
19	Coastal Type	1–150 hp. Sunbeam / 1–220 Renault ...	No.
21	Coastal Type	1–150 hp. Sunbeam / 1–220 Renault ...	No.
4	Parseval Type	2–180 hp. Maybach	**YES.**
6	Parseval Type ...	2–180 hp. Maybach	No.

KINGSNORTH NAVAL AIRSHIP STATION.
Wing Commander C. R. Dane, R.N., in Command.
Telegrams : AIRSHIPS, HOO.

Number	Type.	Engine.	Ready.
1	Coastal Type ...	2–150 hp. Sunbeam	**YES.**
2	Coastal Type ...	2–150 hp. Sunbeam	No.
14	SS Type (B.E. 2C)	75 hp. Renault ...	No.
40	SS Type (Armstrong)	100 hp. Green ...	**YES.**
1	NS Type ...	2–250 hp. R.R. ...	No.
2	NS Type ...	2–250 hp. R.R. ...	Building.
1	SSP Type	75–85 hp. R.R. ...	No.

KIRKWALL NAVAL AIRSHIP STATION.
Flight Lieutenant C. W. C. Brown in Command.

Number	Type.	Engine.	Ready.
41	SS Type (Armstrong)	100 hp. Green ...	No
43	SS Type (Armstrong)	100 hp. Green ...	No.

LARNE NAVAL AIRSHIP STATION.
Caretakers.
Telegrams : AIRSHIPS, WHITEHEAD.

LONGSIDE NAVAL AIRSHIP STATION.
Wing Commander J. N. Fletcher in Command.
Telegrams : AIRSHIPS, LONGSIDE.

Number	Type.	Engine.	Ready.
10A	Coastal Type ...	2–150 hp. Sunbeam	No.
7	Coastal Type ...	2–150 hp. Sunbeam	No.
14	Coastal Type ...	2–150 hp. Sunbeam	**YES.**
18	Coastal Type ...	2–150 hp. Sunbeam	**YES.**

LUCE BAY NAVAL AIRSHIP STATION.
Flight Commander I. H. B. Hartford in Command.
Telegrams : AIRSHIPS, STRANRAER.

Number	Type.	Engine.	Ready.
20	SS Type (B.E. 2 C)	75 hp. Renault ...	**YES.**
23	SS Type (B.E. 2 C)	75 hp. Renault ...	**YES.**
35	SS Type (M.F.) ...	75 hp. Renault ...	**YES.**
38	SS Type (M.F.) ...	75 hp. Renault ...	**YES.**

MULLION NAVAL AIRSHIP STATION.
Squadron Commander Hon. C. M. P. Brabazon in Command.
Telegrams : AIRSHIPS, CURY-CROSS-LANES.

Number	Type.	Engine.	Ready.
9	Coastal Type ...	2–150 hp. Sunbeam	**YES.**
5A	Coastal Type ...	2–150 hp. Sunbeam	No.
22	Coastal Type ...	2–150 hp. Sunbeam	**YES.**

PEMBROKE NAVAL AIRSHIP STATION.
Flight Commander H. C. Fuller in Command.
Telegrams : AIRSHIPS, PEMBROKE DOCK.

Number	Type.	Engine.	Ready.
37	SS Type (M.F.) ...	75 hp. Renault ...	No.
3	Coastal Type ...	2–150 hp. Sunbeam	**YES.**
6	Coastal Type ...	2–150 hp. Sunbeam	**YES.**

POLEGATE NAVAL AIRSHIP STATION.
Flight Commander I. Fraser in Command.
Telegrams : AIRSHIPS, POLEGATE.

Number	Type.	Engine.	Ready.
5	SS Type (B.E. 2 C)	75 hp. Renault ...	**YES.**
6	SS Type (B.E. 2 C)	75 hp. Renault ...	**YES.**
13	SS Type (B.E. 2 C)	75 hp. Renault ...	**YES.**
16	SS Type (B.E. 2 C)	75 hp. Renault ...	**YES.**
30	SS Type (M.F.) ...	75 hp. Renault ...	No
9A	SS Type (B.E. 2 C)	75 hp. Renault ...	**YES.**
12	Coastal Type ...	2–150 hp. Sunbeam	No.

PULHAM NAVAL AIRSHIP STATION.
Wing Captain E. M. Maitland in Command.
Telegrams : AIRSHIPS, PULHAM.

Number	Type.	Engine.	Ready.
28	SS Type (M.F.) ...	75 hp. Renault ...	No.
17	Coastal Type ...	2–150 hp. Sunbeam	**YES.**
26	Coastal Type ...	2–150 hp. Sunbeam	No.
27	Coastal Type ...	2–150 hp. Sunbeam	**YES.**

WORMWOOD SCRUBBS NAVAL AIRSHIP STATION.
Wing Commander C. M. Waterlow in Command.
Telegrams : AIRSTATION, SHEPHERDS, LONDON.

Number	Type.	Engine.	Ready.
32A	SS Type (M.F.) ...	75 hp. Renault ...	Rebuilding
36	SS Type (M.F.) ...	75 hp. Renault ...	No.
42A	SS Type (Armstrong)	100 hp. Green ...	Rebuilding

KITE BALLOON SECTIONS.

Roehampton Naval Training Station.

Squadron Commander H. Delacombe in Command.

No. 1 SECTION—EAST AFRICA.
Flight Lieutenant D. Gill in Command.
H.M.S. "MANICA," 4,120 tons.

No. 2 SECTION—GRAIN.
Flight Lieutenant R. S. Smith in Command.

No. 3 SECTION—
Flight Lieutenant F. R. Sadd in Command.
H.M.S. "CANNING."

No. 4 SECTION—
Re-forming.

No. 5 SECTION—GRAND FLEET.
Flight Lieutenant T. F. Morris in Command.
H.M.S. "MENELAUS," 4,672 tons.

No. 6 SECTION—
Re-forming.

No. 7 SECTION—MUDROS.
Flight Lieutenant B. C. Windeler in Command.

No. 8 SECTION—
Re-forming.

No. 9 SECTION—DUNKIRK.
Flight Sub-Lieutenant C. W. Spencer in Command.
Maintenance Party Only.
Barge "ARCTIC."

No. 10 SECTION—CRANWELL.
Flight Lieutenant K. C. Cleaver in Command

No. 11 SECTION—DUNKIRK
Flight Lieutenant B. Gregg in Command.

No. 12 SECTION—
Re-forming.

No. 13 SECTION—ADEN.
Flight Lieutenant H. E. Crawfurd in Command.

No. 14 SECTION—MESOPOTAMIA.
Commander F. R. Wrottesley, R.N., in Command.

No. 15 SECTION—GRAND FLEET.
Flight Lieutenant E. A. O. A. Jamieson in Command.
H.M.S. "CITY OF OXFORD."

No 16 SECTION—GRAND FLEET.
Flight Lieutenant S. Bell in Command.
H.M.S. "CAMPANIA."

SUMMARY OF ACCESSORIES—W.T.

NOTE.—For machines fitted with power-driven wireless, *see* under lists of machines on stations.

—	Shore sets.	Light transmitters.	Receivers.	—	Shore sets.	Light transmitters.	Receivers.
HOME STATIONS.				**SEAPLANE CARRIERS.**			
Anglesey	YES	5	5	"Ark Royal"	YES	9	.
Barrow	YES	1	3	"Campania"	YES	9	9
Calshot	YES	6	6	"Engadine"		3	3
Cranwell	YES	7	24	"Riviera"		1	3
Dover aeroplanes	YES	2	1	"Vindex"		2	2
Dundee	YES	6	4	Carriers, Port Said	YES	8	2
Eastbourne	YES	..	..				
Eastchurch	YES	5	6				
Felixstowe	YES	12	7				
Grain	YES	3	7	**STATIONS AND FORCES ABROAD.**			
Howden	YES	4	6				
Killingholme	YES	4	7				
Kingsnorth	YES	1	9	Dover-Dunkirk seaplanes	YES	2	2
Kirkwall	YES	2	3	Dunkirk aeroplanes	YES	12	12
Longside	YES	5	5	East African Field Force	YES	3	3
Luce Bay	YES	4	5	Eastern Mediterranean	YES	9	6
Mullion	YES	3	3	Gibraltar	YES	4	1
Pembroke	YES	3	5	Luxeuil		..	..
Polegate	YES	4	4	Vendome		..	..
Westgate	YES	5	5				
Yarmouth	YES	1	9				

DISTRIBUTION OF FORCES.

Command.	Airship Stations.	Aeroplane and Seaplane Stations.	Sub-stations and Landing Grounds.	Seaplane Carriers.	Kite Balloons.	
					Section.	Location.
Admiralty		Hendon (A.) .. Paris (A) Vendome (A) Luxeuil (A.)— No. 3 Wing with	Crystal Pal. Depôt Ochey (A)		No. 2 No. 4 No. 6 } Re-forming. No. 8 No. 12 No. 3	H.M.S. "Canning."
Commodore, Cranwell	Cranwell .. .	Cranwell (A) with Chingford (A) with Eastbourne (A) with Redcar (A) for training	{ Frieston (L) { Windermere (S) Fairlop (L) Ringmer (L)		No. 10 .. Cranwell.	
Captain Supt., White City.	Wormwood Scrubbs		White City Depôt Wormw'd Scrubbs Depôt		Training Roehampton.	
C.-in-C., Home Fleets	Kirkwall (for operations).			H.M.S. "Campania" (S) H.M.S. "Manxman" (S) H.M.S. "Engadine" (S)	No. 16 No. 15 No. 5	H.M.S. "Campania." H.M.S. "City of Oxford." H.M.S. "Menelaus."
V.A.C., Orkneys and Shetlands.	Kirkwall (for administration).		Scapa (shore base for H.M.S. "Campania").			
C.-in-C., Rosyth ..	East Fortune .. Longside .. .. Luce Bay (for administration).	Dundee (S) .. .. East Fortune (A) ..				
R.A.C., E. Coast of England.	Howden	Killingholme (S) .. Redcar (A), under Comm., Cranwell, for training. South Shields (S) (for operations).	..	Fleet Messenger 59 (S) (P.S. "Killingholme")		
S.N.O., Tyne		South Shields (S) (for administration).				
Commodore-in-Charge, Naval Base, Lowestoft	Pulham	Yarmouth (AS) with	{ Aldeburgh (N) .. Bacton (N) .. { Burgh Castle (N) Covehithe (N) .. Holt (N) ..	Fleet Messenger 60 (S) (P.S. "Brocklesby")		
Commodore-in-Charge, Harwich.	..	Felixstowe (AS) ..	Trimley (N) ..			
Commodore (T) ..	..			H.M.S. "Vindex" (AS)		
C.-in-C., the Nore .. Divisional Commander of Air Stations, the Nore.	Kingsnorth	Eastchurch (A) with { Observers' Sch. { Gunnery School { Flying School.. Nore Flight, Felixstowe (S) Grain Island (AS) .. Port Victoria (Depôt) Westgate (AS) with	Leysdown (A) .. { Manstone (A) .. { Detling (A) ..			

A = Aeroplane Force.   S = Seaplane Force.   AS = Mixed Force.   N = Night landing-ground.   L = Landing-ground.

Command.	Airship Stations.	Aeroplane and Seaplane Stations.	Sub-stations and Landing Grounds.	Seaplane Carriers.	Kite Balloons. Section.	Kite Balloons. Location.
Vice-Admiral, Dover..	Folkestone (with sub-station at St. Pol). Polegate	Dover Aerodrome (A) Dover Seaplanes (S) Dunkirk Wings— No. 1, St. Pol (A). No. 4, Petite Synthe (A). No. 5, Coudekerke (A). Seaplane Stn. (S). Repair Depôt ..		H.M.S. " Riviera " (S)	No. 9 No. 11	Barge " Arctic." Dunkirk.
C.-in-C., Portsmouth..		Calshot (S)	Bembridge ..			
C.-in-C., Devonport ..	Mullion	Newlyn (S) .. .. Scilly Isles (S) .. Plymouth (S) ..				
Vice - Admiral, Old Milford.	Pembroke	Fishguard (S) ..				
S.N.O., Holyhead ..	Anglesey .. .. Barrow					
Rear-Admiral, Larne..	Luce Bay (for operations). Larne (Caretakers) ..					
S.N.O., Gibraltar ..		Gibraltar (S) ..				
S.N.O., Malta.. ..		Malta (S)				
S.N.O., Adriatic ..		Otranto (S)				
Vice-Admiral, East Med. Squadron.	Kassandra .. .. (No. 2 Detachment)	Mudros and Aegean bases (AS). No. 2 Wing ..		H.M.S. "Ark Royal" (S). " Empress " (S). ..	No. 7	Mudros.
C.-in-C., East Indies..	.. ..	.. ..		H.M.S. " Anne " (S). H.M.S. "Raven II." (S)	No. 13 No. 14	Aden Mesopotamia.
C.-in-C., Cape ..	.. ..	East African Field Force (A). Cape Station (S) ..			No. 1	H.M.S. " Manica."

A = Aeroplane Force.   S = Seaplane Force.   AS = Mixed Force.   N = Night landing-ground.   L = Landing-ground.

Machines Transferred from Royal Naval Air Service.

To War Office.

AEROPLANES.

Avro 179..	.. ..	80-h.p. Gnome..	13
B.E. 2 C..	.. ..	70-h.p. Renault	36
Bristol Scout	.. ..	None (for 100 Mono) 14 all re-transferred	
Curtiss J N 3	.. ..	90-h.p. Curtiss	90
Curtiss J N 4	.. ..	90-h.p. Curtiss..	11
De Havilland 2 ..	.. ..	100-h.p. Mono	1
H. Farman	.. ..	140-h.p. C. Unne	6
H. Farman	.. ..	150-h.p. C. Unne	1
M. Farman	.. ..	70-h.p. Renault	13
Nieuport (Beardmore) ..		110-h.p. Clerget	20
Nieuport (French)		110-h.p. Rhone	14
Short Bomber	.. ..	250 R.R.	17
Sopwith 9400 S...	.. ..	110-h.p. Clerget	24
Sopwith 9400 S...	.. ..	None	46
Sopwith Triplane	..	130-h.p. Clerget	1
Vickers 32	.. ..	100-h.p. Gnome	8
Vickers 32	.. ..	None	6
Voisin	.. ..	150-h.p. Unne	3
			310

SEAPLANES.

Short 827	.. ..	150-h.p. Sunbeam	1

To Belgian Government.

SEAPLANES.

Short 827 type ..	..	150-h.p. Sunbeam	4

To French Government.

AEROPLANES.

Caudron Twin ..	..	2–100 Anzani	7
Short Bomber ..	..	250-h.p. R.R.	1
Sopwith 9400 ..	..	(Machines without engines).. ..	7
Sopwith 9700 ..	..	110-h.p. Clerget	5
Sopwith 9700 ..	..	(No engines)	16
Sopwith 9400 S. ..	..	110 h.p. Clerget	1
			37

SEAPLANES.

Short 184 type ..	..	225-h.p. Sunbeam	2
Sopwith Baby (Clerget)		None	1
Sopwith Baby ..	..	110-h.p. Clerget	2
			5

To South African Government.

AEROPLANES.

B.E. 2 C ..	.. ..	70-h.p. Renault	2

To Australian Government.

AEROPLANES.

Bristol Scout ..	..	100-h.p. Mono	1
G. W. Box Kites ..	..	60-h.p. Rhone	2
			3

To Northern Aircraft Company.

SEAPLANES.

Nieuport Tractor ..	..	80-h.p. Rhone	2

To Japanese Government.

SEAPLANES.

Short 184 type ..	..	225-h.p. Sunbeam	1
Sopwith Baby ..	..	100-h.p. Gnome	1
			2

To Italian Government.

SEAPLANES.

Sopwith Baby ..	..	100 h.p Gnome	2

Engines Transferred to Royal Naval Air Service.

From War Office.

100-h.p. R.A.F. ..	.. ..	..	111
80-h.p. Renault ..	.. ..	..	36
80-h.p. Clerget ..	.. ..	..	11
			158

For Transfer from Royal Naval Air Service.

No.	Location.	Total.	Type.	H.p.	Engine.	For.
AEROPLANES						
N6015	Parnalls ..		Avro 179 Dual	80	Gnome ..	R.F.C.
N6016	Parnalls ..		Avro 179 Dual	80	Gnome ..	R.F.C.
N6017	Parnalls ..		Avro 179 Dual	80	Gnome ..	R.F.C.
N6018	Parnalls ..		Avro 179 Dual	80	Gnome ..	R.F.C.
N6019	Parnalls ..		Avro 179 Dual	80	Gnome ..	R.F.C.
N6020	Parnalls ..	6	Avro 179 Dual	80	Gnome ..	R.F.C.
?	France	10	H. Fmn. S. Tank	160	C. Unne ..	Roumania.
?	France	16	H. Fmn. L. Tank	160	C. Unne ..	Roumania.
N5235	Mann, Eg.		Sopwith 9400 S.		None ..	Belgian Gov.
N5236	Mann, Eg.		Sopwith 9400 S.		None ..	Belgian Gov.
N5237	Mann, Eg.		Sopwith 9400 S.		None	Belgian Gov.
N5238	Mann, Eg.		Sopwith 9400 S.		None ..	Belgian Gov.
N5239	Mann, Eg.		Sopwith 9400 S.		None ..	Belgian Gov.
N5240	Mann, Eg.		Sopwith 9400 S.		None ..	Belgian Gov.
N5241	Mann, Eg.		Sopwith 9400 S.		None ..	Belgian Gov.
N5242	Mann, Eg.	8	Sopwith 9400 S.		None ..	Belgian Gov.
N5233	C.S.D.	1	Sopwith 9400 S.	110	Clerget ..	
N5527	Sopwith	1	Sopwith 9700	130	Clerget ..	
3118	Manstone	1	H. Page ..	2–250	R.R. ..	French Gov.
SEAPLANES.						
FOR TRANSFER TO R.N.A.S.						
2324	R.F.C. ..	1	B.E. 2 E ..	75	R.R ..	Cranwell.
11 in No.	R.F.C.	1	B.E. 2 C ..	90	R.A.F. ..	C.S.D.
6326	R.F.C. ..	1	B.E. 2 E ..		None ..	C.S.D.
6327	R.F.C. ..	4	B.E. 2 E ..		None ..	C.S.D.
A 101	R.F.C. ..	1	De Havilland 4	190	R.R. ..	

Machines Transferred to Royal Naval Air Service.

From War Office.

AEROPLANES.

Avro 179 Dual ..	..	None	4
B.E. 2 B ..	.. ..	70-h.p. Renault	2
B.E. 2 C ..	.. ..	90-h.p. R.A.F.	2
B.E. 2 C ..	.. ..	None (R.A.F.)..	20
B.E. 2 C ..	.. ..	None (Renault)	10
B.E. 2 E ..	.. ..	75 R.R.	1
B.E. 2 E ..	.. ..	90 R.A.F.	1
B.E. 2 E ..	.. ..	None	2
B.E. 8 ..	.. ..	80-h.p. Gnome	1
Bristol Scout ..	..	80-h.p. Gnome	8
De H. 2 ..	..	100-h.p. Mono	1
M. Farman L. ..	..	70-h.p. Renault	14
M. Farman S. ..	..	80-h.p. Renault	4
R.E. 5 ..	.. ..	120-h.p. A. Daimler	1
R.E. 7 ..	.. ..	None	5
			76

From War Office.

SEAPLANES.

R.A.F. ..	.. ..	90-h.p. Renault	1
R.A.F. ..	.. ..	100-h.p. Renault	1
R.A.F. ..	..	None	1
			3

Engines Transferred from Royal Naval Air Service.

To War Office.

80-h.p. Rhone ..	.. ..	..	2
110-h.p. Rhone ..	.. ..	..	15
135-h.p. C. Unne..	.. ..	..	2
200-h.p. C. Unne..	.. ..	..	4
110-h.p. Clerget ..	.. ..	..	20
90-h.p. Curtiss O.X.	.. ..	..	2
225-h.p. Sunbeam ..	.. ..	..	3
200-h.p. Sunbeam ..	.. ..	..	1
100-h.p. Gnome Mono ..	.. ..	..	12
			61

Leonard Bridgman's wash painting portrays Sopwith Ship's Pup N6452, which made the world's first deck landing, aboard HMS *Furious*, on 2 August 1917, piloted by Sqn Cdr E.H. Dunning DSC, in company with fellow Ship's Pup N6454, fitted with a skid undercarriage and an upward-firing Lewis gun.

RNAS East Fortune

The RNAS air station at East Fortune in Scotland was established in 1915, its main purpose being to defend Edinburgh and the Firth of Forth against attack by German airships. It was assumed that the main threat would come from night attacks from the southeast. These hitherto unpublished photographs have been printed from a relatively recently acquired collection of original glass negatives which unfortunately contained no clues as to dates or the identities of the persons depicted, but evidence suggests that they were almost certainly taken during 1917, the same year that the Disposition of Aircraft featured in this volume was compiled.

Bristol Scout D serial 8992, powered by a 100 h.p. monosoupape rotary, spent its whole life at East Fortune, being delivered to the station's Naval Flying School (NFS) for erection on 30 October 1916. While being flown by Flt Sub-Lt H G Leslie on 13 June 1917 its chassis was completely wrecked and its propeller and 'nosepiece' broken. Then, on 31 July its undercarriage and propeller were broken in the mishap depicted here. It was still with East Fortune NFS on 30 March 1918. In the Disposition it was listed as 'ready', its roles being described as 'C.P. & F.T.'; presumably coastal patrol and flying training.

Personnel pose with another Bristol Scout in a hangar. A noteworthy feature visible here is a curved metal deflector plate on the fuselage underside, in line with the lower wing leading edges. These have been observed on both Bristol Scouts and Sopwith Pups, and though their intended purpose is uncertain, it seems probable that they were fitted to keep either the slipstream or the oil from the rotary engine's total-loss castor oil lubrication system from entering the cockpit.

This Beardmore-built 80 h.p. Le Rhone powered Sopwith Ship's Pup exhibits a similar deflector plate, this time located immediately behind the engine, at the forward fuselage firewall/bulkhead. According to the Disposition, the Sopwith '9901s' were allocated 'for other stations'; actually HMS *Manxman* and 'fleet use'.

A frontal close-up of a Bristol Scout, again with the underfuselage deflector plate in evidence. On this aircraft type an extension of the control column protruded through the cockpit floor, so there must have been a tendency for burnt castor oil to find its way into the cockpit. The propeller bears a Bristol Propeller trademark transfer.

A Sopwith 9901 Ship's Pup after a landing mishap. This aircraft has the Admiralty tripod mounting for a Lewis gun firing upwards through the cut-out in the upper wing centre-section. The transfer on the propeller is the trademark of the Lang Propeller Company.

One of several Beardmore-built Royal Aircraft Factory B.E.2Cs that were on strength at East Fortune in 1917 for night-flying operations. This one, which lacks the wingtip brackets for Holt flares usually fitted to night-flying aeroplanes, is carrying a brace of bombs on carriers immediately aft of the rear undercarriage struts.

A cheery-looking group with a B.E.2C for company. Note the brass ignition switch by the cockpit rim and the priming pump immediately beneath it.

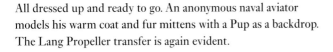

All dressed up and ready to go. An anonymous naval aviator models his warm coat and fur mittens with a Pup as a backdrop. The Lang Propeller transfer is again evident.

Accommodation at East Fortune. The 'beds' appear to be nothing more than boards with mattresses laid on them, and seating takes the form of benches and deck chairs. Presumably to diffuse the light, the lampshades are draped with tasselled covers, apparently embroidered with winged motifs.

A North Sea Class non-rigid airship displays its tapered, trilobal envelope as it sets off on patrol. This is one of the early-form North Sea airships, with a pair of 250 h.p. Rolls-Royce Eagle engines mounted on a framework aft and slightly higher than the crew car, and linked to it by a wooden walkway, with a small cabin between the engines for the two engineers. Troublesome long propeller shafts turned two four-bladed pusher propellers.

An evocative Leonard Bridgman wash painting showing Sopwith 2F.1 Ship's Camel N7129 over HMS *Argus*, the world's first flush-deck aircraft carrier. Both were built by William Beardmore & Co Ltd.

Royal Naval Air Service Communiques Nos 1 to 14

These rare documents, issued by RNAS Headquarters at Dunkirk ("Dunkerque") and covering the period from 2 July 1917 to 31 January 1918, also came to light among Owen Thetford's papers. The first five were produced as sets of single-sided mimeographed pages, but from No.6 onwards they became properly printed reports, printed on both sides of each sheet. They all carried the facsimile signature or authorisation of Wing Captain F.C. Halahan, RN, for the Senior Officer, RNAS. Although units and aircraft types are usually identified, the identities of individual aircraft are frustratingly absent. However, those familiar with personnel will recognise many of the aircrew mentioned.

ROYAL NAVAL AIR SERVICE. FORTNIGHTLY COMMUNIQUE. – NO. 1.

JULY 2ND. Four reconnaissances were carried out by No.2 Squadron to ZEEBRUGGE and OSTENDE to observe shipping. 31 photographs were taken. Shipping normal. Several Smoke Screens seen.

Five offensive patrols were carried out by No. 4 Wing.

ENEMY AIRCRAFT. Two indecisive combats with E.A. driven down in each case.

BOMBING RAID. A bombing attack on shipping in BRUGES DOCKS was attempted by 5 D.H. 4's of No. 5 Squadron, but was not pressed home owing to our formation being attacked by hostile scouts.

JULY 3RD. Three special reconnaissances were carried out by No. 2 Squadron to locate movements of hostile Torpedo craft, reported between NIEUPORT and OSTENDE, and results reported by W/T. Otherwise shipping normal.

Six offensive patrols were carried out by No. 4 Wing.

ENEMY AIRCRAFT. Act.Flight Comdr CHALWICK attacked and drove down a small two seater E.A. out of control in a vertical nose dive. There were also two indecisive combats, but E.A. driven down in each case.

BOMBING RAID. No. 5 Squadron at midday by 5 D.H.4. Machines, four 65lb and forty-eight 16lb bombs were dropped on AMMUNITION DUMP at LICHTERVELDE. – Direct hits causing clouds of smoke. Direct hits on RAILWAY STATION and YARD.

No. 7 Squadron by night. Eight Handley Page machines dropped eighty four 112lb bombs on BRUGES DOCKS. One large explosion caused, also a fire which burnt fiercely for several minutes.

JULY 4TH. Visibility poor. No reconnaissances.

Six offensive patrols by No. 4 Wing.

ENEMY AIRCRAFT. On morning of 4th, a formation of 16 GOTHA twin engine E.A. were met by a flight of 5 Camels of No. 4 Squadron sent to intercept them, and a general running flight took place. Flight. Sub. Lieut. S.E. ELLIS drove down one machine smoking and completely out of control. Flight Commander A.E. SHOOK drove down another machine in flames. Another E.A. engaged by Flight Sub.Lieut. A.J. ENSTONE was driven down damaged, using only one engine, and forced to land near OSTENDE. The same pilot then drove down another machine low over HOLLAND, but apparently under control.

BOMBING RAID. By night. 9 Handley Page machines.
(a). Thirty-six 112lb and twelve 65lb were dropped on GHISTELLES Aerodrome.
(b). Twenty-four 112lb Bombs were dropped on HOUTTAVE-NIEUMUNSTER Aerodrome.
(c). Ten 112lb were dropped on enemy train on BRUGES – OSTENDE – LICHTERVELDE line.
(d). Twelve 112lb were dropped on SEAPLANE BASE, OSTENDE.

JULY 6TH. No reconnaissances. Visibility too poor.

Seven offensive patrols.

ENEMY AIRCRAFT. Act.Flight. Comdr. CHADWICK and Flight Sub.Lieut. S.E. ELLIS destroyed a large 2 seater Albatross [*sic*: the incorrect spelling of Albatros is used throughout the reports. Ed.], which was spotting off NIEUPORT, one wing of the E.A. coming off in the air after it had been driven down smoking.

One other indecisive combat took place.

<u>BOMBING RAID</u>. No. 5 Squadron. D.H.4 machines. By day.

Three 65lb and thirty-six 16lb bombs were dropped on GHISTELLES Aerodrome. The bombs caused a fire in one of the sheds.

<u>JULY 7TH</u>. One coastal reconnaissance by No. 2 Squadron to OSTENDE and ZEEBRUGGE. – No enemy shipping activity.

Six offensive patrols.

<u>ENEMY AIRCRAFT</u>. On information being received that E.A. had sent bombing machines to England, large formations from Nos.3 and 4 Squadrons, and a flight of Seaplane pilots in Pup machines proceeded to try and intercept them on their return, and during these patrols many actions took place with Seaplanes and Fighters E.A. who were sent to escort the E.Bombers home. FLIGHT.SUB.LIEUT.J.S.T.FALL of No. 3 Squadron attacked three hostile single seater Scouts at 18,500 ft, and shot one down in flames. He was then attacked by the other two so spun down 5,000 ft, and then dived for the lines, which he crossed at 2,000 ft.

FLIGHT.SUB.LIEUT.FALL while leading his flight attacked 3 E. Seaplanes, killing the Observer of one of them, and the remainder of his flight continued to drive it down smoking badly, until it crashed in the sea.

FLIGHT.SUB.LIEUT. J.A. GLEN attacked one of the two remaining Seaplanes. Machine dived straight into the water from 15,000 ft and sank at once, only pieces of the planes [i.e. wings] remaining afloat. The third Seaplane was driven down and completely crashed in the sea by FLT.SUB.LT's GLEN, ROCHFORD, FALL, ABBOTT and ARMSTRONG.

FLIGHT. SUB.LIEUT. FALL subsequently attacked and destroyed, in conjunction with FLIGHT SUB LIEUT. GLEN, a third seaplane belonging to another flight of 3. This seaplane also crashed in the water.

<u>ENEMY AIRCRAFT</u>. FLIGHT.SUB.LIEUT. ENSTONE attacked a two-seater Seaplane, which had no passenger, following it down to about 300 ft from the sea, firing all the way, and then he lost sight of it as this machine was very carefully "camouflaged", so that it was difficult to see close to the water. – a seaplane floating floats up was seen here later.

FLIGHT.SUB.LIEUT.BUSBY attacked two two-seater D.F.W.'s and drove one down over the sea out of control.

Several other machines were engaged and driven down, apparently under control.

It is very difficult to accurately assess the machines destroyed, but there is no doubt that in all 3 Seaplanes and one Scout aeroplane were destroyed, and one seaplane and two aeroplanes driven down out of control.

One of our machines fell into the sea, due to engine failure, but was very smartly and gallantly rescued by French Naval Torpedo Craft, from well within range of the enemy shore batteries.

<u>BOMBING RAID</u>. No. 7 Squadron. Handley Page machines. By night.

(a). Fourteen 112lb bombs were dropped on GOUTRODE AERODROME.

(b). Sixty-two 112lb and twenty-four 65lb bombs were dropped on ST DENIS WESTREM AERODROME.

(c). Fourteen 112lb bombs were dropped on RAILWAY LINES, E. of LICHTERVELDE.

(d). Twelve 65lb bombs were dropped on GHISTELLES AERODROME.

This flight was heavily attacked by large formations, but dropped its bombs, and returned safely, though much shot about.

<u>JULY 10TH</u>. One photographic reconnaissance – E. of OSTENDE.

Six offensive patrols were carried out.

Numerous photographs of OSTENDE HARBOUR and ENEMY AERODROMES were taken.

ENEMY AIRCRAFT. A formation of 5 E.A. (D.F.W. 2-Seaters) was attacked by a patrol of No. 3 Squadron and driven Eastwards. There was no decisive result.

A flight of 5 machines of No.4 Squadron attacked three two-seater E.A., and were in time [*sic*: turn?] attacked by 10 enemy Albatross Scouts. ACT.FLIGHT.COMDR.CHADWICK shot down one Scout completely out of control, and assisted by FLIGHT.SUB.LIEUT. R.M. KIERSTEAD, shot down a second completely out of control. Two other Albatross Scouts were driven down but apparently under control. Several other indecisive encounters occurred.

JULY 11TH. Usual offensive patrols.

EMEMY AIRCRAFT. Two indecisive encounters, but the E.A. broke off the fight by diving steeply.

BOMBING RAID. By night. No. 7 squadron. Handley Page machines.
(a). Twenty-four 112lb bombs were dropped on VARSSENAERE AERODROME and DUMP, causing a heavy explosion and big fire.
(b). Eleven 112lb bombs were dropped on ST DENNIS WESTREM AERODROME.
(c). Fifty-one 112lb bombs were dropped on GHISTELLES AERODROME.
(d). Twenty-eight 112lb bombs and twenty-four 50lb bombs were dropped on OSTENDE ELECTRIC POWER STATION and RAILWAY LINES, causing a fire. The RAILWAY SIDING at ZARREN was also fired at by 6 pdr-Davis Gun, - 8 rounds being fired.
(e). Two 112lb bombs were dropped on a train near ST.DENNIS WESTREM.

JULY 12TH. Successful reconnaissances were carried out over OSTENDE HARBOUR, AERODROME and BATTERIES. Plates were exposed and excellent photograph[s] resulted.
Usual offensive patrols.

EMEMY AIRCRAFT. Several indecisive engagements took place owing to the Photographic Reconnaissance being attacked by hostile scouts, which were all drive off, - one machine being drive down but under control.

BOMBING RAID.   No. 5 Squadron. At dawn. D.H.4. and Sopwith Bombers.
(a).   One 65lb, twelve 16lb, and thirty-five Le-Pecq bombs were dropped on GHISTELLES AERODROME, causing a small fire.

No. 7 Squadron. By night. Handley Page machines.
(a).   Fourteen 112lb bombs were dropped on GHISTELLES AERODROME.
(b).   Twelve 112lb bombs were dropped on AERTRYCKE AERODROME, causing a bright flare, possibly a fire.
(c).   Twelve 112lb and twelve 65lb bombs were dropped on HOUTTAVE-NIEUMUNSTER AERODROME.
(d).   Twelve 112lb bombs were dropped on BRUGES DOCKS - N. End.
(e).   Six 112lb bombs were dropped on DUMPS on BRUGES-ZEEBRUGGE CANAL, near BRUGES.
(f).   Twelve 112lb bombs were dropped on RAILWAY JUNCTION on OSTENDE-THOUROUT-BRUGES line.
(g).   Twelve 65lb bombs were dropped on RAILWAY SIDINGS and works south of OSTENDE.

Seaplanes. By Dawn.
Short Seaplanes.
(a).   One 520lb bomb was dropped on ROOT of ZEEBRUGGE MOLE.
(b).   One 520lb bomb was dropped E. of SOLWAY WORKS.

The latter was the objective in both cases, but the mist was so bad, that the pilot could not locate, so he dropped his bomb on the MOLE.

JULY 13TH. Two reconnaissances were carried out over OSTENDE and ZEEBRUGGE, and various points inland. Plates were exposed with good results.

Usual offensive patrols.

JULY 14TH. Usual offensive patrols.

ENEMY AIRCRAFT. FLIGHT.SUB.LIEUT. ENSTONE of No. 4 Squadron intercepted and destroyed an enemy two-seater, thought to have been one of the machines returning from bombing DUNKERQUE. E.A. broke up in the air.

JULY 15TH. One attempted photographic reconnaissance, but weather conditions were unsuitable.

Usual offensive patrols by No. 4 Wing.

BOMBING RAID. No. 7 Squadron. Handley Page machines.

By night.

(a). Thirty-six 112lb bombs and four 65lb bombs were dropped on SOLWAY WORKS, ZEEBRUGGE.

(b). Thirty-seven 112lb bombs dropped on RAILWAY JUNCTIONS and SIDINGS at OSTENDE.

(c). Five-65lb bombs dropped on RAILWAY SIDINGS and AMMUNITION DUMPS at MIDDLEKERKE.

(d). Nineteen 65lb bombs dropped on RAILWAY JUNCTION at THOUROUT.

(e). Three 112lb bombs were dropped on AERTYRKE AERODROME.

(f). MOTOR TRANSPORT convoys on road near LICHTERVELDE and LICHTERVELDE RAILWAY SIDINGS were shelled from a 6 pdr Gun. 10 rounds fired.

CASUALTIES DURING PERIOD 1ST TO 15TH JULY
INCLUSIVE

	KILLED.	SQUADRON.	DATE.
FLIGHT.SUB.LIEUT.	H. ALLEN.	No. 3 Squadron.	6.7.17.
FLIGHT.SUB.LIEUT.	E.W. BUSBY.	No. 4 Squadron	10.7.17.
	Accidentally Killed.		
FLIGHT.SUB.LIEUT.	S.E. ELLIS	No. 4 Squadron	12.7.17.
	Died of Wounds.		
OBSVR.SUB.LIEUT.	C.B. ORFEUR.	No. 2 Squadron.	1.7.17.
	Accidentally Injured.		
ACT.FLIGHT.COMDR.	G.M.T.ROUSE	No. 4 Squadron.	11.7.17

A total over 33 TONS of BOMBS were dropped in period 1st to 15th July inclusive.

HEADQUARTERS.   WING CAPTAIN

  R.N.A.S.   for SENIOR OFFICER. R.N.A.S.

16/7/17.

A.H.C.   July 16th 1917.

SUMMARY OF BOMBING RAIDS WITH WEIGHTS OF EXPLOSIVES DROPPED BETWEEN JULY 1ST AND JULY 15. 1917. INCLUSIVE.

AERODROMES.

TARGET	BOMBS DROPPED	TOTAL
GHISTELLES.	88 – 16 lbs. 35 – 22 lbs. 32 – 65 lbs. 109 – 112 lbs.	16,466 lbs.
HOUTTAVE (EIEUWMUNSTER)	36 – 112 lbs. 12 – 65 lbs.	4,812 lbs.
ST. DENIS WESTREM	73 – 112 lbs. 24 – 65 lbs.	9,736 lbs.
ARSSENAERE.	24 – 112 lbs.	2,688 lbs.
AERTRYCKE.	15 – 112 lbs.	1,680 lbs.
GONTRODE.	14 – 112 lbs.	1,568 lbs.
SEAPLANE BASE OSTEND.	12 – 112 lbs.	1,344 lbs.
BRUGES DOCKS.	102 – 112 lbs.	11,424 lbs.
SOLWAY WORKS.	2 – 520 lbs. 36 – 112 lbs. 4 – 65 lbs.	5,332 lbs.
AMMUNITION DUMPS.	4 – 65 lbs. 48 – 16 lbs.	1,028 lbs.
RAILWAY STATIONS, JUNCTIONS AND SIDINGS.	73 – 112 lbs. 36 – 65 lbs.	10,516.lbs.
OSTEND ELECTRIC POWER STATION AND RAILWAY LINES.	28 – 112 lbs. 24 – 65 lbs.	4,696.lbs.
GRAND TOTAL:		71,290 lbs.

Airco D.H.4s of 5(N) Sqn prepare to take off from their aerodrome at Petit Synthe. Note the white and red(?) radiator frame and shutters of the nearest machine.

When 7 Sqn RNAS moved to its new base at Coudekerque on 2 April 1917 it had already begun exchanging its cumbersome Short Bombers for Handley Page O/100s. One of its Short Bombers is seen here, with a Sopwith 1½ Strutter in the background.

The Sopwith F.1 Camels of 4(N) Sqn ranged up. Five of the unit's aircraft engaged in a "general running fight" with 16 Gotha bombers on the morning of July 4, 1917. (Bruce/Leslie)

Handley Page O/100 3116, piloted by Sqn Cdr D.A. Spenser Grey DSO, becomes the centre of attention at Coudekerque on 4 March 1917, as the first of the type to arrive at the base.

As is the custom with large aeroplanes, 3116 quickly had smaller aeroplanes parked alongside to give an impression of scale. The examples here are a Sopwith Triplane and a Nieuport 17bis of 6 or 11 Sqn, RNAS.

An aerial view of Coudekerque aerodrome shortly after 7(N) Sqn had moved there. Two Handley Page O/100s are visible between the huts and hangars, and four Short Bombers, three with their wings folded, are on the edge of the airfield itself.

A dramatic impression of the view from the O/100's mid-upper position as the bomber approaches Coudekerque aerodrome, which can be seen above the pilots' heads between the centre-section struts.

Taken on 5 June 1917, this air-to-air study shows a Handley Page O/100 of 7(N) Sqn, piloted by Sqn Cdr J. Babington, and carrying His Majesty King Albert of Belgium, approaching Dunkirk.

Sopwith Triplane N5369 of 12(N) Sqn was crashed by Flt Sub Lt Daly on 12 July 1917, Although Daly escaped with minor injuries, the aeroplane was written off. (Bruce/Leslie)

The seaplanes of 4 Wing flew regular anti-submarine patrols. Here, a Short 184, its bomb racks empty, taxies at speed.

An atmospheric air-to-air study of a Short 184, viewed through the interplane bracing of another of its kind.

Airco D.H.4 N5978/B-3[5] of 5(N) Sqn was credited with bringing down a yellow Albatros on 20 July 1917 after bombing Aertrycke Aerodrome. The communiques record such a raid on July 19, not the 20th, and there is no mention of the combat. (Bruce/Leslie)

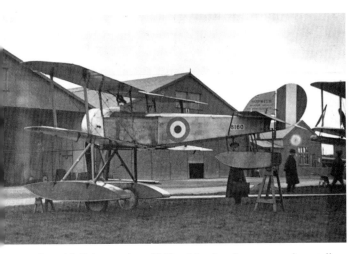

Sopwith Baby seaplane 8160, with a Lewis gun experimentally attached to the port centre-section struts to fire upwards at a 45° angle, flew an anti-Gotha patrol from Westgate on 22 July 1917. (Bruce/Leslie)

Sopwith F.1 Camel B3765 of 3(N) Sqn. Five Camels of this unit intercepted five German seaplanes on their way to attack the Fleet on 26 July, 1917, broke up the formation, drove them back to Ostend and brought one down.

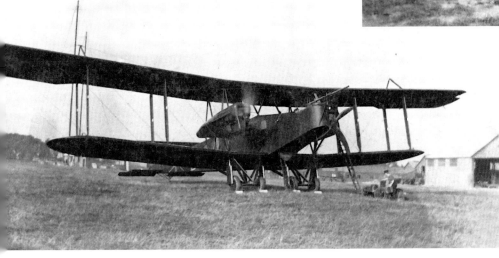

This anonymous Handley Page O/400, said to have been photographed at Redcar, carries a six-pounder Davis gun on its nose. As the Communiques testify, similarly armed O/400s used this weapon against ground targets during bombing raids.

Handley Page O/100s of 7/7A Sqn on
Coudekerque Aerodrome. (Bruce/Leslie)

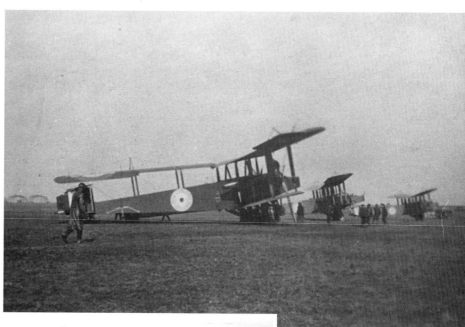

A nasty-looking O/100
crash at Coudekerque. The
underfuselage gunner's
position in line with the wing
trailing edges is shown to
advantage.

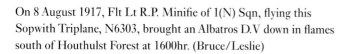

On 8 August 1917, Flt Lt R.P. Minifie of 1(N) Sqn, flying this
Sopwith Triplane, N6303, brought an Albatros D.V down in flames
south of Houthulst Forest at 1600hr. (Bruce/Leslie)

ROYAL NAVAL AIR SERVICE. – COMMUNIQUE NO. 2

<u>JULY 16TH.</u>

Photographic reconnaissances were attempted by No. 2 Squadron to vicinity of BRUGES, but abandoned owing to heavy cloud banks.

Usual offensive patrols by No. 4 Wing, also anti-submarine patrols by Seaplanes.

<u>ENEMY AIRCRAFT.</u>

FLIGHT.SUB.LIEUT BAILEY of No. 4 Squadron in thick clouds indecisively engaged an Albatross Scout, which was observed to side-slip through the clouds, apparently out of control.

<u>JULY 17TH.</u>

Weather unfavourable and much rain, clearing towards evening slightly.

A few offensive patrols by No.4 Wing, also anti-submarine and mine seeking patrol by Seaplanes.

<u>ENEMY AIRCRAFT.</u>

A PATROL OF No. 11 Squadron encountered 3 E.A. Single Seater Albatross Scouts, and some two-seaters. FLIGHT.SUB.LIEUT. A.R. BROWN had two indecisive engagements, the E.A. spinning away and escaping, and on being attacked by 3 E.A., he selected one and drove it down completely out of control, but could not see it crash owing to being attacked. FLIGHT.SUB.LIEUT. H.F. AIREY chased and destroyed a large span two-seater E.A. All the other pilots had indecisive engagements, the E.A. breaking off the combat by spinning away. The hostile formation was completely dispersed.

<u>JULY 19TH.</u>

Weather overcast and unfavourable.

A few fighter patrols by No. 4 Wing and anti-submarine and mine seeking patrol by Seaplanes.

<u>ENEMY AIRCRAFT.</u>

On returning from a bombing raid, the formation of D.H.4's of No. 5 Squadron were continuously attacked by E.A. FLT. COMMDR. CLARKE and OBSVR.LIEUT. ST'JOHN shot down an E.A.

FLIGHT.SUB.LIEUT. GLAISBY and SAW, - ACM, who was acting as Gunlayer, were attacked by E.A. and though the pilot was wounded slightly in the head, and the Gunlayer most painfully wounded in the body, the latter succeeded in shooting down the E.A. Several indecisive engagements occurred, but though much shot about, all machines returned safely.

BOMBING RAID. BY DAY. 5 D.H.4's No. 5 SQUADRON

Six 65lb and fifty-nine 16lb bombs were dropped on AERTRYCKE AERODROME.

<u>JULY 20TH.</u>

A successful photographic reconnaissance was carried out by No. 2 Squadron over ZEEBRUGGE and RAVERSYDE and the coast. Plates were exposed and good photographs obtained. This reconnaissance was attacked by E.A. but they were successfully driven off.

Usual fighter patrols.

<u>ENEMY AIRCRAFT.</u>

Two machines of No. 4 Squadron whilst on patrol were attacked by 4 E.A., 2 above and 2 below. Our machines dived on the two lower ones, and the 2 E.A. from above dived on our machines. One of our pilots failed to return.

<u>BOMBING RAIDS. BY DAY</u> <u>5 D.H.4'S NO. 5 SQUADRON.</u>

Five 65lb and thirty 16lb bombs were dropped on VARSSENAERE AERODROME, causing a fire.

JULY 21ST.

Four successful photographic reconnaissances were carried out by No. 2 Squadron, plates being successfully exposed on the coast.

Usual fighter patrols; an additional 2 patrols were sent to intercept the E.A., which bombed HARWICH and FELIXSTOWE, but saw nothing of them.

<u>BOMBING RAIDS. BY NIGHT. 4 Handley Page. No. 7 SQUADRON.</u>

(a). Twenty-six 112lb bombs were dropped on THOUROUT RAILWAY JUNCTION, causing a large fire and heavy explosions.

(b). Twenty-six 112lb bombs were dropped on MIDDLEKI[*sic*: E]RKE DUMP and sidings.

<u>BY DAY. 5 D.H.4'S. No. 5 SQUADRON</u>

(a). Seven 65lb and forty-eight 16lb bombs were dropped on SNELLEGHEM AERODROME, causing a fire in one of the sheds.

JULY 22ND.

A successful photographic reconnaissance was carried out over BRUGES and DISTRICT.

Usual fighter patrols.; also anti-submarine patrol by Seaplanes.

<u>BOMBING RAIDS. BY DAY. 5 D.H.4'S. NO. 5 SQUADRON</u>

(a). Six 65lb and thirty-six 16lb bombs were dropped on SPARAPPELHOEK AERODROME, causing a large fire amongst Bessonneaux [hangars].

JULY 23RD.

Weather overcast and hazy. No reconnaissance.

Usual fighter patrols and Seaplane anti-submarine Patrol.

<u>ENEMY AIRCRAFT.</u>

An indecisive engagement between a patrol of No. 11 Squadron and a formation of E.A., but weather was too thick.

JULY 24TH.

Weather very bad.

Usual fighter patrols, and seaplane anti-submarine Patrol.

JULY 25TH.

Weather poor.

Several offensive patrols and Seaplane Anti-submarine patrol.

<u>ENEMY AIRCRAFT.</u>

A large two-seater, while spotting for coast batteries firing on the Fleet, was attacked by a patrol of No. 4 Squadron, consisting of Flight Commander Chadwick, Flt. Lieut. ENSTONE, and FLIGHT.SUB.LIEUT. KEIRSTEAD, and driven down completely out of control, 30 miles out to sea.

<u>BOMBING RAID. BY DAY. 5 D.H.4'S. NO. 5 SQUADRON.</u>

(a). Eight 65lb and forty-eight 16lb bombs, were dropped on HOUTTAVE-NIEUWMUNSTER AERODROME. Direct hits were observed, and the large shed set on fire.

(b). Nine 65lb and forty-one 16lb bombs were dropped on VLISSEGHEM AERODROME.

JULY 26TH.

Photographic Reconnaissances were carried out to ZEEBRUGGE and THOUROUT. Plates were exposed over NEW AERODROME, AMMUNITION DUMPS, and RAILWAY JUNCTIONS, with good results.

Usual Fighter Patrols, - Patrols over Fleet, - and anti-submarine patrols by Seaplanes.

ENEMY AIRCRAFT.

A patrol of 5 Camels of No. 3 Squadron, consisting of FLIGHT. LIEUT. FALL, and FLIGHT.SUB.LIEUTS GLEN, BAWLF, ELLWOOD and BEAMISH, intercepted four two-seater E.S. [Enemy Seaplanes?] carrying torpedoes and one single seater E.S., on their way to attack the Fleet. The E.S. were driven back to OSTENDE, and formation broken up entirely, - one Seaplane being seen to crash in the sea 2 miles off the shore.
   Several other indecisive fights took place.

BOMBING RAID. BY DAY. D.H.4 MACHINES, NO. 5 SQUADRON.

Seven 65lb and Twenty-nine 16lb bombs were dropped on VARSSENAERE AERODROME. One direct hit on shed observed.

JULY 27TH.

Photographic Reconnaissances to EECLOO and coast in vicinity of OSTENDE.
Reconnaissance over Barrage at day-light.
Fighter Patrols in AREA and over Fleet.
Usual Anti-Submarine patrol.

ENEMY AIRCRAFT.

A twin-engine Gotha machine on its way to bomb the Fleet was encountered and headed off by a patrol of No. 4 Squadron. FLIGHT.COMMANDER SHOOK; FLIGHT.SUB.LIEUT'S HUNTER and BAILEY, attacked at long range, and E.A. was driven down well inland, - our machines experiencing heavy A.A. fire.

BOMBING RAID. BY NIGHT. HANDLEY PAGE MACHINES. No. 7 SQUADRON.

(a). Twelve 112lb bombs were dropped on GHENT RAILWAY STATION, and SIDINGS.
(b). Twelve 112lb bombs were dropped on various RAILWAY JUNCTIONS and SIDINGS.
(c). Twelve 112lb bombs were dropped on GHISTELLES AERODROME.
   Visibility very bad, and night very dark.

BY DAY. D.H.4 MACHINES OF NO.5 SQUADRON.

(a). Seven 65lb and thirty-two 16lb bombs were dropped on GHISTELLES AERODROME, one direct hit on a shed being observed.

JULY 28TH.

No photographic reconnaissance. Weather too bad.
Reconnaissance at day-break over Barrage.
Usual fighter patrols in AREA and over Fleet.
Anti-Submarine patrol by Seaplanes.

ENEMY AIRCRAFT.

FLIGHT.SUB.LIEUT. R.F.P. ABBOTT who had separated from flight owing to engine trouble was attacked by 3 Scout E.A.. He shot one down completely out of control, and then had to break off the fight owing to his Cowl coming adrift and jamming his propeller and causing him to nosedive. However, he recovered control and made a forced landing on the beach. Machine was considerably shot about.

BOMBING RAID. BY NIGHT. HANDLEY PAGE MACHINES. NO. 7 SQUAD.
(a). Forty-two 112lb and twelve 16lb bombs were dropped on BRUGEOISE WORKS. An explosion caused.
(b). Fifty-two 112lb bombs were dropped on the RAILWAY LINES AND JUNCTIONS at THOUROUT, MIDDLEKIRKE [*sic*] and GHISTELLES, - a series of explosions being caused at the former.

JULY 29TH.

Bad weather all day.

JULY 30TH.

Weather unfavourable.

JULY 31ST.

Weather unfavourable.

CASUALTIES DURING PERIOD 16TH to 31ST JULY INCLUSIVE.

Accidentally Killed.	Squadron.	Date.
Flt.Sub.Lieut. B.H. DALY.	No. 12.	17/7/17.

REPORTED MISSING.	SQUADRON.	DATE.
Flt.Sub.Lieut. F.W. AKERS.	No. 4.	21/7/17.
Flt.Commander A.J. CHADWICK.	No. 4.	28/7/17.
	(Believed drowned).	

WOUNDED		
FLT.Sub.Lieut. L.N. GLAISBY.	No. 5.	19/7/17.
	(Slighty). [*sic*]	
No.F.16741. L.N. SAW. ACM. .2.	No. 5.	19/7.17.
	(Severely).	

A total over 13 TONS of BOMBS were dropped in period 16th to 31st July inclusive.

HEADQUARTERS, R.N.A.S.   WING CAPTAIN.
                                for SENIOR OFFICER. R.N.A.S.

1/8/17
I/W.J.H.

                                August 1st. 1917.

SUMMARY OF BOMBING RAIDS WITH WEIGHTS OF EXPLOSIVES DROPPED BETWEEN JULY 16TH. AND JULY 31ST. 1917 INCLUSIVE.

TARGET.	BOMBS DROPPED.	TOTAL WEIGHT.
AERTRYCKE AERODROME.	6 – 65 lbs.	
	49 – 16 lbs.	1,174 lbs.
VARSSENAERE AERODROME.	12 – 65 lbs.	
	59 – 16 lbs.	1,724 lbs.
SNELLEGHEM AERODROME.	7 – 65 lbs.	
	48 – 16 lbs.	1,223 lbs.

SPARAPPELHOEK AERODROME.	6 – 65 lbs.	
	36 – 16 lbs.	966 lbs.
HOUTTAVE AERODROME.	8 – 65 lbs.	
(NIEUWMUNSTER).	48 – 16 lbs.	1,288 lbs.
VLISSEGHEM AERODROME.	9 – 65 lbs.	
	41 – 16 lbs.	1,241 lbs.
GHISTELLES AERODROME.	12 – 112 lbs.	
	7 – 65 lbs.	
	32 – 16 lbs.	2,311 lbs.
LA BRUGEOISE WORKS.	42 – 112 lbs.	
	12 – 65 lbs.	5,484 lbs.
RAILWAY SIDINGS, JUNCTIONS & STATIONS.	128 – 112 lbs.	14,336 lbs.
	TOTAL	29,747 lbs.

ROYAL NAVAL AIR SERVICE. COMMUNIQUE NO. 3

On the 1st, 2nd, 3rd, 6th and 7th, no flying took place owing to bad weather conditions.

AUGUST 4TH.

During intervals of bad weather, two patrols over the Fleet, were carried out.

BOMBING RAID. BY NIGHT. SHORT SEAPLANES.
Two 520lb bombs were dropped on ATELIERS DE LA MARINE, OSTENDE.

AUGUST 5TH.

No reconnaissances owing to bad weather and low clouds.
Usual fighter patrols over the fleet, and one patrol escorting bombing machines up the coast.

ENEMY AIRCRAFT.
Bombing Flight of No. 5 Squadron was attacked by E.A. whilst approaching their target. FLT.COMMDR. T.F. LE-MESSURIER and GUNLAYER JACKSON engaged 4,- the tail plane of one coming off in the air, which went down completely out of control.

FLT.S.LT. J.S. WRIGHT with GUNLAYER LOVELOCK also drove a machine down out of control about the same time. On the way back, the formation was again attacked by 6 E.A. FLT.COMMDR. T.F. LE-MESSURIER and GUNLAYER JACKSON, and ACT.FLT.COMMDR. R.J. SLADE and GUNLAYER DARBY, each succeeded in driving down an E.A. out of control.

All machines returned safely.

BOMBING RAID. BY DAY. NO. 5 SQUADRON. D.H.4's.
Nine 65lb and Fifty-one 16lb Bombs were dropped on SNELLEGHEM AERODROME. Two direct hits were observed.

AUGUST 8TH.

Weather again too bad for photographs.
Reconnaissance machines and escorts were attacked by E.A. between BLANKERBURGHE and ZEEBRUGGE. (See Enemy Aircraft).

ENEMY AIRCRAFT.
A Reconnaissance by 2 D.H.4's consisting of FLT.COMMDR. F. FOWLER, and OBSVR.LT.R. GOW – (Reconnaissance machine) and FLT. COMMDR. F.E. SANDFORD with SUB.LT. PICKUP as Observer, -Escort, were attacked by 4 E.A. Scouts, one of which was shot down completely out of control.

AUGUST 9TH.

Usual reconnaissance carried out by No. 2 Squadron to ZEEBRUGGE. Weather too bad for photography.
Usual offensive patrols for protection of Fleet and Anti-Submarine and mine seeking patrols by Seaplanes.

BOMBING RAID. BY NIGHT. NO. 7 SQUADRON. HANDLEY PAGE'S.
(a). Twenty-four 65lb and ten-112lb bombs were dropped on ZUIDWEDGE RAILWAY SIDINGS, large clouds of smoke being observed to rise.
(b). Twelve 65lb and thirty-five 112lb bombs were dropped on GHISTELLES AERODROME.
(c). Five 112lb bombs were dropped on THOUROUT JUNCTION and 10 rounds fired from 6 Pndr. Davis Gun.

AUGUST 10TH.

Usual fighter patrols over Fleet. Weather unfavourable for reconnaissance.

ENEMY AIRCRAFT.
Several indecisive combats took place.

BOMBING RAID. BY DAY. NO. 5 SQUADRON. D.H.4'S.
Six 65lb and thirty-nine 16lb bombs were dropped on SPARAPPELHOEK AERODROME.

AUGUST 11TH.
Usual fighter patrols over the Fleet.

America Seaplane accompanied by Escorts carried out a patrol from 6.01 to 8.12 pm. The periscope of a submarine was sighted 8 miles from DRILLSTONE. After turning to attack, no trace of the submarine could be seen. NOTE. Position of DRILLSTONE is approximately 11 miles N.E. of MARGATE.

ENEMY AIRCRAFT.
Several indecisive combats took place in the vicinity of WESTENDE and MIDDLEKIRKE.

BOMBING RAID. BY DAY. NO. 5 SQUADRON. D.H.4's.
A bombing raid was attempted by No. 5 Squadron but owing to bad weather conditions could not be carried out.

AUGUST 12TH.
Two successful photographic reconnaissances were carried out in the vicinity of MIDDLEKIRKE. During these times, observations were made over OSTENDE HARBOUR. Very little shipping of importance was observed. On both occasions the harbour was practically empty, and no war vessels could be seen.

Usual fighter patrols were carried out for the protection of the Fleet.

ENEMY AIRCRAFT.
Little aerial activity was observed during the day.

BOMBING RAID. BY DAY. NO. 5 SQUADRON. D.H.4's.
(a). Ten 65lb and Fifty-one 16lb bombs were dropped on VARSSENAERE AERODROME. Visibility was very good through gaps in the clouds. 6 Hits were observed on the line of sheds on the Eastern side of the Aerodrome and several bombs were observed to explode on the sheds and huts on the Western side. All machines returned safely.

AUGUST 13TH.
Sky was overcast during the greater part of the day. Fighter patrols were carried out and special patrols to intercept hostile machines which were raiding ENGLAND.

ENEMY AIRCRAFT.
At 4-20 pm, four pilots of No. 3 Squadron namely FLT.LT. BEAMISH, and F.S.LTS. HAYNE, HARROWER and ABBOTT, observed 9 GOTHAS heading towards ENGLAND, and started in pursuit catching up E.A. when about 10 miles from the English coast. Pilots harassed the rear of the German formation by firing at long distance. Unfortunately, when getting to close quarters, machines ran out of petrol and were all forced to land.

The GOTHAS were again encountered by four more pilots, namely FLT.COMMDR'S BREADNER and ARMSTRONG, and F.S.LT'S ELLWOOD and CHISAM also of No. 3 Squadron. Pilots promptly gave chase, and attacked formation from the rear, concentrating on the stragglers. Fire was opened from 200 yds range, but had to be broken off owing to all the guns becoming jambed.

SEAPLANE DEFENCE FLIGHT, whilst patrolling over the Fleet of MIDDLEKIRKE, observed an enemy seaplane being fired at by ships on patrol. FLT.COMMDR. GRAHAM. FLT.LT. FISHER and F.S.LT. SLATTER attacked E.A. which was observed to crash into the sea. All the pilots saw wreckage on the water.

AUGUST 14TH.
Five photographic reconnaissances were carried during the day in the vicinity of MIDDLEKIRKE.
Fleet protection patrols were maintained throughout the day. A few E.A. were observed.

<u>ENEMY AIRCRAFT.</u>
A formation of 6 E.A. were observed on one occasion, approaching one of the photographic reconnaissances. Leader of E.A. attacked, and an indecisive combat took place, the remainder of the E.A. turning off.

<u>BOMBING RAID. BY DAY. NO. 5 SQUADRON. D.H.4'S.</u>
A bombing raid was carried out on THOUROUT and GHISTELLES AERODROMES.

(a). Thirteen 65lb and fifty-three 16lb bombs were dropped on the former objective, and a good deal of smoke was observed to rise among the sheds along the OSTENDE-THOUROUT Road.

(b). Six 65lb and twenty-four 16lb bombs were dropped on the latter objective. Several bombs were observed to explode quite close to four large GOTHA machines. All our machines returned safely.

AUGUST 15TH.
Visibility was poor throughout the day, especially to seawards.
Fleet protection patrols were carried out during the day, but no E.A. were observed.

<u>CASUALTIES DURING PERIOD 1ST to 15TH AUGUST INCLUSIVE.</u>

<u>ACCIDENTALLY KILLED</u>	<u>SQUADRON.</u>	<u>DATE.</u>
ACT.FLT.COMDR. F.B.CASEY.	NO. 3.	10/8/17.

<u>DIED OF WOUNDS.</u>

A.M.1.(G/L) S. CURRINGTON	NO. 5.	10/8/17.

NOTE. A Total of nearly SEVEN TONS of BOMBS were dropped in period 1st to 15th August inclusive.

H.Q.R.N.A.S.	WING CAPTAIN.
16.8.17	for SENIOR OFFICER.R.N.A.S.

I/W.J.H.	August 16th. 1917.

SUMMARY OF BOMBING RAIDS WITH WEIGHTS
OF EXPLOSIVES DROPPED BETWEEN AUGUST 1ST.
AND AUGUST 15TH. 1917.

TARGET.	BOMBS DROPPED.	TOTAL WEIGHT
ATELIERS DE LA MARINE, OSTEND.	2 – 520 lbs.	1,040 lbs.
SNELLEGHEM AERODROME.	9 – 65 lbs. 51 – 16 lbs.	1,401 lbs.
GHISTELLES AERODROME.	35 – 112 lbs. 18 – 65 lbs. 24 – 16 lbs.	5,474 lbs.
SPARAPPELHOEK AERODROME.	6 – 65 lbs. 39 – 16 lbs.	1,014 lbs.
VARSSENAERE AERODROME.	10 – 65 lbs. 51 – 16 lbs.	1,466 lbs.
THOUROUT AERODROME.	13 – 65 lbs. 53 – 16 lbs.	1,693 lbs.
RAILWAY SIDINGS AND JUNCTIONS.	15 – 112 lbs. 24 – 65 lbs.	3,240 lbs.
	TOTAL:	15,328 lbs.

The Airco D.H.4s of 5(N) Sqn, seen here, bombed Varssenaere Aerodrome on 12 August 1917, and hits on hangars and other buildings were observed.

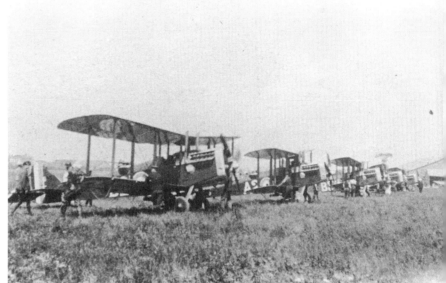

Sopwith Triplane N5459 came on the strength of 1(N) Sqn on 14 August 1917, but after sharing in a victory over an Albatros D.V on 19 September it was itself shot down on the following day by Vzfw Kosmahl of Jasta 26. Its pilot, Flt Sub Lt E.W. Desbarats, escaped injury but became a PoW. (Bruce/Leslie)

Handley Page O/100 1455 of 7A Sqn is bombed up ready for a raid. This machine joined the unit on 22 March 1917. (Bruce/Leslie)

The Airco D.H.4s of 2(N) Sqn carried out a photographic reconnaissance mission on 22 August 1917. One of the unit's aircraft, N5972, built at Yeovil by Westland Aircraft, is seen here. (Bruce/Leslie)

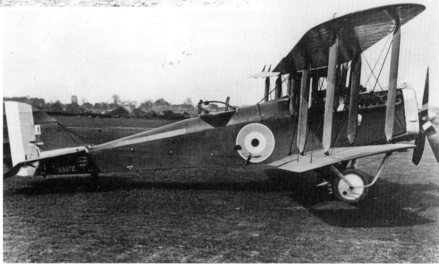

The Sopwith F.1 Camel flown by Flt Cdr Breadner of 3 Sqn was this colourful specimen, B6401. It was also flown by "Tich" Rochford. (Bruce/Leslie)

ROYAL NAVAL AIR SERVICE COMMUNIQUE NO. 4.

The weather was generally good in the early part of the period under review, but the latter part was bad.

AUGUST 16TH.

Photographic Reconnaissance by No. 2 Squadron to OSTENDE in cloudy weather, and some plates were exposed, but results were spoilt by the clouds.

Usual Fighter Patrols to protect the Fleet were carried out.

BOMBING RAID. BY DAY. NO. 5 SQUADRON. D.H.4'S.

(a). Nine 65lb, two 50lb and forty-eight 16lb bombs were dropped on GHISTELLES AERODROME.

(b). Three 65lb, one 50lb and thirty 16lb bombs were dropped on THOUROUT AERODROME.

BOMBING RAID. BY NIGHT. NO. 7 SQUADRON. HANDLEY PAGE'S.

(a). Four 250lb, seven 65lb and seventy-two 112lb bombs were dropped on OSTENDE JUNCTION and SIDINGS, causing a fire.

(b). Sixty 112lb Bombs on THOUROUT JUNCTION and SIDINGS.

(c). Eighteen 112lb bombs on GHISTELLES AERODROME.

MISCELLANEOUS.

Four 16lb bombs were dropped by D.H.4's of No.2. Squadron on ROAD TRANSPORT.

F.S.LT. ABBOTT of No. 3 Squadron was sent on a special mission to attack a hostile aerodrome at dawn with machine gun fire, but failed to find it owing to low clouds and mist. He, on his return, attacked another hostile aerodrome firing 500 rounds at the hangars, and the remainder of his ammunition at men in the trenches from a low height.

FLIGHT.S.LT. HAYNES of same Squadron failed to find his objective for same reasons, and attacked another hostile aerodrome, firing 400 rounds at 3 Albatross Single Seaters on the ground, as his bullets bounced off the sheds. He also fired 50 rounds into the Squadrons quarters. On his return home he shot two horses attached to a wagon on the road, - shot the guard at the railway level crossing, - stampeded a lot of horse transport on the front at MIDDLEKIRKE, and returned safely, all being done at a height of 50 – 100 feet.

AUGUST 17TH.

A reconnaissance was carried out by No. 2 Squadron to ZEEBRUGGE, but plates could not be exposed as weather was too thick. Usual fighter patrols to protect the Fleet.

ENEMY AIRCRAFT.

A Flight of No. 4 Squadron, consisting of FLT.COMMDR. SHOOK, and FLT.SUB.LT'S HUNTER, HODGES, TURNEY and HOWARD, attacked a large two seater E.A. which was trying to get out to sea, probably to spot for shore batteries, on Fleet. Observer of E.A. was shot, but apparently machine though forced down, was still under control.

FLT.SUB.LT. ABBOTT of No. 3 Squadron was attacked by 3 E.A., and though FLT.SUB.LT BAWLF of same squadron came to his assistance, was wounded, and returned to his aerodrome. A patrol of 5 machines of No. 3 Squadron attacked 5 E.A., and FLT.SUB.LT. FALL shot down one E.A. completely out of control. Several other indecisive combats took place.

BOMBING RAID. BY NIGHT. NO. 7 SQUADRON. HANDLEY PAGE'S.

Four 250lb, one hundred and sixty 112lb bombs and twenty-five 65lb bombs were dropped on RAILWAY JUNCTION and AMMUNITION DUMPS at THOUROUT. Direct hits were scored on RAILWAY LINE,

- fires accompanied by explosions were caused near NORTH JUNCTIONS, and also south of the town. A BIG FIRE followed by series of VIOLENT EXPLOSIONS took place at the DUMP, and it was still burning fiercely 1½ hours later.

AUGUST 18TH.

No. 2 Squadron made a reconnaissance to ZEEBRUGGE, but no photographs were taken. Usual patrols over the Fleet.

ENEMY AIRCRAFT.

A flight of 5 machines of No. 4 Squadron observing an R.F.C. R.E.8. machine being attacked by 5 E.A., attacked the E.A. and chased them to GHISTELLES AERODROME, when they were attacked in turn by about 20 hostile scouts and 3 two-seaters, and a general engagement took place. FLT.COMMDR. SHOOK shot down one E.A. which broke up in the air. FLT.SUB.LT. KIERSTEAD attacked and shot down another E.A. completely out of control. Several other indecisive combats took place. FLT.SUB.LT. HODGES was apparently shot down, and is missing. All other machines returned safely.

BOMBING RAID. BY DAY. NO. 5 SQUADRON. D.H.4'S.
(a). Two 65lb and eight 16lb bombs were dropped on TRANSPORT near SCHOORE, at cross roads.
(b). One 65lb and twelve 16lb bombs were dropped on BILLETS and STOREHOUSES near SCHOORE, causing a fire.

This was an attempted raid on SPARAPPELHOEK aerodrome which turned back owing to mistaken signal.

AUGUST 19TH .

Photographic Reconnaissance by No. 2 Squadron to OSTENDE and BLANKENBURGHE, plates being successfully exposed.

Usual fighter patrols over the Fleet.

ENEMY AIRCRAFT.

The bombing flight of D.H.4's of No. 5 Squadron were attacked by E.A. near OSTENDE, but were driven off by a patrol of BRISTOL SCOUTS of No. 48 SQUADRON. R.F.C.

FLT.COMMDR. LE-MESSURIER with GUNLAYER JACKSON engaged two E.A., one of which was shot down completely out of control.

Several other indecisive combats took place.

BOMBING RAID. BY NIGHT. NO. 7 SQUADRON. HANDLEY PAGE'S.
(a). Four 250lb bombs, thirty-two 112lb and nine-65lb bombs were dropped on ST' PIERRE RAILWAY STATION, GHENT.
(b). Fifty-four 112lb bombs were dropped on BRUGES DOCKS.
(c). Twenty-two 112lb Bombs were dropped on THOUROUT RAILWAY STATION.

BOMBING RAID. BY DAY. NO. 5 SQUADRON. D.H.4'S.
Ten 65lb and fifty-four 16lb bombs were dropped on SNELLEGHEM AERODROME, direct hits on sheds and buildings being observed.

AUGUST 20TH.

Photographic reconnaissance by No. 2 Squadron to OSTENDE, ZEEBRUGGE, and COAST BATTERIES. Plates successfully exposed.

Usual Fleet protective fighter patrols, also two Anti-Submarine patrols by Seaplanes. Nothing to report.

<u>BOMBING RAID. BY NIGHT. NO . 7 SQUADRON. HANDLEY PAGE'S.</u>

(a). Fifty-six 112lb bombs were dropped on MIDDLEKIRKE AMMUNITION DUMP.

(b). Four 250lb and forty-two 112lb, and seven 65lb bombs were dropped on BRUGEOISE WORKS.

<u>BOMBING RAID. BY DAY. NO. 5 SQUADRON. D.H.4'S.</u>

A bombing raid was attempted by D.H.4's of No. 5 Squadron, but returned, owing to being attacked by large numbers of E.A.

(a). Nine 65lb and fifty-two 16lb were dropped on various objectives over the lines.

(b). Four 16lb bombs were dropped on SEAPLANE BASE OSTENDE, by Photographic machines of No. 2 Squad.

AUGUST 21ST.

Reconnaissances by No. 2 Squadron to ZEEBRUGGE and Fighter Patrols over the Fleet as usual. Anti–Submarine and mine seeking patrols by Seaplanes.

<u>ENEMY AIRCRAFT.</u>

Several indecisive engagements took place.

AUGUST 22ND.

Photographic Reconnaissances in vicinity of MIDDLEKIRKE by No. 2 Squadron. Plates successfully exposed. Fighter Patrols for protection of the Fleet and to intercept E.A. bombing England.

<u>ENEMY AIRCRAFT.</u>

A large formation of 25 E.A. (scouts) were met by a double patrol of 10 machines of No. 4 Squad., near OSTENDE, and a general engagement took place. FLT.SUB.LT. HEMMING engaged 3 E.A. consecutively two being shot down completely out of control, and possibly the third also. FLT.S.LT. TONKS shot down one completely out of control, and possibly a second as well. FLT.LT. FISHER and FLT.SUB.LT. HICKEY each got down one E.A. out of control, the latter and FLT.SUB.LT. DALY possibly each shotting [sic] down another, but owing to very mixed fighting it is difficult to give details accurately. There were several other combats, but which cannot be considered decisive. All our machines returned safely, but several were much shot about,- FLT.LT. FISHER'S machine having over 100 bullet holes in it, and both petrol tanks pierced. It is possible that this large formation was up to escort the bombers clear of the coast on their way to ENGLAND. FLT. COMMDR. BREADNER and FLT.LT. FALL of No. 3 Squadron met part of the Bombers on their return and opened fire on a GOTHA, killing the Observer but failing to bring down the machine, which emitted puffs of black smoke. During a patrol FLT.SUB.LT. HAYNE and ANDERSON of some Squadron each drove down an E.A. out of control. FLT.LT. KIRBY of the WALMER DEFENCE FLIGHT engaged and brought down a GOTHA twin engine machine off RAMSGATE in the sea.

FLT.COMMDR. HERVEY of DOVER AEROPLANE STATION engaged and brought down a twin engine GOTHA off MARGATE in the sea.

The SEAPLANE DEFENCE FLIGHT (On Air Bag Pups) at DUNKERQUE engaged 12 GOTHAS returning from the bombing raid, meeting them 30 miles out to sea, and chasing them to ZEEBRUGGE, but with no decisive result.

<u>BOMBING RAID. BY NIGHT. NO. 7 SQUADRON. HANDLEY PAGE'S.</u>

Fifty-four 112lb and two 65lb bombs were dropped on MOLE and BATTERIES at ZEEBRUGGE.

<u>BOMBING RAID. BY DAY. NO. 5 SQUADRON. D.H.4'S.</u>

(a). Ten 65lb and fifty-six 16lb bombs were dropped on GHISTELLES AERODROME, causing a fire amongst the Western Sheds.

(b). Three 65lb and twenty 16lb bombs on various objectives.

<u>MISCELLANEOUS.</u>

FLT.SUB.LT'S SPROATT'S engine failed early, so he flew back and got another machine, but was too late to catch the formation, so he attacked and drove down a hostile kite balloon near LEEKE firing 300 rounds at it.

Four 16lb bombs were dropped by Reconnaissance machines of No. 2 Squadron on some destroyers off the Coast, but tho' very close, did not hit them.

AUGUST 23RD.

Reconnaissance by No. 2 Squadron to ZEEBRUGGE.

Usual Fighter Patrols over the Fleet.

<u>ENEMY AIRCRAFT.</u>

A few indecisive actions, but E.A. would not come to close quarters.

<u>BOMBING RAID. BY NIGHT. NO. 7 SQUADRON. HANDLEY PAGE'S.</u>

(a). Forty-two 112lb and fourteen 65lb bombs were dropped on MIDDLEKIRKE DUMP.

(b). Fourteen 112lb bombs were dropped on RAVERSYDE DUMP.

<u>BOMBING RAID. BY DAY. NO. 5 SQUADRON. D.H.4'S.</u>

Fifteen 65lb and sixty-eight 16lb bombs were dropped on HOUTTAVE AERODROME.

AUGUST 24TH and 25TH.

Bad weather. No important flying.

An attempted Bombing Raid was made, but had to return.

AUGUST 26TH.

Bad weather. No Reconnaissances, but several Fighter Patrols over the Fleet were carried out, and at least three enemy spotting machines were driven off, but there was no decisive combat.

<u>BOMBING RAID. BY NIGHT. NO. 7 SQUADRON. HANDLEY PAGE'S.</u>

Four 250lb, nine 65lb and sixty-eight 112lb bombs were dropped on St. DENIS-WESTREM AERODROME. One Handley Page machine failed to return.

AUGUST 27TH & 28TH.

Bad weather. No war flying.

AUGUST 29TH, 30TH.

Weather conditions again unsuitable for any war flying.

AUGUST 31ST.

During the greater part of the day the weather was unfavourable, but cleared towards evening.

<u>BOMBING RAID. BY NIGHT. NO. 7 SQUADRON. HANDLEY PAGE'S.</u>

One hundred and eight 112lb and two 65lb bombs were dropped on GHISTELLES AERODROME. Direct hits were observed on the South side of the Aerodrome, which caused a large conflagration. Hits were also made on the adjacent OSTENDE-THOUROUT RAILWAY LINE.

CASUALTIES DURING PERIOD 16TH to 31ST AUGUST.

ACCIDENTIALLY KILLED.

	Squad.	Date.
FLT.LIEUT. C.J. WYATT.	No. 2.	21.8.17.
OBSR.S.LT. A.J. HUTTY.	No. 2	21.8.17.

MISSING.

FLT.S.LT. C.C.R. HODGES.	No. 4.	18.8.17.
FLT.S.LT. H.H. BOOTH.	No. 7.	26.8.17.
Gunlayer.A.M.. S.A. CANNING.	No. 7.	26.8.17.
Gunlayer. ACM. P.H. YEATMAN.	No. 7.	26.8.17.

NOTE. A total of FORTY-EIGHT TONS of bombs were dropped during the period under review.

H.Q. R.N.A.S.   WING CAPTAIN.
Dunkerque.   for SENIOR OFFICER. R.N.A.S.
1.9.17.

I/W.J.H.   September 1st. 1917.

SUMMARY OF BOMBING RAIDS WITH WEIGHTS OF EXPLOSIVES DROPPED BETWEEN AUGUST 18TH. AND 31ST. 1917 INCLUSIVE

TARGET.	BOMBS DROPPED.	TOTAL WEIGHT
GHISTELLES AERODROME.	126 – 112 lbs.	
	21 – 65 lbs.	
	2 – 50 lbs.	
	104 – 16 lbs.	17,241 lbs.
THOUROUT AERODROME.	3 – 65 lbs.	
	1 – 50 lbs.	
	30 – 16 lbs.	25 lbs.
SNELLEGHEM AERODROME.	10 – 65 lbs.	
	54 – 16 lbs.	1,514 lbs.
HOUTTAVE AERODROME.	15 – 65 lbs.	
	68 – 16 lbs.	2,063 lbs.
ST. DENIS WESTREM AERODROME.	4 – 250 lbs.	
	68 – 112 lbs.	
	9 – 65 lbs.	9,201 lbs.

ZEEBRUGGE MOLE.	54 – 112 lbs.	
	2 – 65 lbs.	6,178 lbs.
BRUGES DOCKS.	54 – 112 lbs.	6,048 lbs.
LA BRUGEOISE WORKS.	4 – 250 lbs.	
	42 – 112 lbs.	
	7 – 65 lbs.	6,159 lbs.
AMMUNITION DUMPS.	112 – 112 lbs.	
	14 – 65 lbs.	13,454 lbs.
RAILWAY STATIONS.	4 – 250 lbs.	
	54 – 112 lbs.	
	9 – 65 lbs.	7,633 lbs.
RAILWAY SIDINGS, JUNCTIONS, TRANSPORT, ETC.	8 – 250 lbs.	
	292 – 112 lbs.	
	34 – 65 lbs.	
	8 – 16 lbs.	37,042 lbs.
VARIOUS.	1 – 65 lbs.	
	12 – 16 lbs.	257 lbs.
	GRAND TOTAL	107,515 lbs.

Sopwith Pup N6203 *Mina* served with 3 Sqn and then with the Seaplane Defence Flight at St Pol, which it joined on 3 July 1917. It subsequently went to 12 Sqn and then the War School at Manston. (Norman Franks)

Taken after the period covered by the communiques, this picture shows the F.1 Camels of C Flight, 3(N) Sqn, preparing to leave Mont St Eloi in March 1918. The nearest machine, B7275, joined the Squadron on 23 March 1918. It was rebuilt twice, as F5948 and F6476.

Kite balloons made tempting but dangerous targets, as they were usually well guarded by anti-aircraft defences. One such as this was attacked by Flt Sub Lt Daly on 2 September 1917.

Another form of German kite balloon over the front, as it might have appeared to an attacking pilot. Although Daly forced the observer to take to his parachute, heavy AA fire prevented him from seeing whether he had destroyed the balloon.

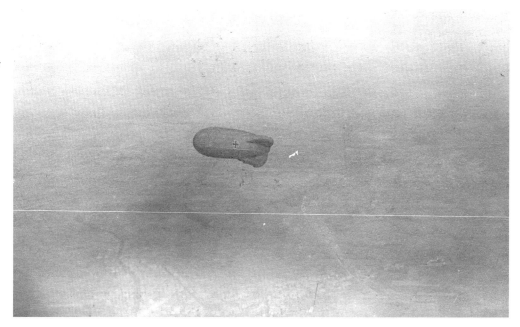

Two views of Westland-built Airco D.H.4 N6000 of 5(N) Sqn, bombed up ready for a mission. This machine joined 5 Sqn on 13 July 1917 and survived until 17 April 1918, by which time its crews had claimed several enemy aircraft out of control. (Bruce/Leslie)

ROYAL NAVAL AIR SERVICE:- COMMUNIQUE NO. 5.

The weather has been very unsettled during the greater part of the period under review, but every opportunity has been taken during the fine periods to carry out operations.

SEPTEMBER 1ST.

A special reconnaissance by No. 2 Squadron to OSTENDE was attempted, but abandoned owing to cloudy weather.

Usual fighter patrols to protect Fleet were carried out, but no E.A. were seen.

SEPTEMBER 2ND.

A reconnaissance by No. 2 Squadron to OSTENDE was made during the afternoon when weather was clear. Fighter patrols to protect Fleet and Escorts to Reconnaissance Machines.

ENEMY AIRCRAFT.

A patrol of 5 Camels of No. 3 Squadron encountered considerable numbers of E.A. near OSTENDE. FLT. COMMDR. BREADNER attacked and destroyed one E.A., the wings coming off, and the same Pilot and his Flight shot down another E.A. completely out of control. FLT.SUB.LT CHISAM attacked 4 Albatross Scouts, shooting down one completely out of control, - being himself attacked and driven down to 50 feet by the remainder, at which height he crossed the lines. The remaining pilots had several indecisive engagements, which were broken off by the E.A. diving or spinning away. All machines were much shot about, and FLT.SUB. LT. HALL was missing.

FLT.SUB.LT'S TURNEY, HUNTER and DALY of No. 4 Squadron while on patrol, attacked one of three two-seater E.A., killing Observer, and then shooting down the E.A. completely out of control. FLT.SUB.LT. DALY attacked a Hostile Kite Balloon, causing the Observer to parachute, but was unable to see if Balloon was destroyed owing to the heavy A.A. fire.

A formation of 10 D.H.4'S of No. 5 Squadron while returning from the bombing raid on VARSSENAERE, were attacked by E.A. and FLT.SUB.LT. SPROATT and P.O. G/L HINKLER shot down one Albatross Scout completely out of control.

BOMBING RAID. BY NIGHT. NOS. 7 & 7A SQUAD. HANDLEY PAGES.

(a). One hundred and ten 112 lb bombs, and two 65 lb bombs were dropped on BRUGES DOCKS and SHIPPING, causing a fire, and columns of smoke at AMMUNITION WORKS AND TORPEDO STORES.

BOMBING RAID. BY DAY. NO. 5 SQUADRON. D.H.4'S.

A bombing raid was attempted on VARSSENAERE AERODROME, but owing to continuous attacks by E.A., the formation was broken up, and bombs dropped as follows:-

(a). Three 65 lb and twenty-three 16lb on VARSSENAERE AERODROME, exploding amongst sheds on the Western side.

(b). Three 65lb and seventeen 16 lb on THOUROUT AERODROME, large clouds of smoke arising.

(c). Two 65lb and eight 16lb bombs on the small aerodrome south of BRUGES.

(d). Eight 65lb and twenty-two 16lb bombs on various RAILWAY objectives and HUTMENTS, causing three separate fires.

SEPTEMBER 3RD.

Machines of No. 2 Squadron SPOTTING for MONITORS bombarding OSTENDE on two occasions during the day. Spotting was hindered greatly by the smoke screens put up by the enemy. TIRPITZ BATTERY replied to monitors fire, but shooting was not good. Enemy machines spotting for shore batteries on Fleet. No decisive engagement took place.

BOMBING RAID. BY NIGHT. NOS. 7 & 7A SQUADRONS. HANDLEY PAGES.

(a). Four 250lb, one-hundred and six 112lb, and eleven 65lb bombs were dropped on BRUGES DOCKS, causing one heavy explosion, and followed by two large fires.

(b). Fourteen 112lb bombs were dropped on VARRSENAERE AERODROME.

(c). Fourteen 112lb bombs were dropped on GHISTELLES AERODROME.

BOMBING RAID. BY DAY. NO. 5 SQUADRON. D.H.4'S.

(a). Nineteen 65lb and eight-four 16lb bombs were dropped on BRUGES DOCKS. Many direct hits on Docks observed, and four separate fires were started.

SEPTEMBER 4TH.

Two photographic reconnaissances by No. 2 Squadron were carried out to OSTENDE. Plates were exposed over the town and the coast to the Eastward as far as the Dutch Frontier. What appears to be a floating boom is being constructed from the tip of ZEEBRUGGE MOLE to S'Eastward.

Usual fighter patrols over Fleet, and offensive sweep carried out by double patrols.

ENEMY AIRCRAFT.

An offensive sweep by 10 Camels of No. 3 Squadron met a formation of 10 E.A., and in the ensuing fight FLT. LT. BEAMISH, and FLT.LT. ROCHFORD each shot down an E.A. completely out of control, the latter's opponent emitting clouds of smoke. Several other indecisive encounters took place, and three enemy spotters were driven off.

The escorting machine to the photographic reconnaissance machine, Pilot FLT.SUB.LT. WARNE-BROWN, Gunlayer PINCHEN (NO.2 SQUAD) was attacked by a two seater E.A. near OSTENDE. The observer of the E.A. was shot and machine shot down making a forced landing on the beach near MIDDLEKIRKE.

BOMBING RAID. BY NIGHT. NOS. 7 & 7A SQUADS. HANDLEY PAGES.

(a). Eighty 112 lb, four 250lb and nine 65lb bombs on BRUGES DOCKS, with many hits, causing two large fires and heavy explosions.

(b). Fourteen 112lb bombs were dropped on GHISTELLES AERODROME.

BOMBING RAID. BY DAY. NO. 5 SQUADRON. D.H.4'S.

Fourteen 65lb and sixty-three 16lb bombs were dropped on BRUGES DOCKS, many direct hits being made, and bursting on or very close to four T.B.D.'S, from whom dense clouds of smoke arose – probably a smoke screen.

SEPTEMBER 5TH.

No reconnaissances. Weather bad, low clouds and very misty.

One offensive sweep by 11 machines and a few fighter patrols. No E.A. seen.

Anti-submarine patrol by Seaplanes. Nothing to report.

SEPTEMBER 6TH and 7TH.

Bad weather. No flying.

SEPTEMBER 8TH.

Special reconnaissance by No. 2 Squadron to OSTENDE – Heavy cloud banks working up, and no shipping visible.

Fighter patrols carried out over the Fleet during the fine weather, which only lasted a few hours. A few indecisive combats took place.

<u>BOMBING RAID. BY DAY. NO. 5 SQUADRON. D.H.4'S.</u>

A raid was attempted on BRUGES HARBOUR, but weather was too bad, so bombs were dropped as follows:- Eight 65lb and thirty-two 16lb bombs on HOUTTAVE AERODROME. Visibility bad.

SEPTEMBER 9TH.

Heavy clouds prevented reconnaissance or photographic work, but weather cleared up in the evening. Fighter patrols were maintained throughout the day for protection of the Fleet. Very few E.A. observed.

<u>BOMBING RAID. BY DAY. NO. 5 SQUADRON. D.H.4'S.</u>

(a). Fourteen 65lb, two 50lb and sixty-four 16lb bombs were dropped on BRUGES DOCKS; clouds of smoke arose and a vessel in Canal was observed to be on fire. A 65lb bomb fell very close to a submarine lying alongside E. Quay of W. Basin.

SEPTEMBER 10TH.

No reconnaissances. Usual fighter patrols for protection of Fleet.

<u>ENEMY AIRCRAFT.</u>

A patrol of 5 Camels of No. 5 Squadron attacked a two-seater D.F.W. machine, and drove it down from 14,000 feet, shepherding it over our side of the lines, and by good judgement preventing the pilot from burning his machine on landing. Machine was captured intact. – Pilot and passenger (who was wounded) being made prisoners.

A patrol of three Camels of No. 4 Squadron encountered an E. Seaplane spotting for shore batteries of Fleet, and FLT.COMMDR. FISHER shot E. Seaplane down, which crashed in the sea,- the crew being killed.

An offensive sweep by 13 Camels of No. 3 Squad was carried out in conjunction with a bombing raid, and a number of E.A. were encountered. FLT.COMMDR. BREADNER, FLT.LT. ROCHFORD, and FLT.SUB. LT. SANDS each shot down on E.A. completely out of control, and in the general engagement probably at least 2 more E.A. were shot down, but they cannot be definitely claimed. The bombing machines, D.H.4'S of No. 5 Squadron were attacked by E.A., and FLT.COMMDR. LE-MESSURIER with Gunlayer JACKSON shot down one E.A. smoking badly, and with its whole tail shaking about as if about to break off. This E.A. had previously smashed 5 trays of Lewis Gun Ammunition in the D.H.4. machine with an explosive bullet and machine was badly shot about.

<u>BOMBING RAID. BY NIGHT. NOS. 7 & 7A SQUADS. HANDLEY PAGES.</u>

(a). Four 250lb, seventy 112lb and seven 65lb bombs were dropped on ST' DENIS WESTREM AERODROME.
(b). Twelve 112lb bombs dropped on GONTRODE AIRSHIP STATION.
(c). Twelve 112lb and two 65lb bombs were dropped on BRUGES DOCKS.
(d). Twelve 112lb and two 65lb bombs were dropped on THOUROUT RAILWAY JUNCTION.
(e). Fourteen 112lb bombs dropped on TRAINS and RAILWAY OBJECTIVES in vicinity of GHENT.

<u>BOMBING RAID. BY DAY. NO. 5 SQUADRON. D.H.4'S.</u>

(a). Thirteen 65lb and fifty-four 16lb bombs were dropped on SPARAPPELHOEK AERODROME, exploding amongst the Hangars and sheds and causing much smoke.

(b). Four 65lb and sixteen 16lb bombs were dropped on the ENGEL AMMUNITION DUMP, starting a large fire, which was still burning when Pilots crossed the lines.

(c). Two 250lb and eight 16lb bombs were dropped on THOUROUT AERODROME, a direct hit with a 50lb bomb on a hangar being observed.

N.B. This was a day of much aerial activity; all our machines returned safely.

SEPTEMBER 11TH.

No reconnaissances owing to unfavourable weather.

Usual Fleet protective patrols.

Special fighter patrol to MARIAKIRKE – GHISTELLES AERODROMES, and escorts to bombers.

ENEMY AIRCRAFT.

Several indecisive encounters took place finishing by the E.A. diving away. The bombers were attacked by 8 E.A. on their return, but E.A. formation was broken up, and driven off successfully.

A special patrol of No. 4 Squadron attacked MARIAKERKE and GHISTELLES AERODROMES from a low height with machine gun fire, in the hope of forcing E.A. up from their Aerodromes but with no result.

BOMBING RAID. BY NIGHT. NOS. 7 & 7A SQUADS. HANDLEY PAGES.

(a). Four 250lb, Ninety-six 112lb and nine 65lb bombs were dropped on THOUROUT AERODROME.

(b). Twelve 112lb, and two 65lb bombs dropped on BRUGES DOCKS, causing a big explosion.

BOMBING RAID. BY DAY. NO. 5 SQUADRON. D.H.4'S.

This raid was attempted on BRUGES DOCKS, but low clouds prevented it, no bombs were dropped as follows:-

(a). Twelve 65lb, two 50lb, and sixty-seven 16lb bombs on ZEEBRUGGE MOLE. Direct hits on SEAPLANE BASE and MOLE causing a fire, and a DESTROYER being hit.

SEPTEMBER 12TH.

Weather very unfavourable – heavy low clouds.

Fighter Patrols were carried out when possible.

BOMBING RAID. BY NIGHT. NOS. 7 & 7A SQUADS. HANDLEY PAGES.

A bombing raid was attempted but had to return owing to low thick clouds, without reaching objective – BRUGES DOCKS.

(a). Twelve 112lb and two 65lb bombs dropped on GHISTELLES AERODROME.

(b). Fourteen 112lb bombs dropped on THOUROUT RAILWAY STATION, - courses being steered by compass. –Night very dark and clouds thick & low.

The two machines were piloted by FLT.SUB.LT'S JOHNSON and ALLEN.

SEPTEMBER 13TH.

Weather very bad, - prevented flying.

Only a few fighter patrols were carried out.

SEPTEMBER 14TH.

Owing to bad weather, little flying could be done.

A photographic reconnaissance was made to ZEEBRUGGE, but no plates were exposed, owing to bad weather.

A few fighter patrols were carried out for the protection of Fleet. Very few E.A. were seen.

<u>BOMBING RAID. BY DAY. NO. 5 SQUADRON. D.H.4'S.</u>

A bombing raid was attempted by D.H.4'S of No. 5 Squadron, but had to return owing to bad weather.

SEPTEMBER 15TH.

No reconnaissances. Usual fighter patrols for protection of Fleet, and special sweeps over the Fleet during preparations for the bombardment of OSTENDE. Very little enemy aircraft activity.

<u>BOMBING RAID. BY DAY. NO. 5 SQUADRON. D.H.4'S.</u>

A bombing raid was carried out on enemy shipping at sea, along the coast from OSTENDE to ZEEBRUGGE.

Sixteen 65lb, two 50lb, and eighty-four 16lb bombs were dropped on DESTROYERS, and TRAWLERS. ONE DIRECT HIT amidships with a 65lb bomb was made on a large DESTROYER by FLT.SUB.LT. SPROATT and GUNLAYER P.O. HINKLER, causing large clouds of smoke, and all boats were lowered. The vessel was last seen very low in the water, steaming slowly for OSTENDE.

Two bombs were seen to burst close to two vessels, probably TRAWLERS, which were also sunk.

<u>MISCELLANEOUS.</u>

Arrangements were made by the Fleet to bombard OSTENDE, but this had to be cancelled at the last minute owing to the failure of the W/T in the Spotting Machine.

<u>CASUALTIES DURING PERIOD 1ST to 15TH SEPTEMBER.</u>

NAME	SQUAD.	DATE.
FLT.SUB.LT N.D. HALL. (Missing)	5.	3/9/17.
FLT.SUB.LT G.E.C. HOWARD. (Wounded)	4.	3/9/17.

NOTE: A total of over FORTY TONS of bombs have been dropped during the period under review.

Headquarters,
R.N.A.S. Dunkerque.   WING CAPTAIN.
16/9/17   for SENIOR OFFICER.R.N.A.S.

I/W.J.H.   September 16th. 1917.

SUMMARY OF BOMBING RAIDS,
WITH WEIGHTS OF EXPLOSIVES DROPPED
SEPTEMBER 1ST. – 15TH.1917.

TARGET.	BOMBS DROPPED.	TOTAL.
ST. DENIS WESTREM AERODROME.	4 – 250 lbs. 70 – 112 lbs. 7 – 65 lbs.	9,295 lbs.
GHISTELLES AERODROME.	40 – 112 lbs. 2 – 65 lbs.	4,610 lbs.

THOUROUT AERODROME.	4 – 250 lbs.	
	96 – 112 lbs.	
	12 – 65 lbs.	
	2 – 50 lbs.	
	25 – 16 lbs.	13,032 lbs.
VARSSENAERE AERODROME.	3 – 65 lbs.	
	23 – 16 lbs.	563 lbs.
HOUTTAVE AERODROME.	8 – 65 lbs.	
	32 – 16 lbs.	1,032 lbs.
SPARAPPELHOEK AERODROME.	13 – 65 lbs.	
	54 – 16 lbs.	1,709 lbs.
GONTRODE AIRSHIP SHED.	12 – 112 lbs.	1,344 lbs.
BRUGES DOCKS.	8 – 250 lbs.	
	320 – 112 lbs.	
	73 – 65 lbs.	
	2 – 50 lbs.	
	211 – 16 lbs.	46,061 lbs.
GHENT DOCKS.	5 – 112 lbs.	560 lbs.
ZEEBRUGGE MOLE AND HOSTILE SHIPPING.	12 – 65 lbs.	
	2 – 50 lbs.	
	67 – 16 lbs.	1,952 lbs.
HOSTILE SHIPPING OFF OSTEND.	19 – 65 lbs.	
	2 – 50 lbs.	
	84 – 16 lbs.	2,679 lbs.
AMMUNITION DUMPS.	14 – 112 lbs.	1,568 lbs.
RAILWAY STATIONS.	21 – 112 lbs.	2,352 lbs.
RAILWAY SIDINGS, JUNCTIONS, TRAINS AND TRANSPORT.	14 – 112 lbs.	
	9 – 65 lbs.	
	24 – 16 lbs.	2,537 lbs.
VARIOUS.	7 – 65 lbs.	
	24 – 16 lbs.	839 lbs.
	GRAND TOTAL:	90,133 lbs.

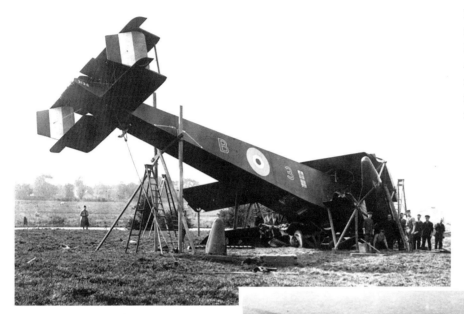

Handley Page O/100 3135 of 7A Sqn is recorded as being badly damaged while landing after a raid on 4 September 1917. Although the communique reports two night raids by 7 and 7A Sqns that night, no mention is made of any losses or mishaps. (Bruce/Leslie)

Sopwith F.1 Camel B6242 joined 3(N) Sqn on 11 September 1917, just missing the action on the previous day, when a DFW reconnaissance aircraft was forced down by the squadron and captured. Named *Fidgety Phil*, this Camel subsequently served with the unit as the Walmer Defence Flight, as seen here, and had several enemy aircraft to its credit. (Bruce/Leslie)

This is the DFW C.V which four Camels of A Flight, 3(N) Sqn, led by Flt Cdr R.F. Redpath, forced down intact at Furnes-Adinkerke on 10 September 1917, after driving it down from 14,000ft and shepherding it over the lines. It was flown to the UK by "Tich" Rochford a fortnight later, and is believed to have been C4686/17, which was allocated the captured aircraft serial XG13 and is thought to have been sent to Canada. (Bruce/Leslie)

A rather hazy but unusual air-to-air study of a 7 Sqn Handley Page O/100 up from Coudekerque.

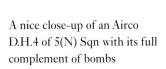

A nice close-up of an Airco D.H.4 of 5(N) Sqn with its full complement of bombs

Curtiss H.12B Large America flying boat 8662 at Great Yarmouth. As well as making attacks on several U-Boats in its lifetime and sinking UB20 in company with 8676 on 29 July 1917, this aircraft also bombed the British submarine E41 on 21 March 1918. (Bruce/Leslie)

ROYAL NAVAL AIR SERVICE COMMUNIQUE.—No. 6.

The weather was generally bad in the earlier part of the past fortnight, but improved towards the end of the month though still unsettled..

September 16th.

A Photographic Reconnaissance was carried out by No. 2 Squadron over Zeebrugge Mole and Lock Gates, plates being exposed with good results.

The usual Fighter Patrols, for protection of Fleet and to Drive off Enemy Spotting Machines were carried out, also Anti-submarine Patrol by Seaplanes.

Enemy Aircraft.

While on Anti-submarine Patrol the large America Seaplane was attacked by two Enemy Seaplanes, one of which was shot down in flames by escorting Camels, Pilots— Flight Commander Graham and Flight Sub-Lieut. Slatter, and seen to crash. The chase of the second had to be abandoned owing to darkness.

A Patrol of five Camels of No. 3 Squadron met eight E. A. Albatross Scouts in formation, Flight Commander Armstrong shot down and destroyed one E. A. and drove down another completely out of control. There were several indecisive Combats, and a Hostile Kite Balloon was attacked but no result observed.

Bombing Raid by day, No. 5 Squadron, D. H. 4's.

A Raid was attempted on Bruges Docks in forenoon, but formation returned owing to bad visibility and strong westerly wind.

In the afternoon another attempt was made, also unsuccessful, but bombs were dropped on Ghistelles Aerodrome. Thirteen 65-lb., two 50-lb., and sixty-eight 16-lb. bombs, were dropped on Ghistelles Aerodrome, bombs falling among sheds, and a house near shed on N.E. corner being destroyed.

September 17th, 18th, 19th.

No flying owing to unfavourable weather.

September 20th.

Weather still very bad, a few Fighter Patrols were carried out.

Bombing Raid by day, No. 5 Squadron, D. H. 4's.

(a) Two 65-lb., two 50-lb. and sixteen 16-lb. bombs were dropped on Aertrycke Aerodrome.
(b) Fifteen 65-lb. and sixty-five 16-lb. bombs were dropped on Sparappelhoek Aerodrome. Weather very bad and visibility much hindered by heavy banks of clouds.

September 21st.

Photographic Reconnaissance was attempted but weather was too unfavourable. The usual Fighter Patrols for protection of Fleet were carried out, and several Enemy spotters were driven off.

Bombing Raid by day, No. 5 Squadron, D. H. 4's.

(a) Four 65-lb., three 50-lb. and thirty-two 16-lb. bombs were dropped on Aertrycke Aerodrome, the bombs dropping close to the sheds.
(b) Seven 65-lb. and forty-four 16-lb. bombs were dropped Sparappelhoek Aerodrome, the western sheds being hit; other bombs all exploded on the Aerodrome.
(c) Two 65-lb. and eight 16-lb. bombs were dropped on Thourout Aerodrome. Bombing Machines were attacked on the way back by many E.A. but succeeded in driving them off with the assistance of a Patrol of Bristol Fighters of No. 48 Squadron, R.F.C.
(d) Eight 250-lb., eighty-two 112-lb. and fifteen 65-lb. bombs were dropped on Thourout Railway Station and Junction. Good shooting appears to have been made and no traffiic was observed on the railway until two days afterwards. Strong westerly wind and visibility not good.

Miscellaneous.

Four 16-lb. bombs were dropped on Thourout Railway Station by a D. H. 4 Machine of No. 5 Squadron. Four 16-lb. bombs were dropped on Ostende Docks by Photographic Escorting Machines of No. 2 Squadron.

September 22nd.

Photographic Reconnaissance by No. 2 Squadron to Ostende, plates being successfully exposed of result of bombardment by large Monitor. Spotting for Monitor was carried out successfully by No. 2 Squadron, considerable damage being caused, and large enemy batteries opened fire but did no damage to ships.

Anti-Submarine Patrol

Was carried out by large America, Pilots—Flight Sub-Lieuts. Magor and Lusk, with escort of Camels of Seaplane Defence Flight, and a large Enemy Submarine, about 200 to 250 feet long, was observed fully blown and attacked, two 230-lb. bombs being dropped at about 800 feet and striking just behind Conning Tower as she was half submerged, causing her to heel over on her side and sink. Wreckage, large bubbles and oil were observed subsequently.

Enemy Aircraft.

A low Patrol of No. 4 Squadron, consisting of Flight Sub-Lieuts. Hunter, Turney and Burt, attacked and shot down a two-seater Enemy Seaplane which was evidently spotting for shore batteries. The Pilot and portions of the Machine being salved by one of our T.B. Destroyers. Flight Sub-Lieut. Burt had a forced landing in the sea, and was picked up by same Destroyer. Subsequently Flight Sub-Lieut. Hunter shot down one Enemy Seaplane which was seen to crash in the sea and sink, and another was forced to land heavily in the sea, with Observer shot and Machine evidently damaged, by Flight Sub-Lieut. Turney at a point about 22 miles N.E. of Ostende.

Bombing Raids by night, No. 7 and 7a Squadrons H.P.'s.

(a) Four 250-lb., fifty-four 112-lb. and seven 65-lb. bombs were dropped on Thourout Railway Station and Junction, starting a small fire.

(b) Eight 250-lb., twenty-eight 112-lb. and sixteen 65-lb. bombs were dropped on Cortemarck Railway Station and Junction, a large fire being started and three direct hits observed.

Miscellaneous.

The escort to Photographic Reconnaissance, dropped eight 16-lb. bombs on Docks at Ostende, exploding on Railway Sidings.

September 23rd.

Weather unfavourable. A Photographic Reconnaissance and Bombing Raid were attempted, but had to return. Anti-Submarine Patrol, nothing sighted.

Enemy Aircraft.

Information being received that a large formation of 22 E.A. were near the lines, 14 Machines of No. 3 Squadron were sent to engage them. In the general melee which took place, it was difficult to see what happened, but Flight Sub-Lieut. Harrower and Flight Lieut. Beamish each shot down one E.A. completely out of control, and there were many other indecisive fights, the E.A. either diving or spinning away.

September 24th.

Two Photographic Reconnaissance were carried out by No. 2 Squadron, and plates successfully exposed in each case.

Usual Fighter Patrols for protection of Fleet and escorts for Bombers, also to drive away Hostile Spotters, were carried out.

An Anti-Submarine Patrol was carried out in the evening, but the Short Machine stalled and spun into the sea while straightening up to bomb some Destroyers, both pilot and passenger being missing.

Enemy Aircraft.

A high Patrol of No. 4 Squadron met a large formation of E.A. Scouts, and in the action that followed, Flight Sub-Lieut. Keirstead shot one E.A. down in flames, and another completely out of control. A number of other indecisive combats took place then, also while escorting the Bombing Machines, and when driving off Enemy Artillery Spotters.

One Patrol of No. 4 Squadron on return from Patrol attacked the Enemy Front Line Trenches from 1,000 feet, firing about 2,000 rounds.

Bombing Raid by day, No. 5 Squadron, D. H. 4's.

Nineteen 65-lb. and eighty-four 16-lb. bombs were dropped on Varssenaere Aerodrome. Visibility good, several direct hits were observed on sheds and huts, and on 26 E. A. lined up on Aerodrome, among which many bombs fell and which probably were considerably damaged.

September 25th.

Photographic Reconnaissance by No. 2 Squadron attempted, but had to return owing to bad visibility. Usual Fighter Patrols for protection of Fleet. Spotting was carried out by No. 2 Squadron for a large Monitor firing on Ostende, on the occasion of the visit of the American Admiral and various Admiralty Officers. Hostile heavy batteries replied, and smoke screens were put up over Ostende within half a minute of first round.

N.B.—As reprisals for this shoot, the 15-inch Leugenboom Gun bombarded Dunkirk from 8-0 p.m. to 11-30 p.m., firing about 20 rounds.

Enemy Aircraft.

Whilst Patrolling over Fleet, two Camels of Seaplane Defence Squadron encountered four E. two-seater Seaplanes and two single-seater Seaplanes, and attacked them at once. Flight Commander Graham shot down a two-seater E. S. in the sea, and Flight Sub-Lieut. Slatter shot down a single-seater E. S. which broke up entirely. One of the E. S. landed near the damaged two-seater, and was fired on on the water and could not get off. Subsequently Flight Commander Graham had an engine seizure, his oil tank being shot through, and landed near a British Destroyer who rescued him and salved his machine.

Bombing Raid by day, No. 5 Squadron, D. H. 4's.

Sixteen 65-lb. and seventy-two 16-lb. bombs were dropped on Sparappelhoek Aerodrome, direct hits being secured on Northern Sheds and a fire started. From fifteen to twenty Eneny Scouts were lined up on Aerodrome, which were well straddled.

Miscellaneous.

Flight Commander Graham and Flight Sub-Lieut. Slatter attacked Enemy Gotha type bombing machines by night, who were bombing Dunkirk from about 1,200 feet, indecisively. Both Pilots landed safely.

September 26th.

No Reconnaissances, sky being overcast all day and clouds low.

Fleet Protective Patrols, no E. A. sighted.

Anti-Submarine Patrol was carried out, nothing sighted.

Bombing Raid by night, No. 7 and 7a Squadrons, H. P.'s.

(a) Twelve 250-lb., seventy-four 112-lb. and twenty-two 65-lb. bombs were dropped on Thourout Railway Station and Junction.

(b) Four 250-lb., twenty 112-lb. and six 65-lb. bombs were dropped on Lichtervelde Railway Station and Junction.

(c) Four 250-lb., thirty 112-lb. and eight 65-lb. bombs were dropped on Cortemarck Junction, one direct hit being observed at fork of Junction.

Weather cloudy, bombs dropped from 2500 feet to 4000 feet, it being necessary to damage these Junctions to hold up enemy reserve troops during our attack east of Ypers.

It was intended to send 10 machines, two trips each, but after four of second trip had gone weather got too bad.

Miscellaneous.

Flight Sub-Lieut. Burt of No. 4 Squadron left in very thick weather to attack an Enemy Aerodrome with bombs and machine gun fire, but visibility was very bad at 200 feet, so four 16-lb. bombs were dropped on Heyst.

September 27th.

Photographic Reconnaissances by No. 2 Squadron, good photos being obtained of Ostende and large coast batteries, and a further Photographic Reconnaissance was made later of coast near Zeebrugge. Usual Fighter Patrols and Escorts. A few indecisive combats.

Two Pilots were lost by collision when on Patrol, both machines falling 15000 feet locked together into the sea.

Anti-Submarine Patrol.

A report being received of a damaged enemy submarine, W/T machines from No. 2 Squadron located her after a search, about 18 miles N.N.W. of Dunkerque, and British destroyers were informed and directed to the spot. Destroyers opened fire and the W/T machines also fired about 50 rounds from Lewis gun, and submarine submerged.

Bombing Raid by day, No. 5 Squadron, D. H. 4's.

Thirteen 65-lb. and sixty-eight 16-lb. bombs were dropped on St. Denis Westrem Aerodrome, and on two groups of 15 and 8 Gothas drawn up on Aerodrome, among which many bombs burst. Smoke also arose from the sheds in two places.

N.B. The very large multi-engined machine was observed on the Aerodrome.

September 28th.

Special Photographic Reconnaissances to Zeebrugge Lock Gates to locate fall of bombs on previous night, and also to photograph Uytkerke Aerodrome, both of which were successfully accomplished. Usual Fighter Patrols over Fleet, and to escort bombers.

Anti-Submarine Patrol.

During the day the same damaged submarine as was seen yesterday was reported, and a further search was made by No. 2 Squadron with no result, as weather was misty and low clouds.

Enemy Aircraft.

During the bombing raid on Dunkerque by night Flight Sub-Lieut. Slatter of the Seaplane Defence Squadron went up in Sopwith Pup and had an indecisive engagement with a Gotha twin engine machine. He landed safely subsequently.

Bombing Raids by night, No. 7 and 7a Squadrons, H.P.'s.

(*a*) Four 250-lb., thirty-two 112-lb. and six 65-lb. bombs were dropped on St. Denis Westrem Aerodrome.

(*b*) Eight 250-lb., forty-six 112-lb. and eighteen 65-lb. bombs were dropped on Lock Gates, Zeebrugge.

(*c*) Fourteen 112-lb. bombs were dropped on Gontrode Airship Shed.

Bombing Raid by day, No. 5 Squadron, D. H. 4's.

A further raid was attempted at St. Denis Westrem but visibility was bad, and clouds low, so bombs were dropped as follows :— Thirteen 65-lb. and sixty 16-lb. bombs were dropped on Houttave Nieumunster Aerodrome.

September 29th.

No Reconnaissances. Usual Fleet Protective Patrols and escorts to bombers, and driving away enemy spotters.

Anti-submarine Patrol was carried out, a hostile submarine being sighted 30 miles N. of Dunkerque by large America, Pilots Flight Sub-Lieuts. Magor and Lusk. Submarine was half submerged when first observed and dived quickly, two 230-lb. bombs being dropped and falling about 200 to 250 feet ahead of the "feather" caused by her periscope as it submerged. Submarine disappeared, but it is feared that the bombs were too far ahead of her. Seaplane remained on the spot for 15 minutes but nothing more was seen.

Bombing Raid by day, No. 5 Squadron, D. H. 4's.

Eighteen 65-lb., ninety-two 16-lb. and two 10-lb. bombs were dropped on St. Denis Westrem Aerodrome. Hits were secured on Bessoneaux and shed and bombs fell very close to four Gotha twin engine machines on Aerodrome, and also to one large multi-engined machine. There were three other similar Gothas on Aerodrome.

September 30th.

Two successful Photographic Reconnaissances were carried out by No. 2 Squadron to Zeebrugge, Bruges and the coast, also heavy coast batteries.

Usual Fleet Protective Patrols and escorts. Several night fighter patrols were carried out against hostile machines bombing Dunkerque. Anti-submarine Patrol carried out—nothing seen, visibility being bad.

Enemy Aircraft.

Flight Lieut. Price and Flight Sub-Lieut. Slatter of Seaplane Defence Squadron were up in "Pups" for two hours by night with object of attacking E. A. bombing Dunkerque. Several encounters took place, which were broken off by E. A. being lost sight of. Flight Sub-Lieut. Slatter had a running fight with a twin engine Gotha machine, and when attacking from the rear experienced considerable difficulty owning to "slip stream" from Gotha's propellers. Eventually the Gotha's port engine stopped, followed by starboard engine and machine dived steeply, and was lost to view, probably having to make a forced landing.

Flight Lieut. Enstone of No. 4 Squadron attacked two Albatross Scouts and shot one down completely out of control.

A patrol of No. 9 Squadron attacked a hostile patrol of five Albatross two-seaters. Flight Sub-Lieut. Stackard shot down one completely out of control, and assisted Flight Commander Fall and Flight Sub-Lieut. Wood to shoot down another which was observed to crash.

Several other indecisive fights took place during the day.

Bombing Raids by night, No. 7 and 7a Squadrons, H. P.'s.

(a) Eight 250-lb., fifty 112-lb. and four 65-lb. bombs were dropped on Lock Gates, Zeebrugge.

(b) Eight 250-lb., two 112-lb. and seventeen 65-lb. bombs were dropped on St. Denis Westrem Aerodrome, one large shed being destroyed by fire, subsequently confirmed by photography by R.F.C.

(c) Twelve 112-lb. and one 65-lb. bombs were dropped on Brugeoise Works and moving trains.

One H.P. machine carrying five Lewis guns, pilot and four gun-layers, and eight 65-lb. bombs patrolled for four hours 10 miles to seaward of Ostende to intercept E. A. night bombers on England, and to observe activity and lighting of E. Aerodromes by night. Three E. A. were met and two attacked, one of which was probably forced to land in the sea, as she went down very steeply. The eight 65-lb. bombs were dropped on Thourout Aerodrome.

A long distance raid by night was made by Flight Commander Brackley, with Observer Sub-Lieut. Bewsher on the Railway Bridge across the Meuse at Namur, on which objective four 250-lb. and eight 65-lb. bombs were dropped, two of the 250-lb. bombs hitting the western end of bridge from a height of 4,400 feet on second run over target. The time for the 250 mile flight was $4\frac{1}{4}$ hours. Much valuable information was obtained from the observations made on this flight.

Casualties during period 16th to 30th September.

Name.	Unit.	Date.
KILLED.		
Flight Sub-Lieut. E. J. K. Buckley	No. 4 Squadron	27/9/17
Flight Sub-Lieut. K. V. Turney	No. 4 Squadron	27/9/17
MISSING.		
Flight Sub-Lieut. A. W. Phillips	Seaplanes	25/9/17
C.P.O. E. A. Boyd, F. 3632	Seaplanes	25/9/17
WOUNDED.		
Flight Commander P. S. Fisher	No. 4 Squadron	25/9/17
Flight Sub-Lieut. G. Harrower	No. 3 Squadron	23/9/17
Flight Sub-Lieut. N. P. Playford	No. 5 Squadron	21/9/17

F. C. HALAHAN,

WING CAPTAIN, R.N.,

FOR SENIOR OFFICER, R.N.A.S.

HEADQUARTERS, R.N.A.S.,

DUNKERQUE.

Summary of Bombing Raids carried out by the R. N. A. S.

From September 16th to 30th, 1917, inclusive,

With weights of Explosives dropped.

TARGET.	BOMBS DROPPED.	TOTAL LBS.
GHISTELLES AERODROME.	13 — 65-lbs. 2 — 50-lbs. 68 — 16-lbs.	2,033
HOUTTAVE AERODROME.	13 — 65-lbs. 60 — 16-lbs.	1,805
AERTRYCKE AERODROME.	6 — 65-lbs. 5 — 50-lbs. 48 — 16-lbs.	1,408
VARSSENAERE AERODROME.	19 — 65-lbs. 84 — 16-lbs.	2,579
SPARAPPELHOEK AERODROME.	38 — 65-lbs. 181 — 16-lbs.	5,366
THOUROUT AERODROME.	10 — 65-lbs. 4 — 16-lbs.	714
GONTRODE AIRSHIP SHED AND AERODROME.	14 — 112-lbs.	1,568
ST. DENIS WESTREM AERODROME.	16 — 250-lbs. 66 — 112-lbs. 60 — 65-lbs. 160 — 16-lbs. 2 — 10-lbs.	17,872
ZEEBRUGGE LOCK GATES.	24 — 250-lbs. 96 — 112-lbs. 38 — 65-lbs.	19,222
ZEEBRUGGE MOLE.	4 — 65-lbs.	260
OSTENDE DOCKS INCLUDING ATELIERS DE LA MARINE.	12 — 16-lbs.	192
LA BRUGEOISE WORKS.	11 — 112-lbs.	1,232
TRAINS AND TRANSPORT.	1 — 112-lbs. 1 — 65-lbs.	177
RAILWAY STATIONS.	40 — 250-lbs. 288 — 112-lbs. 74 — 65-lbs. 4 — 16-lbs.	47,130
RAILWAY BRIDGE AT NAMUR.	4 — 250-lbs. 8 — 65-lbs.	1,520
HOSTILE SUBMARINES. (One Sunk).	4 — 230-lbs.	920
VARIOUS.	4 — 16-lbs.	64

Grand Total - 104,062 lbs.

N.B.—A total of over FORTY-SEVEN TONS of BOMBS have been dropped during the period under review.

PRINTED AT ROYAL NAVAL AIR SERVICE HEADQUARTERS, DUNKERQUE, 1917.

A Curtiss Large America and its crew. In addition to a Lewis machine-gun, the nose position is also provided with a moveable plate camera for oblique air-to-ground photography.

Another 3(N) Sqn Seaplane Defence Flight Pup was N6179 *Baby Mine*, which is recorded elsewhere as bringing down a Gotha bomber on 29 September 1917, while piloted by Flt Sub Lt L.H. Slatter. The communique covering this period gives 30 September as the date for this incident. (Bruce/Leslie)

A Sopwith Triplane of 9(N) Sqn, the unit that engaged five "Albatros two-seaters" on 30 September 1917 and brought one down and sent another down "completely out of control".

A group of Handley Page crews of 3 Wing RNAS. From the left: Flt Sub Lts J.F. Jones and M.A. Hains, Lt Cdr E.W. Stedman, and Flt Sub Lts E.B. Walker, D.R.C. Wright, Pepperel and Paul Bewsher. Bewsher, a poet, had two books of verse published during the war, *The Dawn Patrol* (1917) and *The Bombing of Bruges* (1918), and his account of night bombing, *Green Balls*, first appeared in 1919.

A DFW C.V two-seater sets off on a reconnaissance. One of these fell to the guns of Sopwith F.1 Camel B3893, flown by Flt Lt A.R. Brown of 9(N) Sqn, over Ostende on 13 October 1917.

ROYAL NAVAL AIR SERVICE COMMUNIQUE. No. 7.

The weather generally has been bad during the period under review, and on days on which flying has been possible it has been most unsettled. On several days flying was impossible.

October 1st.

No photographic reconnaissances. Usual fighter patrols for protection of fleet, and escorts to bombers.

An anti-submarine patrol was carried out by seaplanes, but saw nothing.

Enemy Aircraft.

The patrol of five Camels of No. 4 Squadron sent out to escort bombers have had several encounters with Albatross scouts during which Flight Sub-Lieut. Gossip shot down one E.A., which had been previously engaged by Flight Sub-Lieut. Tonks, completely out of control.

Flight Sub-Lieut. Hill of same patrol engaged and shot down a two-seater Albatross, which crashed in the sea and broke up two miles off Ostende.

Flight Sub-Lieuts. Rochford and Hayne of No. 3 Squadron attacked a two-seater E.A. off Ostende and shot the observer and E.A. broke off the fight by diving.

Bombing Raids by night, Nos. 7 and 7a Squadrons, H.P's.

(a) Four 250-lb., thirty-two 112-lb. and six 65-lb. bombs were dropped on St. Denis Westrem Aerodrome, a direct hit being scored on large shed on south side of ground, which burst into flames, and apparently spread to other buildings. This fire was observed from a distance of 30 miles.

(b) Eight 250-lb. and sixteen 65-lb. bombs were dropped on Zeebrugge Lock Gates.

Bombing Raid by day, No. 5 Squadron, D.H. 4's.

Fourteen 65-lb. and fifty-six 16-lb. bombs were dropped on St. Denis Westrem Aerodrome. Several direct hits on sheds, which were set on fire in S.E. corner of Aerodrome. Confirmation by R.F.C. escort machines.

Observers report large shed bombed by H.P.'s on previous night was completely gutted. R.F.C. photographs confirmed this later in the day.

October 2nd.

Usual fighter patrols and escort to bombers.

Night patrol by two machines of Seaplane Defence Squadron against E.A. bombing Dunkerque, but no combats.

Enemy Aircraft.

Flight Sub-Lieuts. Banbury and Redgate together shot down one E.A. at close range, which fell completely out of control. Both pilots belong to No. 9 Squadron which has joined No. 4 Wing from being attached to R.F.C. Flight Commanders Fall and Edwards of No. 9 Squadron, attacked and shot down an E.A. quite out of control.

Bombing Raids by night, Nos. 7 and 7a Squadrons, H.P's.

(a) Six 250-lb. and twenty-eight 112-lb. bombs were dropped on Zeebrugge Lock Gates.

(b) Four 112-lb. bombs were dropped on Ghistelles Aerodrome by one pilot to lighten his machine, whose engines were not pulling well.

Bombing Raid by day, No. 5 Squadron, D.H. 4's.

Eight 65-lb., four 50-lb., forty-eight 16-lb. and two 10-lb. bombs were dropped on St. Denis Westrem Aerodrome. A fire was started on south side of Aerodrome, and bombs fell among eight Gotha machines lined up close to sheds on N.E. side, straddling sheds and machines which were covered by the smoke of bursting bombs.

October 3rd.

Bad weather during the day and no flying.

Bombing Raids by night, Nos. 7 and 7a Squadrons, H.P's.

(*a*) Four 250-lb. and twenty 112-lb. bombs were dropped on St. Denis Westrem Aerodrome.

(*b*) Eight 250-lb. and twenty-three 112-lb. bombs were dropped on Zeebrugge Lock Gates.

(*c*) Four 250-lb. and four 112-lb. bombs were dropped on Thourout Railway Station.

(*d*) One 250-lb. and two 112-lb. bombs were dropped on Bruges Docks. The search lights made so much glare that after several attempts, as pilot could not locate objective, he dropped

(*e*) Three 250-lb. and four 112-lb. bombs on Ghistelles Aerodrome, whose landing lights were observed to be lit.

Visibility generally was very poor.

October 4th, 5th, 6th, 7th, 8th and 9th.

No flying. Heavy gales and rain with low thick clouds.

October 10th.

No photographic reconnaissances, but a few fighter patrols carried out during forenoon. One patrol on return journey descended to 800 feet and fired at enemy trenches, Lombartzyde. A pilot of another patrol, being heavily shelled by A.A., descended to 500 feet and scattered the gun's crew, one man being observed to fall.

Bombing Raids by night, Nos. 7 and 7a Squadrons, H.P.'s.

Between 01.10 and 04.50 sixteen 250-lb. and fifty-five 112-lb. bombs were dropped on Thourout Station and Junction.

Four 250-lb. and thirty-two 112-lb. bombs were also dropped on Lichtervelde Station and Junction.

October 11th.

Unfavourable weather conditions made only a few patrols possible, a few E.A. being seen but no combats reported.

A sweep, during a bombing raid, fired into enemy trenches at Lombartzyde and an offensive patrol in the afternoon again attacked these trenches on their return.

Flight Sub-Lieut. Black failed to return from the patrol.

Bombing Raid by day, No. 5 Squadron, D.H. 4's.

About noon, fourteen 65-lb., fifty 16-lb. and two 10-lb. bombs were dropped on Sparappelhoek Aerodrome, hangars on north and south-west sides being straddled, and a shed on south-east side reported as hit.

October 12th.

Unfavourable weather conditions rendered war work of any importance impossible.

October 13th.

Unfavourable weather again rendered photographic or coastal reconnaissances impossible.

Some fighter patrols were carried out during the forenoon, during one of which a D.F.W. was brought down in flames over Ostende by Flight Lieut. A. R. Brown.

A patrol which went up to intercept an E.A. over Dunkerque attacked it on her return, and the patrol leader, Squadron Commander Huskisson, succeeded in getting within 200 yards, and it is thought, disabled the observer as he was no longer visible, and E.A. stopped firing.

October 14th.

Two photographic reconnaissances were carried out during the day in the direction of Middlekerke, during one of which an indecisive engagement took place with two E.A. who approached from Ostende.

Two other indecisive engagements took place in the course of offensive patrols from No. 4 Wing.

October 15th.

Bombing Raid by night, Nos. 7 and 7a Squadrons, H.P's.

A bombing raid was carried out over Bruges Docks on the night of the 14th and morning of 15th. Twelve 250-lb. and fifty-seven 112-lb. bombs were dropped on the target, and hits are claimed on the land between W. and E. bassins, a number also falling among the docks, but the intensity of searchlights and A.A. made accurate observation difficult.

A photographic reconnaissance and a considerable number of escort and offensive patrols took place during the day. During the course of these, several E.A. formations were encountered, and two E.A. are reported as driven down over Ostende and St. Pierre Capelle by No. 4 Wing.

Flight Sub-Lieut. Oakley failed to return from one of these patrols. In connection with this a report has been received from 4th Army that a British machine was seen to land near Niewland Polde at 12.20, and that the pilot was wounded and taken prisoner. As the R.F.C. had no casualties in this area to-day it is thought this must refer to Flight Sub-Lieut. Oakley.

Bombing Raid by day, No. 5 Squadron, D.H. 4's.

A day bombing raid was carried out by D.H. 4's, the target being Varssenaere Aerodrome, over which fourteen 65-lb., two 50-lb., sixty 16-lb. and one 10-lb. bombs were dropped. Some of the sheds on E. side of Aerodrome are reported as being hit and other damage is considered possible on Bessoneaux in N.W. corner, but heavy clouds made any accurate observations difficult,

Seven 16-lb. bombs were, in addition, dropped on Houttave Aerodrome.

During the return of this raid several encounters with E.A. formations are reported. Flight Commander De Mesurier with Gun-layer Jackson engaged two E.A. and drove them off, the first going down out of range, spinning, and the second, which dived and attacked at very close range, after receiving a tray from rear gun, gliding away with engine stopped.

Bombing Raid by night, Nos. 7 and 7a Squadrons, H.P.'s.

A night raid by H.P.'s was also carried out over Bruges Docks on which twelve 250-lb. and fifty-seven 112-lb. bombs were dropped. Intense searchlight and active A.A. again rendered observation difficult, but W. and E. bassins were again well straddled, result of bombs falling amongst the docks.

Casualties during period 1st to 15th October.

MISSING.

Name.	Unit.	Date.
Flight Sub-Lieut. N. Black	No. 9 Squadron	11/10/17
Flight Sub-Lieut. W. E. B. Oakley	No. 9 Squadron	15/10/17

F. C. HALAHAN,

WING CAPTAIN, R.N.,

for SENIOR OFFICER, R.N.A.S.

HEADQUARTERS, R.N.A.S.,

DUNKERQUE.

Summary of Bombing Raids carried out by the R. N. A. S.

From October 1st to 15th, 1917, inclusive,

With weights of Explosives dropped.

TARGET.	BOMBS DROPPED.		TOTAL LBS.
GHISTELLES AERODROME.	3 — 250 lbs. 8 — 112 lbs.		1,646
HOUTTAVE AERODROME.	7 — 16 lbs.		112
ST. DENIS WESTREM AERODROME.	4 — 250 lbs. 20 — 112 lbs. 14 — 65 lbs. 56 — 16 lbs.		5,046
VARSSENAERE AERODROME.	30 — 65 lbs. 2 — 50 lbs. 118 — 16 lbs. 4 — 10 lbs.		3,978
ZEEBRUGGE LOCK GATES.	14 — 250 lbs. 51 — 112 lbs.		9,212
BRUGES DOCKS.	9 — 250 lbs. 42 — 112 lbs.		6,954
RAILWAY STATIONS, SIDINGS AND JUNCTIONS.	24 — 250 lbs. 91 — 112 lbs.		16,192

Grand Total - 43,140 lbs.

N.B.—A total of over NINETEEN TONS of BOMBS have been dropped during the period under review.

Printed at Royal Naval Air Service Headquarters, Dunkerque, 1917.

Camel B3884 of 9(N) Sqn had several victories and shared victories to its credit while serving with the unit, and added a couple more to its tally during its subsequent Service life. (Bruce/Leslie)

On 21 October 1917 Sopwith Triplane N5387 *Peggy* of 1(N) Sqn, flown by Flt Sub Lt H.leR. Wallace, sent an enemy two-seater down out of control south of Comines. It joined 12(N) Sqn on 6 December. (Bruce/Leslie)

Daly of 12(N) Sqn was responsible for this Sopwith Triplane crash.

The Sopwith Triplanes of 1(N) Sqn lined up on 28 October 1917. (Bruce/Leslie)

Above and right: Sopwith F.1 Camels of 9(N) Sqn at Bray Dunes, displaying an assortment of garish personal fuselage markings. In the line-up picture, B3884 is on the extreme left and B6327 is on the right. The latter was with the squadron from 19 October 1917 to January 1918. (Bruce/Leslie)

ROYAL NAVAL AIR SERVICE COMMUNIQUE.—No. 8.

Weather has been bad for flying during the fortnight, gales and low clouds making flying impossible on several days.

October 16th.

A few fighter patrols over Fleet and to drive off spotters were carried out, but weather generally was too unsettled for reconnaissances or photographic work.

Enemy Aircraft.

Flight Commander Fall of No. 9 Squadron, observing a large enemy two-seater close under clouds, climbed above the clouds this side of lines, and then returned, dived on the E.A., and shot him down in flames, the observer falling out of the machine.

October 17th.

No photographic work or reconnaissances—weather conditions made them impossible.
A few fighter patrols were carried out.

Enemy Aircraft.

A patrol of five Camels of No. 4 Squadron had a long indecisive action with five E.A. two-seaters at 8,000 feet, above which were 10 single-seater E.A. at 15,000 feet, the two-seaters acting as decoys for the scouts, which all broke off the fight as soon as the Camels were reinforced by five R.F.C. Pups. The Camels, on the way back, fired their remaining ammunition at German transport on the roads, from low altitude.

Flight Sub-Lieut. Redgate of No. 9 Squadron engaged and shot down an E.A. single-seater completely out of control.

Flight Commander Fall of same squadron, engaged and drove down an E.A. single-seater rotary-engined " V " strutter scout in a spin from 13,000 feet to 500 feet. This machine was probably quite out of control.

Flight Commander Price and Flight Sub-Lieut. Pinder of Seaplane Defence Squadron engaged two enemy seaplanes, the latter shooting one E.S. down to the sea where it crashed and broke up, one mile off Zeebrugge Mole.

October 18th.

Weather still unsettled.

A photographic reconnaissance to Zeebrugge by Flight Sub-Lient. Ovens and Observer-Lieut. Chapman of No. 2 Squadron was carried out, and plates exposed successfully.

Usual Fleet Protective Patrols and escorts to bombers and reconnaissance machines.

Bombing Raid by day, No. 5 Squadron, D. H. 4's.

Eleven 65-lb., two 50-lb. and sixty 16-lb. bombs were dropped on Varssenaere Aerodrome. Bombs fell well among sheds and hangars. A.A. fire was heavy, nearly all the machines being hit in several places.

October 19th.

Sky overcast, bad visibility.

A few fighter patrols were carried out, but very few E.A. seen, and all declined to engage.

October 20th.

No reconnaissances.

Machines of No. 2 Squadron went to vicinity of Ostende to spot for Monitor firing, but the latter did not open fire, so machines returned.

At 2.30, Monitor opened fire, one round being spotted, the spotting machines then were unable to continue, owing to dense smoke screens. Pilots, Flight Commanders Robinson and Sandford, and Observer Sub-Lieuts. Anderson and Pickup.

Usual Fighter Patrols and escorts to Fleet and spotters.

Bombing Raid by night, Nos. 7 and 7a Squadrons, H.P.'s
(2 Machines).

Two 250-lb., twelve 112-lb. and eight 65-lb. bombs were dropped on Bruges Docks. Visibility very poor.

Bombing Raid by day, No 5 Squadron, D. H. 4's.

Ten 65-lb., two 50-lb. and forty-eight 16-lb. bombs were dropped on Engel Aerodrome. Bombs exploded well among hangars, and a fire was caused among buildings on south-western side.

October 21st.

Photographic reconnaissances were carried out to Breedene to search for new aerodrome reported, and of Ostende harbour to photograph results of bombardment. Pilots, Flight Commander Robinson and Flight Sub-Lieut. Brewerton, and Observer Sub-Lieuts. Anderson and Nicholson, all of No. 2 Squadron. Plates were successfully exposed.

Usual fighter patrols and escorts to spotters and bombers.

Spotting was carried out for Monitor firing on Ostende at about noon. After first spot had been given, spotting machine, Pilot, Squadron Commander Fellowes, Observer Sub-Lieut. Stennett, was attacked by 6 H.A., and W/T gear put out of action, and observer slightly wounded. The second W/T machine, Pilot, Flight Sub-Lieut. Warne-Browne and Observer Sub-Lieut. White attempted to carry on spotting, but this was rendered impossible by smoke screens. This latter machine drove off the E.A. who attacked Squadron Commander Fellowes' machine, shooting one E.A. down out of control apparently, but the E.A. was not seen to crash, as both pilot and observer were much too busy to look.

Enemy Aircraft.

A patrol of five Camels of No. 4 Squadron, when on offensive patrol near Ghistelles, encountered about 20 E.A., some two-seaters and some scouts, and attacked them at once. Enemy formations were reinforced by eight or ten single-seater E.A. Flight Commander Shook shot down an Albatross D III. scout out of control, and was then wounded himself. Flight Sub-Lieut. Keirstead destroyed a similar E.A., the port wings falling off, and shot down another, which was attacking Flight Commander Shook, completely out of control. A fourth E.A. was shot down in flames, and is attributed to Flight Sub-Lieut. Eyre, who subsequently, after the combat had been broken off, was missing, though he got away from the main fight alright. All the other machines returned safely.

It is interesting to note that the last eight or ten E.A. to join the fight were rotary-engined "V" strutters.

On arriving over their objective the bombing formation of No. 5 Squadron were attacked by a number of E.A. scouts, and many combats took place.

Flight Commander Le Mesurier and Gun-layer Jackson shot away the propeller of one E.A. which undoubtedly crashed quite out of control, Flight Lieut. Shaw and Gun-layer Naylor shot down another out of control, and the R.F.C. escorting flight of No. 48 Squadron shot down yet another. The bombers were much shot about.

Flight Sub-Lieut. Humphrey of No. 12 Squadron, when on patrol near Gravelines chased two E.S., one a two-seater, and one scout, to within six miles of Margate then opening fire, on which E.S. turned and flew off to S.E., and Flight Sub-Lieut. Humphrey landed at Manstone with his petrol exhausted.

Bombing Raids by day, No. 5 Squadron, D. H. 4's.

(a) Six 65-lb., two 50-lb. and thirty-one 16-lb. bombs were dropped on Vlisseghen Aerodrome, bursting well among the sheds.

(b) Eight 65-lb., two 50-lb. and forty 16-lb. bombs were dropped on Houttave Aerodrome, causing a fire owing to a direct hit on a shed. A machine getting off, near which a bomb burst, was observed to crash on edge of Aerodrome.

Bombing Raid by night, No. 7 and 7a Squadrons, H.P's.

Two 250-lb. and eight 65-lb. bombs were dropped on Bruges Docks. Visibility very bad.

October 22nd.

No reconnaissances. Usual fighter patrols, but practically no E.A. seen.

Bombing Raid by day, No 5 Squadron, D. H. 4's.

During the afternoon, a raid was attempted on St. Denis Westrem Aerodrome, but owing to heavy low clouds and mist the bombs, consisting of six 65-lb., four 50-lb., forty-eight 16-lb. and one 10-lb., were dropped on Zeebrugge Mole and vicinity. Two direct hits reported on a vessel alongside the Mole, causing a fire, and a barge was also hit and set on fire. Several hits made on Mole and buildings.

Bombing Raid by night, Nos. 7 and 7a Squadrons, H.P.'s.

Two 250-lb., twelve 112-lb. and eight 65-lb. bombs were dropped on Melle Railway siding, near Ghent. Visibility poor.

October 23rd.

Bad weather. Rain. No flying.

October 24th.

A reconnaissance was carried out in a short spell of fine weather over Zeebrugge, Bruges, and Ostende. No other flying except a few fighter patrols, and no E.A. seen.

October 25th.

No flying. Gale of wind blowing, very squally.

October 26th.

Weather very bad, so that little flying was possible. A few patrols, but no E.A. seen.

Bombing Raids by day, No. 5 Squadron, D. H. 4's.

(a) Four 65-lb. and twelve 16-lb. bombs were dropped on Thourout Railway Station.
(b) Four 16-lb. bombs were dropped on Varssenaere.

These two objectives were detailed in conjunction with the Military Operations in the vicinity of Passchendael, and although it was raining and the clouds thick and low, two pilots, Flight Sub-Lieuts. Lupton and Dickson, with Observer Sub-Lieut. Pattison and Gun-layer Smith volunteered to go, and carried out their mission successfully, returning and landing in the dark.

October 27th.

Weather much finer, enabling a photographic reconnaissance to be carried out to Bruges and Zeebrugge by Flight Lieut. Chisholm and Observer Sub-Lieut. Nicholson of No. 2 Squadron. Plates were successfully exposed. A reconnaissance well out to sea was also carried out by Flight Sub-Lieut. Warne-Brown and Observer Sub-Lieut. White of the same Squadron.

Photographs were also taken of the objectives bombed by No. 5 Squadron during the bombing raids.

Usual fighter patrols and escorts to bombers and photographic reconnaissances.

Enemy Aircraft.

A large number of E.A. were encountered during the day and several combats took place. A flight of five Camels of No. 9 Squadron, led by Flight Commander Edwards, observing nine E.A. scouts diving on four Camels of the same squadron, attacked the E.A. and shot down one completely out of control. Several indecisive combats also took place.

Flight Lieut. Slatter of Seaplane Defence Squadron, during a long range action between British and enemy destroyers, the latter accompanied by many E.A. bombers, attacked a single E.A. scout detached from the main body, and shot it down in the sea out of control. Subsequently he attacked another isolated E.A. which dived away and joined up with the main body who were bombing the destroyers. Flight Lieut. Slatter was able to give some good comments on the destroyer action and the fall of shot, and then returned to make his report.

Bombing Raids by night, Nos. 7 and 7a Squadrons, H.P.'s.

(a) Twelve 250-lb. and thirty-three 112-lb. bombs were dropped on Lichtervelde Railway Station. Direct hits caused a large explosion, followed by many small ones, possibly a truck load of ammunition.

(b) Twelve 250-lb. and fifty-eight 112-lb. bombs were dropped on Thourout Railway Station. Bombs fell close to a moving train, which stopped at once. An explosion was also caused.

(c) Sixteen 112-lb. bombs were dropped on Cortemarck Railway Junction.

Bombing Raids by day, No. 5 Squadron, D. H. 4's.

(a) Four 65-lb., four 50-lb. and thirty-eight 16-lb. bombs were dropped on Sparappelhoek Aerodrome.

(b) Four 65-lb. and sixteen 16-lb. bombs were dropped on Engel Aerodrome.

(c) Eight 16-lb. bombs were dropped on Ostende—Thourout Railway Line, just south of Engel.

Bombers were attacked by E.A. on several occasions, one pilot being wounded.

October 28th.

Very hazy most of the day, photographic work not possible.

Anti-submarine patrol by large America seaplane, and mine-seeking patrols by D.H. 4 of No. 2 Squadron were carried out, also usual offensive patrols and escorts to bombers.

Enemy Aircraft.

Considerable E.A. activity.

Flight Commander Brown and Flight Lieut. Banbury of No. 9 Squadron attacked a formation of seven E.A. and shot down one E.A. which was observed to crash.

Flight Lieut. Lawson of Seaplane Defence Squadron attacked and drove off an E. seaplane, two-seater, which was about to attack British destroyers which were in action with enemy destroyers, causing her to drop her bombs and dive away.

There were several other indecisive combats.

Bombing Raids by night, Nos. 7 and 7a Squadrons, H.P.'s.

(a) Twenty-three 112-lb. bombs were dropped on Engel Aerodrome.

(b) Eight 112-lb. bombs were dropped on Cortemarck Railway Junction.

(c) Thirty 112-lb. bombs were dropped on Lichtervelde Railway Junction.

(d) Fifteen 250-lb. and twenty-four 112-lb. bombs were dropped on St. Denis Westrem Aerodrome. One machine failed to return.

Bombing Raids by day, No. 5 Squadron, D. H. 4's.

(a) Seven 65-lb., one 50-lb., forty-one 16-lb. and two 10-lb. bombs were dropped on Varssenaere Aerodrome.

(b) One 50-lb. and two 16-lb. bombs were dropped on Railway Line and Dump at Stahill-Brugge, N.W. of Varssenaere.

October 29th.

No photographic work. A mine-seeking patrol was carried out by No. 2 Squadron.

Usual Fleet protective and offensive patrols and escorts to bombers.

One anti-submarine patrol by large America seaplane carried out.

Night patrols over Dunkerque aera during bomb raid by Seaplane Defence Squadron.

Bombing Raids by night, Nos. 7 and 7a Squadrons, H.P.'s.

(a) Six 250-lb., thirty-two 112-lb. and twenty-four 65-lb. bombs were dropped on Hoboken Yard and the large Station De Sud, and adjacent Railway Sidings. Big explosions and several fires occured, which were seen as long as Antwerp was in sight.

(b) Two 250-lb. and eight 65-lb. bombs were dropped on three trains close to La Pinte Junction near Ghent, bombs exploded close to them on the track.

(c) Two 250-lb. and eight 65-lb. bombs were dropped on Bruges Docks.

(d) Twelve 112-lb. bombs were dropped on a very large, brightly illuminated factory near Duren. This machine, Pilot, Flight Lieut. Gardner, Observer, Sub-Lieut. Terrell, started for an objective in Germany, but when about half-way, encountered rain and bad weather, with low clouds, and machine had to fly at about 1,500 to 2,500 feet. Weather being so bad, the original objective had to be abandoned, and the factory near Duren was bombed, one direct hit being made, and all other bombs fell within factory compound. The return journey was made in even worse conditions, in heavy rain for two hours, steering by compass only, and the machine was landed safely after $7\frac{1}{2}$ hours at the R.F.C. Aerodrome at Droglandt, about 15 miles from Dunkerque, and flew back to its aerodrome next morning.

October 30th.

Bad weather. Only a few fighter patrols all day.

During the night three machines of Seaplane Defence Squadron patrolled for defence of Dunkerque from enemy bomb raids. There were three indecisive engagements.

Bombing Raids by night, Nos. 7 and 7a Squadrons, H.P.'s.

(a) Fourteen 112-lb. bombs were dropped on Sparappelhoek Aerodrome.

(b) Two 250-lb. and twenty 112-lb. bombs were dropped on Varssenaere Aerodrome.

October 31st.

A photographic reconnaissance by Flight Commander Robinson and Observer Sub-Lieut. Andrews of No. 2 Squadron was carried out to Bruges and district. Plates were exposed, but conditions were poor. Machine was attacked by E.A. (see Combats).

Usual Fleet protective patrols and escorts.

Anti-submarine patrol was carried out by large America seaplane.

Enemy Aircraft.

While acting as escort to the photographic machine, Flight Sub-Lieut. Brewerton, with Gun-layer Pinchen of No. 2 Squadron were attacked by six E.A., one of which was shot down completely out of control by Gun-layer Pinchen, who was wounded in the arm.

Flight Commander Fall of No. 9 Squadron shot down an E.A. completely out of control, and the same pilot and his flight killed or badly wounded the observer of a two-seater Albatross.

Bombing Raids by night, Nos. 7 and 7a Squadrons, H.P.'s.

(a) Fourteen 250-lb. and thirty-eight 112-lb. bombs were dropped on Lichtervelde Railway Junction causing two big explosions on the track, and dense columns of smoke.

(b) Eight 250-lb. and forty 112-lb. bombs were dropped on Thourout Railway Junction.

Bombing Raids by day, No. 5 Squadron, D. H. 4's.

(a) Seven 65-lb., four 50-lb. and thirty-three 16-lb. bombs were dropped on Aertrycke Aerodrome.

(b) Eight 16-lb. bombs were dropped on large shed three miles E. of Beerst. Bombers were attacked by E.A., but these were driven off.

Honours Awarded between 16th and 31st October.

NAME	UNIT	AWARDED
Acting Flight Commander R. Grahame, D.S.C.	Seaplane Defence Squadron	D.S.O.
Acting Flight Commander P. S. Fisher, D.S.C.	No. 4 Squadron	D.S.O.
Acting Flight Commander S. T. Edwards	No. 9 Squadron	D.S.C.
Acting Flight Commander E. R. Brown	No. 9 Squadron	D.S.C.
Flight Sub-Lieut. F. R. Johnson	No. 7 Squadron	D.S.C.
Flight Commander G. E. Hervey	Dover	D.S.C.
Flight Lieut. L. H. Slatter	Seaplane Defence Squadron	D.S.C.
Flight Lieut. V. R. Gibbs	No. 7A Squadron	D.S.C.
Aircraftsman, 1st Class, J. Conley, O. No. F 16254	No. 7A Squadron	D.S.M.
Air Mechanic (Gun-layer) J. R. Barber, O. No. F 3771	No. 7 Squadron	D.S.M.

Casualties.

MISSING.

NAME	RANK	SQUADRON	DATE
Eyre, E. G. A.	Flight Sub-Lieut.	No. 4	21/10/17
Andrews, G.	Flight Sub-Lieut.	No. 7A	27/10/17
Oakley, W. E. B.	Flight Sub-Lieut.	No. 9	15/10/17
Kent, G. A.	L.M. (G.-L.), O. No. J 5381	No. 7A	27/10/17

WOUNDED.

Shook, A. M.	Flight Commander	No. 4	21/10/17
Stennett, W. R.	Observer Sub-Lieut.	No. 2	21/10/17
Pinchen, S. H.	A.M. 1 (G.-L.), F 2932	No. 2	31/10/17

Summary of Bombing Raids carried out by the R. N. A. S.

From October 16th to 31st, 1917, inclusive,

With weights of Explosives dropped.

TARGET.	BOMBS DROPPED.	TOTAL LBS.
ST. DENIS WESTREM AERODROME.	15 — 250 lbs. 24 — 112 lbs.	6,438
SPARAPPELHOEK AERODROME.	14 — 112 lbs. 11 — 65 lbs. 8 — 50 lbs. 71 — 16 lbs.	3,819
VARSSENAERE AERODROME.	2 — 250 lbs. 20 — 112 lbs. 18 — 65 lbs. 3 — 50 lbs. 105 — 16 lbs. 2 — 10 lbs.	5,760
ENGEL AERODROME.	23 — 112 lbs. 14 — 65 lbs. 2 — 50 lbs. 64 — 16 lbs.	4,610
VLISSEGHEM AERODROME.	6 — 65 lbs. 2 — 50 lbs. 31 — 16 lbs.	986
HOUTTAVE AERODROME.	8 — 65 lbs. 2 — 50 lbs. 40 — 16 lbs.	1,260
ZEEBRUGGE LOCK GATES, MOLE, ETC.	6 — 65 lbs. 4 — 50 lbs. 48 — 16 lbs. 1 — 10 lbs.	1,368
BRUGES DOCKS.	18 — 250 lbs. 69 — 112 lbs. 24 — 65 lbs.	13,788
DUREN (LARGE FACTORY).	12 — 112 lbs.	1,344
ANTWERP. (COCKERILL'S YARDS AND MAIN RAILWAY SIDINGS.	6 — 250 lbs. 32 — 112 lbs. 24 — 65 lbs.	6,644
RAILWAY STATIONS, JUNCTIONS, LINES, SIDINGS AND TRAINS.	50 — 250 lbs. 235 — 112 lbs. 22 — 65 lbs. 1 — 50 lbs. 22 — 16 lbs.	40,652
VARIOUS	8 — 16 lbs.	128

Grand Total - 86,797 lbs.

N.B.—A total of over THIRTY-EIGHT TONS of BOMBS have been dropped during the period under review.

PRINTED AT ROYAL NAVAL AIR SERVICE HEADQUARTERS, DUNKERQUE, 1917.

November 1st.

Unfavourable weather. No work of importance carried out.

November 2nd.

Weather poor. Mist and rain.

November 3rd.

Weather still unfavourable.

Enemy Aircraft.

One patrol only, carried out by No. 9 Squadron. Several two-seater Albatross, escorted by eleven E. A. Scouts were attacked between Middlekerke and Slype. The two-seaters were driven back. No results.

November 4th.

Weather fine, considerable mist at low altitudes. Photographic reconnaissance to Ghent was abandoned owing to clouds. No. 2 Squadron.

Usual Fleet and anti-submarine patrols were carried out.

Enemy Aircraft.

A patrol of three Camels of No. 4 Squadron observed and engaged a formation of five Rumpler two-seaters which were spotting for enemy destroyers firing on the Fleet. The Rumplers were escorted by two seaplane scouts, and three Albatross two-seaters. Flight Sub-Lieut. Gossip attacked an Albatross two-seater, shot the observer dead, and drove the machine into the water. A second Albatross was also probably destroyed, and the formation broken up.

A patrol of five Camels of No. 9 Squadron was attacked by seven Albatross Scouts. Flight Commander Fall drove one machine down which fell on its back, stalled, and was last seen spinning through the clouds.

Indecisive actions took place between five Camels of No. 9 Squadron and four E. A.

During the attack by E. A. on the bombing formation, Flight Lieut. Shaw with A. M. (G/L) Naylor, drove his adversary down, and Flight Sub-Lieut. Mason with A. M. (G/L) Burne, shot one down completely out of control. A. M. (G/L) Burne was wounded in the leg.

Bombing Raid by day, No. 5 Squadron, D. H. 4's.

Three 65-lb., seven 50-lb., forty-six 16-lb. and two 10-lb. bombs were dropped on Engel Aerodrome. The sheds were well straddled, but the formation being heavily attacked by E. A. rendered the observation of results extremely difficult. Several of our machines were badly shot about, but all returned safely.

November 5th.

Weather misty. No war work of importance.

November 6th.

Weather overcast. One pilot and observer failed to return from local flight.

November 7th.

Owing to unfavourable weather conditions, little war work could be carried out during the day. A few fighter patrols were attempted, but had to be abandoned owing to clouds and bad weather.

Bombing Raid by night, Nos. 7 and 7a Squadrons, H.P.'s.

Raid on Thourout and Lichtervelde Railway Stations and Junctions.

Twelve 250-lb. and twenty-six 112-lb. bombs were dropped on Thourout. The junctions were well straddled, and direct hits observed on the lines.

Eight 250-lb. and forty-six 112-lb. bombs were dropped on Lichtervelde. A train proceeding from Lichtervelde to Roulers was bombed, and a large fire seen S.W. of Lichtervelde. Bombs exploded close to junction. All machines returned safey.

November 8th.

Weather conditions continue very unfavourable.   Fighter Patrols were carried out over Nieuport Sector and the Fleet.

November 9th.

Enemy Aircraft.

E. A. were very active throughout the day.   A patrol of No. 9 Squadron attacked six Albatross two-seaters, and drove two down over Middlekerke.   A patrol of three Camels of No. 4 Squadron had indecisive actions with two spotting machines, which were driven down. Two Gothas were engaged near Pervyse by pilots of No. 1 Squadron, and driven down towards Ghistelles.   Flight Sub-Lieut. Tonks, of No. 4 Squadron, observed a D. F. W. two-seater, flying west, it was however forced to recross the lines north of Pervyse by A. A. fire over Furnes.   After a running fight, during which several hundred rounds were fired by Flight Sub-Lieut. Tonks, E. A. was attacked at close range and driven down completely out of control over Schoore, the observer in the D. F. W. did not fire a shot.

A D. F. W. seen to be spinning spirally near Pervyse, was attacked by Acting Flight Commander Enstone, of No. 4 Squadron.   The machine was last seen spinning completely out of control.   The result of this fight is confirmed by the Belgians and No. 9 Squadron.   It is believed that the machine had been previously hit, but was then only just under control.

November 10th.

Weather continued very bad, low clouds, and showers prevented any war work.

Bombing Raid by night, Nos. 7 and 7a Squadrons, H. P.'s.

On the night of November 9th, seven machines attempted an attack on St. Denis Westrem Aerodrome.   Owing to extremely unfavourable weather only one machine, piloted by Flight Sub-Lieut. Johnson, reached the objective on which fourteen 112-lb. bombs were dropped, well straddling the hangars.

The remainder of the pilots attacked the alternative target—Bruges Dock—dropping twelve 250-lb. and forty-six 112-lb. bombs.   Excellent shooting appears to have been made and many hits observed, a large fire being caused in docks.

On the return journey all machines encountered very heavy rain storms.   Nevertheless all machines returned safely.

November 11th.

The continuation of poor weather conditions prevented any photographic reconnaissances or bomb raids being carried out.

Enemy Aircraft.

Several hostile formations were sighted during the day.   A pilot of No. 4 Squadron while on a test flight observed E. A. proceeding towards Furnes, consisting of three Gothas, nine two-seaters, believed to be D. F. W.'s, and three scouts, with black wings, white cross, and it is believed rotary engines.   Pilot attacked rearmost Gotha, but had to break off engagement owing to both guns jambing.

Six large machines were seen coming from Ostende.   Immediately our patrol was sighted E. A. turned at Westende Bains, and flew back.   Two more of these machines were seen to go into a spin after an encounter with an R. F. C. patrol.   From further information, this patrol encountered a big formation of these large E. A., destroying two and driving one down out of control.

November 12th.

Bad weather conditions, with mist and low visibility impeded the observers in their observations during the submarine and Fleet patrols.   There was nothing to report.

Enemy Aircraft.

A patrol of five Sopwith Triplanes, No. 1 Squadron, attacked several Albatross scouts and two-seaters in the neighbourhood of Dixmude, with indecisive results.

A patrol of Camels, No. 9 Squadron, drove off several enemy scouts which were attacking allied machines. Other indecisive combats took place. Flight Lieut. Kinkhead and Flight Sub-Lieut. Forman, No. 1 Squadron, attacked and destroyed a new type of scout near Dixmude. After several attacks he nose-dived and was seen to be on fire.

NEW TYPE SCOUT.—Slightly larger than a Triplane with Fokker planes, Albatross tail with large fin, two single struts and large fuselage. Stationary engine. Climb the same as Triplane at 6,000 feet. Pilot sitting well behind the mainplane.

Bombing Raid by day, No. 5 Squadron, D. H. 4's.

A raid was carried out on Vlisseghem Aerodrome, over which eight 50-lb., twenty-nine 16-lb. and two 10-lb. bombs were dropped. No direct hits were observed, but bombs fell close to the sheds. All machines returned safely.

Acting Flight Lieut. G. L. Trapp reported killed from No. 10 Squadron, attached R.F.C.

November 13th.

Weather conditions much improved, but not sufficiently so to enable photographic work to be carried out. Special W/T patrols and Fleet patrols were carried out.

Enemy Aircraft.

E. A. was very active during the day, numerous encounters and indecisive combats taking place. During the morning, patrols from Nos. 1, 4 and 9 Squadrons, chased and engaged formations of Gothas, in one case the observer in the Gotha was probably killed by two pilots of No. 1 Squadron as he ceased firing after several attacks. In all encounters the E. A. were driven back over their lines. A patrol from No. 4 Squadron, which went up to intercept E. A., observed two formations of Albatross Scouts, one of nine, and the other of six machines, closing on a formation of Pups and Camels. Flight Sub-Lieut. Gossip attacked two of the E. A., one was brought down completely out of control, in the second case the result was indecisive. Flight Commander Rowley of No. 1 Squadron, attacked an Aviatik, shooting him down completely out of control E. of Nieuport. The patrol also indecisively engaged a number of two-seaters and scouts during the day. During the afternoon, high offensive patrol, six Camels from No. 9 Squadron, had encounters with several Enemy machines. Flight Commander Fall and Flight Sub-Lieut. Wood attacked three Albatross Scouts. The rearmost machine was destroyed, followed down, and seen to crash in the floods. The machine hit a fence and turned over on its nose, partly upside down. This was confirmed by another pilot in the flight. On returning from replenishing ammunition, Flight Commander Fall attacked an Albatross two-seater, it was last seen at 500 feet spinning on its back completely out of control and was most probably destroyed.

Bombing Raid by day, No. 5 Squadron, D. H. 4's.

At 1-30, Houttave Aerodrome was attacked by eight machines, three 65-lb., eleven 50-lb., sixty-four 16-lb. and two 10-lb. bombs were dropped on objective. A number of bombs were seen to explode amongst, and in close proximity to the sheds, and one direct hit is reported on the sheds on the S. side of the road. A considerable number of E. A. were sighted but did not get near enough to attack our formation. All machines returned safely.

November 14th.

No war work of importance was possible owing to bad weather conditions.

November 15th.

Overcast sky and clouds prevented reconnaissance and photographic work from being attempted.

Enemy Aircraft.

During the morning, No. 1 Squadron high offensive patrol of five Camels encountered a formation of seven Albatross scouts, and two two-seaters. The patrol dived on the E. A.; in the general fight which ensued Flight Lieut. Kinkhead shot down a scout, which was seen to crash amongst some shattered buildings near Beerst. After two more indecisive combats Flight Lieut. Kinkhead shot down another Albatross completely out of control to N. of Dixmude. Flight Sub-Lieut. Findlay, firing from 20 yards range, brought down a scout completely out of control. Another E. A. was also driven down. One of our machines was badly shot about.

While on a special mission, Squadron Commander Dallas, D.S.C., observed several E.A. near Houthulst Forest, and joining up with some S.E.5's he attacked a D.F.W. two-seater. After receiving several bursts the enemy purposely spun for 4,000 feet followed by Squadron Commander Dallas who fired another long burst; E.A. then dived, and his tail plane was seen to crumple up, after which he got into a flat spin, crashing on the ground at Roggevelde. A small body of troops was also attacked, the remaining ammunition being expended on two D.F.W. two-seaters.

Indecisive fights took place between two Camels (No. 1 Squadron), a scout, and two two-seaters, in which the E.A. were driven eastwards.

In the evening a patrol of eight Camels from No. 9 Squadron observed two Gothas over Dunkerque, but were unable to engage them as E.A. were lost in the clouds.

Bombing Raid by day, No. 5 Squadron, D.H. 4's.

A bombing raid was attempted on Uytkerke Aerodrome. Owing to very high wind of over 60 miles per hour from the N. the formation was unable to proceed to objective, and eight 50-lb., thirty-two 16-lb. and one 10-lb. bombs were dropped on sheds N. of Handzaeme. No results could be observed owing to heavy banks of clouds. All machines returned safely, though one crashed owing to a forced landing, pilot and passengers uninjured.

Casualties during period 1st to 15th November.

NAME	SQUADRON	DATE
MISSING.		
Flight Lieut. W. S. Magrath	No. 1	9/11/17
Flight Sub-Lieut. H. P. Salter	No. 2	6/11/17
Observer Sub-Lieut. H. W. White	No. 2	6/11/17
INJURED.		
Flight Commander J. Robinson	No. 2	13/11/17
Observer Sub-Lieut. W. S. Anderson	No. 2	13/11/17

Honours.

NAME	UNIT	AWARDED
Wing Commander C. L. Courtney	No. 4 Wing	D.S.O.
Observer Lieut. R. W. Gow, D.S.C.	No. 2 Squadron	D.S.O.
Flight Commander F. C. Armstrong	No. 3 Squadron	D.S.C.
Flight Lieut. H. F. Beamish	No. 3 Squadron	D.S.C.
Flight Sub-Lieut. G. W. Hemming	No. 4 Squadron	D.S.C.
Flight Sub-Lieut. E. T. Hayne	No. 3 Squadron	D.S.C.
Flight Sub-Lieut. J. E. L. Hunter	No. 4 Squadron	D.S.C.

F. C. HALAHAN,
WING CAPTAIN, R.N.,
FOR SENIOR OFFICER, R.N.A.S.

HEADQUARTERS, R.N.A.S.,
DUNKERQUE.

Summary of Bombing Raids carried out by the R. N. A. S.

From November 1st to 15th, 1917, inclusive,

With weights of Explosives dropped.

TARGET.	BOMBS DROPPED.	TOTAL LBS.
ST. DENIS WESTREM AERODROME.	14 — 112 lbs.	1,568
ENGEL AERODROME.	3 — 65 lbs. 7 — 50 lbs. 46 — 16 lbs. 2 — 10 lbs.	1,301
HOUTTAVE AERODROME.	3 — 65 lbs. 11 — 50 lbs. 64 — 16 lbs. 2 — 10 lbs.	1,789
VLISSEGHEM AERODROME.	8 — 50 lbs. 29 — 16 lbs. 2 — 10 lbs.	884
SHEDS NORTH OF HANDZAEME.	8 — 50 lbs. 32 — 16 lbs. 1 — 10 lbs.	922
BRUGES DOCKS.	12 — 250 lbs. 46 — 112 lbs.	8,152
RAILWAY STATIONS, JUNCTIONS, TRAINS AND SIDINGS.	20 — 250 lbs. 72 — 112 lbs.	13,064

Grand Total - 27,680 lbs.

N.B.—A total of over TWELVE TONS of BOMBS have been dropped during the period under review.

Printed at Royal Naval Air Service Headquarters, Dunkerque, 1917.

Airco D.H.4 N5992 of the 5th Wing crashed after an abortive bombing raid on Aertrycke ("Uytkerke") Aerodrome on 15 November 1917. Because of adverse weather, Handzaeme was bombed instead, with inconclusive results. The communique reports that "all machines returned safely, though one crashed owing to a forced landing …". (Bruce/Leslie)

Curtiss H.12 Large America 8670 bombed a U-Boat 23 miles south of the Needles on 18 November 1917, though the communique reports that an overcast sky restricted operations to two patrols by Camels. (Bruce/Leslie)

Sopwith F.1 Camel B6420 of 1(N) Sqn at Dover. This aircraft joined the unit on 9 November 1917. (Bruce/Leslie)

Camels of 9(N) Sqn, with B3884 on the right and B6327, flown by Flt Sub Lt H.F. Stackard, on the left. (Bruce/Leslie)

Having served initially with 10(N) Sqn, Sopwith Triplane N5379 was repaired after being damaged by fire on the night of 1 October 1917 and was flying with 12(N) Sqn by 29 November. (Bruce/Leslie)

Numerous Handley Page O/100s in the 28-aircraft batch 3115-3142 served with 7(N) Sqn, and quite a number of those were brought down in German territory. This is one of them, but unfortunately the last two digits of its serial number are obscured by the starboard rudder.

During the period under review the weather has been very bad, strong gales and low clouds being almost continuous. This has rendered bombing raids impossible.

November 16th and 17th.

Owing to unfavourable weather, fog and low clouds, no war work was carried out.

November 18th.

The sky was overcast throughout the day, it was only possible to carry out two patrols.

Enemy Aircraft.

Five Camels from Seaplane Defence Squadron attacked four hostile seaplanes which had been reported off La Panne. A running fight ensued in which tracers were seen to enter the rearmost E. A., who afterwards appeared in difficulties. Gun jambs greatly hampered our pilots, who, nevertheless, engaged the seaplanes at a height of 200 feet to within one mile of Ostende.

A flight of five Camels from No. 1 Squadron attacked several E. A. at long range, without result. The low clouds prevented the delivery of a proper attack.

November 19th.

The sky was completely overcast, no war work was carried out.

November 20th.

No war work of any importance could be carried out owing to the unfavourable weather conditions.

Enemy Aircraft.

In the afternoon E. A. were observed S. of Nieuport, one of our patrols from No. 9 Squadron left in pursuit, but on arrival E. A. had already been driven back by other Allied machines.

Flight Sub-Lieut. Knott saw a company of enemy infantry crossing a bridge N. E. of Dixmude, and descending to 500 feet, fired some 300 rounds into them, killing some and scattering the remainder.

Flight Sub-Lieut. Redgate afterwards engaged two D 3 Albatross scouts at 10,000 feet S. of Pervyse, diving on to the tail of one and firing into him at 100 yards range. E. A. was observed to crash about three miles behind enemy lines.

November 21st.

Drizzle and clouds prevented any war work being carried out.

November 22nd.

It was only possible to carry out a few patrols owing to the continuation of bad weather. Nothing of importance to report.

November 23rd.

A reconnaissance was carried out by No. 2 Squadron to Ostende, Bruges, and Zeebrugge. The visibility over Ostende was poor, making observations very difficult. Better results were obtained over Bruges and Zeebrugge. One of the escorting machines had a short indecisive encounter with an E. A. over Nieuport.

Enemy Aircraft.

A patrol of three Camels, No. 9 Squadron, encountered nine Albatross scouts at 14,000 feet near Houthulst Forest. Flight Commander Banbury and Flight Sub-Lieut. Hales engaged and shot down one of the E. A., it being last seen spinning on its back completely out of control.

Five Camels of No. 4 Squadron observed two E. A. flying above a formation of six Albatross scouts. During the ensuing combat Flight Sub-Lieut. Tonks attacked one of the E. A. at close range, firing 200 rounds and shooting him down completely out of control. Flight Sub-Lieut. Tonks was, however, immediately attacked by six more scouts and was forced to spin, and fall to within 500 feet. Although the E. A. were still attacking him, he had to stop his engine to prevent the compass vibrating, in order to pick up the W., being too low to take any bearings. This allowed the E. A. to close up again and the pilot did not shake them off until within 50 feet of the floods. In the same fight Flight Sub-Lieut. Hickey engaged a scout painted bright yellow, shooting it down out of control.

November 24th and 25th.

Owing to unfavourable weather no war work was carried out.

November 26th.

A few fighter patrols were carried out, but no decisive engagements took place.

November 27th.

Bad weather prevented any war work being carried out.

November 28th.

Little war flying could be performed owing to the unfavourable weather.

Whenever the weather permitted, fighter patrols were carried out. Several short engagements with E. A. took place, in all cases they were driven back over the lines.

November 29th.

Adverse weather conditions prevented much war work being carried out, several patrols having to return owing to the low clouds and mist.

Enemy Aircraft.

Four Camels from No. 1 Squadron dived on four Albatross Scouts from 14,000 feet near Middlekerke. Flight Commander Minifie, D. S. C., fired 100 rounds into one of the E. A., shooting it down completely out of control. Flight Sub-Lieut. Forman attacked two others, driving one down out of control; the second one, however, escaped. A third machine was forced into a voluntary spin. Several other indecisive engagements took place during the day.

November 30th.

The usual patrols were attempted, but in most cases were forced to return owing to the low clouds and mist. Nothing of importance to report.

Honours during period 16th to 30th November.

NAME	UNIT	AWARDED
Flight Lieut. R. G. Gardner	No. 7 Squadron	D.S.C.
Observer Sub-Lieut. T. Terrell	No. 7 Squadron	D.S.C.
Acting Flight Commander J. S. T. Fall	No. 9 Squadron	Bar to D.S.C.
Observer Sub-Lieut. W. H. Pattison	No. 5 Squadron	D.S.C.
Flight Sub-Lieut. E. Dickson	No. 5 Squadron	D.S.C.
Flight Sub-Lieut. C. R. Lupton	No. 5 Squadron	D.S.C.
Flight Lieut. N. A. Magor	Seaplanes	D.S.C.
S. H. Pinchen, L.M. G/L, F 2932	No. 2 Squadron	D.S.M.

Promotions for Meritorious War Service.

Flight Sub-Lieutenant E. T. Hayne, D.S.C., to Flight Lieutenant.

The following Acting Promotions have also been made :

Flight Commander R. Graham to command The Seaplane Defence Squadron, with the rank of Acting Squadron Commander.

Flight Commander L. S. Breadner to command No. 3 Squadron, with the rank of Acting Squadron Commander.

Flight Lieutenant L. H. Slatter to command "B" Flight, Seaplane Defence Squadron, with the rank of Acting Flight Commander.

Flight Lieutenant B. S. Wemp to command "A" Flight, No. 2 Squadron, with the rank of Acting Flight Commander.

Flight Lieutenant F. E. Banbury to command "C" Flight, No. 9 Squadron, with the rank of Acting Flight Commander.

Flight Sub-Lieutenant A. C. Burt to command "C" Flight, No. 4 Squadron, with the rank of Acting Flight Lieutenant.

The following C.P.O.'s and P.O.'s in the command have been promoted to Warrant Officer, Second Grade, to date 1st Oct. 1917.

	NAME	OFFICIAL NUMBER	UNIT
C.P.O. II., R.H.,	Percy Coyle	218288	Walmer.
,, ,,	A. E. Gliddon	345713	No. 1 Squadron.
,, ,,	B. Cheesman	346288	Depot.
,, ,,	P. V. Milner	F. 3563	Seaplane Defence Squadron.
,, ,,	T. S. Jobling	F. 249	No. 5 Squadron.
C.P.O. III., E.,	R. Tuck	271357	Depot
,, ,,	E. Parrett	M. 733	No. 1 Aircraft Park.
,, ,,	E. J. Wright	270593	Dover Seaplanes.
C.P.O. II., S.,	J. H. Turner	F. 1780	Depot.
,,	G. M. Guy	F. 7107	Dover Seaplanes.
C.P.O. III., G.,	A. E. Le Sueur	F. 3413	R. F. C.
P.O., G.L.,	B. Hinckler	F. 311	No. 5 Squadron.
,, ,,	J. Mc Young	F. 3652	No. 7 Squadron.

Casualties.

NIL.

F. C. HALAHAN,

WING CAPTAIN, R.N.,

FOR SENIOR OFFICER, R.N.A.S.

HEADQUARTERS, R.N.A.S.,
DUNKERQUE,
2ND DECEMBER, 1917.

PRINTED AT ROYAL NAVAL AIR SERVICE HEADQUARTERS, DUNKERQUE, 1917.

ROYAL NAVAL AIR SERVICE COMMUNIQUE.—No. 11.

Throughout the fortnight under review, the weather has been generally misty with low clouds.

December 1st, 2nd and 3rd.

Owing to the very unfavourable weather conditions, low attached clouds, and high wind, no war work could be carried out.

December 4th.

Visibility throughout the day was poor. No reconnaissance or bomb raids could be carried out.

Enemy Aircraft.

Several indecisive encounters took place during the day, and on several occasions E. A. were driven back over their lines.

Four Camels from No. 1 Squadron attacked an Albatross Scout, grey in colour, over Foret d' Houthulst. Flight Sub-Lieut. Findlay fired 350 rounds into him at 25 yards range, and E. A. fell over, and side-slipped several thousand feet, and then dropped into the clouds completely out of control. Flight Lieut. Kinkhead sighted a two-seater D.F.W., S.E. of Dixmude, firing 200 rounds into him at point blank range. The E. A. went down in a vertical nose-dive, completely out of control.

Two two-seaters and a scout were attacked single-handed over Ostende, the result was indecisive.

Three Camels from the Seaplane Defence Squadron attacked an Aviatik two-seater near Zarren. Flight Sub-Lieut. Pinder dived, and opened fire at 50 yards. After the first burst, the observer in the E.A. stopped firing, and E.A. did a turning dive. Flight Sub-Lieut. Mackay then attacked, and was fired on by the E.A. which then went down completely out of control. Our pilots were then driven off by seven Albatross Scouts, and forced to climb into the clouds.

December 5th.

The weather was fine throughout the day, though the visibility was somewhat impeded by haze.

A special North Sea Patrol was carried out by four D.H. 4's from No. 2 Squadron. Three of the machines were forced to land in England. Nothing of importance to report. No. 2 Squadron also carried out a coastal reconnaissance to Zeebrugge, during this flight several combats took place.

Bombing Raid by day, No. 5 Squadron, D. H. 4's.

Sparappelhoek Aerodrome was attacked by five machines, three others accompanying them, as escorts. Ten 50-lb. and thirty-two 16-lb. bombs were dropped over the target and were seen to fall near the sheds, but no direct hits were observed.

Four 16-lb. bombs were also dropped on a train leaving Engel dump.

All machines returned safely.

Enemy Aircraft.

During the afternoon, E. A. activity was above the normal.

The escort to the Reconnaissance machines was attacked by a number of E. A., both scouts and two-seaters, while off Wenduyne, a running fight ensued as far as Nieuport, in the course of which one of the D. H. 4's was badly shot about.

During the various combats, four Camels (S. D. S.), Flight Sub-Lieuts. Paynter, Cooper, Mackay and Pinder, attacked two Albatross two-seaters, the pilots dived on the E. A. in turns, firing at close range, the second E. A., meanwhile, attacking one of our other Camels whose guns were frozen. The first E. A. was again attacked by two Camels and forced shorewards, being eventually brought down in the sea, after a burst by Flight Sub-Lieut. Pinder, who, descending to 50 feet, observed pilot half submerged in his machine and the observer swimming 20 yards away.

While on a special mission, Flight Sub-Lieut. Rosevear attacked and destroyed an Albatross Scout at Vladsloo, E. of Dixmude.

During the afternoon the rear of a formation of No. 10 Squadron Camels was attacked by one of four Albatross Scouts. Flight Lieut. Curtiss dived on this machine firing a long burst into it at 15 yards range. The E.A. went into a vertical nose-dive, smoking profusely and was observed to crash.

A number of indecisive combats took place and several E.A. were driven back over the lines during the day. In addition, two enemy K.B.'s were attacked without apparent result to the balloons, but in one case a parachute was seen to fall and open out.

A pilot of No. 9 Squadron fired into enemy trenches E. of Nieuport piers, and along the Yser canal S.E. of Nieuport, also at a machine gun between Westende Bains and Nieuport piers at which he fired about 150 rounds, finishing at 25 yards range. The machine gun had then ceased firing.

December 6th.

Photographic Reconnaissance.

A successful photographic reconnaissance was carried out by No. 2 Squadron over Zeebrugge, and the coast between Blankenberghe and De Haan. Interesting photographs were obtained of two lines of buoys in the neighbourhood of the tip of the mole.

Bombing Raid by Night, Nos. 7 and 7a Squadrons, H.P.'s.

During the evening of the 5th, five H.P.'s carried out a raid on the following objectives :
St. Denis Westrem, four 250-lb. and twenty-three 112-lb.
Bruges Docks, four 250-lb. and three 112-lb.
Engel Aerodrome, three 112-lb.
Various Railway Traffic, twenty-five 112-lb.

Detached clouds rendered observations very difficult, but good results seem to have been obtained on all targets.

All machines returned safely.

Bombing Raid by day, No. 5 Squadron, D. H. 4's.

A raid was carried out at midday by seven bombers and three escorts on Uytkerke Aerodrome, over which the following bombs were dropped : ten 50-lb. and forty 16-lb. They were seen to explode among the living quarters and huts W. side of the road, one of which appeared to receive a direct hit. Other bombs burst close to sheds on E. side of road, setting one on fire. All machines returned safely.

Enemy Aircraft.

During a special early patrol to intercept enemy bombers, several combats took place between pilots of No. 1 Squadron and enemy machines. Flight Lieut. Rosevear, D.S.C., encountered an E.A. two-seater near Ostende which was flashing a white light, after receiving 200 rounds at point blank range the E.A. plunged vertically downwards, completely out of control. A Gotha with lights on was attacked by another pilot, but unfortunately the latter was caught in the back-wash while coming up under his tail. After regaining control he was unable to see the Gotha. Squadron Commander Dallas, D.S.C., attacked a two-seater D.F.W. near Ostende. The E.A. spun and fell over, the ultimate result could not be observed, however, as the pilot was attacked by six E.A. and was forced to retire. The D.F.W. was very probably out of control. During this early patrol, Flight Lieut. Kinkhead attacked a two-seater E.A. at close range near Foret d'Houthulst. The E.A. stalled and dived vertically, but owing to the uncertain light was soon lost to view. It seems probable that the E.A. was completely out of control.

Flight Commander Fall, whilst on a solo Offensive Patrol, attacked a D.F.W. (colour, mottled yellow and brown), S. E. of Ypres. The machine was seen to crash near Courtrai. Flight Commander Fall also observed a D. 5 Albatross near Staden. Diving on him from out of the sun he delivered a surprise attack at close range. The machine was last seen still diving on its back at 1,000 feet and was therefore, most probably destroyed.

Five Camels of No. 1 Squadron encountered a number of E.A. N. of Passchendaele. In the general fight which followed, both Flight Commander Ridley and Flight Lieut. Kinkhead shot an Albatross scout down completely out of control. In both cases the machines were still out of control when within a short distance of the ground, and were, therefore, probably destroyed.

Three Camels (No. 4 Squadron) went up in pursuit of an E.A. observed over Dunkirk. The E.A. was sighted off La Panne, but before our machines commenced the attack, a French or Belgian Spad closed up and opened fire, eventually driving the E.A. into the sea where it was seen to crash.

A flight from No. 9 Squadron attacked an Albatross two-seater, W. of Courtrai. The E.A. was followed down to 2,000 feet and shot down by Flight Lieut. Winter and Flight Sub-Lieut. Knott who saw it crash into the ground.

A large number of rounds of ammunition were fired into enemy trenches during the day. Ghistelles Aerodrome, a train near St. Pierre Capelle, and a "flaming onion" battery E. of Nieuport were also attacked.

December 7th.

Owing to unfavourable weather conditions no war work was carried out.

December 8th.

Anti-submarine patrol was carried out by Seaplane. Nothing to report.

W/T Spotting for Monitors.

During the morning, while in a position to observe, the spotting machine was recalled. It is possible that this gave the Germans the clue that opening fire was meditated. In the afternoon firing was again attempted, this time three E.A. were waiting for the spotter which was unfortunately detached from its escort. The machine made three attempts to spot, but each time was attacked and eventually had to retire. It is believed that during the attack one of the E.A. was driven down.

Bombing Raid by Day, No. 5 Squadron, D.H. 4's.

During the morning six bombers accompanied by four escorts attacked Aertrycke Aerodrome over which twelve 50-lb. and fifty-six 16-lb. bombs were dropped. Visibility was only fair, as target was partially obscured by clouds. Endeavours were made to photograph the Aerodrome and results, but the clouds interfered. Bombs were seen to explode close to the S.E. group of sheds. A.A. fire was very accurate, all machines but one being hit. The bombing formation was attacked on its way back.

Enemy Aircraft.

When returning from a sweep inland beyond Ostende, Flight Commander Minifie encountered a two-seater D.F.W. and attacked from close range. The E.A. went into a a nose-dive, and was seen to crash E. of Dixmude.

A flight of six Camels (No. 9 Squadron) dived on two Albatross scouts and one two-seater. Flight Sub-Lieut. Knott attacked the two-seater from very close range firing about 300 rounds.

The E.A. was last seen completely out of control turning on its back. This machine was probably destroyed. Whilst on a solo Offensive Patrol, Flight Commander Fall attacked two Albatross scouts near Ypres. After a fairly long fight one of the E.A. folded up and spun down. The other scout chased Flight Commander Fall back part of the way to the lines.

The bombing formation was attacked by five E.A., during the ensuing fight three E.A. were driven down, probably damaged.

December 9th.

Rain and low clouds all day, no war work carried out.

December 10th.

No. 2 Squadron attempted two photographic reconnaissances in the neighbourhood of Ghent, but had to abandon them owing to engine trouble.

Spotting machines and their escorts, No. 2 Squadron, left with a view to operating with the monitors, but a signal was received cancelling same.

All machines, therefore, carried out an offensive patrol.

Bombing Raid by day, No. 5 Squadron, D. H. 4's.

A bomb raid was carried out at noon on Varssenaere Aerodrome. Twelve 50-lb. and sixty 60-lb. bombs were dropped. Bombs were seen to drop close to and among sheds on E. and W. side of the aerodrome and on the new sheds in the N.E. corner.

All machines returned safely.

During the raid, photographs were taken of Varssenaere and Houttave Aerodromes.

Enemy Aircraft.

During a patrol over Roulers, Ypres district, eight Camels of No. 10 Squadron encountered an Albatross scout at 9,000 feet. E.A. was attacked by Flight Sub-Lieut. Clark and Flight Commander Macgregor in turn. The machine went down out of control and then burst into flames.

A flight from Seaplane Defence Squadron observed a two-seater Aviatik between Dunkirk and Bergues. One of the pilots attacked, but had to retire owing to temporary stoppage of both guns.

Whilst carrying out a fighter patrol over the Fleet, four Camels from Seaplane Defence Squadron observed five Albatross scouts 10 miles N. E. of Ostende. E. A. were engaged and driven back to Ostende by two of the pilots. Shortly afterwards, six large two-seaters and one small two-seater were seen making for the Fleet. On being attacked, all the E.A.'s turned back to Ostende. Two E.A.'s were engaged with indecisive results, and a third was driven down in a nose-dive by Flight Sub-Lieut. Pinder. Owing to the light, it was impossible to determine if machine was completely out of control or not.

During an offensive sweep between Nieuport and Dixmude, a flight from No. 9 Squadron drove four E.A.'s down towards Ostende, and afterwards engaged a D.F.W. near Pervyse. Flight. Sub-Lieuts. Redgate, Wood and Knott dived on the E.A., firing about 1,000 rounds. The Observer was evidently hit in the first burst as he did not reply. The E.A. then caught fire and turned over on its back, and was still seen burning at 1,000 feet.

December 11th.

Owing to unfavourable weather conditions, little work could be carried out during the day. During one of the coast patrols several ground targets were attacked.

Bombing Raid by Night, Nos. 7 and 14 Squadrons, H.P.'s.

A bomb raid was carried out on the evening of the 10th on Oostacker Aerodrome and Bruges Docks.

Visibility at first was fairly good, but soon afterwards deteriorated considerably, so much so, that the last machine to leave was forced to land, as the ground by then could not be seen.

Eight 250-lb. and forty 112-lb. bombs were dropped on this objective; and on Bruges Docks, eight 250-lb. and fifty-four 112-lb. bombs were dropped.

Bombs were seen to explode among the sheds just N. of the E. Bassin, and the Docks in general were well straddled.

All machines returned safely.

December 12th.

Two photographic reconnaissances were attempted by No. 2 Squadron, but had to be abandoned owing to thick clouds over all objectives.

Anti-submarine patrol was carried out by Seaplanes. Nothing to report.

Owing to weather few fighter patrols could be carried out.

Bombing Raid by Night, Nos. 7 and 14 Squadrons, H.P.'s.

On the evening of the 11th and morning of the 12th a bomb raid was carried out on Bruges Docks.

Four 250-lb. and thirty-four 112-lb. bombs were dropped, but owing to the low clouds results were difficult to observe. It was noted, however, that one of the bombs caused a particularly large explosion.

All machines returned safely.

Enemy Aircraft.

While making a sweep round by Ghistelles and Dixmude, nine Camels from No. 10 Squadron encountered six Albatross scouts. A general engagement took place in which one of our machines was attacked and shot down by an Albatross. Flight Commander Macgregor immediately attacked the E.A. and drove him down out of control.

Other indecisive engagements took place.

Confirmation of the destruction of this E.A. has since been received from the Belgians, who state that a British and a hostile machine were seen to go down at this time, near Leke.

During the course of the patrols several hundred rounds were fired into enemy trenches.

December 13th.

During the day the sky was completely overcast, with low clouds and mist.

It was only possible to carry out a very little war work.

Search patrols were carried out for missing C.M.B., and an airship reported to be in trouble. Information was received later that the airship had landed in Holland and the crew interned.

Fleet protection patrols were also carried out, no E.A. were seen.

December 14th.

Unfavourable weather prevented any war work being carried out.

December 15th.

Owing to unfavourable weather conditions, no operations of importance could be carried out.

Honours during period 1st to 15th December.

Name	Unit	Awarded
Acting Flight Commander J. S. T. Fall	No. 9 Squadron	2nd Bar to D.S.C.

Promotions.

Name	Unit
Warrant Officer D. S. W. Hambley, to Lieutenant, R.N.V.R.,	Aircraft Depot.
Warrant Officer T. Martin, to Lieutenant, R.N.V.R.	
Official No. F 6834 Petty Officer (W/T) M. B. Egan, to Warrant Officer, II.,	No. 1 Wing.

Acting Promotions.

Name	Unit
Flight Lieut. R. Collishaw, D.S.O., D.S.C., to Acting Flight Commander	Seaplane Def. Squad.
Flight Lieut. R. R. Winter to Acting Flight Commander	No. 9 Squadron
Flight Lieut. J. Chisholm, to Acting Flight Commander	No. 2 Squadron
Flight Sub-Lieut. C. F. Brewerton, to Acting Flight Lieutenant	No. 2 Squadron
Flight Sub-Lieut. J. G. Manuel, D.S.C., to Acting Flight Lieutenant	No. 10 Squadron

Casualties.

Missing.

Name	Unit	Date
Flight Sub-Lieut. J. G. Clark	No. 10 Squadron	12/12/17

F. C. HALAHAN,
Wing Captain, R.N.,
for Senior Officer, R.N.A.S.

Headquarters, R.N.A.S.,
Dunkerque,
18th December, 1917.

Summary of Bombing Raids carried out by the R. N. A. S.

From December 1st to 15th, 1917, inclusive,

With weights of Explosives dropped.

TARGET.	BOMBS DROPPED.		TOTAL LBS.
ST. DENIS WESTREM AERODROME.	4 — 250 lbs. 23 — 112 lbs.		3,576
SPARAPPELHOEK AERODROME.	10 — 50 lbs. 34 — 16 lbs.		1,044
UYTKERKE AERODROME.	10 — 50 lbs. 40 — 16 lbs.		1,140
AERTRYCKE AERODROME.	12 — 50 lbs. 56 — 16 lbs.		1,496
VARSSENAERE AERODROME.	12 — 50 lbs. 60 — 16 lbs.		1,560
OOSTACKER AERODROME.	8 — 250 lbs. 40 — 112 lbs.		6,480
ENGEL AERODROME.	3 — 112 lbs.		336
BRUGES DOCKS.	16 — 250 lbs. 91 — 112 lbs.		14,192
RAILWAY LINES, SIDINGS, TRAFFIC, ETC.	25 — 112 lbs. 4 — 16 lbs.		2,864

Grand Total - 32,688 lbs.

N.B.—A total of over FOURTEEN TONS of BOMBS have been dropped during the period under review.

PRINTED AT ROYAL NAVAL AIR SERVICE HEADQUARTERS, DUNKERQUE, 1917.

Camels of 10(N) Sqn ready for the day's work. Aircraft B6299 joined the unit on 16 November 1917. Flown by Flt Cdr N.M. MacGregor, it claimed four Albatros D.Vs destroyed or driven down before it was transferred to 9 Sqn on 4 February 1918. The aircraft immediately behind it, B6204, has the greeting "'allo! Lil Bird" painted around its individual letter on the fuselage side. (Bruce/Leslie)

Camel B3882, which served with 6, 10 and 12 Sqns, joined 10 Sqn on 30 August 1917. (Bruce/Leslie)

Handley Page O/100 number 3121 of 14 Sqn crashed and overturned a mile northeast of Coudekerque on the night of 12 December, while returning from a raid on Bruges Docks, and was written off. The communiques reported that "All machines returned safely". (Bruce/Leslie)

Sopwith F.1 Camel B3881 of A Flight, 9(N) Sqn at Leffrinhouche Aerodrome, displaying a cartoon of music hall comedian George Robey on its fin.

Another shot of a 9(N) Sqn Camel, possibly B3881 again, though the fin adornment is lacking.

A German kite balloon about to ascend. On 22 December a pilot of 9 Sqn upset a German observer's Christmas by forcing him to take to his parachute east of Dixmunde.

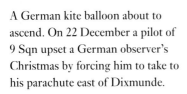

During the fortnight under review the weather has been generally unfavourable, with low clouds, mist, and sleet.

December 16th.

Owing to the very unfavourable weather conditions, no war work of importance could be carried out.

December 17th.

A very high wind and low clouds prevented any work being carried out.

December 18th.

Reconnaissance.

A Photographic Reconnaissance was attempted by No. 2 Squadron in the vicinity of Ghent, but had to be abandoned on account of low clouds which stretched far inland over the objective.

The Reconnaissance, therefore, took photos of the West Cappelle—Ramscappelle district.

The bombing formation took photographs of Engel Aerodrome and Dump.

Bombing Raid by Day, No. 5 Squadron, D.H. 4's.

During the afternoon a raid was carried out on Engel Aerodrome and Dump by five bombers accompanied by three D.H. 4's as escort.

Eight 50-lb. and thirty-two 16-lb. bombs were dropped. Two 50-lb. bombs were observed to explode close to the S.W. sheds of the aerodrome, from which all Bessoneaux had been removed. The dump was well straddled, and bombs were seen to burst on the railway sidings and sheds. Visibility was good.

Encounters with E.A. took place whilst commencing the return journey.

All machines returned safely.

Enemy Aircraft.

Whilst starting the return journey, the bombing formation was attacked by E.A. Flight Commander Sproatt with A./G.L. Naylor engaged two Albatross scouts at short range. The first was shot down in flames by Flight Commander Sproatt. A./G.L. Naylor fired at the second machine which was observed to go down in a spin and was last seen in a nose dive.

Several other E.A. were attacked and successfully driven off.

On one occasion a patrol of six Camels, No. 9 Squadron, attacked two Albatross scouts and a new unknown type with pointed wing tips and elevators. One of these was driven down and forced to land by Flight Sub-Lieut. Taylor, who followed it to within 30 feet of the ground and fired a number of rounds into it.

A returning photographic machine attacked E.A. two-seater over Bergues without decisive result.

During the day many other encounters with E.A. took place without any decisive results. Difficulty was experienced with the guns owing to the intense cold. In three other cases it is thought that the observer was killed or wounded as no fire was returned.

The unknown type of scout described by R.F.C. is stated to be a Pflaz scout.

December 19th.

Photographic Reconnaissance.

A Photographic Reconnaissance was carried out by No. 2 Squadron over Oostacker, Mariakerke and Ghent, including the docks at Ghent and railway centres. Thirty-two plates were exposed with good results.

Spotting Operations.

Spotting operations were carried out by No. 2 Squadron for ships firing on Ostende. On the way home the machines were attacked by E.A.

Bombing Raid by Night, Nos. 7 and 14 Squadrons, H.P.'s.

During the night 18th—19th, a raid was carried out on La Brugeoise Works, Bruges; twelve 250-lb. and seventy-four 112-lb. bombs were dropped. Visibility was extremely good, enabling good observations to be made. The northern end of the works was hit and a large fire was started which was still burning when machines re-crossed the lines. The remainder of the works were also straddled and bombs were seen to explode among the main buildings. All machines returned safely.

Bombing Raid by Day, No. 5 Squadron, D.H. 4's.

At noon, Vlisseghem Aerodrome was attacked by six machines. Twelve 50-lb. and fifty 16-lb. bombs were dropped on the objective. A number were observed to explode among the group of sheds on the west side of the aerodrome, and a direct hit was reported on one of the smaller sheds.

The bombing formation was attacked on the return journey. One machine failed to return.

Enemy Aircraft.

Returning from Vlisseghem while escorting the bombers, Flight Commander Sproatt with A./G.L. Naylor attacked an Albatross Scout. It was observed to spin down rapidly and a few seconds afterwards, to fall to pieces in the air. Other E. A. were driven off.

While escorting D.H. 4 Spotters, three Camels of Seaplane Defence Squadron encountered two Albatross two-seaters between Ostende and Zeebrugge. Flight Sub-Lieut. Mackay attacked one diving towards Zeebrugge and fired two bursts, the observer then stood up holding up his hands, and was shortly afterwards seen to fall out of the machine, which went down out of control. Later, Flight Commander Collishaw carried out a surprise attack on four Albatross scouts, shooting one down out of control.

A patrol of No. 4 Squadron encountered a formation of six enemy scouts of new type with rotary engine, dihedral bottom plane, straight top plane with extensions, and a very good climb. They were working in two formations, one above the other, the lower one was broken up, the other taking no part in the fight.

Many other indecisive engagements took place during the day.

December 20th and 21st.

Owing to unfavourable weather conditions, no war work of importance could be carried out.

December 22nd.

Owing to unfavourable weather conditions, no reconnaissance could be carried out during the day.

Enemy Aircraft.

A pilot of No. 9 Squadron attacked a Kite Balloon east of Dixmude, forcing the observer to jump out in a parachute.

Flight Commander Fall, while on a solo offensive patrol, attacked a two-seater Albatross, S.E. of Quesnoy. The E.A. went down completely out of control and was seen to crash in a field.

Five Camels of No. 10 Squadron had engagements with four Albatross scouts. The results were indecisive, but it is probable that one of the E. A. was damaged and one out of control.

December 23rd.

Bombing Raid by Night, Nos. 7 and 14 Squadrons, H.P.'s.

During the evening of the 22nd a raid was carried out on the following aerodromes. Eight machines took part in the raid.

Mariakerke, twenty-eight 112-lb. bombs. Bombs were observed to burst close to and among the sheds and buildings in the N.W. and N.E. portions of the aerodrome.

St. Denis Westrem, four 250-lb. and twenty-two 112-lb. bombs. Two direct hits were claimed and in addition, a certain number of bombs were observed to burst close to the sheds and hangars.

Oostacker, twelve 250-lb. and thirty-two 112-lb. bombs. Two direct hits were claimed, bombs also burst among principal group of sheds.

Many useful observations were made by pilots and observers during the raid.

All pilots and machines returned safely.

December 24th.

No reconnaissance or fighter patrols could be carried out owing to weather conditions.

Bombing Raid by Night, Nos. 7 and 14 Squadrons, H.P.'s.

On the night of 23rd—24th, the following raid was carried out by six machines:—

St. Denis Westrem Aerodrome, fourteen 112-lb. bombs.

Bruges Docks, eight 250-lb. and forty 112-lb. bombs.

Ghistelles Aerodrome, fourteen 112-lb. bombs.

Visibility was poor and became worse, making observation of results very difficult.

December 25th, 26th and 27th.

Heavy banks of clouds, high winds with snow and sleet, made flying impossible.

December 28th.

Fighter Patrols were maintained during the greater part of the day. Nothing of importance to report.

December 29th.

Owing to the unfavourable weather conditions no reconnaissances or bomb raids could be carried out.

Fighter Patrols were maintained up to noon, but then low clouds and mist prevented any further flying during the day. Nothing of importance to report.

December 30th and 31st.

Unfavourable weather conditions prevented any war work being carried out.

Honours during period 16th to 31st December.

Name	Unit	Awarded
Flight Sub-Lieutenant W. L. Jordon	No. 10 Squadron	D. S. C.

Acting Promotions.

Name	Unit
Squadron Commander P. F. M. Fellowes, to Acting Wing Commander	No. 1 Wing
Flight Lieut. H. McClelland, to Acting Flight Commander	"A" Squadron
Flight Sub-Lieut. O. W. Redgate, to Acting Flight Lieutenant	No. 9 Squadron
Naval Schoolmaster G. Roberts, to Acting Warrant Schoolmaster	No. 1 Wing

Casualties.

Missing.

Name	Unit	Date
Flight Sub-Lieut. S. S. Richardson	No. 5 Squadron	19/12/17
A.C. 1 (G./L.) R. A. Furby, O. No. F 13925	No. 5 Squadron	19/12/17

Killed.

Name	Unit	Date
Flight Sub-Lieut. D. R. C. Wright	No. 10 Squadron	23/12/17
Flight Sub-Lieut. T. M. Greeves	No. 12 Squadron	23/12/17

F. C. HALAHAN,

WING CAPTAIN, R.N.,

for Senior Officer, R.N.A.S.

HEADQUARTERS, R.N.A.S.,

DUNKERQUE,

2ND JANUARY, 1918.

Summary of Bombing Raids carried out by the R. N. A. S.

From December 16th to 31st, 1917, inclusive,

With weights of Explosives dropped.

TARGET.	BOMBS DROPPED.	TOTAL LBS.
ST. DENIS WESTREM AERODROME.	4 — 250 lbs. 36 — 112 lbs.	5,032
ENGEL AERODROME, DUMP AND SIDINGS	8 — 50 lbs. 32 — 16 lbs.	912
MARIAKERKE AERODROME.	28 — 112 lbs.	3,136
VLISSEGHEM AERODROME.	12 — 50 lbs. 50 — 16 lbs.	1,400
OOSTACKER AERODROME.	12 — 250 lbs. 32 — 112 lbs.	6,584
GHISTELLES AERODROME.	14 — 112 lbs.	1,568
BRUGES DOCKS.	8 — 250 lbs. 40 — 112 lbs.	6,480
LA BRUGEOISE WORKS	12 — 250 lbs. 74 — 112 lbs.	11,288

Grand Total - 36,400 lbs.

N.B.—A total of over SIXTEEN TONS of BOMBS have been dropped during the period under review.

PRINTED AT ROYAL NAVAL AIR SERVICE HEADQUARTERS, DUNKERQUE, 1918.

ROYAL NAVAL AIR SERVICE COMMUNIQUE.—No. 13.

During the fortnight under review the weather has been generally very bad. High winds, low clouds and snow storms having greatly curtailed flying.

January 1st and 2nd.

Owing to unfavourable weather conditions, little war work could be carried out, only a few fighter patrols being maintained. Nothing to report.

January 3rd.

Intermittent snow storms throughout the day made flying difficult. Fighter patrols were maintained whenever possible.

A bomb raid was attempted on Ghistelles Aerodrome by No. 5 Squadron, but had to be abandoned.

Enemy Aircraft.

Several indecisive engagements took place during the day. A pilot of No. 10 Squadron being forced down to 200 feet over Ostende, eventually escaping in the clouds. Two of our pilots failed to return from a general engagement near Lille.

Flight Sub-Lieut. Day, Seaplane Defence Squadron, went in pursuit of a hostile photographic machine over Dunkirk. Overtaking it near Bruges he fired 300 rounds at point blank range, E. A. dived very steeply and disappeared in the clouds. It is considered highly probable that this machine was destroyed.

January 4th.

A successful photographic reconnaissance was carried out by No. 2 Squadron over Bruges Docks and La Brugeoise Works. A number of plates were exposed and interesting results obtained.

Bombing Raid by Day, No. 5 Squadron, D.H. 4's.

At noon a bomb raid was carried out on Ghistelles Aerodrome. Fourteen 50-lbs. and fifty-three 16-lb. bombs were dropped on the objective. Bombs were observed to explode close to and among the sheds on the S.W., S. and E. sides of the aerodrome, and a direct hit with a 50-lb. bomb on a shed on the south side is reported, and confirmed by photographs taken during the raid.

Enemy Aircraft.

E. A. were inactive during the day. Pilots of No. 9 Squadron drove three Aviatik two-seaters E. over Middlekerke. After several attacks one of these was driven down.

January 5th.

Weather conditions prevented any war work being carried out.

January 6th.

Owing to the unfavourable weather conditions only fighter patrols could be carried out during the day.

Visibility throughout the day was extremely poor. A certain number of engagements with E. A. in the vicinity of the forest of Houthulst took place, but all with indecisive results.

January 7th.

The unfavourable weather conditions prevented aerial work to any great extent. Patrols over the Fleet were maintained.

Three E. A. were observed approximately 20 miles off Nieuport in close proximity to our patrol vessels. The E. A. were successfully driven back in the direction of Middlekerke.

January 8th.

No flying was possible owing to clouds and high wind.

January 9th, 10th and 11th.

No war work of importance could be carried out owing to the weather, low clouds and mists prevailing.

January 12th.

A Fleet patrol and an offensive sweep were the only operations possible, owing to the weather.

January 13th.

No reconnaissance could be carried out.

Bombing Raid by Day, No. 5 Squadron, D.H. 4's.

At noon a bombing raid was carried out on Engel Dump. Six 50-lb. and twenty-four 16-lb. bombs were dropped. A direct hit with a 50-lb. bomb is reported on one of the sheds, and immediately afterwards a large cloud of smoke was seen to arise.

All machines returned safely.

Enemy Aircraft.

Little E.A. activity was observed during the day.

750 rounds were fired into enemy trenches from the air at Nieuport.

January 14th.

Weather conditions prevented coastal reconnaissance being carried out during the day.

Enemy Aircraft.

Twenty-four E.A. were observed during the day, a number of indecisive engagements taking place.

In the course of a general fight between six Albatross scouts and two two-seaters and a patrol of No. 10 Squadron, Flight Commander Curtis brought an Albatross down completely out of control. This was confirmed by one of the other pilots.

A flight of No. 9 Squadron fired 1,600 rounds into enemy trenches and machine gun emplacements E. of Nieuport Piers.

January 15th.

No operations were carried out during the day.

Honours during period 1st to 15th January.

Name	Unit	Awarded
Flight Commander G. W. Price	No. 8 Squadron	D.S.C.
Flight Lieut. S. M. Kinkhead	No. 1 Squadron	D.S.C.

Acting Promotions.

Name	Unit
Flight Commander C. T. Maclaren, to Acting Squadron Commander	No. 6 Squadron
Flight Commander R. Collishaw, to Acting Squadron Commander	No. 13 Squadron
Flight Lieut. J. S. Wright, to Acting Flight Commander	No. 6 Squadron
Flight Lieut. G. L. E. Stevens, to Acting Flight Commander	No. 6 Squadron
Flight Lieut. R. M. Bayley, to Acting Flight Commander	No. 2 Squadron
Flight Lieut. C. F. Brewerton, to Acting Flight Commander	No. 2 Squadron
Flight Lieut. R. M. Keirstead, to Acting Flight Commander	No. 4 Squadron
Flight Lieut. O. W. Redgate, to Acting Flight Commander	No. 9 Squadron
Flight Lieut. C. R. Lupton, to Acting Flight Commander	No. 5 Squadron
Flight Lieut. W. A. Curtis, to Acting Flight Commander	No. 10 Squadron
Flight Lieut. V. R. Gibbs, to Acting Flight Commander	No. 14 Squadron
Flight Lieut. G. M. Day, to Acting Flight Commander	No. 13 Squadron
Flight Lieut. P. E. Beasley, to Acting Flight Commander	No. 13 Squadron
Flight Sub-Lieut. A. W. Wood, to Acting Flight Lieutenant	No. 9 Squadron

For further Honours and Promotions, see Temporary Memoranda Nos. 210, 211 and 212.

Casualties.

ACCIDENTALLY KILLED.

Name	Unit	Date
Flight Sub-Lieut. C. R. Barber	No. 2 Squadron	7/1/18
Observer Sub-Lieut. H. R. Easby	No. 2 Squadron	7/1/18

DIED OF WOUNDS.

Flight Sub-Lieut. H. Willis	No. 5 Squadron	15/1/18

DIED OF INJURIES.

A. L. Jefferies, Act. A.M. 1 (A), O. No. F 27501	No. 5 Squadron	13/1/18

WOUNDED.

A. Foster, A.M. 2 (Act. G.-L.), O. No. F 11691	No. 5 Squadron	13/1/18

INJURED.

E. Whittaker, A.M. 1 (A), O. No. F 2192	No. 5 Squadron	13/1/18

MISSING.

Flight Sub-Lieut. A. G. Beattie	No. 10 Squadron	3/1/18
Flight Sub-Lieut. F. Booth	No. 10 Squadron	3/1/18
Flight Sub-Lieut. A. J. Dixon	No. 8 Squadron	4/1/18

F. C. HALAHAN,

WING CAPTAIN, R.N.,

FOR SENIOR OFFICER, R.N.A.S.

HEADQUARTERS, R.N.A.S.,

DUNKERQUE,

18TH JANUARY, 1918.

Summary of Bombing Raids carried out by the R. N. A. S.

From January 1st to 15th, 1918, inclusive,

With weights of Explosives dropped.

TARGET.	BOMBS DROPPED.		TOTAL LBS.
GHISTELLES AERODROME.	14 —	50 lbs.	1,548
	53 —	16 lbs.	
ENGEL DUMP.	6 —	50 lbs.	684
	24 —	16 lbs.	

Grand Total - 2,232 lbs.

N.B.—A total of nearly ONE TON of BOMBS has been dropped during the period under review.

PRINTED AT ROYAL NAVAL AIR SERVICE HEADQUARTERS, DUNKERQUE, 1918.

Sopwith Camel B6330 served with 9(N), 10(N), 9(N) again and then 213Sqn. A Sopwith Triplane of 1(N) Sqn is visible in the background on the left. (Bruce/Leslie)

Sopwith F.1 Camels of A Flight of 210(N) Sqn, RAF, in 1918. The nearest aircraft, B6298, was flown by Canadian ace W.M. Alexander, and the pilots of the next two machines were Lts F.V. Hall and D.L. Nelson.

Taken on 2 January 1918, when the weather was "unfavourable" for operations, this shot depicts Robinson, Gow and Russell of 2(N) Sqn with Airco D.H.4 A7845. (Bruce/Leslie)

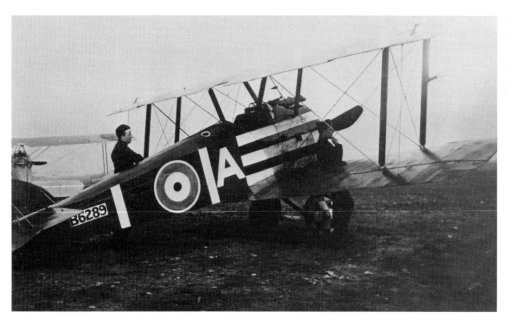

Sopwith Camel B6289 joined 10(N) Sqn on 26 September 1917, but moved to 9(N) Sqn on 4 February 1918, and went with them to Dover. (Bruce/Leslie)

These personnel of 5(N) Sqn, posing for the camera in 1918, seem blissfully unaware that the Rolls-Royce Eagle engine of the Airco D.H.4 behind them is about to burst into life when the ground crew swing the propeller.

During the fortnight under review the weather has been fair, but on several days mist and low clouds prevented much work being carried out.

January 16th and 17th.

No war flying was carried out owing to unfavourable weather.

January 18th.

Reconnaissance.

No. 2 Squadron carried out a special coastal reconnaissance over Zeebrugge, and to a point 15 miles north of the Mole at a height of 7,000 feet.

Visibility was poor, and observations could only be made through gaps in the clouds.

Owing to adverse weather conditions no other war work could be carried out during the day.

January 19th.

W/T Spotting.

No. 2 Squadron carried out spotting for the monitor firing on Ostende.

Firing was opened at 5.30. Good shooting appears to have been made. After the third shot the enemy put up their usual dense smoke screens; nevertheless spotting was able to be continued.

Batteries in action against the Fleet: Turpitz, Deutschland (Jacobinessen), and a battery near Blankenberghe.

Very few E.A. observed.

January 20th.

No flying was carried out through the day owing to rain and low clouds.

January 21st.

Only a few fighter patrols could be carried out. Nothing to report.

January 22nd.

The weather greatly impeded flying, at times the sky was completely overcast, several showers of rain occurring.

Photographic Reconnaissance.

A photographic reconnaissance was carried out by No. 2 Squadron to Zeebrugge and Ostende. The only clear patch in the sky, however, was at Zeebrugge, and two plates were exposed over the Solway Works.

Enemy Aircraft.

Six hostile seaplanes were observed about 20 miles off Blankenberghe.

A flight of No. 3 Squadron gave chase, and drove E.A. to within five miles of Blankenberghe. The rearmost E.A. were attacked, and one of them was driven down into Ostende. Hostile T.B.D. fired on our pilots.

Few other E.A., were observed during the day. Nothing else of importance to report.

January 23rd.

Photographic Reconnaissance.

At noon, during the short period of fine weather, two machines were despatched from No. 2 Squadron on a photographic reconnaissance.

The only clear patches were at Zeebrugge, and plates were exposed over the Mole and Donkerlok battery. All other objectives were covered with clouds, Ostende being invisible. No E.A. were seen.

In the afternoon two special patrols were despatched to search for reported enemy shipping off Schouwen Bank. Owing to low clouds, patrols were carried out at heights ranging from 200 to 6,000 feet.

Enemy Aircraft.

Eight Camels of No. 3 Squadron carried out an offensive sweep south of Ostende, Thourout and Roulers. When over Foret D'Houthulst our formation met seven E.A. (four D.F.W.'s and three Scouts, new type). Flight Lieut. Anderson dived on one D.F.W., driving him down out of control. A general engagement ensued, in which many indecisive combats took place, and all the E.A. were driven down.

One of our machines failed to return.

While patrolling at 7,000 feet over Staden, 10 Camels of No. 10 Squadron observed three E.A. two-seaters and an Albatross Scout just above the clouds. These dived through the clouds and were followed by a part of our patrol. Below the clouds they were joined by five more Albatross Scouts. In the general engagement which followed, one of the two-seaters was driven down out of control by Flight Commander Curtiss, and observed to break up in the air. An Albatross was driven down completely out of control by Flight Commander Alexander.

Other indecisive combats took place, from which one of our machines failed to return, he was last seen spinning down with an E.A. scout, both machines being observed to crash simultaneously.

January 24th.

Reconnaissance.

A special reconnaissance was carried out by No. 2 Squadron to observe enemy shipping.

Two hundred and fifty rounds were fired at coast and trenches from heights between 1,500 and 2,000 feet.

One of our machines when over Ostende at 2,000 feet was hit by shrapnel, and was compelled to make a forced landing on the beach at La Panne.

E.A. Activity.

Few E.A. were observed during the day. Two of our pilots saw a formation of 16 E.A. in the vicinity of Houthulst Forest. They had the appearance of a new type of machine with dihedral on top plane and rotary engine. Good climb and speed.

A special patrol by two machines of No. 9 Squadron, fired 1,200 rounds into enemy trenches behind Nieuport. Flammenwerfer, A.A. and machine guns were fired at these two machines, one of which was hit in several places.

January 25th.

Photographic Reconnaissance.

A photographic reconnaissance was carried out by No. 2 Squadron. Forty plates were exposed between Selzaete, Bruges, and Westcappelle. A few rounds were fired at E.A. east of Bruges.

A second reconnaissance was also carried out. Plates were exposed over Jacobinessen battery, Turkijen battery, and the Ateliers de la Marine. A number of E.A. were seen, and visibility was good.

Bombing Raid by Day, No. 5 Squadron, D.H. 4's.

A bombing raid was carried out on Varseenaere Aerodrome.

Eight 50-lb., eight 20-lb., and thirty-five 16-lb. bombs were dropped on the objective.

A direct hit is reported among a group of twelve small sheds at the north-east corner of the aerodrome.

Photographs were secured of the Ostende-Thourout railway (north-west of Engel), and of the objective.

Enemy Aircraft.

While over Ostende the escort to photographic machine was attacked by three E.A., who, after firing at close quarters, dived away to allow A.A. guns to fire at our machine, which was hit in several places.

A flight of No. 9 Squadron observed a machine go down in flames from 10,000 feet. No other machine was seen in the vicinity.

A Pilot of No. 13 Squadron pursued an E A. which was seen over Dunkerque and sighted it near Dixmude. A large number of other E.A. were seen and several indecisive engagements took place. In one instance six German triplanes (with rotary engines and lower plane less span than the other two) were encountered.

Another Pilot of the same Squadron fired 500 rounds into enemy trenches and huts near Pervyse from a height of 15 feet.

Two of No. 9 Squadron Pilots on special patrol attacked six E.A. over Cortemarck, who, however, showed no fight. A large number of rounds were fired without decisive results.

January 26th.

Owing to the unfavourable weather conditions little war flying was possible.

Enemy Aircraft.

Between 23.25 and 01.05 on the evening of the 25th—26th, a special patrol of two machines (No. 10 Squadron) went up in search of enemy machine spotting for the long range gun which was shelling Dunkerque. Spotting machine, however, could not be observed.

One of the pilots after searching between Dunkerque and Zuydcoote for the E.A. crossed the lines, and proceeded beyond Lichtervelde and Thourout, but saw no signs of activity in this area.

The second machine crossed the lines further north and observed an aerodrome east of Ostende, and south-east from the revolving light at De Haan, which Pilot attacked from a height of about 300 feet, firing about 240 rounds.

It would appear that the aerodrome referred to was Vlisseghem.

An offensive sweep was also attempted but had to be abandoned owing to bad visibility.

January 27th.

The low clouds and bad visibility prevented any reconnaissance work.

Bombing Raid by Day, No. 5 Squadron, D.H. 4's.

Aertrycke Aerodrome and Engel Dump were attacked by seven machines and three escorts. Two 50-lb. and eight 25-lb. bombs were dropped on Engel Dump at 11.50.

Six 50-lb. and twenty-four 16-lb. bombs were dropped on Aertrycke Aerodrome at 11.55. Visibility was fair, but both targets were almost completely obscured by clouds. This rendered observation of results impossible.

Enemy Aircraft.

Very few E.A. were seen and no combats took place.

January 28th.

Bombing Raid by Day, No. 5 Squadron, D.H. 4's.

Eight 50-lb., eight 25-lb., and twenty-seven 16-lb bombs were dropped on Aertrycke Aerodrome. Several explosions were observed among the two groups of hangars and sheds. A direct hit is also reported on a Hervieux hangar.

Two 50-lb. and six 16-lb. bombs were dropped on Engel Aerodrome. Sheds and hangars were well straddled, but no direct hits were reported.

Four 16-lb. bombs were also dropped on Engel Dump. Bombs were observed to burst among the sheds on the siding.

On the return journey four E.A. were engaged at long range without decisive result.

Enemy Aircraft.

While carrying out an offensive sweep over the Ypres—Dixmude—Roulers area, a patrol of eight Camels from No. 3 Squadron attacked eight E.A. Flight Lieut. Glen and Flight Commander Rochford closed with a D.F.W. two-seater. The observer was badly wounded or killed by Flight Commander Rochford, as he did not return fire, and was right down in the cock-pit with his gun pointing upwards. The same two pilots and Flight Sub-Lieut. Devereux attacked a second D.F.W. over Foret d'Houlthulst, which went down out of control, the observer being badly wounded.

Flight Sub-Lieut. MacLeod attacked a D.F.W. two-seater from the side, and after firing about 100 rounds the machine went up on one wing tip and spun down completely out of control.

Several other E.A. were attacked during the day indecisively.

January 29th.

Photographic Reconnaissance.

A photographic reconnaissance was attempted by No. 2 Squadron, but had to be abandoned on account of mist and haze.

Bombing Raid by Day, No. 5 Squadron, D.H. 4's.

A bombing raid was carried out on Coolkerke Aerodrome. Twelve 50-lb., four 25-lb., and forty-eight 16-lb. bombs were dropped on the objective at 13.08, which was well straddled. Bombs were seen to burst among the sheds, and a fire broke out.

Enemy Aircraft.

During a high offensive patrol a flight from No. 3 Squadron engaged two formations of Albatross scouts. Flight Commander Armstrong attacked five Albatross scouts, one of which turned over on its back and fell in a spin, out of control. A number of indecisive combats took place, two E.A. being driven down.

Fourteen E.A. of various types were encountered by a flight from No. 9 Squadron. Two E.A. were driven down in spinning nose-dives, but owing to the continuous fighting that took place ultimate results could not be observed.

An E.A. which was being shelled by our A.A. between Dunkerque and Nieuport, was indecisively attacked by a No. 10 Squadron pilot. On returning he himself was heavily shelled by our A.A.

While on a Fleet Patrol, five Camels of No. 13 Squadron engaged two hostile seaplanes off Blankenberghe. One was attacked by the whole patrol in turn, and after bursting in flames, fell in the sea 100 yards from Piers. The flight consisted of Flight Commander Slatter, Flight Lieut. Paynter, and Flight Sub-Lieuts. Greene, Cooper, and Mackay.

Throughout the day the vicinity of Roulers and Menin was patrolled by large E.A. formations, and a good many indecisive combats took place.

January 30th.

Reconnaissance by No. 2 Squadron, D.H. 4's.

A low Fleet Patrol was carried out, but a good reconnaissance was unable to be made owing to bad visibility.

A photographic reconnaissance was carried out in the afternoon. Forty plates were exposed between Selzaete, Bruges and Westcappelle.

Bombing Raid by Day, No. 5 Squadron, D.H. 4's.

Oostcamp Aerodrome was attacked by seven machines. Fourteen 50-lb. and sixty 16-lb. bombs were dropped on the objective at 13.15.

The three groups of sheds and hangars to the southward were straddled, and a direct hit is reported on a hangar, from which fire and dense smoke arose.

On the return journey bombing formation was attacked by E.A.

One of our machines failed to return.

Enemy Aircraft.

Six Albatross Scouts were attacked by a flight from No. 3 Squadron over Gheluvelt. Flight Commander Rochford, Flight Lieuts. Ellwood and Glen had a decisive combat with two of the machines, both of which were attacked at close quarters and driven down out of control.

A patrol of No. 13 Squadron sighted three E.A. off Ostende. Flight Commander Day and Flight Lieut. Paynter dived on the leader, both firing a number of rounds. The E.A. was suddenly observed to explode and the machine fell in small pieces. It is presumed that a bomb was hit. The other two E.A. dived for Ostende.

Immediately after leaving their objective the bombing formation was attacked by a number of E.A. scouts. One E.A. was observed to go down into a spin, but the final result could not be observed.

Various other engagements took place during the day with indecisive results.

One of our pilots whilst on patrol, was compelled to make a forced landing on the water. Both pilot and machine were saved.

January 31st.
Reconnaissance by No. 2 Squadron, D.H. 4's.

A patrol over the Fleet was carried out by W/T machine and escort. No observations could be made over Ostende owing to dense clouds.

A photographic reconnaissance was carried out at midday. Plates were exposed over Breedene, but on account of mist no accurate observations of Ostende could be made.

On the return journey five E.A. were sighted, but on fire being opened these machines made off in the direction of Ostende.

Later in the day a second photographic reconnaissance was carried out to the east of Bruges. Plates were exposed between Selzaete, Bruges, and Knocke.

Bombing Raid by Day, No. 5 Squadron, D.H. 4's.

A bombing raid was carried out on Engel Aerodrome and Dump. Four 50-lb. and forty-one 16-lb. bombs were dropped on the aerodrome. Two direct hits are reported, one on a group of small huts, and the other on the eastern-most hangar, and a fire broke out in each case.

Three 50-lb. and eight 16-lb. bombs were dropped on Engel Dump. Two direct hits are claimed, and a fire was observed to break out in the south-east corner of the dump.

All machines returned safely.

Enemy Aircraft.

Three E.A. were encountered by one of our patrols east of Dixmude at 15,000 feet. E.A. were followed and eventually engaged over Thourout, with indecisive results.

Very few E.A. were observed during the day.

Honours during period 16th to 31st January.

Name	Unit	Awarded
Acting Flight Commander N. M. Macgregor	No. 10 Squadron	D.S.C.

Acting Promotions.

Name	Unit
Flight Commander R. Graham, D.S.O., D.S.C., to Acting Squadron Commander	No. 13 Squadron

Casualties.
Missing.

Name	Unit	Date
Flight Sub-Lieut. H. S. J. E. Youens	No. 3 Squadron	23/1/18
Flight Sub-Lieut. R. A. Blyth	No. 10 Squadron	23/1/18
Flight Sub-Lieut. J. H. T. Carr	No. 12 Squadron	25/1/18
Flight Sub-Lieut. F. T. P. Williams	No. 5 Squadron	30/1/18
F 23539, A.C. 1 (G.-L.) C. A. Leitch	No. 5 Squadron	30/1/18

Wounded.

Name	Unit	Date
Flight Sub-Lieut. A. A. Cameron	No. 10 Squadron	18/1/18
Flight Sub-Lieut. J. E. Beveridge	No. 9 Squadron	22/1/18

F. C. HALAHAN,
Wing Captain, R.N.,
for Senior Officer, R.N.A.S.

Headquarters, R.N.A.S.,
Dunkerque,
4th February, 1918.

Summary of Bombing Raids carried out by the R. N. A. S.

From January 16th to 31st, 1918, inclusive,

With weights of Explosives dropped.

TARGET.	BOMBS DROPPED.		TOTAL LBS.
AERTRYCKE AERODROME	14 —	50 lbs.	
	8 —	25 lbs.	
	51 —	16 lbs.	1,716
COOLKERKE AERODROME	12 —	50 lbs.	
	4 —	25 lbs.	
	48 —	16 lbs.	1,468
OOSTCAMP AERODROME	14 —	50 lbs.	
	60 —	16 lbs.	1,660
VARSSENAERE AERODROME	8 —	50 lbs.	
	8 —	20 lbs.	
	35 —	16 lbs.	1,120
ENGEL AERODROME	6 —	50 lbs.	
	47 —	16 lbs.	1,052
ENGEL DUMP	5 —	50 lbs.	
	8 —	25 lbs.	
	12 —	16 lbs.	642

Grand Total   -   7,658 lbs.

N.B.—A total of nearly THREE AND A HALF TONS of BOMBS have been dropped during the period under review.

Printed at Royal Naval Air Service Headquarters, Dunkerque, 1918.

Truing-up of Aeroplanes

This publication, 'No 5', issued by the Air Department on 1 September 1916, gives the basic information to enable ground crew to assemble and rig aeroplanes, and then goes into greater detail with regard to aircraft of particular configurations and of specific types. An appendix of diagrams illustrates the methods of truing up different types of landplanes and seaplanes then in service with the RNAS.

TRUING-UP

OF

AEROPLANES.

AIR DEPARTMENT,
1st September 1916.
No. 5.

CHAPTER I.

GENERAL PRINCIPLES.

A.—Selection of Materials.

Before commencing to erect an aeroplane care must be exercised in the examination of all parts to be used. Attention must be paid to the following:—

(1) *Metal Parts.*—There must be no signs of rust or flaws, especially in the wires.

(2) Bolts and nuts employed should be accurately machined all over.

(3) Piano or spoke wire should not have been previously bent and must be free from kinks.

(4) Stranded wire or cable should be regularly twisted and not frayed at any point.

There should be no trace of white powdery deposit on the lay of wire rope. All splices should have at least two complete tucks before the strands are tapered, and the splices should be served with waxed cord or wire.

Extra flexible cable is to be invariably employed for all controls. In other parts of the machine where cable is employed flexible cable of 7 × 7 or 1 × 19 construction is to be employed. These latter types of cable do not splice so well as the extra flexible, but a more efficient joint than that obtained by splicing may be made in the following manner:—

The end of the wire cable is bent round to form an eye, and the parts of the cable which are thus brought into contact are carefully tinned, and then either served round with a series of bands of copper wire or fitted with a series of flattened copper ferrules. If wire serving is employed the serving must not be too neatly done, but the wire is to be wound round the two parts of the cable so as to leave small spaces of about twice the diameter of the wire between adjacent coils. In addition, about ⅜-inch of bare cable should be left between adjacent ferrules or bands of wire serving. These latter, and also the bare cable between them, are then carefully soldered over. When soldering or tinning, a blow lamp is on no account to be used. An ordinary soldering iron is to be employed.

This type of joint should never give an efficiency of less than 100 per cent. The thimble employed in the eye should be of solid construction, and the hole through which the eye of the cable passes should have a suitable radius as in the case of spliced wire.

(5) Tubing should be perfectly straight and should not show signs of having been previously bent and subsequently straightened. The inside should be carefully inspected for signs of rust; it should then be carefully oiled internally and its ends should be finally plugged with wood to prevent the entrance of water or damp.

(6) The threads of bolts, nuts and screws should be clean, and not worn or burred, and there should be no slackness in the nut.

(7) Strut sockets and other metal fittings should not be bent out of their original shape. Such fittings should also not be used if they show signs of having been bent and subsequently straightened. In the case of aluminium sockets, care must be taken that there are no cracks, especially where the sockets have been previously subjected to severe stress. Eye-plates and eye-bolts should show no signs of wear or fracture.

(8) Metal work must either be bent hot all over or bent cold; local heating must not be employed unless carried out along the whole width of the plate.

(9) Sticky tape should never be used to cover up strainers or ferrules, or to bind wires where they cross. The tape does not provide protection against rust and it hides the rust when formed. When employed on strainers it also prevents the locking-wire from being seen. Where bracing wires cross they should not, as a general rule, be bound together unless they touch and so are liable to chafe one against the other. In this case it is necessary to bind the wires, when waxed twine or iron wire only is to be employed.

(10) Great care should be taken that all bracing wire is fully stretched before being used, or the machine will soon go "soggy," and need re-truing. This stretching can best be done by putting a proof load on to the finished wire, after splicing (if possible) equal to the normal load which will be borne by it in flight. Heavy gauge thimbles should be employed in the eye of a splice so as to prevent the eye elongating, and the attachment holding the eye should have a sufficient radius to prevent it from closing the top of the eye.

Wood Parts.—The correct wood for the various parts of the aeroplanes must always be employed. There should be no signs of flaws and the wood should be properly seasoned. Struts must be straight; any departure from a straight line is liable to be accentuated by end pressure to a sufficient extent to involve collapse or fracture. Signs of dry rot and wormholes should be looked for most carefully before varnishing.

Fabric.—Fabric should show no signs of deterioration. In covering a plane, fabric that has already been doped should not be re-employed.

B.—Fitting of Accessory Parts.

(1) All internal drift wirings and any metallic fixings covered by the fabric must be painted with some rust- and dope-resisting material, such as "Velure," enamel or "Velure,"

A (12)30853 Wt 36999—P 1908 2500 10/16 E & S A 2

Page 4

varnish. If enamel is employed it should be of light colour, otherwise it may hide rust when the latter has once formed.

(2) *Turnbuckles or Wire Strainers.*—

(a) Turnbuckles should be a good fit on the screwed ends of the barrel. There should be no "shake" between the two parts nor should they be too tight a fit. The thread should be perfectly uniform. In the event of the turnbuckle being a tight fit, there is a risk of the wires being twisted in tightening up.

(b) Turnbuckles must not be worked upon with pliers or other tools. A wire, passed through the hole provided in them, must be employed when adjusting them, the eyebolts being held by the fingers or a wire.

(c) Turnbuckles must not be screwed up to the limit of their screw threads. The wire itself must be shortened when necessary, or a new one fitted.

(d) Turnbuckles must always have the whole of their thread engaged, and the barrel must not be covered with tape.

(e) *In no circumstances is it permissible to saw off any portion of the turnbuckle.*

(3) *Lubrication of Pulleys, &c.*—All pulleys and fair leads for the wires must be lubricated with grease and not with oil.

(4) *Fitting of cocks.*—In all cases where cocks are employed in petrol or oil systems, care is to be taken that they are so fitted that when in their correct working positions their handles point downwards, otherwise the effect of vibration will tend to alter their setting. In cases where cocks have T handles, arrangements must be made to secure them in their working positions.

(5) *Petrol and Oil Piping.*—Piping of all kinds must be arranged with a proper regard to the amount of vibration to which it will be subjected. Long unsupported lengths must be avoided. In metal piping it is generally advisable to insert a joint of specially prepared rubber tubing close to any unions, as the latter frequently become a seat of fracture. Although the special rubber tubing is prepared to resist the action of petrol and oil, it will nevertheless gradually deteriorate, and will require examination at short intervals, though this can be partially avoided by keeping the ends of the copper tubes close together. Chokes in pipes are frequently caused by deterioration of the lining of the tubing.

(6) *Bolts and Nuts.*—Care must be taken that when small bolts and nuts are tightened up with a spanner they are not overstrained.

If a nut be tightened up too much the bolt will have an initial stress put into it, and the further stress due to its normal

Page 5

load may be sufficient to cause the bolt to fracture. Where bolts are fitted on wooden members of an aeroplane, washers of ample diameter are to be fitted under the head of the bolt and the nut to prevent these from crushing the wood when tightened up.

(7) *Locking Devices.*—All bolts and nuts, &c., must be secured in some *positive manner* to prevent them from slacking back. An ordinary split pin fitted above a nut is useless for the purpose, unless the nut is washered up to the split pin and the nut a tight fit on the bolt.

The following are the most general methods of securing nuts:—

(a) Castellated nut fitted with split pin.

(b) End of bolt (or stud) riveted over the top of the nut.

(c) Check nut fitted over an ordinary nut, and a split pin fitted to bear on the upper nut.

(d) The thread at the end of the bolt may only be burred in exceptional cases, such as when fitted in an inaccessible place.

(e) Spring washers are often fitted underneath nuts, but this is *not* a positive lock.

(f) With turnbuckles, a wire is fitted passing through the hole in the barrel and secured to both eyebolts. Great care must be taken that the keep wire is put on properly.

(g) Before putting fabric on to the wings or other parts the greatest care should be taken that all nuts are locked in the requisite manner, that all turnbuckles are fitted with keep wires, and that all internal steel work is protected by a good quality paint or varnish against the formation of rust.

(8) *Tension of Bracing Wires.*—Wires which are in inaccessible places, such as the internal wiring of wings, are usually put on with rather greater initial tension than ones which can be easily tested.

(9) *Notes on Covering and Doping of Planes.*—It is found that the best dopes at present on the market are those made by Messrs. Cellon and Messrs. The British Emaillite Company. Both these firms manufacture non-poisonous dopes which for every reason are preferable to those containing tetrachlorethane. "Emaillite" 11a and c, or "Cellon" N.P. 2 are dopes to be recommended.

Both of the firms mentioned above now issue comprehensive "Doping Schemes," the instructions contained in which must be rigidly adhered to in order to obtain satisfactory results. In the case of machines to be used in tropical climates "Cellon" should be used, and the upper surfaces of the wings finally varnished with an approved non-actinic pigment varnish, such as P.C. 10, a khaki-coloured acetate paint, which protects the dope from the actinic rays of the sun's light, thereby preventing decomposition.

The under surfaces of the wings should receive two coats of some approved transparent varnish, such as V.114.

When covering planes prior to doping, the surfaces of the wing-framework in contact with the fabric should be left bare and not varnished.

The fabric is to be put on in the approved manner either by—

(1) Sewing to the ribs, or
(2) Fixing it down by cane strips.

If the first method is employed, the string is to be waxed to prevent its becoming slack. It must be further secured by a double knot at three points along the length of the rib, so that in case of the string breaking the whole of the fabric does not become loose on the rib; the pitch of the stitch must not exceed 4 inches, except in the case of abnormally large machines.

If method 2 is employed, brass screws must be used to secure the cane strips, which must be carefully bored to avoid splitting.

The joints in the fabric should be made of the balloon seam type with double stitching, and the fabric should be laid over the leading edge and sewn up to the trailing edge. The fabric should be fairly taut, but *not too taut*, before doping is commenced.

When doping with "Cellon" or "Emaillite," the first coat should be put on with about 2 parts dope, 1 part thinning; the second coat 4 parts dope, 1 part thinning, then three or more coats of undiluted dope.

The surface of the wing should be finished up with 2 coats of Pigment Varnish. The fabric must on no account be sand-papered to obtain a smooth surface. Pigment Varnish is employed on the upper surfaces of wings, &c., only, and its object is to form a screen through which the actinic rays of light from the sun cannot pass, and thus to protect the fabric from deterioration under the action of sunlight.

Doping should be carried out in as dry an atmosphere as possible. Successive coats of dope are to be put on as soon as the preceding coat is dry.

(10) *Fabric on Fuselage.*—In machines whose fuselage is covered with fabric, it is the Admiralty practice to have the joint in the fabric laced so as to provide a ready means of inspecting the fuselage or tuning it up.

If the lacing is carried out with a single cord, then in the event of the cord breaking, the cover of the fuselage is liable to strip off, foul the elevator and prevent it from working. When lacing up fuselages, the cord is to be securely fastened *by double knots* at *every 12th pair of eyes*, so as to prevent the cover from stripping off in the event of the lace breaking.

CHAPTER II.

TRACTOR BIPLANES.

The first operation to be proceeded with is the truing-up of the fuselage.

Truing-up of the Fuselage.—The usual method of construction adopted in the fuselage is that indicated in the diagram (Figs. 1 *a* and *b*).

Side elevation on Plan.

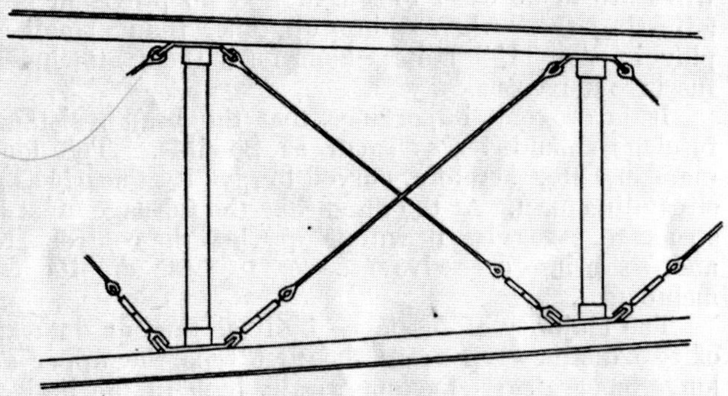

FIG. 1a.

Cross Section.

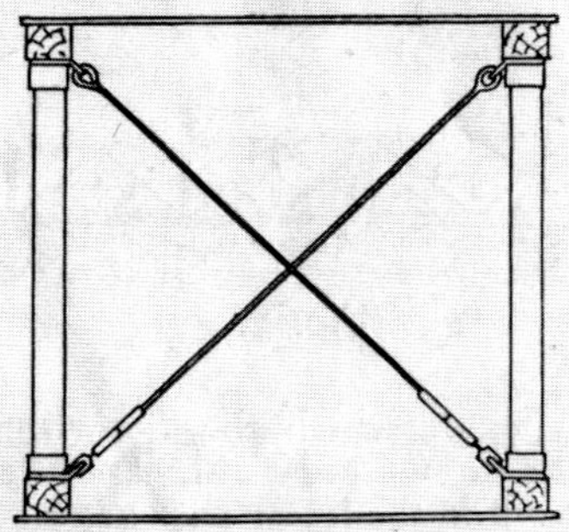

FIG. 1b.

The fuselage is a braced structure, usually of rectangular section. The four longitudinal members or "longerons," are connected at intervals by vertical and horizontal struts which form transverse frames or panels of more or less rectangular or trapezoidal shape. Each of the panels formed by the longerons and a pair of these struts are braced together with diagonal wiring, so as to make each panel into a stiff frame and so render the fuselage structure capable of taking the bending moment due to the tail loading, rudder, &c.

The transverse sections are similarly traced by diagonal wires which run transversely across the inside of the fuselage forming the panels, having the main longerons for corners. These provide the fuselage with the necessary rigidity to resist torsion.

The bracing wires are usually fitted with turnbuckles which enable their lengths to be adjusted within limits, and so allow of the fuselage being trued up. In B.E. machines swaged rods are fitted in place of the bracing wires. The butted ends of these are threaded opposite hands and screw into fork-end attachments which render them adjustable.

In most of the machines built by Messrs. Short the bracing wires are made dead to length, and no provision is made for adjusting them when truing up, other than a small amount of play in the "U" bolts which form their attachment to the fuselage longerons.

It is of great importance that the head resistance of the fuselage should be as small as possible. The longitudinal members are, therefore, curved to give it as nearly as possible a streamline form. At the same time the fuselage must be a rigid structure, otherwise it will whip when the controls are worked and so bring excessive stresses to bear on its component members.

The majority of fuselages built at present date are of one of two distinct types; in the first type the upper and lower longerons are curved symmetrically both in the horizontal and vertical planes about the axis of the fuselage, e.g., the B.E. biplane (see Fig. 2).

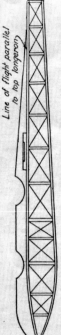

FIG. 2.

In the other type, of which the Sopwith machine is an example, the top longerons are straight except for the short portion at the nose while the lower ones are curved (see Fig. 3).

In machines of the former type the line of flight is parallel to the axis of the fuselage, while in the latter it is parallel to the upper longeron in the normal flying position. In practically all machines the datum line from which the machine is tuned up, whether parallel to the axis or to the upper longeron, is parallel to the centre line of the crankshaft. As will be seen later, this gives a line from which all pusher machines can be trued up. It is obvious that if any of the bracing wires become altered in length the whole of the structure may alter in shape and so get out of truth, and since its length is great compared with the cross section, any such alteration will have an exaggerated effect on the trim of the machine. It is therefore necessary that the fuselage should be periodically checked for true alignment, and,

if necessary, re-trued up. The foremost consideration in connection with a fuselage is that its axis shall be true.

Symmetrical Type Fuselage.—With this type of fuselage, when under construction, each of the transverse struts, on all four sides of the fuselage, is bisected in length and the middle point marked as at (a) (Fig. 4).

It is the Admiralty practice that all contractors shall permanently mark in these points with black paint.

If the fuselage structure is in truth, a line stretched between two points at the middle of the struts situated at each of its ends will cut each of the intermediate struts at its middle point. If they do not, the fuselage is out of truth, and the diagonal bracing wires must be suitably readjusted until these points come truly in line.

If the fuselage is very much out of truth, the operation of truing up is much facilitated by the following procedure:—

Line of flight parallel to top longeron

FIG. 3.

The intersection of the centre lines of each of the strut ends and of the longitudinal members is accurately marked with a dot, as shown in Fig. 4. If the panel BCDE is in truth the points A and A¹ will both be situated on the axis of the side of the fuselage, and in this case it is obvious from the symmetrical form of the fuselage that the two diagonals of the panel, viz., BD and CE, will be equal. On the other hand, if A¹ is not on the axis of the side of the fuselage, then one of these diagonals will be greater than the other.

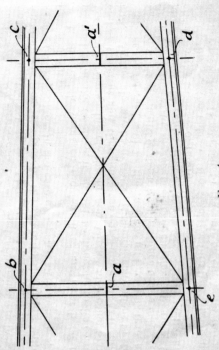

FIG. 4.

This method of truing up a fuselage of this type is carried out as follows:—The fuselage is placed on trestles and, commencing with one of the side panels at its forward end, the distance between the diagonal points B and D is measured with a trammel and checked against the length of the other diagonal CE. Should these diagonals be unequal, then by slackening out one diagonal wire and tightening up the other, the panel can be adjusted until they are equal.

The operation is then repeated on the next panel, and so on along the whole fuselage.

When truing up by this method, great care must be taken to see that all the strut sockets are fitted to the longerons in their exact and true positions. If one socket is out of place, it will cause the diagonals of each of the panels on either side of it to be of uneven length.

If the fuselage is being completely built up, this can be checked by putting the longerons alongside each other, and comparing the positions for the struts as marked on the longerons. If, however, the fuselage is already built up and only requires re-truing, the position of the strut sockets can be checked by a plumb bob on set square or spirit level.

As a check on the foregoing method of truing up, and also in cases where the fuselage is only slightly out of truth, the alignment of the fuselage should be checked by a line stretched along the length of the fuselage coinciding with the middle points of the struts at each of its ends. This line can be tied directly on to the forward strut, but at the aft end, owing to the taper of the fuselage, it will be necessary to clamp a batten across one of the after frames, and to attach the line to this well clear of the fuselage so as to leave the line free to take up its true position. The line must be kept very taut during the process of truing up and not allowed to sag at all. The coincidence of the line and the points marked at the middle of the intermediate struts can be checked approximately by eye, but as a final check it should be tested at several points by squaring off from the side of the struts to the string with a square (see Fig. 5), or, in the case of tapered strut-members, by means of a level.

If the middle point on the length of any strut is off the centre line of the fuselage, it should be brought to its correct position by slackening off the bracing wires which come to one end of the strut and tightening the opposing wires at its other end. As has already been stated, it is most convenient to start work at the forward end of the fuselage and get this true, and then to work gradually to the aft end. Since errors may occur in joining the strut socket positions on the longerons, the alignment of the centre line of the fuselage is to be the final check for the trueness of the fuselage structure.

Having got the sides of the fuselage into true alignment a similar procedure is adopted to true up or check its top and bottom surfaces.

The panels of these surfaces are cross-wired in the usual manner, but in addition the four longerons are braced together so as to give the fuselage torsional rigidity. Consequently, if any panel of either the upper or lower surface of the fuselage is found not in truth, then, before any adjustments of the panel wiring are made, care must be taken to see that these bracing wires which are in a plane perpendicular to the axis of the fuselage are sufficiently slack to allow the requisite adjustment to be made in the upper and lower horizontal panels without causing them to be overbraced.

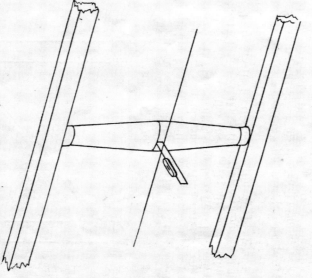

Fig. 5.

In the case of B.E. machines the upper and lower surfaces of the fuselage are filled in with three-ply wood. These panels should therefore remain permanently in truth; should they, however, get damaged and out of truth, they can only be adjusted by fitting new three-ply. In such a case it is probable that new longerons would also be required.

The next operation consists of "squaring up," the fuselage by means of the transverse bracing wires already referred to. These transverse wires bring the sides and upper surface of the fuselage perpendicular to each other. The operation of truing up may be considerably facilitated by employing a sliding trammel. This instrument consists of two light battens held together by metal clips which allow the two battens to slide

manner as has already been described for the former type of body structure.

Initial tension of Bracing Wires.—The greatest care must be taken in adjusting the tension of all bracing wires, otherwise they may be set up sufficiently overstrained to cause them either to break themselves or to deform the structure when the additional flying load is put upon them. In all cases a panel must be adjusted by first slacking off one diagonal and then tightening the other.

When the adjustments are completed and the machine is correctly trued up, the bracing wires *should all be taut,* and care should be taken to ensure that *the degree of tension is uniform throughout the whole of the various panels* of the fuselage. This presents no great difficulty so far as the panels of the outer surface of the fuselage are concerned, but in certain cases may prove difficult as regards the transverse bracing.

If the initial tension in any wire is excessive, not only is the wire likely to fail when additional forces are brought to bear on it in flight, but large compressive stresses are thrown on to the compression members, even if the wire does not actually fail. Further, if the initial tension of the bracing wires varies in different panels, some of the members may commence to give and so throw the whole structure of the fuselage out of truth the first time the machine is taken into the air.

In certain cases where a machine comes into the workshops to be trued up, it may be found that by merely slightly slacking off certain bracing wires true alignment may be regained.

When in the course of truing up a structure it is necessary to tighten up one or more wires and at the same time slack off others in the same or adjacent panels, the slacking off should invariably be carried out first.

The final operation in truing up with regard to the fuselage is to check the position of the main-wing spar sockets. These should be fixed absolutely symmetrically on each side of the fuselage, otherwise difficulties will be experienced when fitting the wings.

The vertical distances from the upper longerons to the centres of the main wing spar sockets should first be checked from the drawing; if no drawing is available it will suffice if these measurements are equal for the corresponding sockets on each side of the fuselage.

Next, the positions of these sockets must be symmetrical along the length of the fuselage; this can be checked in the following manner.

With the fuselage still fixed on trestles and with its axis level fore-and-aft and top surface level athwart-ship, run a plumb-line up from the centre of each main-wing spar socket on to the top of the upper longeron.

Where this line meets the upper surface of the longeron, a pencil line across the upper

over but keep them parallel to each other, so that their total length can be easily adjusted. The length of a diagonal of any one panel can thus be measured and compared with that of the opposite diagonal of the same panel (*see* Fig. 6). Should the two diagonals of any one transverse panel not be equal, the diagonal bracing wires are adjusted until they are so, and the sides of the fuselage are then of necessity perpendicular to one another.

When the transverse panels at the front of the fuselage have been checked and found true, the adjustment of the remainder of the cross wires can also be fairly accurately checked by sighting along the length of the fuselage from the forward cross wires to the middle of the stern post; all the remaining cross wires should intersect along this line of sight, which, if the fuselage is true, will be the centre line of the whole fuselage structure.

Fuselages of the "Sopwith" type.—With this type of structure the procedure of checking the alignment or setting-up is rendered more simple than in the former case by the top longerons being absolutely straight for their whole length. It is only necessary to check this straightness of the longerons to ensure that the side panelling of the fuselage is true. This can be very simply carried out by employing a long straight-edge placed in contact with the top of these longerons and then adjusting the diagonal bracing wires of the panels till straightness is secured. For ordinary checking purposes, if no straight-edge is available, a string should be stretched taut along the top of each upper longeron, level with its upper surface. If this string is kept to one side of the longeron's surface, so as to be free to take up a straight position, it will provide a good guide as to the alignment. When the sides have been lined up correctly, the truing up of the panels of the top and bottom surfaces of the fuselage and the "squaring up" of its cross section panels may be proceeded with in exactly the same

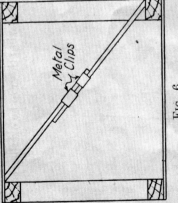

Fig. 6.

surface of the longerons. The point of intersection of this line with the centre line of the longerons should then be marked by a dot or, still better, a pin. The distance of each of these points (each pair being taken separately) to the centre of the rudder post, or some other convenient point known to be in vertical plane through the centre line of the fuselage, is then taken with a steel tape. These should be equal for each pair of points. If these distances are not equal, then either the spar sockets are out of their symmetrical positions, or else the fuselage itself is out of truth.

* *Truing up the Plane.*—The next procedure is to true up the main planes. The usual form of construction employed in wings is shown diagrammatically in Fig. 7. The main framework comprises two main spars "*aa*" and "*bb*"; and a certain number of main ribs "*cc*" fixed at right angles to these main spars. The rectangles or panels formed by the intersection of the main ribs or drift struts and the main spars are braced together by means of diagonal bracing wires which form the wing structure into a rigidly braced structure, and give the wing sufficient rigidity to resist the drift forces brought to bear on it during flight.

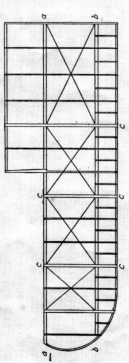

FIG. 7.

But for this bracing the wing would fold back under the action of these drift forces. A number of light ribs are fitted in between the main ribs in order to support the fabric in an efficient manner and give the whole wing section the necessary profile or section.

The most common type of wing structure is very simple to true up, since the front and rear spars of the main planes are rigidly parallel. To check this alignment the intersection of the centre lines of the spars and the main drift struts or compression ribs are accurately found and marked with a hard pencil. The trueness of the wing structure is then tested by taking each separate panel in turn and comparing the lengths of its diagonals by means of a trammel. If in any particular panel the lengths of the two diagonals are found to be unequal they

* It is of the utmost importance that when a plane has to be supported on trestles, the trestles shall be placed under the main spars, and not under the lighter ribs, which have very little strength, and so are likely to get deranged if carelessly handled.

must be made equal by adjusting the lengths of the diagonal bracing wires in the manner already described for truing up the fuselage. When each panel has been dealt with in this way the whole wing should be in perfect alignment.

When erecting a new plane or adjusting an old one, great care must be taken to see that the strut sockets or box rib fastenings are exactly opposite each other on their respective spars. This can be done by direct measurement or by placing the spars alongside each other before commencing erection of the wings. If the box ribs or drift struts are not fixed in their true positions on the main spars, the diagonals in each panel will not be equal, hence it is necessary to check their positions most carefully.

When all the panels have been trued up in this manner both front and rear spars should be perfectly straight along the whole of their respective lengths. This should be checked either by testing with a straight-edge or else by stretching a line along the spars, on top of each spar and just over its edge, and then observing whether the edge of the spar is parallel to the string along its whole length. The straightness of the spars must be taken as the final test for the true alignment of the wing structure.

In the case of the Henry Farman and similar types of wings, the spars of the main planes are not parallel to each other, and the wings must be trued up by getting the rear spar straight along its whole length and at the same time perpendicular to the end or box rib of the centre plane.

This is best carried out as follows:—

(1) Take the centre panel of the plane, and since the main spars are parallel in this panel, true the panel up by adjusting the diagonal bracing till the diagonals of the panel are equal.

(2) The next panel outboard on either side of the centre panel can be trued up in a similar manner since the main spars are still parallel over this length.

(3) The main front spar commences to sweep back after the above panel is past. The rear spar of this next panel can, however, be brought into line with the rear spar of the centre three panels by stretching a line over the rear spar of these panels and parallel to it, and then adjusting the bracing of the next panel till its main spar forms a continuation of the rear main spar of the three centre panels.

This alignment of the rear spars may also be checked by dropping plumb-lines from the edge of the rear spar at different points along its length and sighting these to see that they are all truly in line.

When all the planes are quite true, they may be covered with fabric and doped. In some cases, however, it may be preferable to erect the machine in skeleton form before proceeding to cover the wings. Before putting on the fabric great care must be taken that all turnbuckles are fitted with keep wires and all nuts properly locked. In putting the fabric on it must only be stretched to a moderate degree, otherwise the shrinkage which occurs during the process of doping may deform the plane. It is of the utmost importance that the leading edge of the planes shall be of the correct profile or cross-section, as on this, in a large measure, depends the efficiency of the wings. If difficulty has been experienced previously due to the leading portion of the wing distorting or losing its profile, intermediate "riblets," or false ribs should be inserted between the front main spar and the leading edge of the plane between each pair of ordinary ribs. These give the fabric the centre support necessary.

Erection.—The fuselage is set up on two trestles in the normal position, with the datum line and opposite points on the upper surface of the top longerons horizontal. In those types of machine where the datum line corresponds with the axis of the fuselage (as in the B.E. type), this may be obtained by clamping a straight-edge or batten along the side of the fuselage with its upper edge coinciding with the "Centre Line" marks on the middle of the vertical struts.

A level is placed on this batten and the fuselage packed up on the trestles until the top of the batten is horizontal. Fuselages in which the datum line is parallel to the top longerons may be packed up into the correct position by levelling up the top longerons themselves. This latter method may be applied whether the longerons are straight and parallel to the "Datum Line" over the whole length of the fuselage, as in the Sopwith machines, or only at the front part of the fuselage, as in the Short and Avro types. It will generally be found that when the machine is set up with the datum line horizontal, the engine bearers are also horizontal.

The fuselage is now levelled up in the transverse direction by placing a level on the top longerons of the fuselage at right angles to the axis of the fuselage. When the fuselage is levelled in both directions it should be fixed quite firmly by clamping it to the trestles so as to prevent any accidental displacement.

A very simple type of level which greatly facilitates the process of setting up the fuselage and wings can be constructed out of two large glass tubes, the lower ends of which are connected by a long piece of rubber tubing, and whose upper ends are open to the atmosphere. This apparatus is filled with water to a point about halfway up the two glass tubes. Since the water will always find its own level in the two tubes, it is merely necessary to hold one of the tubes against each of the vertical struts at the opposite end of the fuselage, and then to adjust the trestles till the surface of the water in each tube

coincides with the marks at the middle of the respective end struts. The axis of the fuselage will then be accurately horizontal, assuming that the fuselage has been itself trued up correctly.

The next operation is the erection of the landing chassis, the construction of which differs in almost every type of machine.

In truing this up, the adjustments which have to be most carefully checked are (a) that the skids are parallel to one another and symmetrical about the axis of the fuselage, and (b) that the angle at which they are inclined to the horizontal is correct.

Taking the B.E. chassis as an example, the construction is explained in Fig. 8.

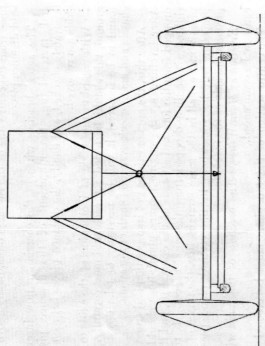

FIG. 8.

Before any attempt at erecting is commenced it should be seen that all the struts fit well home in their respective sockets, and also that each pair of corresponding struts are exactly the same and of the correct length.

The skids should also be placed alongside each other and checked for symmetry as regards the positions of their various fittings for mounting the undercarriage.

The skid struts are then fitted into their sockets on the skids and the whole lifted into place and packed up as nearly as possible in their true position under the fuselage.

To facilitate the erection of the under-carriage, two pieces of wood, cut to the correct length, are fixed as distance

A 30853   B

pieces between the two skids, one near the front end, and the other near the rear of the skid. These distance pieces hold the skids parallel to one another, and at the correct distance apart.

The distance between the skids is now accurately bisected along these distance pieces, and the bisecting points marked with a hard pencil. These bisecting points between the skids are now brought approximately under the centre line of the fuselage and jury wiring inserted in the under-carriage structure so as to hold it in position.

A plumb-line should now be dropped from each end of the fuselage, and immediately under the centre line of the fuselage; the skids are then moved by adjusting the jury wiring till the bisecting points on their distance pieces come in the direct line between these two plumb-lines. This is checked by sighting, but in addition it is also advisable to drop plumb-lines from the centre line of the fuselage immediately above the skid distance pieces.

The actual bracing wires of the chassis are now inserted and tautened up, the alignment of the distance pieces accurately checked, and finally, the distance pieces between the skids are removed.

With regard to the angle of inclination of the skids to the ground, this should be tested for each skid most carefully. If found to be incorrect, it will be necessary to take down the chassis and again check over the length of the struts.

After this, the engine can be got into position and trued up. After levelling up the engine bearers, plumb-lines should be dropped from the fore and aft ends of the crankshaft, and these sighted with a line dropped from the rudder post. If these plumb-lines are all in the same straight line, the thrust of the propeller will lie somewhere in the vertical plane passing through the axis of the machine.

Erection of Main Wings.—The erection of the main wings can now be commenced.

The centre section of the top plane must be erected and trued up before anything further is attempted. The struts are first checked for length, from the drawing, and are then erected in their sockets on the upper side of the fuselage. The centre section of the plane is placed in position on top of these struts, and the necessary bracing wire inserted for this centre structure.

In most English machines the struts supporting the centre section are all truly vertical when the fuselage datum line is horizontal. This greatly assists the truing up of the centre section. The struts are brought vertical by means of a plumb-line, the bracing wires to this centre structure being adjusted as necessary. The centre fore-and-aft line of the centre plane section should now lie vertically over the centre line of the fuselage. In the case of some American machines, the struts

are symmetrically inclined fore and aft, and also inwards towards the axis of the fuselage. In this case it is necessary to bisect accurately. The distance between the tops of the forward and aft struts on each side of the centre panel is, in this case, accurately bisected, and the middle points marked. From each of these points a plumb-line is dropped; then the fore-and-aft inter-strut wiring is adjusted until these lines come exactly midway between the bottoms of the struts on the upper longerons of the fuselage. The inward splay of the struts is next checked by a plumb-line from the side of the centre panel alongside each centre panel strut. The transverse inter-strut wiring is then adjusted till the splay of each separate pair of centre plane struts is the same. The centre line of the centre plane should then lie vertically over the centre line of the fuselage. This can be checked by plumb-lines.

In a few types of machines the centre section struts are inclined forward, and to check their slope it will be necessary to drop a plumb-line from each extremity of the leading edge of the centre section. If the stagger of the struts is incorrect, the incidence wires should be adjusted until the plumb-lines come vertically over the correct points previously marked on the two longerons of the fuselage, as obtained from the working drawings.

Great care must be taken to ensure that the angle of incidence of the centre section is exactly correct, since, if it is not so, it will be found after the machine is finally erected that the whole of the top plane is out of truth. The angle of incidence of the centre panel should therefore be checked; if it is found to be incorrect, the fault will probably be found in the length of the supporting struts from the top of the fuselage, or the position of these strut sockets. These should, therefore, be most carefully re-checked before commencing to erect.

The bottom planes can now be erected into their approximately true positions, the inner ends being connected up to their respective sockets or fittings on the sides of the fuselage, and the outer ends supported on trestles. The upper planes are then ready for erection. The lengths of the interplane struts, and their fit into their respective sockets on the planes must be checked.

A scaffold is erected above the lower plane alongside each pair of interplane struts, and a man stationed alongside each strut.

The upper plane is then lifted to somewhere near its correct position, and the interplane struts fitted into their sockets on it. The whole is then lowered into position, and the lower ends of the struts entered into their respective sockets on the lower plane. The interplane bracing wires can now be attached to their respective fittings. In re-erecting a machine in which the exact lengths of the bracing wires are not definitely known,

When the upper plane is true the next operation is to get the lower plane parallel to the upper one. This is done by checking the stagger of the planes.

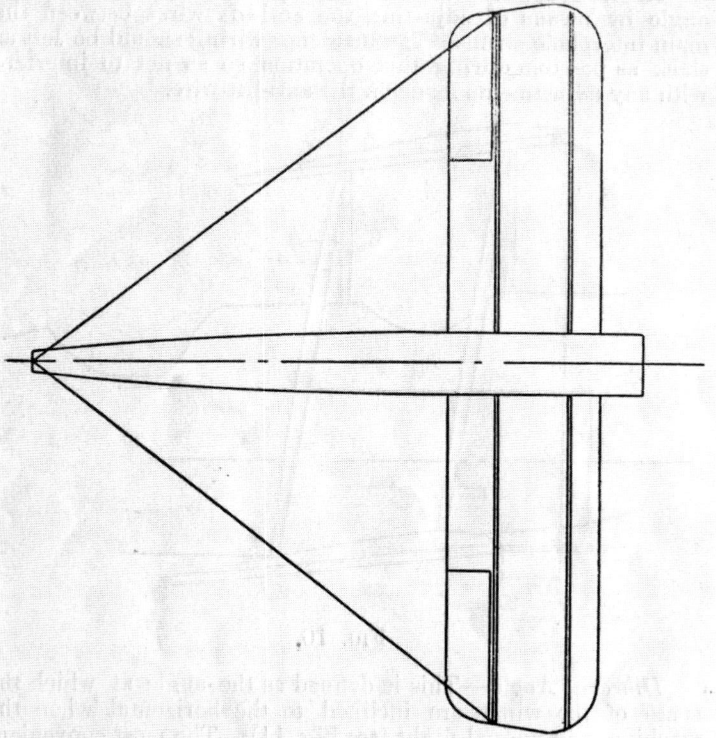

FIG. 9.

Stagger.—The stagger is the horizontal distance that the top plane projects in front of the bottom plane when the datum line of the fuselage is horizontal. This is checked directly by dropping plumb-lines from various points along the leading edge of the upper plane, and measuring the horizontal distance from this line to the leading edge of the bottom plane. (*See* Fig. 10.)

At the inner end of the planes the stagger is fixed by the position of the strut socket.

A line should be dropped from the leading edge of the top plane at the inner end and the stagger measured. This operation should be repeated at several points along the length of the planes, in order to make certain that the stagger of the top plane is uniform over the whole span of the machine.

If the stagger is not correct then the lower plane is not symmetrically placed relative to the fuselage, and the inner end of the lower planes will require planing in exactly the same

it is most convenient to fit temporary or jury interplane wiring at first, and to replace this later when the main planes are tuned up and the correct lengths of wire known. If, however, the lengths of the wires are known, this step is unnecessary.

Another method of erection sometimes adopted is to erect the whole main cell completely on the ground, wire it up, and afterwards lift it up and attach it to the fuselage as a complete unit.

The main cells have now to be trued up with regard to the dihedral angle, angle of incidence, stagger, &c.; these operations must be carried out in a definite order.

Truing up the Main Planes.—The first operation consists in getting the leading edges of the upper main planes into the correct positions relative to the axis of the fuselage.

The wings must be so placed that they are symmetrical about the axis of the fuselage, and in addition their leading edges must be given the correct "sweep back" (if any) relative to the centre section. A swept-back wing is very rare in British machines, and in general the leading edges of the wings are perpendicular to the axis of the fuselage.

The checking of the above characteristics of the wings necessitates two separate operations. In the first place a steel tape is stretched from the centre of each of the outer front strut sockets in turn to the centre of the rudder post. If the distances between these points as shown on the tape are equal, then the wings are symmetrical about the axis of the fuselage (*see* Fig. 9) in a horizontal plane.

Previous to checking the symmetry of the wings it should be ascertained that the corresponding strut sockets on the main spars are at an equal distance from the centre line of the fuselage, and are at corresponding points on the width of the main spars.

Secondly, if there is no "sweep back" to the wings, their alignment should be checked, since the two wings may be symmetrically placed on each side of the axis of the fuselage, and yet not be perpendicular to the axis of the fuselage.

This is best done by hanging plumb-lines against the leading edge at the inner and outer ends of each wing. By sighting along these four lines it can at once be seen whether the wings are in true alignment. If on checking the position of the wings in the foregoing manner it is found that either or both are not in the correct position, it will be necessary to plane a small amount off one end of the wooden box ribs forming the outside of the centre section, or off the main plane where it abuts the centre section. In practice, a small piece of packing may be inserted temporarily, and the thickness of this adjusted until the wings are brought square, and the correct amount may then be taken off the box rib at the end of the wing section.

manner as that described above for bringing the upper plane symmetrical to the axis of the fuselage.

The front spar must next be set up to the correct dihedral angle by means of adjusting the anti-lift wires between the main interplane struts. The incidence wiring should be left as slack as possible during this operation, so as not to interfere with any adjustments made on the anti-lift wire.

Dihedral Angle.—This is defined as the angle at which the spars of the wings are inclined to the horizontal when the machine is in normal flight (*see* Fig. 11). The most convenient

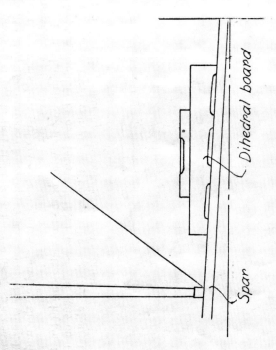

Fig. 10.

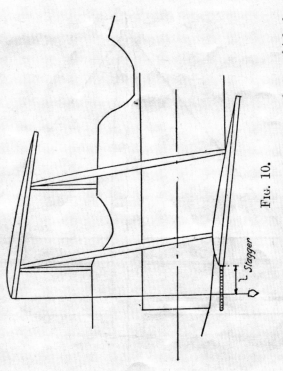

Fig. 11.

method of checking this is by means of a dihedral board. This board is cut to the correct dihedral angle, and, consequently, if one of its sides be placed on a main spar of the wing, the other side of the board will be horizontal if the spar is at its correct dihedral angle (*see* Fig. 12).

This dihedral board is placed on top of the wing's front spar, and the anti-lift bracing wires are adjusted until the upper edge of the board becomes horizontal, as shown by a level. When this edge of the board is level, the spar will be inclined at the correct angle to the horizontal. When the dihedral angle of the main planes is zero, the latter can be adjusted to their true horizontal positions by applying the water-level direct to the main spar itself.

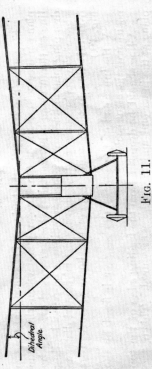

Fig. 12.

The rear spar should now be set up in an exactly similar manner, by adjusting its own anti-lift wires. If the truing up with the dihedral board is performed with care, the angle of incidence should now be correct everywhere along the planes at the end of this operation.

Angle of Incidence.—In workshop practice the angle of incidence of a wing surface is defined as the angle that, when the machine is in its normal flight attitude, the chord of the lower surface of the plane makes with the horizontal. For convenience in the erecting shop it is usually given in terms of Fig. 13, *i.e.*, the vertical distance between the respective levels of the leading and trailing edges of the wing's under surface.

In order to check the incidence of the lower main planes, a wooden batten is placed vertically, with its lower end on the floor and its upper end in contact with the leading edge of the lower plane.

A straight-edge is then placed with its upper edge in contact with the trailing edge of the plane, and is then brought up

22

23

horizontal by means of a level. Whilst in this position it is steadied by being held to the vertical batten.

The distance *AB* can then be measured off directly with a rule.

This gives the incidence to which the wing is set. If the uniformity of the angle of incidence along the plane is merely being checked, the following method should be employed.

At about four places along the length of each of the planes a piece of string is tied right round the plane. This string will follow the contour of the upper surface of the wing, but at the lower side it will coincide with the chord of the under surface.

If the incidence of the wing is the same all along its length, *i.e.*, the machine is one in which there is no wash-out on the wings, its truth can at once be seen by sighting along the strings; they should all be parallel to one another.

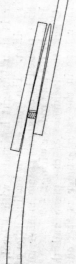

Fig. 13.

In truing up a wing the angle of incidence should first be carefully measured at the inner end of the planes, where the incidence is fixed by the position of the main spar sockets, in the fuselage; then, working outwards, the incidence should be checked at various points along the length of the plane to see that it is uniform.

As a final check, strings should be put round the plane at various points, and these sighted in the manner already explained.

If the angle of incidence is found to be incorrect at any point, it should be corrected by adjusting the anti-lift wires to the rear spar at that point, and on no account by adjusting the incidence wiring, which does not in reality control the incidence.

The lower plane should now be in truth, and, if the struts are all of correct length, the upper plane also. The incidence

of this should be checked in the same way as that of the lower plane.

The lift wires are now carefully adjusted to the correct tension, and finally the incidence wires should all be tautened up correctly.

To adjust the ailerons, battens are held tangential to the camber of the upper and lower surfaces of the wings just in front of the aileron hinge, and the aileron should be fixed midway between these (*see* Fig. 14). When fitting the aileron

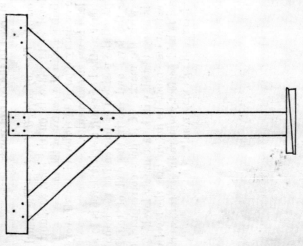

Fig. 14.

control cables the ailerons are packed up to a position about ¼-in. below the mean position shown in Fig. 14. The exact amount will vary with different machines and is a matter of experience. This is done by means of a tee batten (*see* Fig. 15). The control column or wheel is held in its neutral position, and the control wires are adjusted to be just taut with the ailerons in this position.

Fig. 15.

The Tail Plane.—The exact angle of incidence of the tail plane is generally obtained by actual flight and is fixed definitely according to the flying balance of each individual machine. The centre of the tail plane is set up to the correct angle of incidence on the fuselage, ignoring, for the time being, its outer ends. The plane must be placed so that its main spar is perpendicular to the axis of the fuselage. This is tested by measuring the distances of the extremities of the tail plane from some point on the axis of the fuselage, in a similar manner to that used in setting up the leading edge of the main planes symmetrically with the axis of the machine. The rear spar is then brought horizontal with a level, and secured in this position. The front spar or leading edge of the tail plane is then treated in exactly the same manner and secured into position by the stay rods or wiring.

Check the incidence of the plane and then set up the elevator flaps in the same manner as that employed for the ailerons, adjusting the control wires so as to be just taut when the control column is vertical.

Check the movement of all controls up and down, seeing that the range of movement is correct in both directions.

Put the rudder bar in its midship position, and block it there. Fit the rudder wires and make them just taut when the rudder is neutral, and check the rudder movement to right and left, to obtain its travel and also to see that sufficient slackness has been allowed in the control wires.

Note on the Use of Spirit Levels.—The usual method of using a level is to place it on the spar, &c., and then adjust until the bubble is in the centre of the tube.

As the ordinary type of spirit level is usually very inaccurate, this may lead to erroneous results.

The proper method of using a spirit level is to mark with a soft lead pencil the position of one end of the bubble and then to reverse the level and see if the end of the bubble still coincides with the mark. If it does correspond, the spar, or whatever is being tested, will be accurately level.

The greatest care must be taken that the level whenever it is employed is held perfectly square in the transverse direction, otherwise false readings may result.

CHAPTER III.

"PUSHER" TYPE MACHINES.

Maurice Farman (1913) *Machines.*—The first operation consists in truing up the upper and lower main planes themselves. These are in turn assembled and placed on trestles. They are now adjusted by means of the internal drift wiring, until the main spars are in true alignment. This is checked either by sighting along the spars or by getting a line stretched along exactly as explained for "Tractor" type machines.

Erecting the Main Cell.—The positions of the strut sockets on the top and bottom planes is checked for symmetry, and in addition the struts are to be checked for length.

When the planes are in truth, the centre section of the lower plane is got into a horizontal position on trestles and is packed up until the chord of the lower surface and each main spar are perfectly horizontal, this being checked by means of a level.

The struts are now erected in their sockets and the centre section of the upper plane got into position, the whole being wired up with *temporary bracing wires.*

The wiring is now adjusted until the struts are all perfectly vertical, as shown by a plumb-line, and the main spars of the lower centre section are 9 mm. higher at the point where they are cut by the plane of symmetry than at the ends. This hog or arch in the two main spars is obtained by tautening up the lift and checking the anti-lift bracing wires in the two inner panels. The adjacent sections of the main cell are then assembled on to the centre section, and the whole wired up and adjusted in the same manner, the chord of the lower surface and each of the main spars being horizontal, and the struts truly vertical. Proceeding outwards the whole of the main cell is erected and trued up in the same manner.

Finally a line should be stretched across the span of the wings, between the struts situated at opposite ends of the main cell, at a distance of, say, $\frac{1}{4}$ inch above the spar. If the adjustments have been correctly made this will be at a uniform distance above the spar right across the planes, except at the centre section where the spar is arched so as to take the weight of the nacelle, engine, &c.

Erection of Tail Cell.—The tail cell is erected in exactly the same manner as the main cell, but the main spars are not hogged at the centre of the tail. The upper and lower planes are first trued up; the lower plane is then placed on trestles with the chord of the lower surface horizontal, and the whole cell is assembled with temporary wiring which is adjusted until all the struts are perfectly vertical.

Tail Booms.—These should all be laid out on the floor and checked for length, the position of the sockets, &c. They are then assembled with the cross struts and the bracing wires inserted. The whole is then erected, suitably supported on chocks and fitted on to the main and tail cell units. The centre panels of the tail boom unit is now trued up by trammelling its diagonals and adjusting its bracing wires until the latter are equal. The two outside panels are now trued up, the bracing wires being adjusted until the booms are straight and in true alignment, this being tested either by sighting or by running a line along the booms.

The main cell and the tail cell should now be in their correct positions relative to each other. This is now checked by running a line through from the front strut of the main cell at a height of ·965 metres (3 ft. 2 ins.) from the top of the main cell at a height of ·715 metres (2 ft. 4·1 ins.) from the top of its main spar. This line should then cut the rear strut of the main cell at a height of ·94 metre (3 ft. 1 in.) above the top of the rear spar. Should it cut this strut at any other point the length of all the tail boom members should be re-checked, and, if necessary, the tail boom wiring readjusted till this measurement is correct. The nacelle may now be got into position and secured, and the under-carriage assembled.

Erection of Under-Carriage.—The vertical distance from the bottom of the front spar to the top of the skid is 1·06 metres (3 ft. 5·7 ins.) and from the bottom of the rear spar to the top of the skid is 1·05 metres (3 ft. 5·3 ins.). The under-carriage is erected on exactly the same principle as that adopted for the tractor.

Angle of Incidence.—The machine has now to be set up in the flying position. This is effected by packing up the tail of the machine until the engine bearers in the nacelle are perfectly horizontal.

The incidence of the main and tail planes is now checked in the same manner as already explained in connection with tractor machines.

The incidence of the plane has already been defined as the vertical distance from the leading edge of the plane to a horizontal straight-edge in contact with the trailing edge. The incidence of the tail plane checked in this way should be 3·5 cms. (1·38 ins.). The incidence of the centre section and the whole of the right-hand wing is uniform and equal to 9 cms. (3·54 ins.). In the Maurice Farman machine the left-hand wing is arranged with a greater angle of incidence than the right-hand wing, the increased lift so obtained being employed to produce a moment which balances the propeller torque. The increased incidence is obtained by sloping the rear spar of this wing slightly downwards by means of the rear anti-drift wires. When correctly adjusted the angle of incidence at the

extreme left-hand strut should be 10·5 cms. (4·13 ins.), at No. 2 strut 10 cms. (3·94 ins.), and at No. 3 strut 9·5 cms. (3·74 ins.). The last operation consists in replacing the temporary wiring by the final bracing wires, when the correct lengths of the latter have been found. The incidence wiring is finally tautened up correctly.

The erecting and adjustment of control gear, &c. is effected in exactly the same way as in tractor type machines, with the exception of the elevator. If a front elevator is provided, then the top surface of this should be horizontal when the tail or rear elevator is fixed in its neutral position.

"America" Type Curtiss Flying Boats.

Hull.—The boat is levelled in the transverse direction carefully. The fore-and-aft position of the planes and the hull is not of such great importance, as the relation of the planes and the hull in this direction are fixed by the short wing bases which form part of the hull itself, and cannot therefore be adjusted.

Main Planes.—These are assembled on trestles and checked for truth by diagonal measurements in the usual manner, the adjustments being made by means of the internal bracing wires. The joint plates and sockets are then fitted and the struts checked over for length, fit into sockets, &c.

The floats should be temporarily fixed in place on the lower planes before erecting, a centre line being marked on the float and this made to come vertically under a centre line marked on the rib. Final adjustments are made after the planes have been trued up.

Lower Planes.—These are got into place on the boat, being packed up into position at a dihedral angle of 1° 45', *i.e.*, 6 inches rise measured on the distance between the centre of the outer strut and the point where the plane abuts the short wing base which is built into the hull.

A trestle is placed near the outer strut and the wing packed up at the inner end. It is then slipped into position and bolted up to the socket which should have been previously fixed in place.

Centre Section.—The centre section is next erected. The centre struts are first got into position. The engine bearer struts and engine bearers are now connected up on the bench, and the horizontal cross struts attached to them. These units are now picked up and dropped into the fore and aft engine strut bottom sockets, and at the same time the horizontal strut is pushed into the socket on the centre strut. The centre section of the top plane is now lifted up and got into place on the struts. Four men are required, one at each corner. Lastly the section is wired and trued up in the same manner as that described for a tractor centre plane section.

The truing up of the centre section is extremely important and must be most carefully carried out, as the truth of the whole machine depends on this.

The engine bearer struts are now to be squared up by overall diagonal measurement or by getting the struts vertical by means of a plumb-bob, the centre strut being neglected for the time being. The rear struts are set up in a similar manner.

The incidence of the centre section is now carefully checked. If incorrect, the lengths of the struts should be re-checked. It is necessary to make certain that the diagonal struts are vertical in the fore-and-aft direction and that the diamonds formed by the engine bearers and engine bearer struts do not bulge forward at the engine bearers. A slight camber or hollow aft may be tolerated, provided it is very small, as the engine thrust tends to cause it to bend in the opposite direction in flight. The truth of this diamond formed by the engine bearers and the engine bearer struts, should be tested by trying whether the diagonals bisect. A plumb-line hung from the centre of the upper socket is the handiest method.

Erecting the Main Planes.—At each end of the plane scaffolds are erected across the lower plane at a convenient height, and cross boards placed athwartships across these at the fore-and-aft sides of the plane. A man is required at each engine strut and outer strut. After the struts have been tried in their sockets for fit, the plane is lifted high enough to let the outer struts be slipped into the top sockets and made fast. The plane is next got into the inner joint plates, and bolted up. The outer struts are now lowered into position in the bottom sockets. The inner struts should be eased into the sockets and made fast, and finally the bottom end of the outer strut is secured.

The temporary wiring is next got into place in all the bays, and the pylons erected, so as to be ready for the extensions.

The main planes are now ready for truing up.

Truing up the Main Planes.—The procedure is similar to that employed in truing up ordinary tractor machines.

The alignment of the leading edges of the planes is first checked.

The flying wires are adjusted until the dihedral of the front and rear spars of the lower plane are correct (1·75-in.). The angle of incidence of the lower plane should now be uniform along the length of the plan; the actual value being 4½°. If necessary the flying wires may need a final adjustment to correct this.

The upper plane is got into truth by getting the struts perfectly vertical with a plumb-line, and the angle of incidence is then checked. If this is found incorrect anywhere, the lengths of the struts must be re-checked.

Plane Extensions.—Suitable scaffolding is put up and the plane extensions erected. The plane is slid into the joint plates and bolted up, the wiring made fast both to the pylons and the lower plane wiring plate.

The incidence of the extension is then checked, and, if necessary, modified by altering the length of the wires from the pylon. The lift wires are then adjusted in the usual manner.

The ailerons may then be attached. The plane extensions should now be trued up in exactly the same way as the main planes.

When all is complete it is as well to test the main plane, extension, and centre section, for alignment across the whole span of the machine, by dropping plumb-lines at intervals over the leading edge of the lower plane and sighting along these.

The ailerons may be attached to the extension planes before erecting the latter, and the whole erected as a complete unit. If they are erected after the extensions are in place, the alignment of the extension should in this case be re-checked after the ailerons are attached.

Measurements are now taken for the length of the cables, and permanent bracing wires substituted for the temporary wiring. Care must be taken to see that no bay is left inadequately wired while this is proceeding, or distortion is certain and serious damage is likely to be done.

Fin.—This is fitted to the mortice on the hull, the front socket put on and also the clips attached to the boat, and finally the stays are fixed. The fin should be tested for plumb, both before and after fixing stays.

Tail Plane.—The tail plane is slipped over the fin and fixed to clips. The tail is set at right angles to the axis of the main struts, *i.e.*, set neutral at first. The stays should then be fixed. It is to be borne in mind that the exact final setting of the tail is experimental and depends on trial flight. It will in most cases differ slightly from boat to boat, even though they are of exactly the same design.

The rudder and elevators are next put in place. Both are to be wired before erection.

The tail plane should be parallel to the cellule. When the machine is in the flying position the incidence of the fixed plane should be as shown in Fig. . If in flight the machine pushes too much against the pilot, another degree more incidence should be put in the tail. If the pilot has to pull, a degree less of incidence should be given. The incidence can be altered by adjusting the steel quadrant on the front spar of the tail, and the four wires which pull from the middle of the front spar.

In horizontal flight, with the engine running full out, there should be a distinct pressure against the pilot's hand.

The axis of the motor is parallel to the line of flight, *i.e.*, when the main cellule struts are vertical the crank shaft is horizontal.

CAUDRON BIPLANE, G.4. TYPE.

Truing the Cellule.—The front spar of the top plane is set truly horizontal and in correct alignment.

The control lever should be set in a vertical position and fastened so as to be immovable.

The tail of the machine should be packed up until the cellule struts are exactly perpendicular.

The incidence measured between *the lower face of the front spar and the lower face of the back spar* should now be checked in this position.

Beneath the nacelle the spars should be level.

Above the left-hand skid the bottom of the back spar should be 12 mm. lower than the bottom of the front spar.

Above the right-hand skid the bottom of the back spar should be 12 mm. higher than the bottom of the front spar.

Under the right- and left-hand cellule struts both spars should be level; also the spars of the top plane extension.

In practice, if the struts are all of the correct length, it is only necessary to true the lower plane.

The tail booms and skids can now be trued. The left-hand side should be trued up first, then the right-hand side aligned with it.

The machine should be kept in the same position, *i.e.*, the main cellule strut vertical, and a batten placed on the back spar of the bottom plane.

When this batten is horizontal the top of the back skid should be 34·5 cm. below the bottom of the guide.

Two parts of the left-hand tail boom form a straight line. On the other hand the two parts of the right-hand tail boom form a line broken upwards at the large tail boom strut.

APPENDIX.

DIAGRAMS SHOWING THE METHOD OF TRUING UP DIFFERENT TYPES OF AEROPLANES AND SEAPLANES.

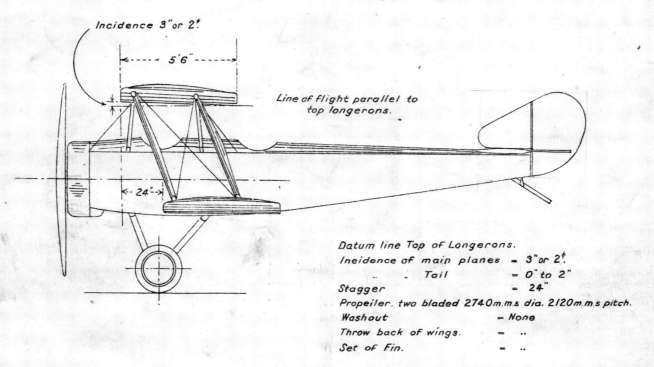

SOPWITH 1½ STRUTTER.
110 H.P CLERGET.

Incidence 3" or 2½"

5'6"

Line of flight parallel to top longerons.

24"

Datum line Top of Longerons.
Incidence of main planes = 3" or 2½"
          "   Tail   = 0" to 2"
Stagger   = 24"
Propeller. two bladed 2740 m.m.s dia. 2120 m.m.s pitch.
Washout   = None
Throw back of wings.   = ..
Set of Fin.   = ..

4659.

Malby & Sons.Lith

SOPWITH 1½ STRUTTER.
110 H.P. CLERGET.

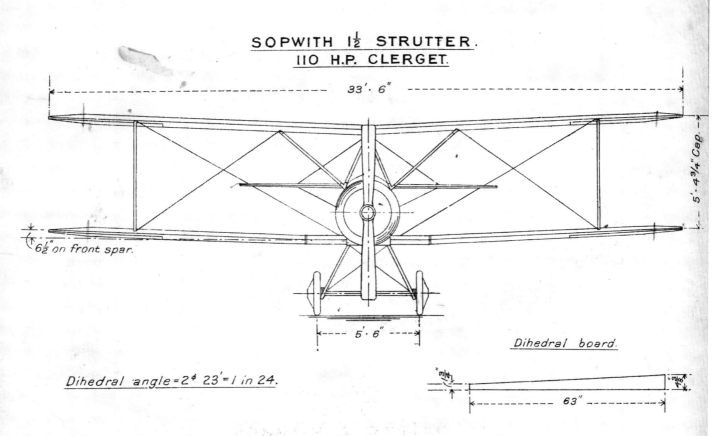

33'· 6"

5'· 4¾" Cap.

6½" on front spar.

5'· 6"

Dihedral angle = 2° 23' = 1 in 24.

Dihedral board.

63"

4659.

Malby & Sons.L

SOPWITH 2 SEATER.
SCOUT.
80 HP GNOME.
1051 — 74.

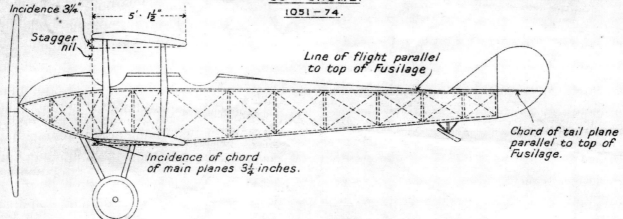

Incidence 3¼"

Stagger nil.

5'. 1½"

Line of flight parallel to top of Fusilage

Chord of tail plane parallel to top of Fusilage.

Incidence of chord of main planes 3¼ inches.

Datum Line — Top of Top Longerons.
Incidence of Chord of Main Planes 3¼ Inches.
Wash out — Nil.
Stagger — Nil.
Incidence of Chord of Tail Planes Zero.
Throw back of Wings — Nil.
Set of Fin — Nil.
Struts of Main Cell. Forward Length 63¹⁄₁₆" overall.
    "   "   "   Back   "   63⅝"
Propeller — Chauviere 2 blades 2·60 m. dia. 1·60 m. Pitch.

4659

Malby & Sons. Lith.

SOPWITH 2 SEATER.
SCOUT.
80 GNOME.

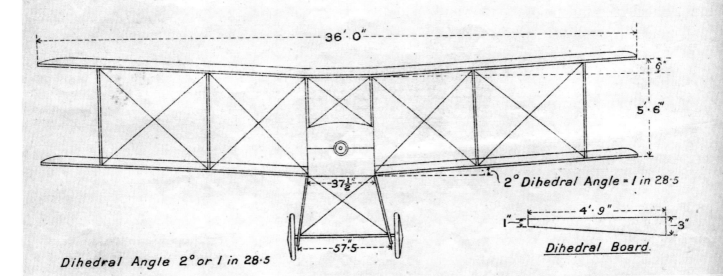

36'. 0"

6"

5'. 6"

2° Dihedral Angle = 1 in 28·5

37½"

57·5

4'. 9"

1"

3"

Dihedral Board.

Dihedral Angle 2° or 1 in 28·5

Malby & Sons. Lith.

9

150 H.P. SOPWITH PUSHER.

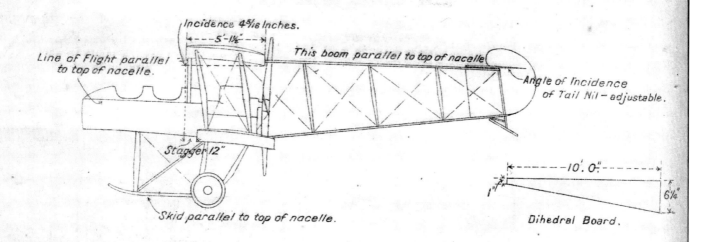

Incidence 4⁵⁄₁₆ Inches.

5'-1½"

Line of Flight parallel to top of nacelle.

This boom parallel to top of nacelle

Angle of Incidence of Tail Nil – adjustable.

Stagger 12"

Skid parallel to top of nacelle.

10'. 0"

1"

6¼"

Dihedral Board.

Line of Flight parallel to top of nacelle.
Incidence of Main Planes 4⁵⁄₁₆ Inches.
Wash out – Nil.
Stagger – 12"
Incidence of Tail Planes Nil – adjustable.
Throw back of Wings – Nil.
Set of Fin – Nil.

Dihedral angle 1 in 22·86
Skids parallel to top of nacelle.
Spacing of skids 4' 10" Centres.
Propeller fitted Laing 4 bladed. 2·9m. dia. 2·0 m. Pitch.

SOPWITH SCHNEIDER CUP.
MACHINE 1436-47.

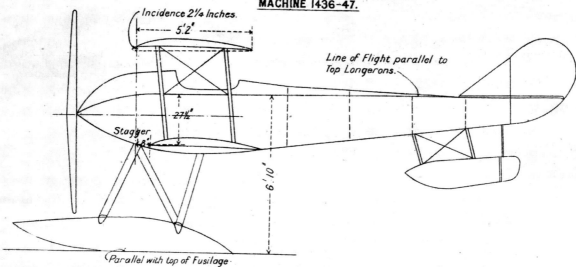

Incidence 2¼ Inches.

5'2"

Line of Flight parallel to
Top Longerons.

27½"

Stagger
8"

6'10"

Parallel with top of Fusilage.

Datum Line Top of top of Longerons.
Incidence of Chord of Main Planes 2¼ Inches.
Wash out — Nil.
Stagger 8"
Incidence of Chord of Tail Planes Zero degrees.
Throw back of Wings — Nil.
Set of Fin — Nil.
Struts of Main Cell For.d Struts overall 51⅞"
          "   "   "   " Aft.   "   51¼"
Propeller Long 2 Blades 2·65"m. Diam. 2·10 m. Pitch

4659

Malby & Sons. Lith

SOPWITH SCHNEIDER CUP.

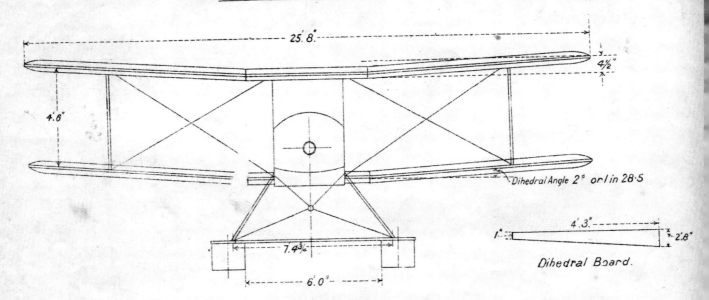

25' 8"

4½"

4'6"

Dihedral Angle 2° or 1 in 28·5

4'3"

1"

2'8"

Dihedral Board.

7'4¾"

6'0"

Dihedral Angle 2° or 1 in 28·5

659

Malby & Sons. Lith

2

SOPWITH BABY SEAPLANE.

110 HP CLERGET.
100 HP GNOME.

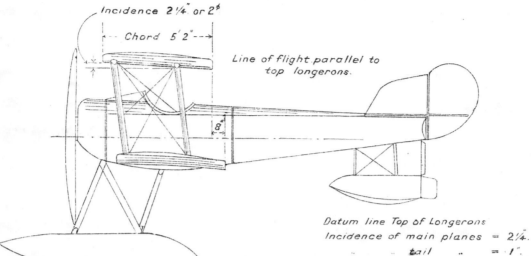

Incidence 2¼" or 2⅝"

Chord 5' 2"

Line of flight parallel to top longerons.

Datum line Top of Longerons
Incidence of main planes = 2¼"
" " tail " = 1".
Stagger = 8"
Propeller two bladed 2650 m.m.s dia. 2250 m.m.s (Clerg
2650 m.m.s dia. 2100 m.m.s (Mono)
(Pitch)
Washout = None
Throw back of wings. = ..
Set of Fin. = ..
.. " Air Rudder. = 2"

4659.

Malby & Sons Lith.

2

SOPWITH BABY SEAPLANE.

110 HP CLERGET.
100 HP GNOME.

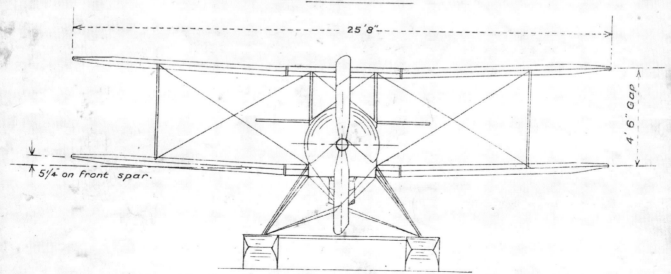

25' 8"

4' 6" Gap

5¼" on front spar.

Dihedral Angle 2°-40' or 1 in 21·5.

DIHEDRAL BOARD.

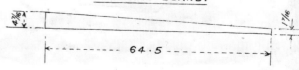

64·5

559.

Malby & Sons Lith.

AVRO BIPLANE.
TYPE 504.

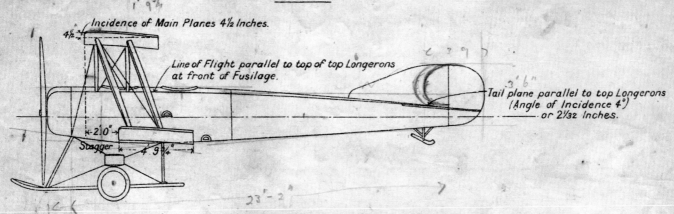

3

aileron

1' 9½"

Incidence of Main Planes 4½ Inches.

4½

Line of Flight parallel to top of top Longerons
at front of Fusilage.

3' 6"

Tail plane parallel to top Longerons
(Angle of Incidence 4°)
or 2 1/32 Inches.

← 2 10" →

Stagger

4' 9¾"

23' 2"

Line of Flight parallel to top Longeron at front part of Machine.
Incidence of Main Planes 4½ Inches.
Wash out — Nil. adjustments (lateral) made by washing in L.H. plane.
Stagger 2'.0".
Incidence of Tail Planes 2 1/32" or 4°.
Throw back of Wings — Nil.
Set of Fin — Perpendicular and parallel to line of flight.
Propeller fitted "Avro" 9'.0". Dia. 6'.0". Pitch.

4659

Malby & Sons Lith.

3

AVRO BIPLANE.
TYPE 504.

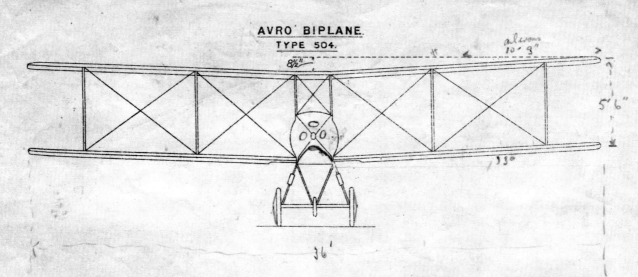

aileron
10' 3"

8½"

5' 6"

11°

36'

Dihedral 8½ Inches can be
Checked by Cord between
Wing tips.

The dihedral angle is fixed by the
Setting Staff shown.
This is used to Measure the distance
between the points shown in the Sketch.
These points are marked on the Planes
by means of small Aluminium Plates.

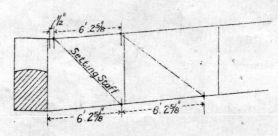

½"

6'.2⅝"

Setting Staff

6'.2⅝"

6'.2⅝"

6'.2⅝"

8'.3¾" long

Timber

4659

Malby & Sons, Lith.

AMERICA FLYING BOAT.
TYPE

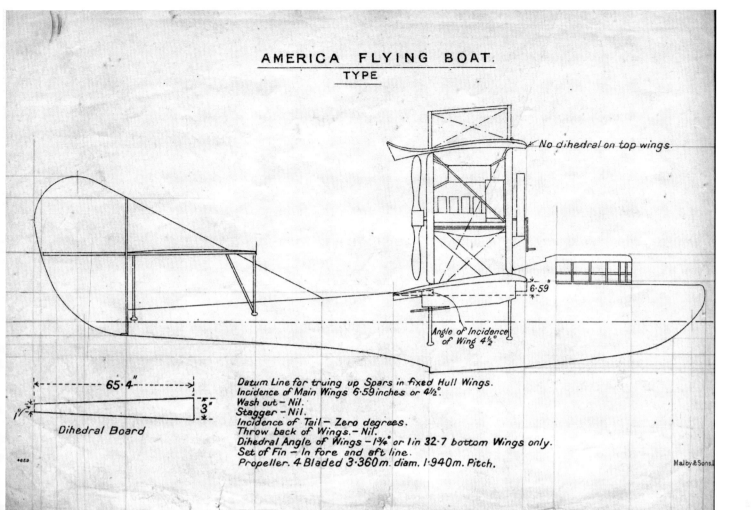

No dihedral on top wings.

6·59"

Angle of Incidence of Wing 4½°

65·4"

1"

3"

Dihedral Board

Datum Line for truing up Spars in fixed Hull Wings.
Incidence of Main Wings 6·59 inches or 4½°.
Wash out – Nil.
Stagger – Nil.
Incidence of Tail – Zero degrees.
Throw back of Wings. – Nil.
Dihedral Angle of Wings – 1¾° or 1 in 32·7 bottom Wings only.
Set of Fin – In fore and aft line.
Propeller. 4 Bladed 3·360 m. diam. 1·940 m. Pitch.

Malby & Sons.L.

15

MAURICE FARMAN 1914 MACHINE.
WITH MONOPLANE TAIL.

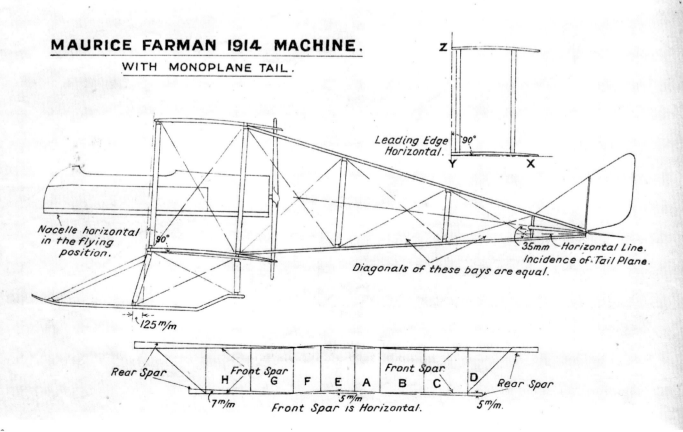

Z

Leading Edge Horizontal.

90°

Y   X

Nacelle horizontal in the flying position.

90°

35mm Horizontal Line.
Incidence of Tail Plane.

Diagonals of these bays are equal.

125 m/m

Rear Spar   Front Spar   Front Spar   Rear Spar

H   G   F   E   A   B   C   D

7 m/m   5 m/m   5 m/m.

Front Spar is Horizontal.

10

135 H.P. CANTON UNNE SEAPLANE.
SHORT.

Dihedral Nil.

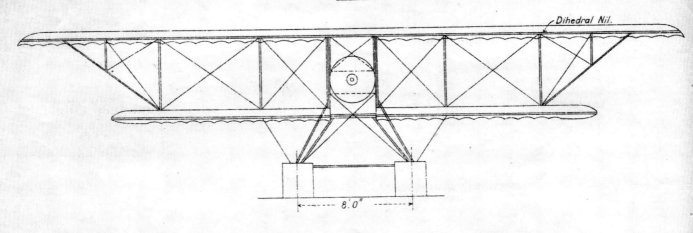

8'0"

Dihedral Angle - Nil.

Malby & Son

77 10

135 H.P. CANTON UNNE SEAPLANE.
SHORT.

Stagger - nil.

Incidence of Main Planes 5¼ Inches

Datum Line parallel to top Longeron at
forward end.

Incidence of Tail Plane 1$\frac{27}{32}$ Inches

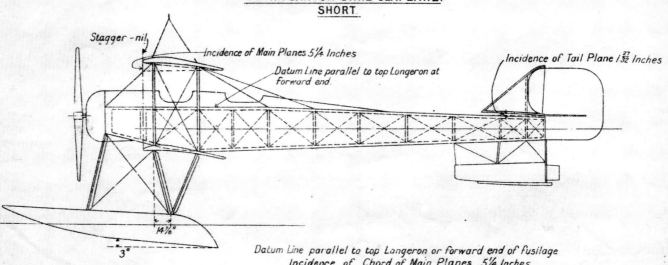

14⅞"

3°

Datum Line parallel to top Longeron or forward end of fusilage
Incidence of Chord of Main Planes 5¼ Inches
    "   "   "   Tail   "   1$\frac{27}{32}$ Inches
Stagger - nil
Inclination of Bottom of Floats 3°
Propellor Tractor Type 105" Diam, 64" Pitch.

Malby & Sons.Lith.

200 H.P. CANTON UNNE SEAPLANE.
SHORT.

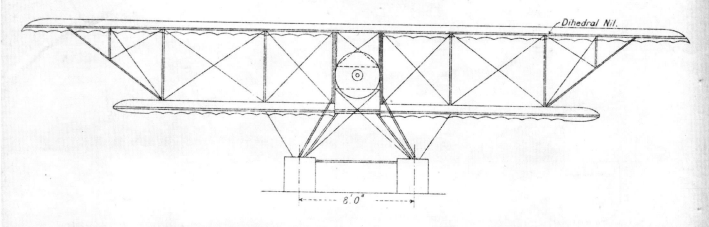

Dihedral Nil.

8'0"

Dihedral Angle - Nil.

4659   2500. 12. 16.

Malby & Sons Li

19

200 H.P. CANTON UNNE SEAPLANE.
SHORT.

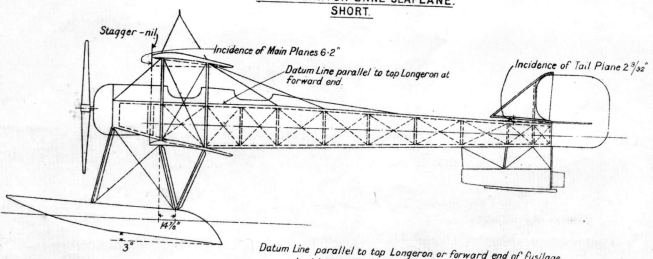

Stagger - nil.

Incidence of Main Planes 6·2"

Datum Line parallel to top Longeron at forward end.

Incidence of Tail Plane 2 ³/₃₂"

14 ⅞"

3°

Datum Line parallel to top Longeron or forward end of fusilage.
Incidence of Chord of Main Planes   6·2"
    "   "   "   Tail   "   2 ³/₃₂"
Stagger - nil.
Inclination of Bottom of Floats 3°
Propellor Tractor Type 114 " Diam, 73" Pitch.

4659

Malby & Sons Lith

225 H.P. SHORT - SEAPLANE.

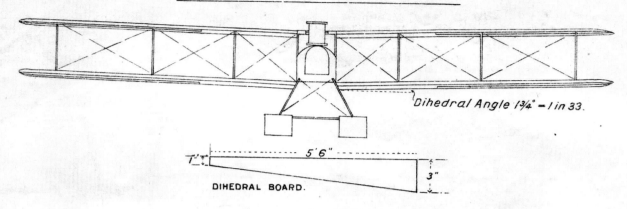

Dihedral Angle 1¾° = 1 in 33.

5´6"

1´

3"

DIHEDRAL BOARD.

4

SHORT 225 H.P. SUNBEAM.
SEA PLANE.

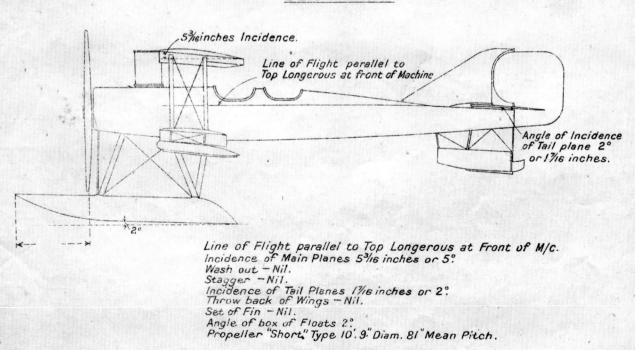

5³⁄₁₆ inches Incidence.

Line of Flight parallel to
Top Longerous at front of Machine

Angle of Incidence
of Tail plane 2°
or 1⁷⁄₁₆ inches.

2°

Line of Flight parallel to Top Longerous at Front of M/c.
Incidence of Main Planes 5³⁄₁₆ inches or 5°.
Wash out — Nil.
Stagger — Nil.
Incidence of Tail Planes 1⁷⁄₁₆ inches or 2°.
Throw back of Wings — Nil.
Set of Fin — Nil.
Angle of box of Floats 2°.
Propeller "Short" Type 10´. 9." Diam. 81" Mean Pitch.

6

BRISTOL SCOUT.

with 3% or 5% Dihedral.

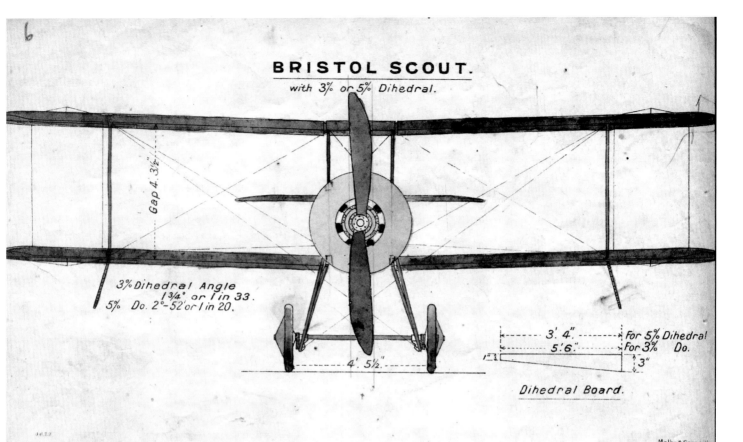

Gap 4. 3½"

3% Dihedral Angle
1¾° or 1 in 33.
5% Do. 2°-52'or 1 in 20.

4'. 5½"

3'. 4" ········· For 5% Dihedral
5'.6" ········· For 3% Do.

3"

Dihedral Board.

Malby & Sons, Lith.

23

BRISTOL SCOUT.

ENGINE 80 H.P. GNOME.

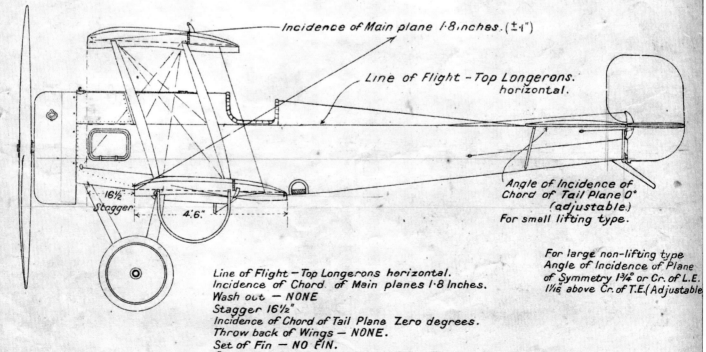

Incidence of Main plane 1·8 inches. (±¼")

Line of Flight — Top Longerons.
horizontal.

Angle of Incidence of
Chord of Tail Plane 0°
(adjustable.)
For small lifting type.

16½"
Stagger

4'.6".

For large non-lifting type
Angle of Incidence of Plane
of Symmetry 1¾° or Cr. of L.E.
1¹⁄₁₆ above Cr. of T.E.(Adjustable)

Line of Flight — Top Longerons horizontal.
Incidence of Chord. of Main planes 1·8 Inches.
Wash out — NONE
Stagger 16½"
Incidence of Chord of Tail Plane Zero degrees.
Throw back of Wings — NONE.
Set of Fin — NO FIN.
Propeller Two Blade Bristol. 2·5 m. Dia   2·2 m.Pitch.

4658. 2500. 12. 16

Malby & Sons.

B.E.2C. MACHINE.

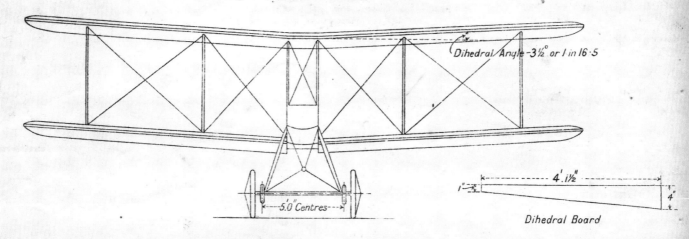

Dihedral Angle -3½° or 1 in 16·5

Dihedral Board

4' 1½"
1" 3
4"

-5'.0" Centres-

Dihedral Angle -3½° or 1 in 16·5
Distance between Centres of Skids 5'.0"

4659

Malby&Sons

B.E.2C. MACHINE.

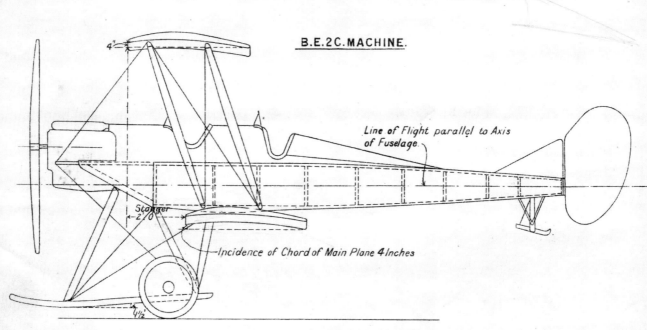

4"

Line of Flight parallel to Axis
of Fuselage.

Stagger
2'.0"

Incidence of Chord of Main Plane 4 Inches

4½°

Line of Flight Parallel to Axis of Fuselage
Incidence of Chord of Main Plane 4"
Wash out – Nil.
Stagger 2'.0"
Incidence of Chord of Tail Plane Zero.
Throw back of Wings – Nil.
Set of Fin – Nil.
Angle of Skids 1½°.
Propeller fitted Special R.A.F. design.

4659

Malby &

✗✗✗

WHITE TRACTOR SEAPLANE.
225 SUNBEAM ENGINE.

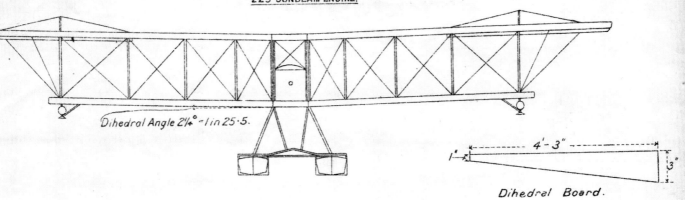

Dihedral Angle 2¼° = 1 in 25·5.

Dihedral Board.

4'-3"

1"

3"

Dihedral Angle 2¼° = 1 in 25·5. on the leading edge.

Malby & Sons, Lith

4659

9

WHITE 225 H.P. TRACTOR.
SEAPLANE.
SUNBEAM ENGINE.

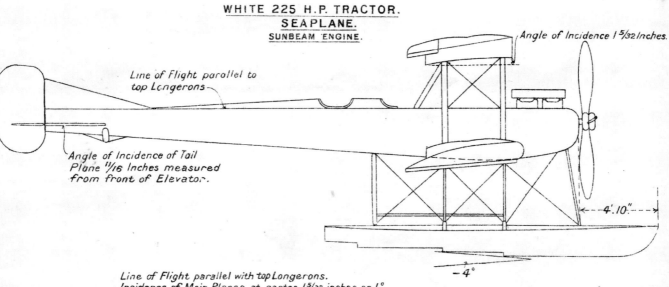

Angle of Incidence 1⁵/₃₂ Inches.

Line of Flight parallel to
top Longerons

Angle of Incidence of Tail
Plane ¹¹/₁₆ Inches measured
from front of Elevator.

4'.10"

-4°

Line of Flight parallel with top Longerons.
Incidence of Main Planes at centre 1⁵/₃₂ inches or 1°.
Wash out is 1·6°.
Stagger—Nil.
Incidence of Tail ¹¹/₁₆ Inches or 1°.
Throw back of Wings — Nil.
Set of Fin — Nil.
Front two steps of Floats at −4° to line of flight.
Propeller Lang 2 bladed 11'. 6". Dia. 6'. 6¾" Pitch.
　　　　　　　　11'. 10". Dia. 6'. 6¾" Pitch.

4659

Malby & Son

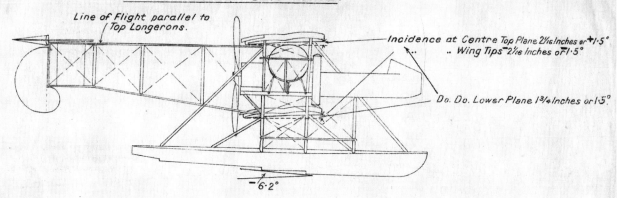

225 SUNBEAM
WHITE PUSHER SEAPLANE.

Line of Flight parallel to Top Longerons.

Incidence at Centre Top Plane 2¹⁄₁₆ Inches or +1·5°
" Wing Tips 2¹⁄₁₆ Inches or +1·5°

Do. Do. Lower Plane 1¾ Inches or 1·5°

−6·2°

Line of Flight parallel to top Longerons.
Incidence at Centre Top Plane 2¹⁄₁₆ Inches or 1·5°
....."......"...."... Lower ..." .. 1¾ ...."....."....."...
....."......"...." Wing Tips −1·5°
Wash out is 3°.
Stagger 5" on leading edge.
Angle of Tail leading edge ⁷⁄₁₆ inches above trailing edge.
Dihedral Angle on Front Spar 1·04° or 1 in 55·2.
Throw back of Wings 1·25° or 1 in 46.
Set of Fin − Nil.
Front two steps of Floats −6·20° to line of Flight.
Propeller 4 Bladed Lang.

4659

Malby & Sons, Lith

CAUDRON BIPLANE.
G. .TYPE.

Right Hand.

−12ᵐ/ₘ   +12ᵐ/ₘ

Left Hand.

−12ᵐ/ₘ   +12ᵐ/ₘ

The front spars are horizontal
(i.e. Dihedral Angle is nil.)

The inclination of the rear spars are exaggerated.

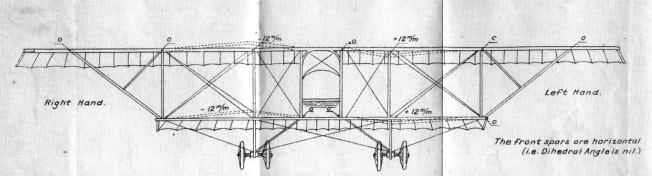

Datum Line. shown in sketch.
Incidence of Chord of Lower Main Plane 8¹⁄₈ Inches or 9½°.
....."......"...."... Top ....",....."... 12 ..."....."...11½°.
Wash out − Nil.
Stagger − Nil.
Incidence of Chord of Tail Plane 4¼ Inches or 4²⁄₂
Throw back of Wings − Nil.
Dihedral − Nil.
Set of Fin − Parallel to longitudinal axis of Machine.
Propeller fitted Gremont 2·60m. Diam.

80 H.P. Gnome

1·45 m pitch at 1m from centre of boss.

100 H.P. Anzani { Grémont . 2·50 m Diam.
1·90 m. pitch at 1m from
Centre of boss.

Stagger. nil.

Line of Flight

Datum Line

Incidence of chord of
Tail Plane 4½ or 4¼ In

0·73 M.   0·52. M.   0·345. M.

Incidence of chord of Lower Main Plane 9½° or 8¹⁄₈ Inches.
....."......"...."...."...."... Top ....",....."...11½° or 12 Inches.

4659.

Malby & Sons, Lith

SHORT 150 H.P. SEAPLANE.

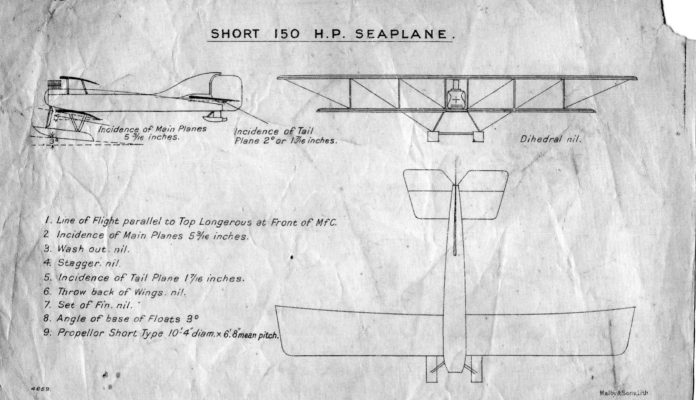

Incidence of Main Planes
5 3/16 inches.

Incidence of Tail
Plane 2° or 1 7/16 inches.

Dihedral nil.

1. Line of Flight parallel to Top Longerous at Front of MfC.
2. Incidence of Main Planes 5 3/16 inches.
3. Wash out. nil.
4. Stagger. nil.
5. Incidence of Tail Plane 1 7/16 inches.
6. Throw back of Wings. nil.
7. Set of Fin. nil.
8. Angle of base of Floats 3°
9. Propellor Short Type 10'4" diam. x 6'8" mean pitch.

4659.

Malby & Sons, Lith.

Maurice Farman, 1913 (80 h.p. Renault), with Biplane Tail.

LENGTHS OF STRUTS.

These Lengths are the Centre Lines of the Struts.

	Front.	Rear.
A - - - -	199·8 m/m	200·2 m/m.
B - - - -	”	”
C - - - -	”	”
D - - - -	190·8 m/m	191·2 m/m.
E - - - -	199·8 m/m	200·2 m/m.
F - - - -	”	”
G - - - -	”	”
H - - -. -	190·8 m/m	191/2 m/m.

ERECTING.

At B and F angle XYZ = 90°.

Lower plane get B and F in horizontal line on trestles and struts B and F vertical (front and rear).

Tauten landing wires till centre portion of front and back spars are cambered 5 m/m.

Wing portion of planes :—

Port : Angle XYZ = 90° and both front and rear spars horizontal.

Starboard : Front spars horizontal.

Rear spars tuned by dihedral boards, viz., Port wing, 1 in.—416 up.

Front elevator horizontal in flying position and tail elevator forms continuation of the upper and lower surface of tail planes. Incidence as shown in diagram.

Incidence at A E F and B = 90 m/m.
 ”   ”   H = 100 m/m.
 ”   ”   G = 95 m/m.
 ”   ”   C = 85 m/m.
 ”   ”   D = 80 m/m.

N.B.— The incidence is taken between back and front spars and not from trailing edge.

A 30853

The Drawings

These are the sketches and drawings made by Mr Howard Earl when he was a draughtsman at the RNAS seaplane repair station at Port Victoria, Isle of Grain, in Kent. In most cases the originals were in the form of meticulously annotated detail sketches recorded in a draughtsman's pad with scale grids on the pages. Although, owing to tragic circumstances, the original book has now been lost, Mr Earl very kindly allowed me to borrow the book and copy it when I met him many years ago. Two drawings, those for the redesigned fuselage for Sopwith B.1 N50, which turned the aircraft into the first Grain Griffin, and for arresting gear for a Sopwith 2.F1 Camel (apparently never fitted), were copied from large originals, also now lost. I am delighted that these unique records have now been made available to all researchers.

Draughtsman Howard Earl made meticulous measurements of a French Letord twin-engine bomber, presumably when one visited Port Victoria/Grain. It was probably a Letord 4, as seen here, with a nosewheel and a raised nose gun ring, features evident in his sketches.

An airborne study of an RNAS Caudron G.4, another French twin-engine type subjected to Howard Earl's tape measure.

One of the last types to be measured by Howard Earl was the Fairey N.10, the first of the Fairey III series that were to become prolific in the RAF and Fleet Air Arm in the interwar years.

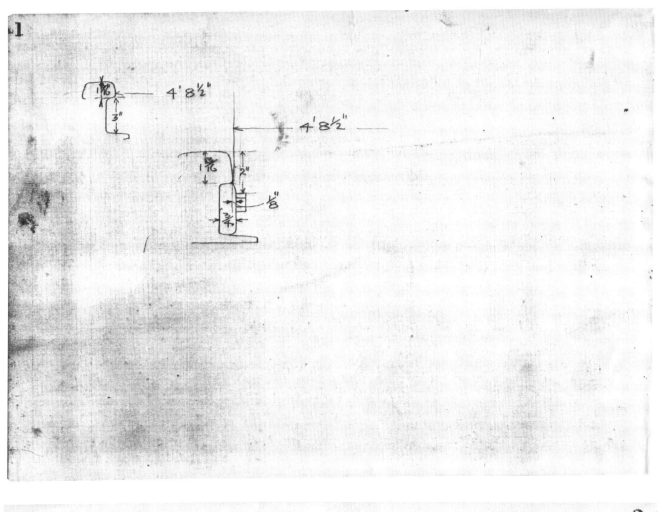

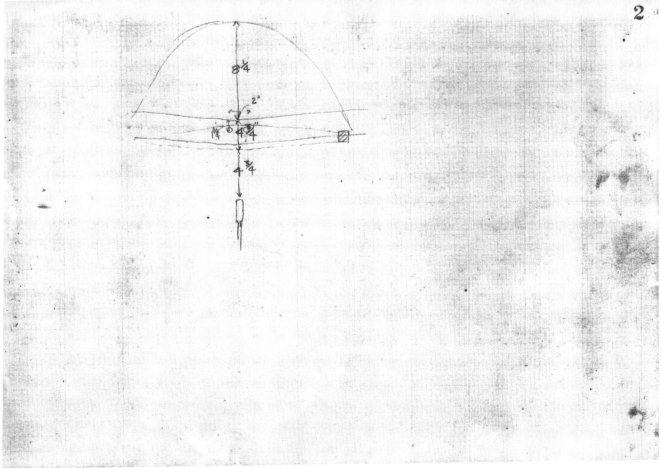

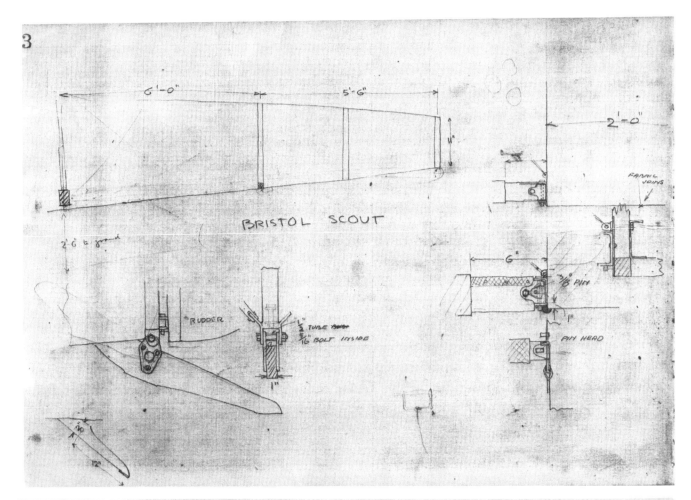

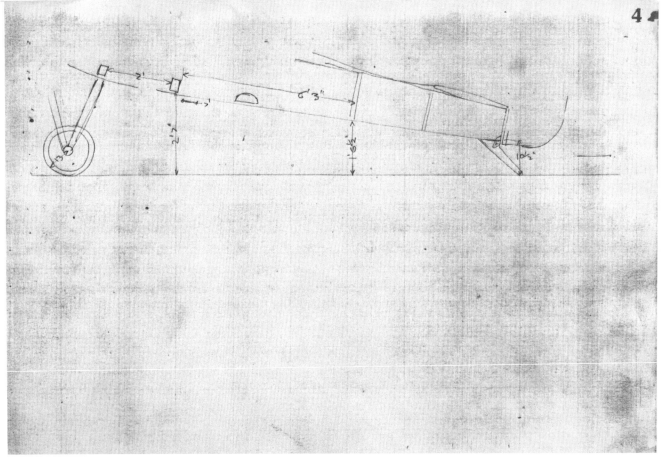

Sopwith Admiralty Type 860 seaplane 852

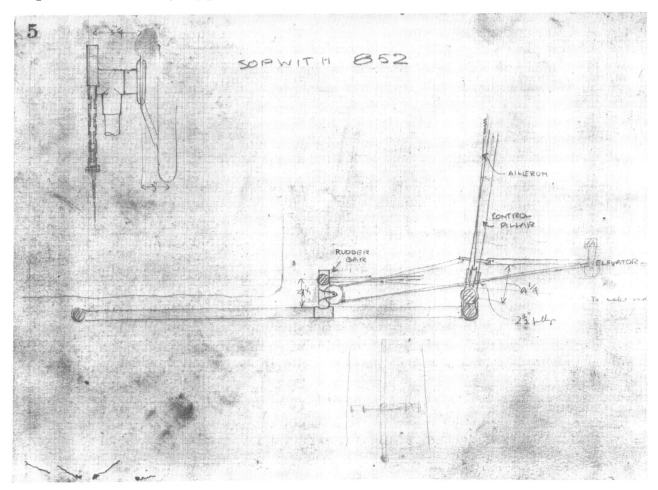

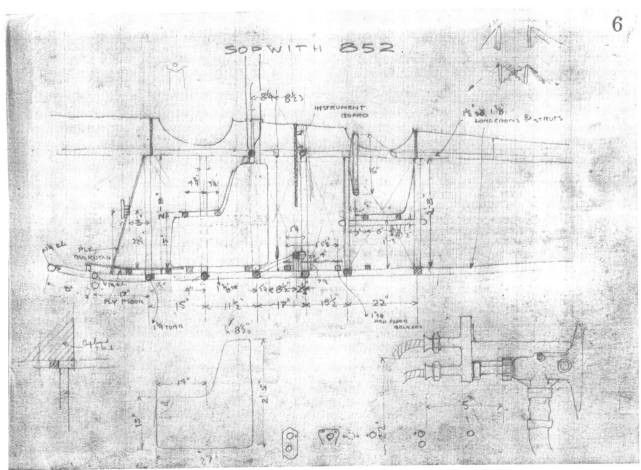

Sopwith Admiralty Type 860 seaplane 852

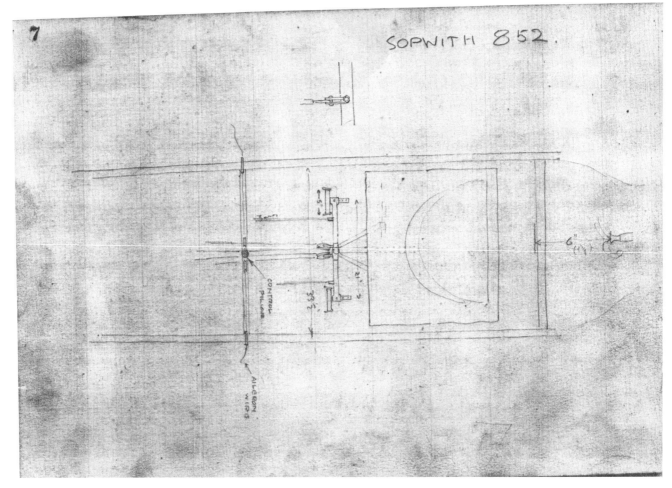

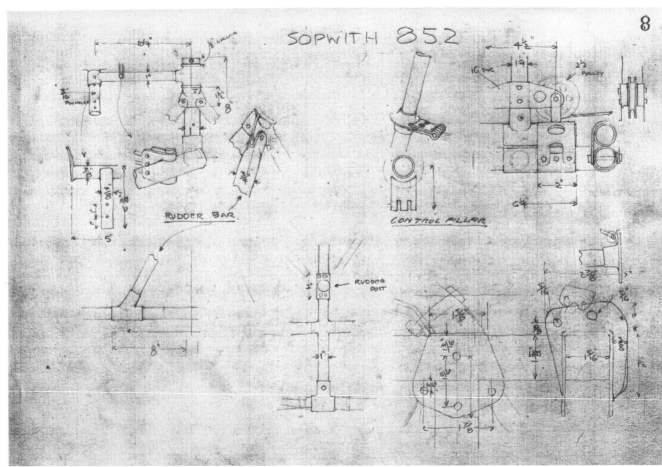

Sopwith Admiralty Type 860 seaplane 852

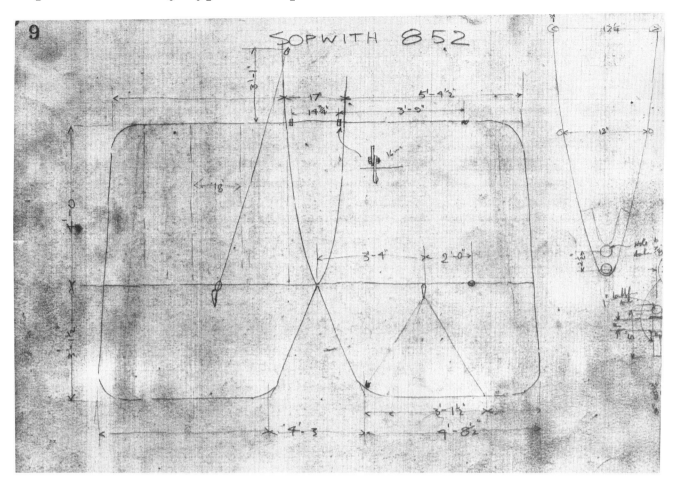

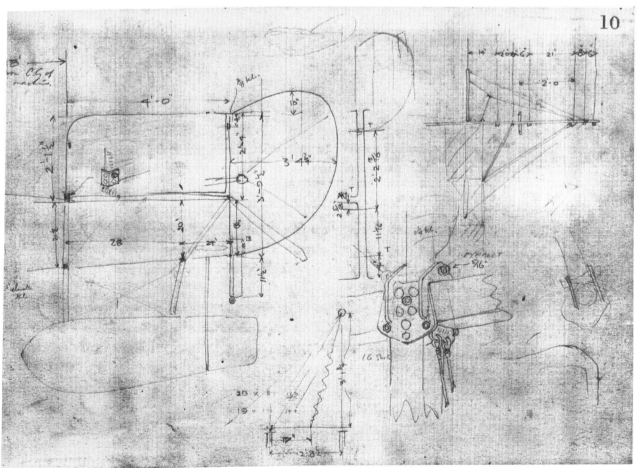

Sopwith Admiralty Type 860 seaplane 852?

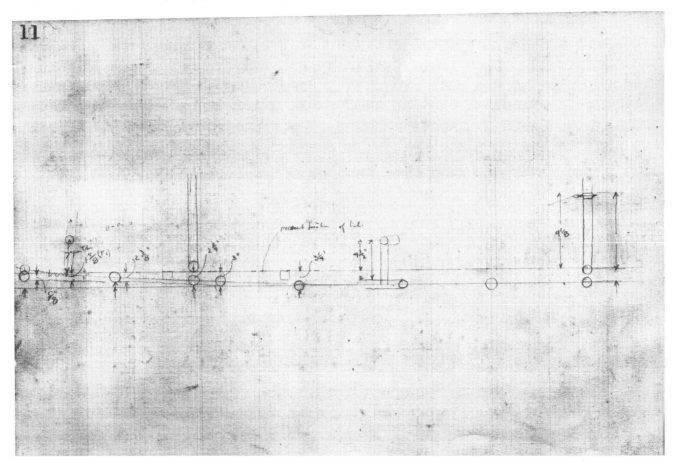

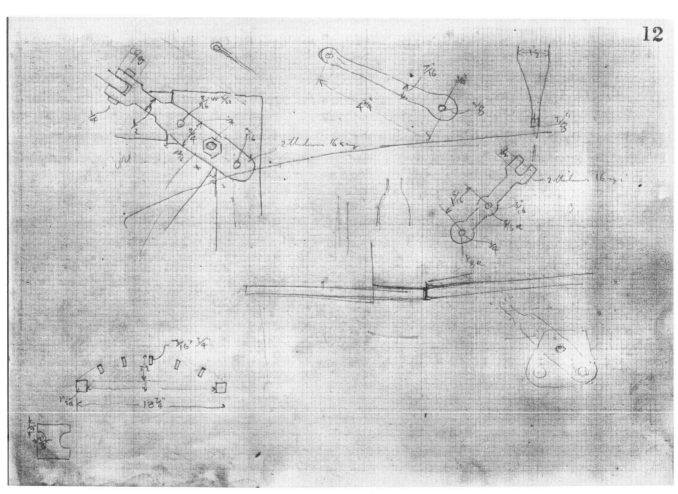

NO· 4 SHED

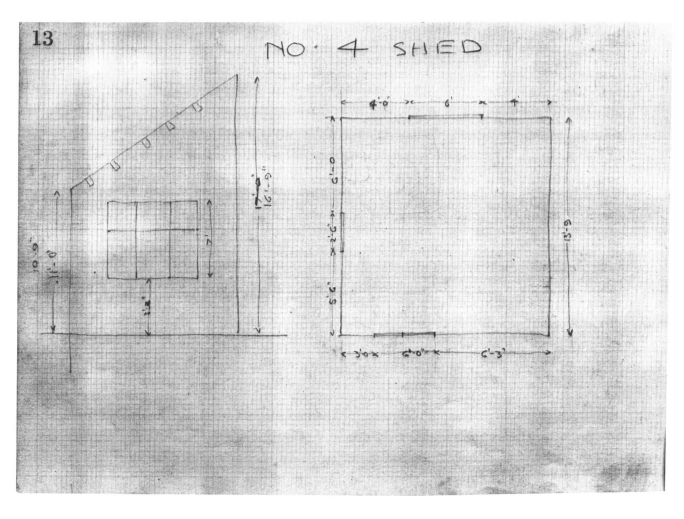

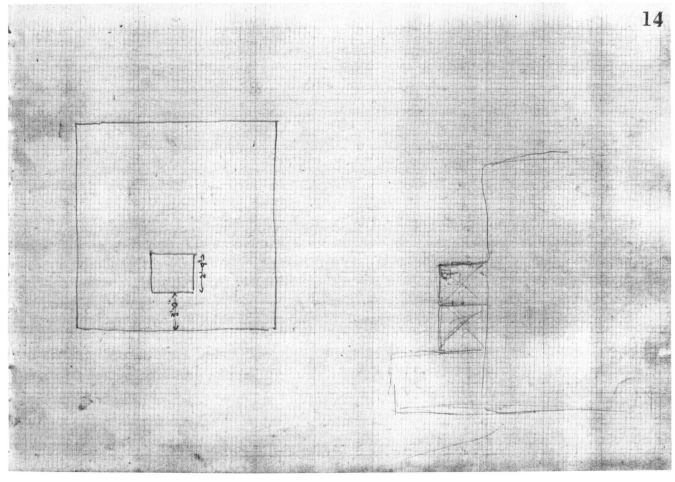

Wight Baby seaplane

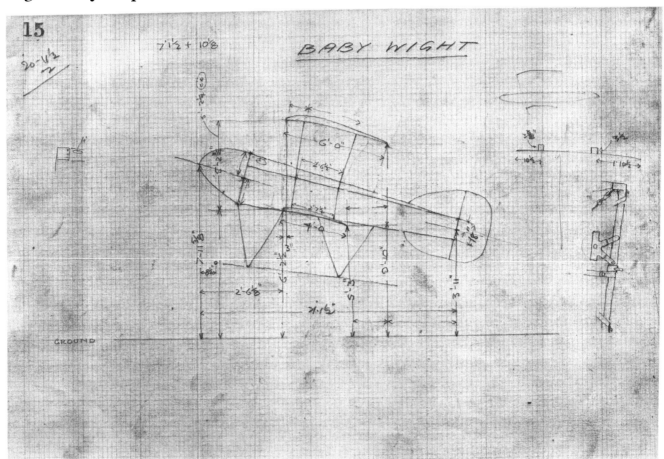

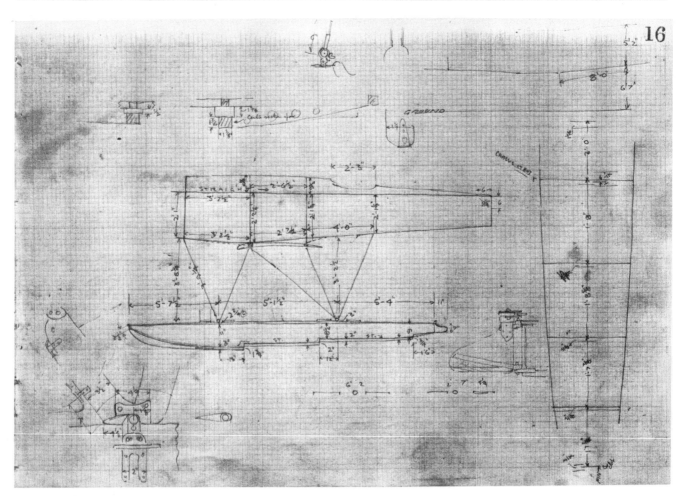

Wight Baby seaplane

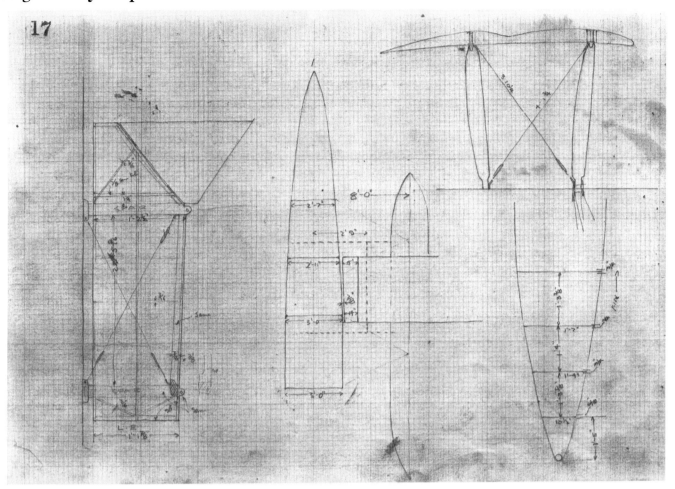

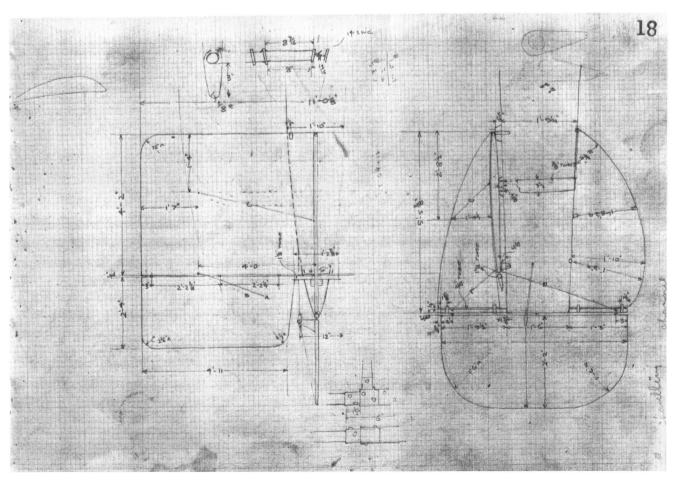

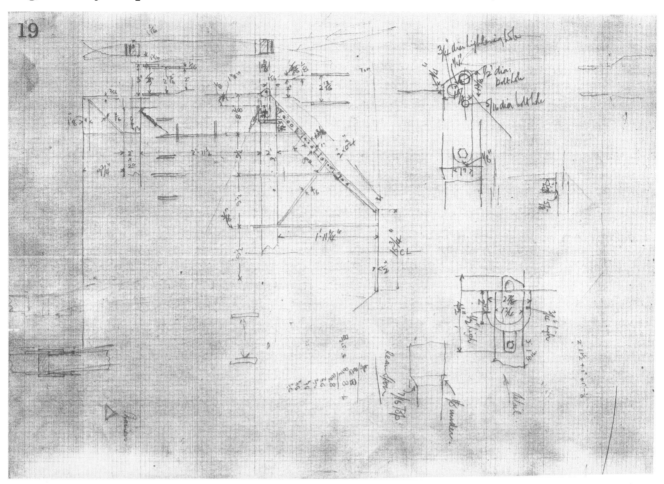

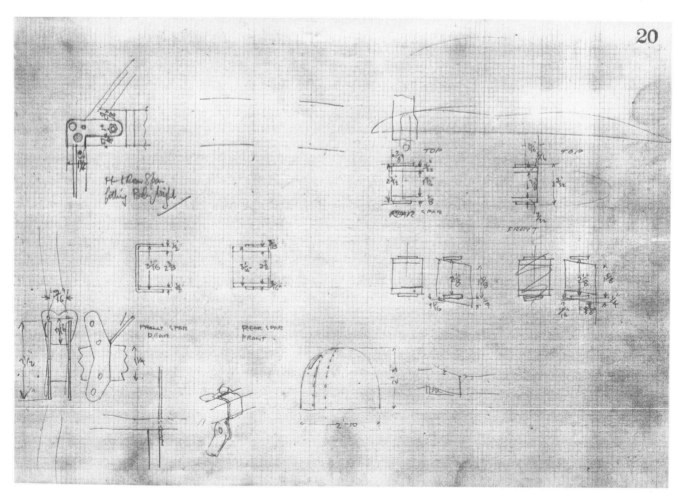

Bristol Scout No. 8058

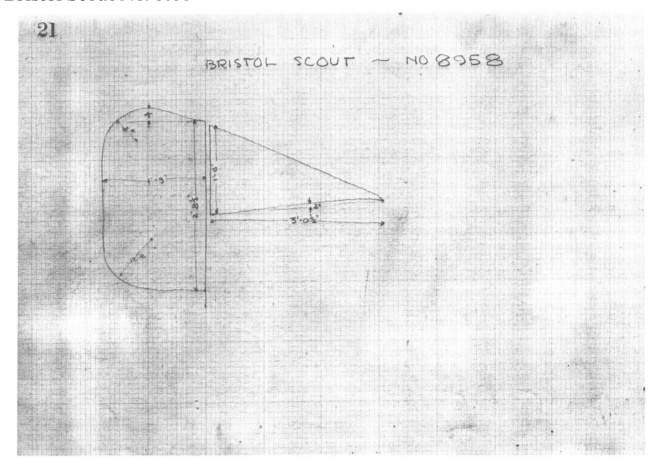

Maurice Farman F.40

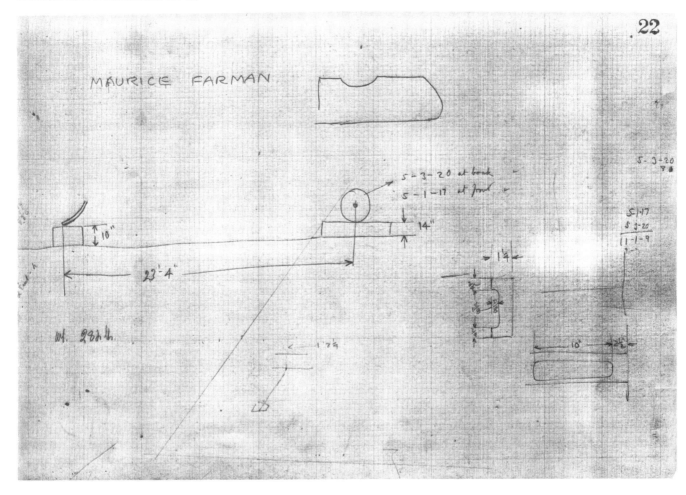

Maurice Farman F.40

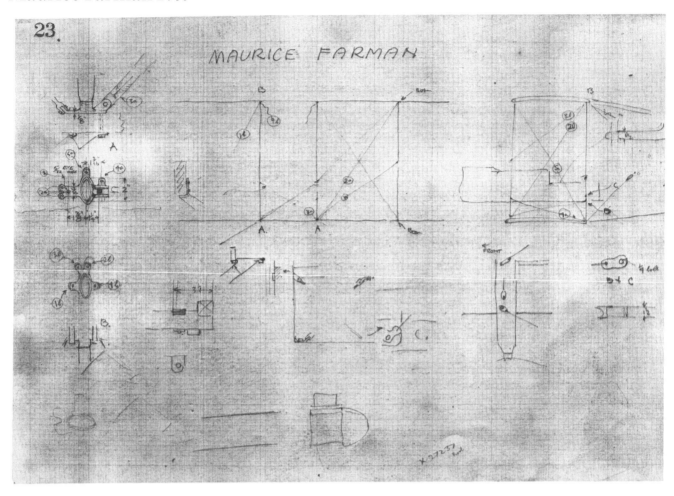

Sopwith Camel?

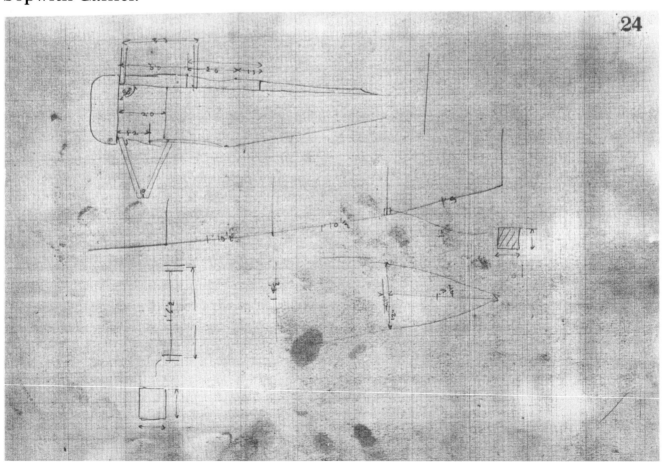

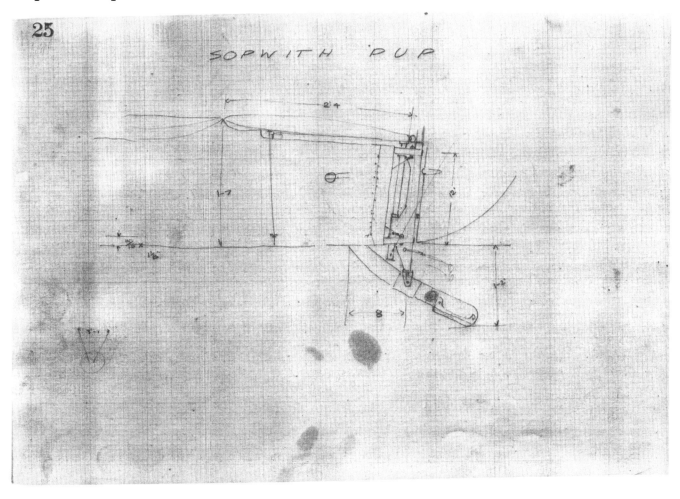

SOPWITH PUP

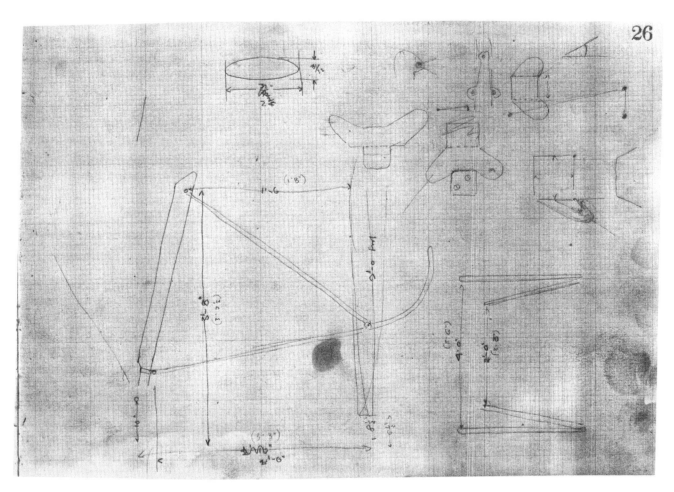

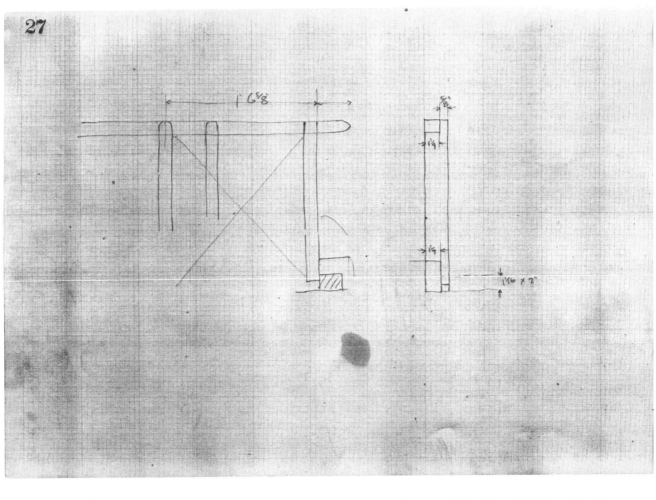

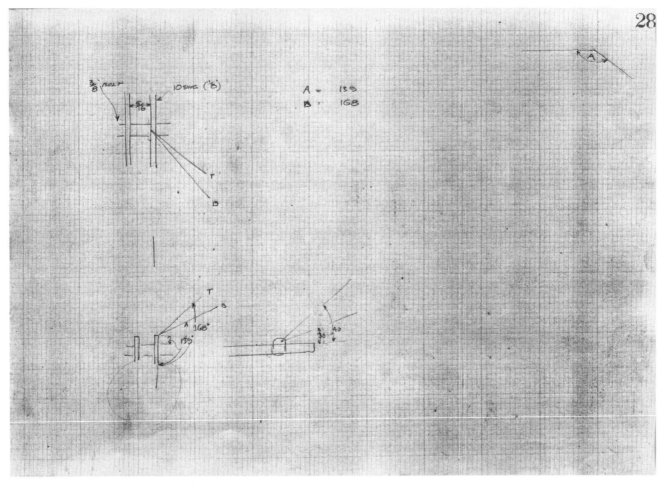

A = 135
B = 168

Sopwith Camel

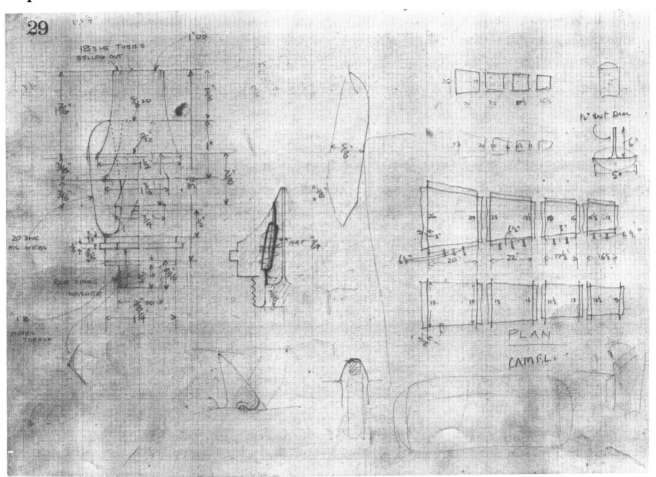

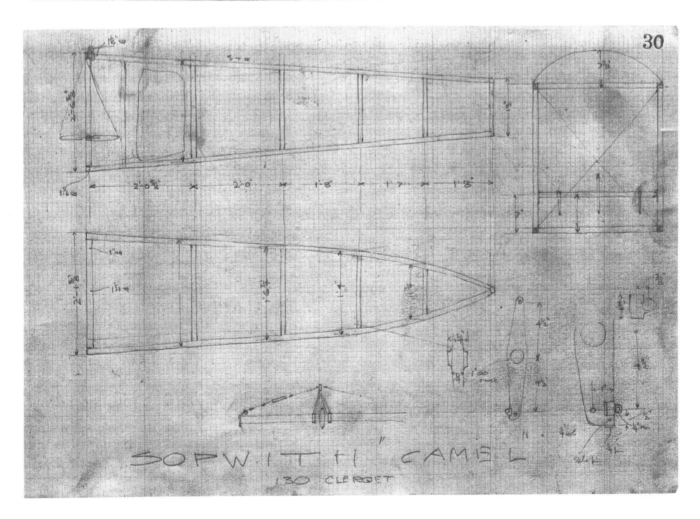

Sopwith Camel

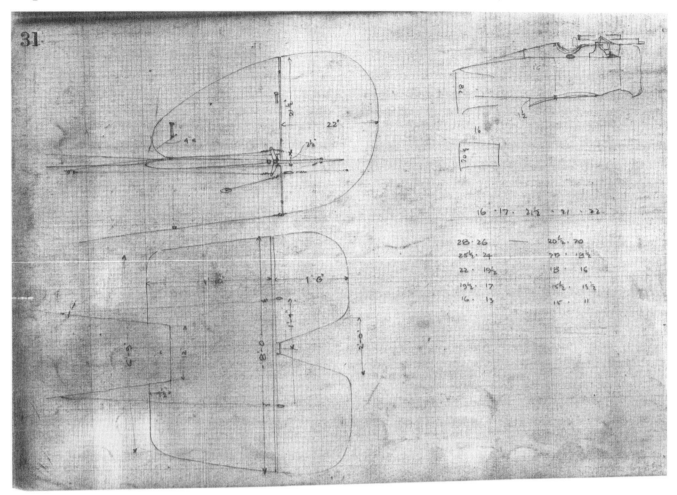

Flotation bag installation

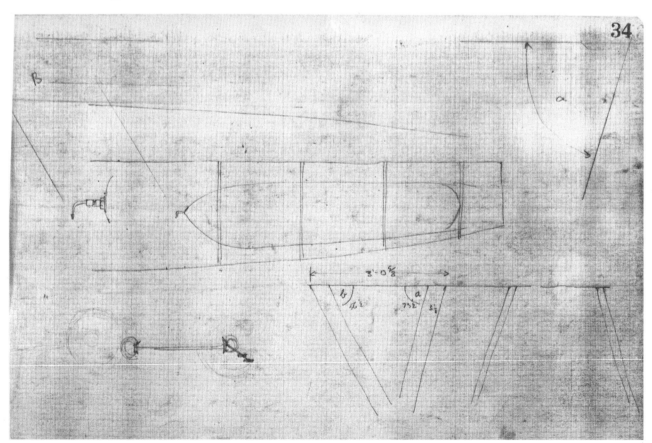

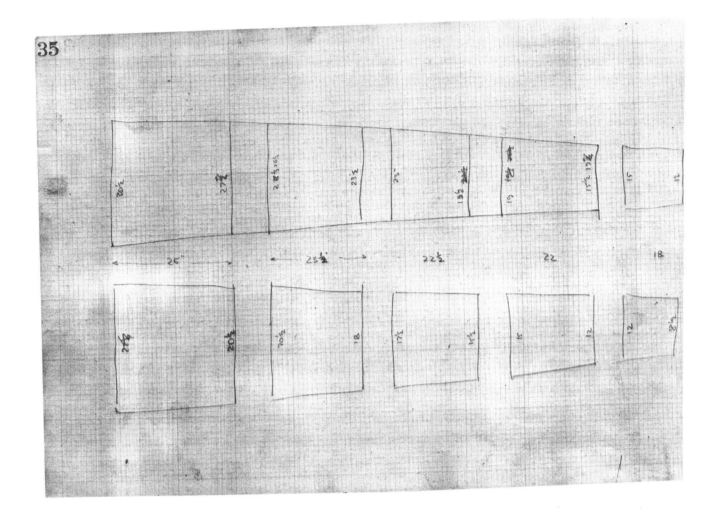

Voisin LA No 2010

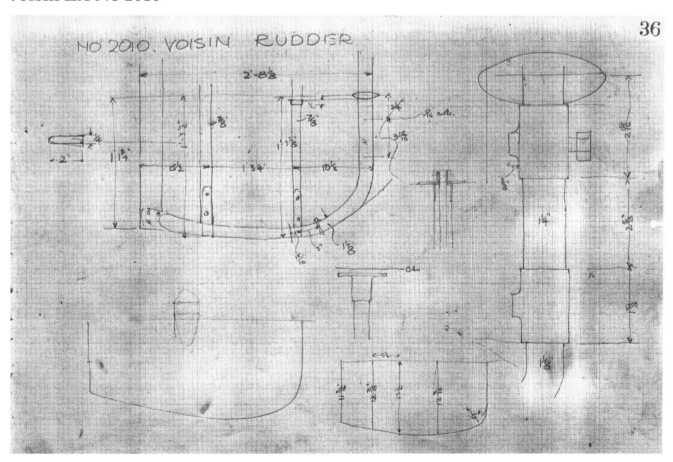

Sopwith N.50: from B1 to Grain Griffin

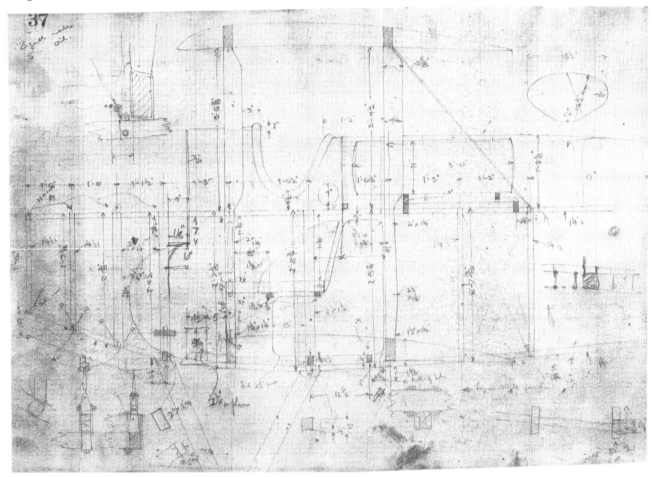

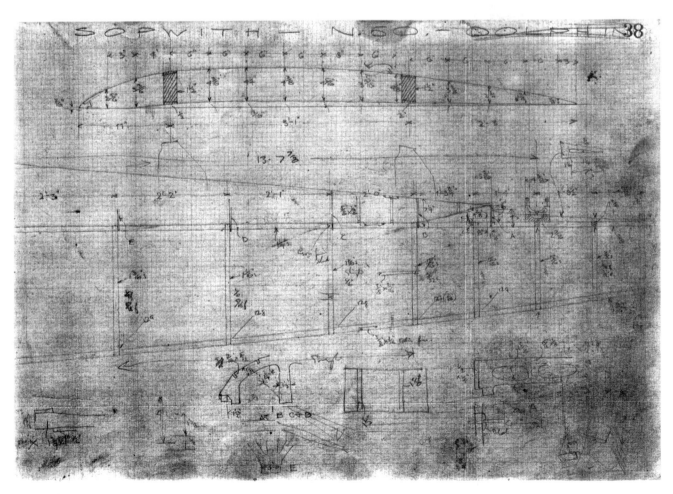

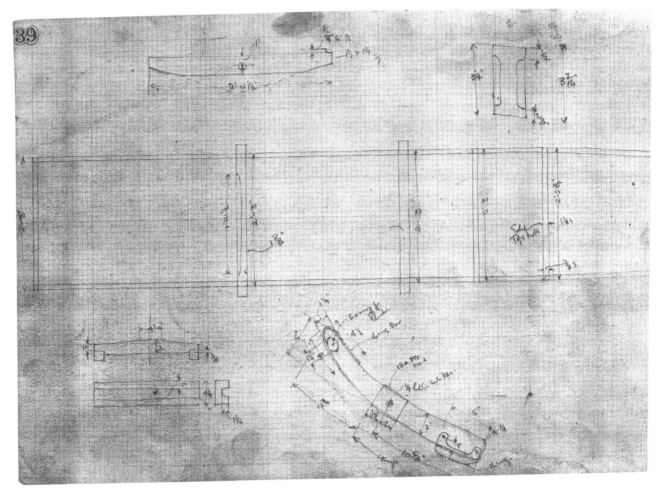

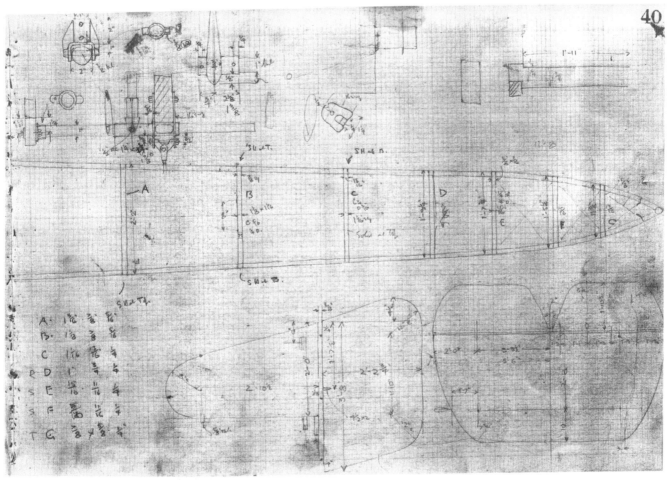

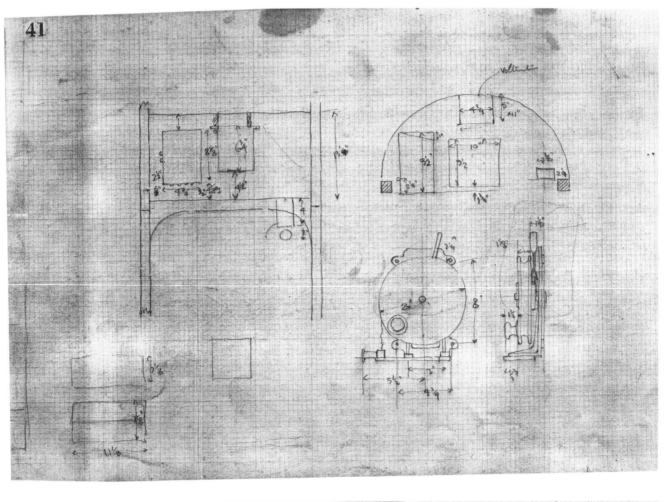

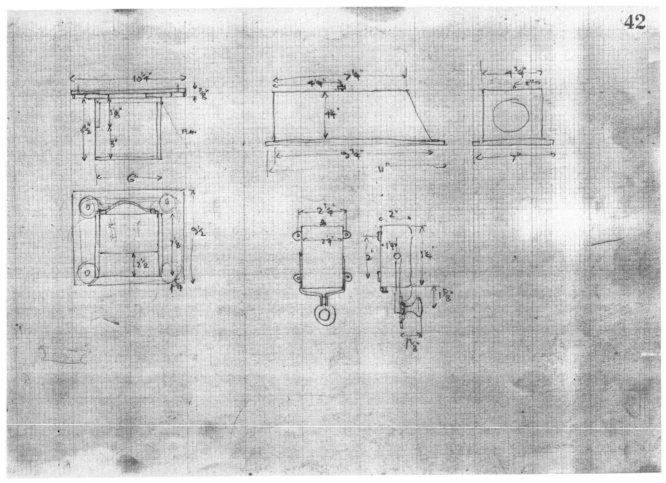

Engine mounting

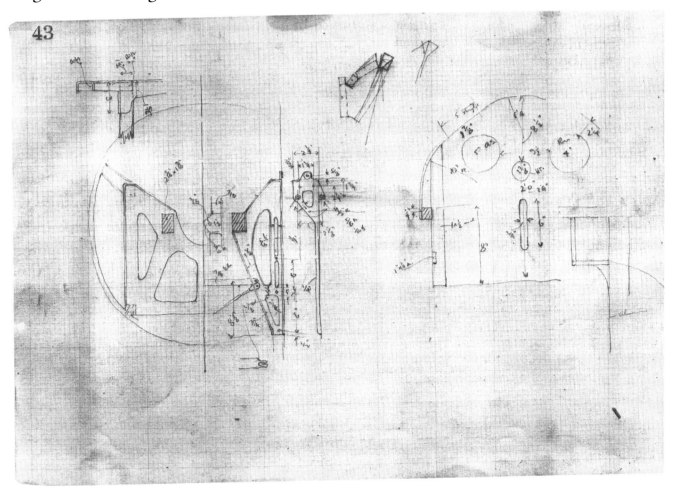

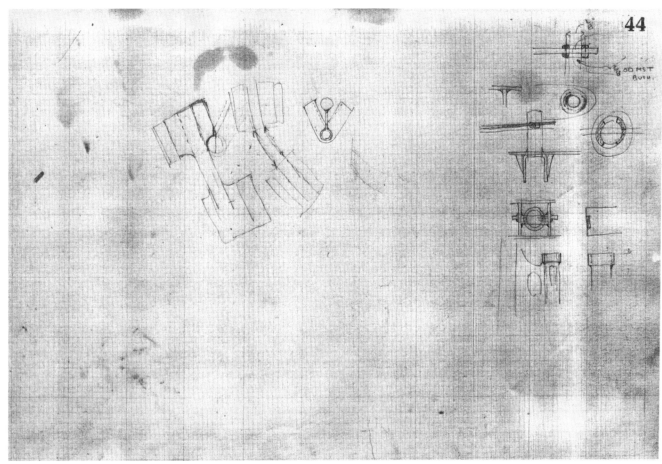

Caudron G.4 twin

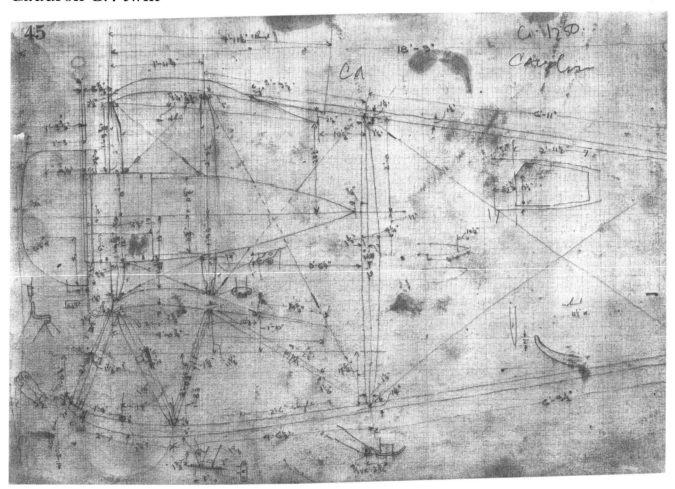

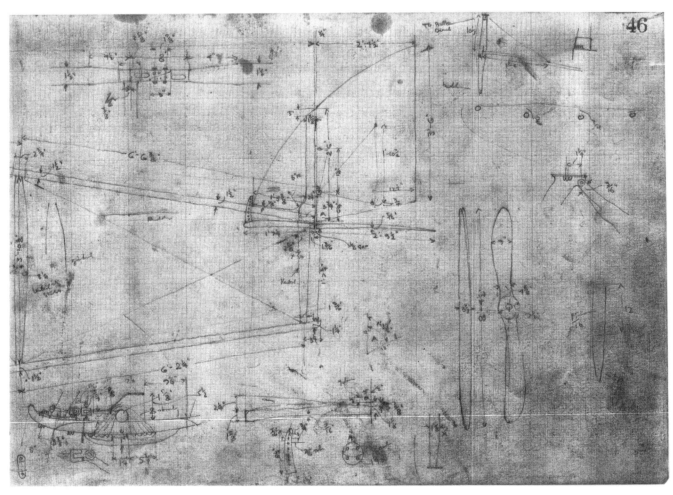

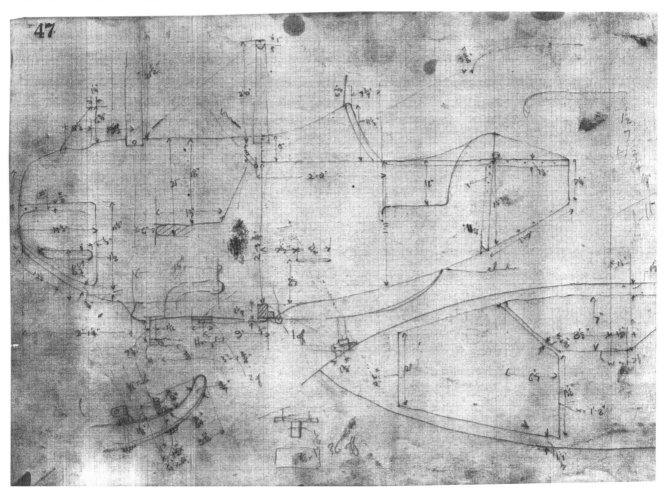

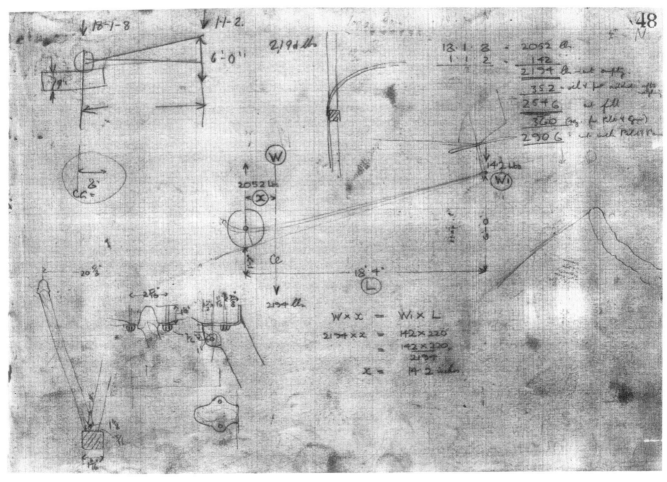

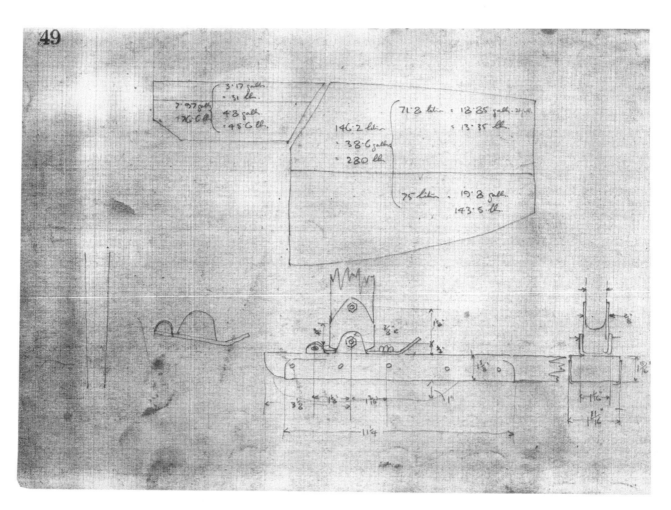

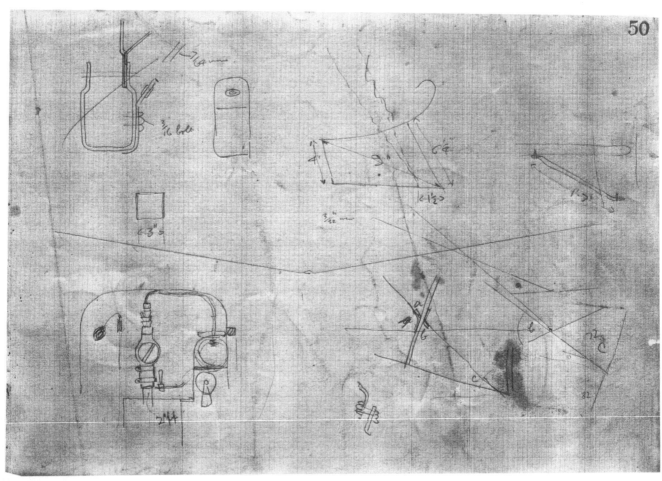

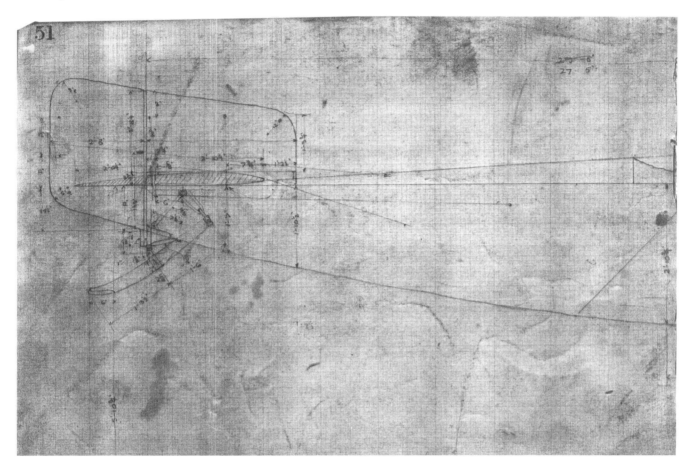

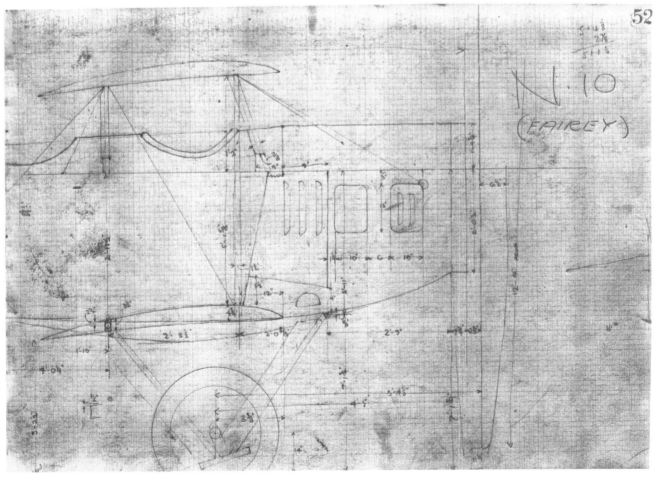

Fairey N.10

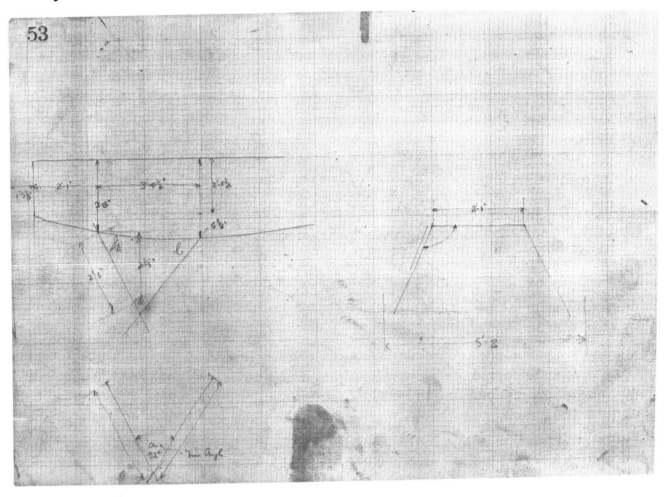

Sopwith 1½ Strutter

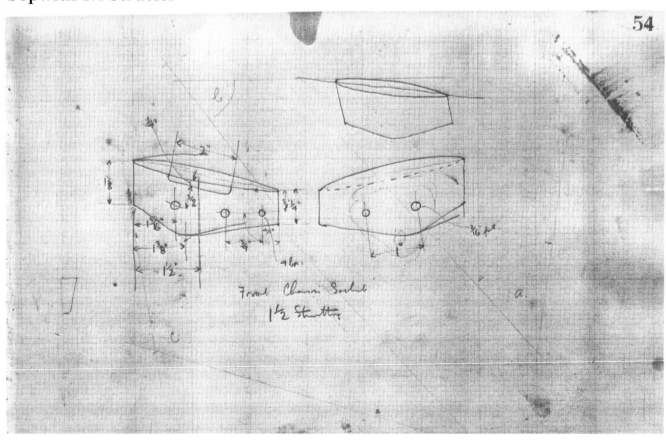

Front Chann Socket
1½ Strutter

Skids for Sopwith Pup, 1½ Strutter, Camel, and N.50

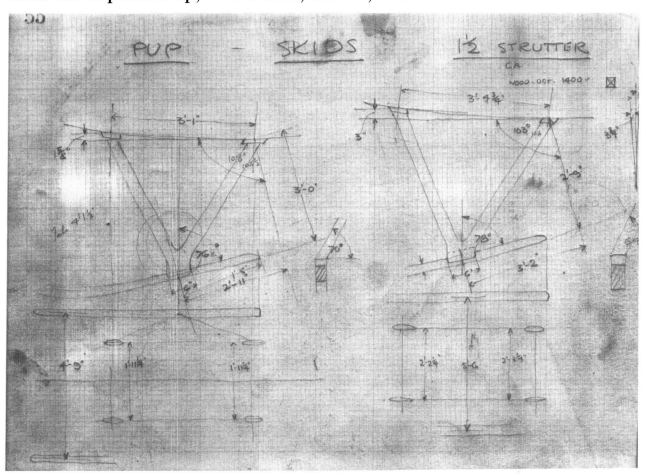

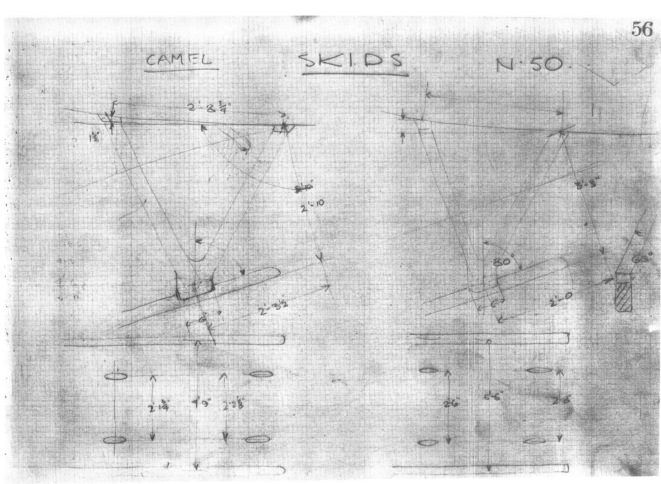

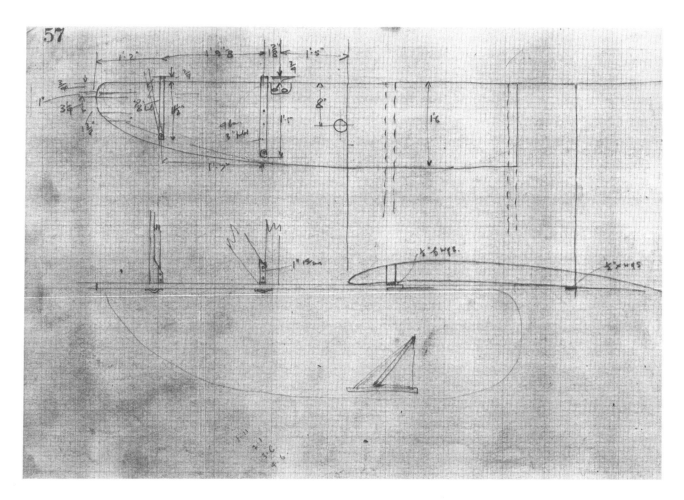

Oxygen bottle to inflate air bags

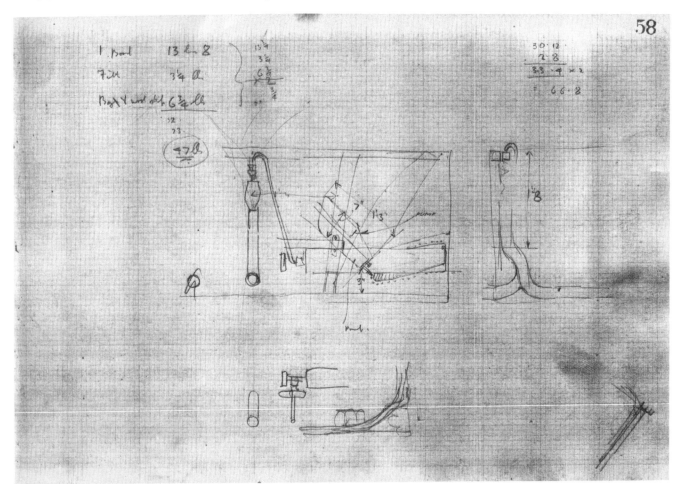

French Letord Bomber

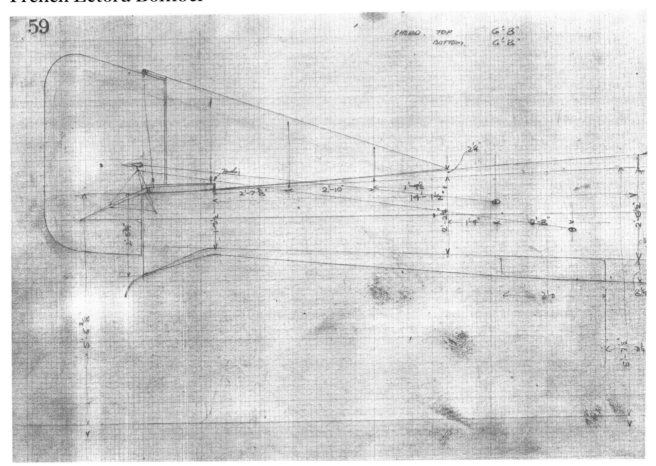

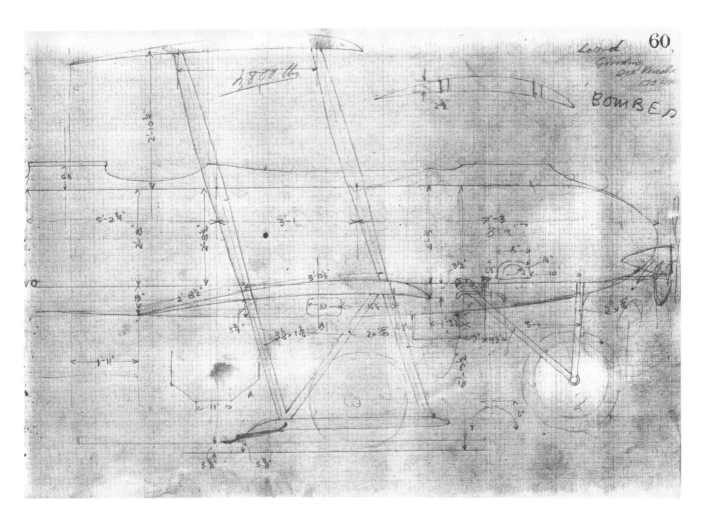

French Letord Bomber

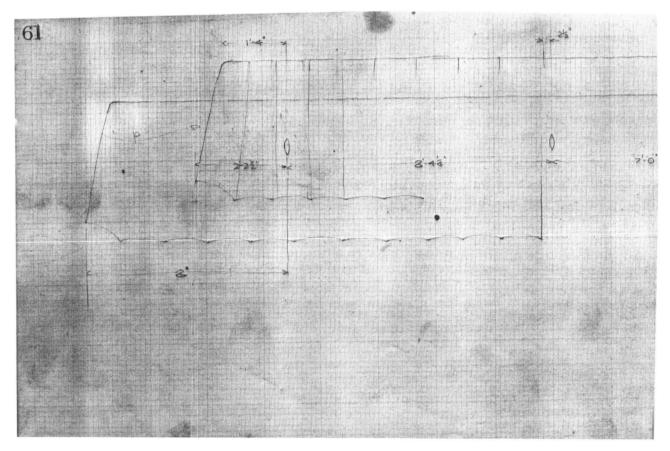

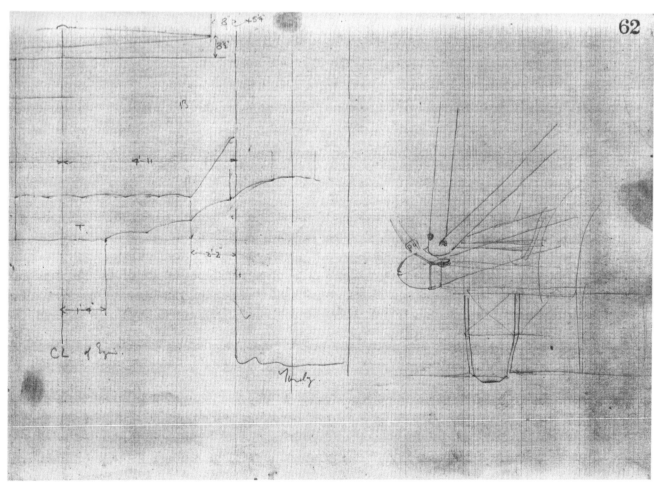

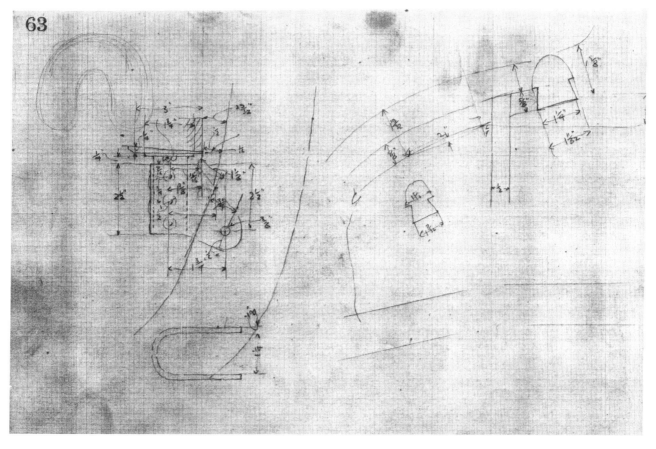

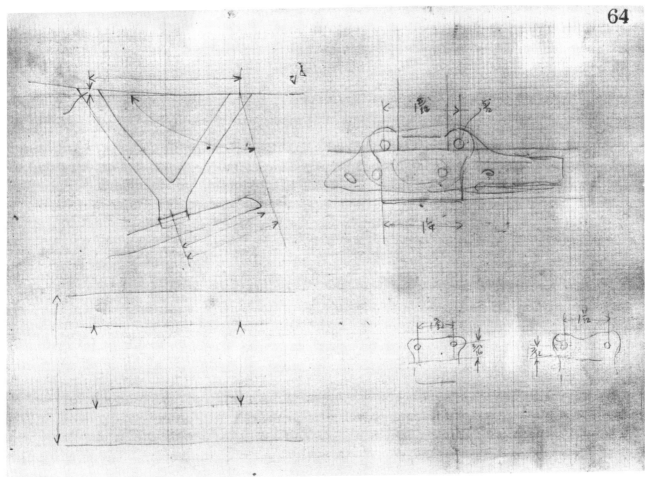

Fuselage cross-section

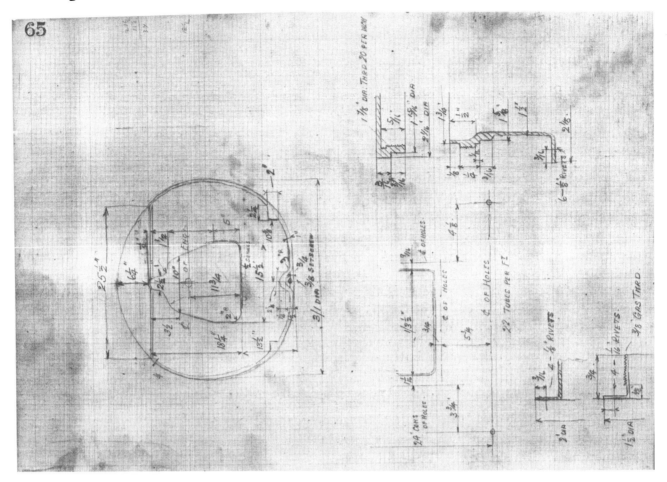

Upper wing centre section

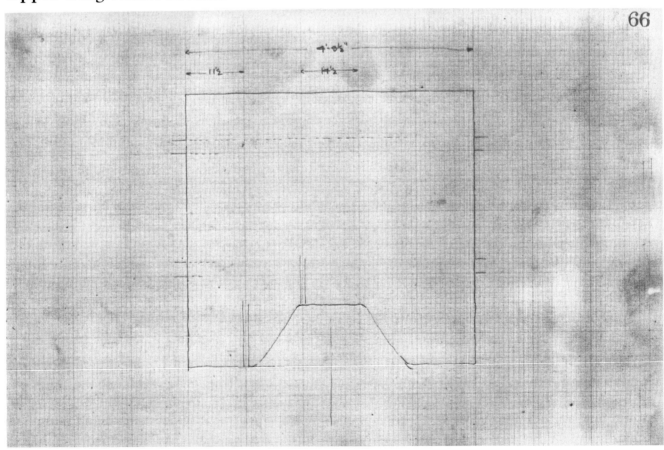

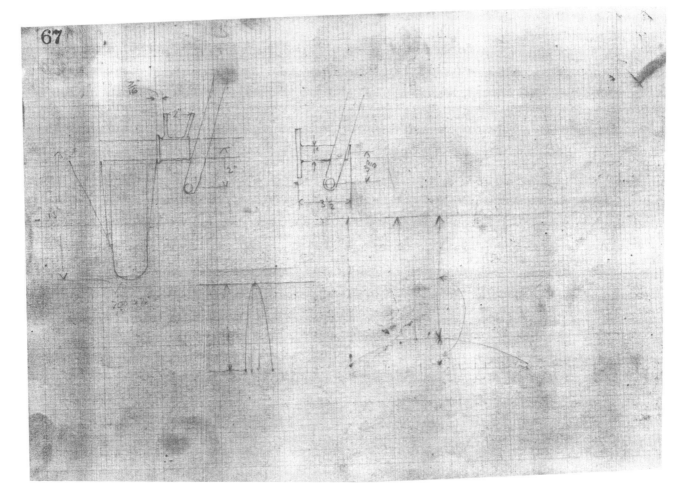

Dyott Bomber – fin and rudder

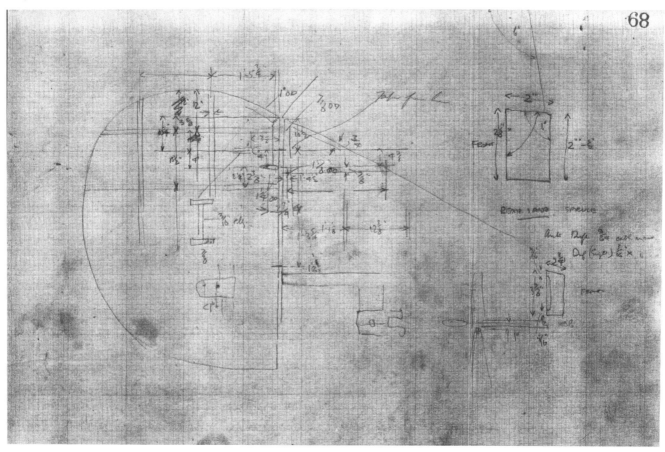

Dyott Bomber

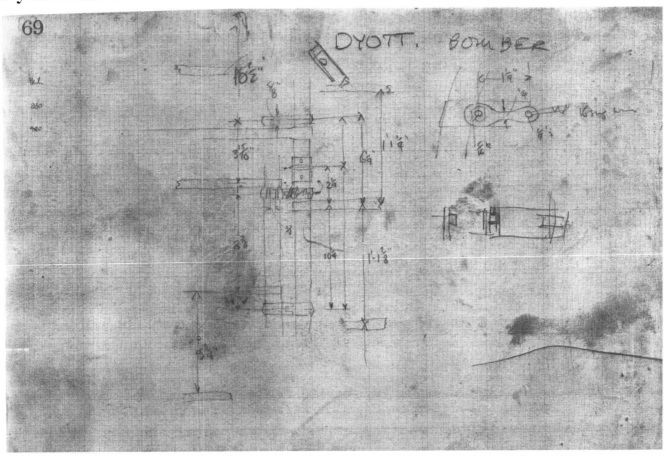

Parnall Panther and 'Bristol'

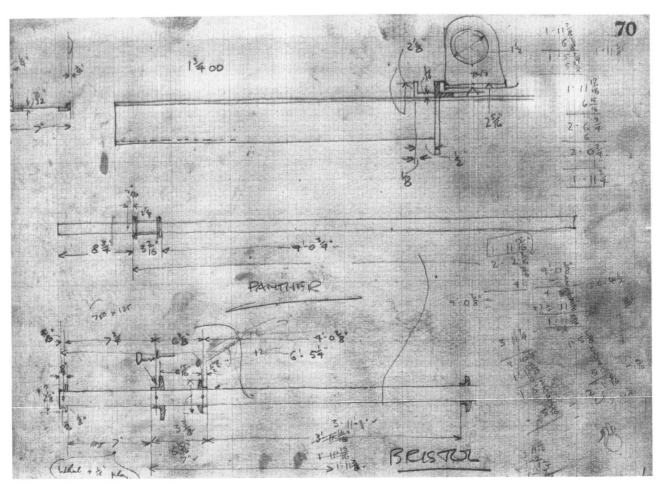

Parnall Panther

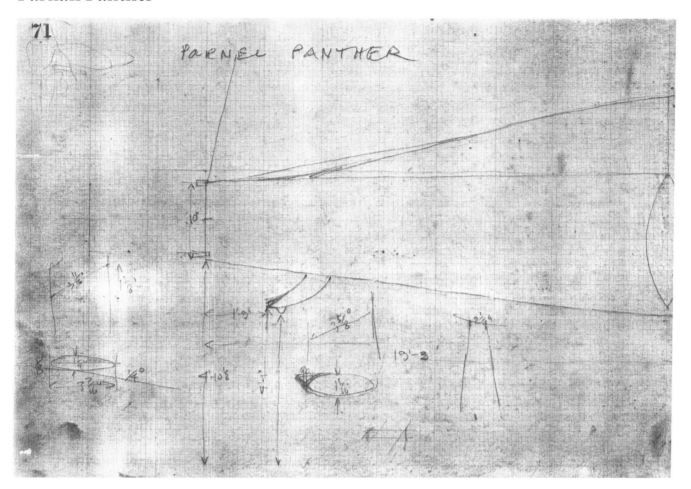

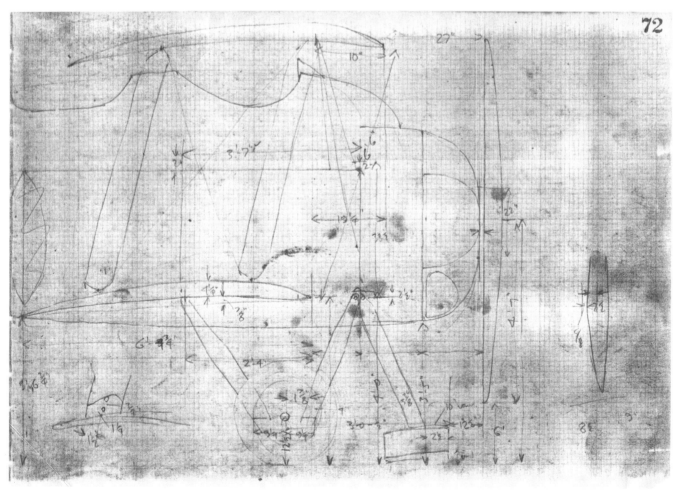

Hook arresting gear for Sopwith 2F.1 Camel

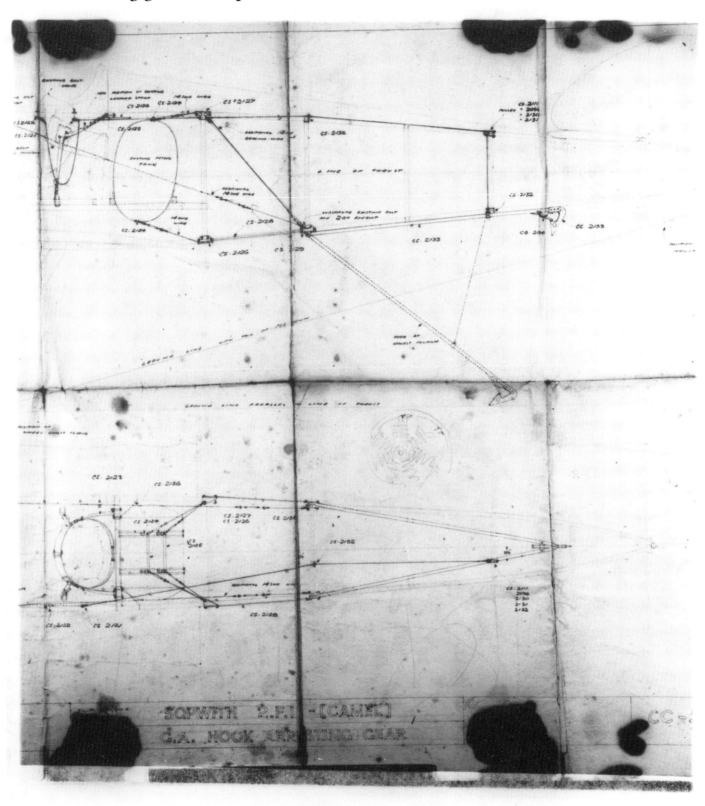

SOPWITH 2.F.1 - [CAMEL]
G.A. HOOK ARRESTING GEAR

N50 Grain Griffin fuselage

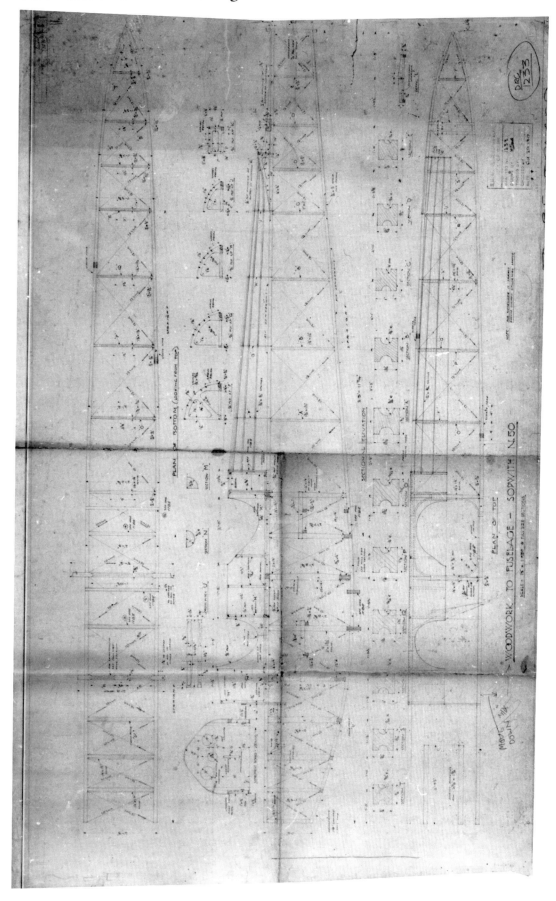